W9-AML-331

The Gatsby Affair

The Gatsby Affair

Scott, Zelda, and the Betrayal That Shaped an American Classic

Kendall Taylor

ROWMAN & LITTLEFIELD
Lanham • Boulder • New York • London

Published by Rowman & Littlefield
An imprint of The Rowman & Littlefield Publishing Group, Inc.
4501 Forbes Boulevard, Suite 200, Lanham, Maryland 20706
www.rowman.com

Unit A, Whitacre Mews, 26-34 Stannary Street, London SE11 4AB

Distributed by NATIONAL BOOK NETWORK

British Library Cataloguing in Publication Information Available

Library of Congress Cataloging-in-Publication Data

Names: Taylor, Kendall, 1941– author.
Title: The Gatsby affair : Scott, Zelda, and the betrayal that shaped an
  American classic / Kendall Taylor.
Description: Lanham, Maryland : Rowman & Littlefield, [2018] | Includes
  bibliographical references and index.
Identifiers: LCCN 2018008344 (print) | LCCN 2018008820 (ebook) |
  ISBN 9781538104941 (ebook) | ISBN 9781538104934 (cloth : alk. paper)
Subjects: LCSH: Fitzgerald, F. Scott (Francis Scott), 1896–1940—Marriage. |
  Fitzgerald, F. Scott (Francis Scott), 1896–1940—Characters—Jay Gatsby. | Authors,
  American—20th century—Biography. | Fitzgerald, Zelda, 1900–1948—Marriage. |
  Fitzgerald, Zelda, 1900–1948—Relations with men. | Authors' spouses—United
  States—Biography. | Married people—United States—Biography. | Fitzgerald,
  F. Scott (Francis Scott), 1896–1940. Great Gatsby.
Classification: LCC PS3511.I9 (ebook) | LCC PS3511.I9 Z8725 2018 (print) |
  DDC 813/.52 [B]—dc23
LC record available at https://lccn.loc.gov/2018008344

Printed in the United States of America

For my daughter,
Dre
Never Doubt the Power of Perseverance

It was a sad love affair holding no promise and too impassioned to be dignified. None of them, in their fervor and necessity to contribute to their brilliant and embittered world, remembered the fact that, what counts is not the kiss, but the loyalties which are broken, the threads of fidelity which are frayed.

—Zelda Fitzgerald

Contents

Preface

$\mathcal{L}$ife has its defining moments, pivotal events that change people forever when nothing remains the same. Zelda Sayre Fitzgerald had three: a sexual assault in Montgomery, Alabama, when she was fifteen; her marriage to F. Scott Fitzgerald; and a brief affair with the French aviator Edouard Jozan. When my last book on the Fitzgeralds was published, critics generally agreed, it was the most authoritative and complete account of their tortured marriage. However, there was one important aspect I did not fully explore. That was Zelda's affair with the Frenchman, its impact on the couple's life and work, and the role it played in her mental breakdown. Although Edouard has always interested Fitzgerald followers, there has been little agreement about his impact on their lives, and in an otherwise well-researched case history, the pilot has remained a mystery.

In his groundbreaking biography *The Far Side of Paradise*, Arthur Mizener ignored Edouard completely, commenting instead on Zelda's infatuation with another Frenchman, Rene Silvy. Andrew Turnbull, who knew the Fitzgeralds when they lived on his parents' property, in his study, *Scott Fitzgerald*, only conjectured that either she was bored, trying to make Scott jealous, or the seduction of the moment proved too strong. By the time Nancy Milford interviewed Edouard for her 1970 book *Zelda: A Biography* he could not, or would not, recall details of their relationship. The only other interview he gave, three years later, to Zelda's Montgomery friend Sara Mayfield for *Exiles from Paradise*, provided little new information. While Sara had the advantage of being Zelda's confidant, Edouard remained circumspect in his answers and shared only the scantiest of details. Silence over the liaison remained intact. Later studies, including those by Scott Donaldson, Andre Le Vot, James Mellow, Jeffrey Meyers, Sally Cline, and Linda Wagner-Martin, offered no additional insights. Nonetheless, fascination with the Frenchman persisted, with the interlude making its way into literary narrative. Tennessee Williams dramatized it on Broadway in *Clothes for a Summer Hotel*, and French author Gilles Le Roy drew on the affair for his steamy novel *Alabama Song*, which won France's top literary prize, the Goncourt. Most recently, Therese Fowler renewed interest in Edouard by fictionalizing him in *Z: A Novel of Zelda*, which topped best seller lists.

The pilot remained a shadowy figure until I heard from his daughter, Martine, who had read my earlier biography and wanted to share information about her father. "Of all the books I have read so far about the Fitzgerald saga," she wrote,

> this is the one which gives a true insight into the complexity of Zelda's personality, her intelligence and most of all an insight about her alleged mental illness. As I read your book, it made me understand how Zelda would have fascinated my father; her beauty surely, because my dad always had an eye for beautiful women, and had an incredible charm because of his good looks, but I also think that what captured his attention was not only the great intelligence of Zelda, but also her absence of conformism, her appetite for life, and really her tendency to live dangerously, a trait my father possessed also and which put him in all sorts of troubles. The daring qualities of Zelda must have fascinated him, and he must have been amused, entertained and ready to play.

Martine's acute observations began an exchange that has continued over the years, and she and her brother, Pierre, provided important biographical information about the Jozan family, access to their father's papers, and insights into his character.

Zelda met Edouard Jozan in 1924, while he was a flight instructor at Frejus near the Fitzgeralds' villa on the French Riviera. Southern France seemed the ideal place for Scott to finish writing *The Great Gatsby*. After arriving that June, he established a strict work schedule and forbade interruptions. Zelda accommodated by going to the beach, where after a swim in the Mediterranean, she would practice her French with some naval pilots from the nearby base. Edouard was the handsomest of the group, and she was instantly attracted. In contrast to Scott, who was slight with an almost feminine face, Edouard was square-jawed, athletic, and muscular. Confident and charismatic, he exuded dominance, which benefited him as a naval officer and made him attractive to women. Accustomed to their attention, he was experienced in his response. Zelda and Edouard were soon observed together, strolling through the marketplace and drinking aperitifs at seaside bistros. When Gerald and Sara Murphy saw them at the beach, they suspected an affair, but Scott seemed oblivious to what was happening and later would say, "I liked [Edouard] and was glad he was willing to pass the hours with Zelda. It gave me time to write. It never occurred to me that the friendship could turn into an affair." Given Zelda's previous history with men, this seems hard to believe.

Five weeks into the affair, Zelda confessed that she loved the Frenchman and asked Scott for a divorce. He was dumbstruck. There had been other dalliances on both sides, but this was different. Offering no excuses or apologies, Zelda was prepared to abandon her family for Edouard. That was unfathomable to Scott, who never ceased agonizing over her betrayal or punishing her for it. He demanded they both come before him and profess their love, but Edouard was unwilling to jeopardize his military career and promptly left. The confrontation that never took place in life made its way into Scott's first draft of *The Great Gatsby*, where Gatsby tells Nick Carraway that Daisy suddenly had appeared with packed suitcases wanting them to run off together. "I tried to explain to her that we couldn't do that, and I only made her cry." It was a mistake for someone like him with lofty ambitions to fall in love, but he had let himself go, and that was it. Likely, this is what Edouard told Zelda during their final days together. That she hardly knew French and he barely spoke English contributed to Zelda's misinterpretation of his intentions, but she also was blinded by passion and embroiled in something completely unfamiliar.

To a degree the affair was also a creation of Zelda's and Scott's imaginations. Scott encouraged it to generate a love triangle that would infuse *The Great Gatsby* with emotional tension, and Zelda was testing her appeal on a new conquest. None of this was lost on the Frenchman, who later observed, "They both had a need of drama; they made it up and perhaps they were the victims of their own unsettled and a little unhealthy imagination." Nonetheless, from the moment Zelda asked Scott for a divorce, the power shifted in their marriage and he grasped control.

That Zelda loved the Frenchman is apparent, but how could a five-week affair become such a tipping point? Partially, because the emotional upheaval Zelda experienced after the affair's wrenching conclusion was magnified by something else, a traumatic memory of the brutal side of passion. It had remained dormant until resurrected by Edouard's rejection and magnified her response to his sudden departure. "She had forgot all about that year of her life until she was grown and married," Zelda wrote, "and tragedy had revivified its traces, as she then saw, from the beginning." Trauma can generate psychoses, sometimes the brain's way of coping, and in this instance calamitous forces were released, a Greek tragedy—French style—triggering profound depression that culminated in Zelda's first suicide attempt. By the time she questioned how much a heart can hold, she had ample time to experience its capacity for pain. "When one really can't stand it anymore," she wrote, "and the limits are transgressed and one thing has become another, poetry registers itself on the hospital charts and heartbreak has to be taken care of, but heartbreak perishes in public institutions." There was before Edouard and after, simple as that.

Old wounds also opened for Scott. His first love, Ginevra King, had rejected him for a naval pilot, and once again, he was vanquished by a more powerful suitor. Unable to undo Zelda's infidelity, he assumed ownership and incorporated the betrayal into stories and novels, exploiting in fiction what he could not control in life. What Edouard would not say to his face—"Your wife doesn't love you. She loves me."—repeatedly was played out as a stand-alone scene. Jay Gatsby makes this declaration to Tom Buchanan in *The Great Gatsby*, and Tommy Barban announces it to Dick Diver in *Tender Is the Night*. With authorial agency, Scott now could wield power over circumstances, have characters make different choices and alter outcomes; it took the sting out of a compromised marriage.

For some writers the separation between personal and literary life is indistinguishable. That was the case for Zelda and Scott, who continually rewrote their personal histories. For Scott, nothing was off limits, whether his wife's affair with Edouard or the names of her sedatives, and he looked for material in every detail of life, observing in one notebook entry that if you found a drug good for two things—for example, if paraldehyde or choral were also ink eradicators—then you had a climax. The incidents of each day were memories for tomorrow. Much of Scott's fiction stemmed from a few powerful experiences, expressed in different guises, and he believed there were only two or three great and moving experiences in our lives, so extraordinary that it didn't seem anyone else has been so dazzled and astonished before, and we tell those two or three stories repeatedly in some new disguise as long as people will listen. The Jozan affair became that singular event for the Fitzgeralds, a decisive and determining experience continually revisited. It played a pivotal role in Zelda's two novels, and but for it, *The Great Gatsby* would be more about lost illusions than adultery and betrayal, and Jay Gatsby, initially based on Edouard Jozan, a different character.

Zelda was brought up to be protected by men and lacked the resources to guard herself from those she charmed. From Scott's perspective, she was soft where she needed to be hard and strong where she should have been yielding. Aware of this contradiction, Zelda readily admitted it was difficult to be someone who wanted to be a law unto herself but also kept safe and protected. When she selected Scott over other suitors, she had several objectives. He provided a way out of the South into the broader world she desired, and she believed she could help with his writing. Zelda had given considerable thought to matrimony and bemoaned the fact that, for the average woman, which she was not, one either became a man's secretary or got married; it seemed the same to her. It was exciting to imagine that Scott might evolve into a celebrated author, and she become famous herself. And where better to accomplish that than New York City? Her Montgomery friend Tallulah Bankhead was already there appearing on Broadway, and Zelda considered herself equally talented. Until the last moment, however, she wavered. Her family vehemently opposed the marriage, and while she hated to admit it, she was not physically attracted to Scott. It was already clear he drank too much, and though her father brought this to her attention, she didn't listen, probably because she was overdrinking herself. On the positive side, Scott appeared more worldly than her other beaux, had attended Princeton, and seemed to offer the best route to an urbane life.

What Zelda really wanted was a man with the strength and idealism of her father, but someone with whom she could find emotional fulfillment. Scott knew he was not that person: "All our lives, since the day of our engagement, we have spent hunting for some man Zelda considers strong enough to lean on. I am not." Throughout her youth, she had fantasized about finding such an individual and recognized him in Edouard. His heroic mind-set recalled a generation of courageous Southerners who had fought for the Confederacy, and she romantically compared their star-crossed tryst to that of Tristan and Isolde. While her intense feelings were authentic, the relationship she envisioned was not. Although Edouard cared about Zelda and was sorry to cause her pain, he considered their liaison a summer romance without obligations.

Named for a heroine in a romantic novel, Zelda grew up with dreamy notions about love. But after her sexual initiation through assault, she dispensed with sentimentality along with moral principles and gave little consideration to what others thought. That she was being adulterous with Edouard never crossed her mind, and what began as a harmless interlude set into motion a series of tectonic consequences that became a turning point in the Fitzgeralds' life, with Scott writing in his notebook that what had happened never could be repaired. His Midwestern Puritanism and Catholic upbringing considered a woman's adultery a mortal sin and grievous injustice to the spouse, punishable by the highest severity. In the catechism of the church, it not only broke the sixth commandment but also destabilized the institution of marriage and shattered the contract upon which it was based. Although twice in his ledger Scott remarks on his role in the affair, he would later place the blame on Zelda, accusing her of becoming involved with Edouard to sabotage his writing. He never forgave her, and she accepted the consequences, considering it one of two actions that had sealed her fate—the first being her marriage.

From this juncture, Scott set out to neutralize Zelda, so there would be no future incidences. In revenge, he began a relationship with seventeen-year-old Lois Moran, already a successful Hollywood actress and trained ballerina, and taunted Zelda by lauding the young star's talent and ambition. Before marrying Scott, Zelda had assured him that she would never become personally ambitious, but now she plunged headlong into achieving something on her own, first as a ballet dancer, then a writer. Scott was so threatened by her determination that he continually placed obstacles in her path. One author in a literary family was enough, and having witnessed his value as a man challenged, he was not going to have his celebrity compromised. Unable to see her way out of the chaos she had created, and with little hope for the future, in spring of 1929, Zelda suffered her first psychic breakdown. Her symptoms were right out of the *Diagnostic and Statistical Manual of Mental Disorders*, or *DSM*, that indispensable handbook for naming mental disorders. When she appeared for her initial psychological evaluation, her thinking was scattered, she was fraught with anxiety, she could not eat or sleep, and she was experiencing hallucinations. She had also attempted suicide with an overdose of sleeping pills.

Swiss psychiatrist Eugen Bleuler met with her for three hours before presenting his diagnosis of schizophrenia to Oscar Forel, director of Prangins, a sanitarium near Lake Geneva in Switzerland. Bleuler had coined the term only ten years earlier, but it soon became the most common diagnosis on admission papers. It was so widely employed that by 1930 almost anyone could find themselves institutionalized under that rubric. What hysteria had been to the nineteenth century, schizophrenia became to the twentieth. Psychiatrists believed that women were more susceptible to this condition, based on their observation that many of their patients were sad and confused females, suffering from "lovesickness." Generally, they were brought to sanitariums by fathers or brothers, as was the case for Zelda's friend Sara Mayfield, for Vivienne Elliott married to T. S., and for Lucia Joyce, daughter of James Joyce, who also was evaluated by Bleuler, and as might be expected, diagnosed as schizophrenic and taken to Prangins Clinic.

Forel, who had opened Prangins only a year earlier, held patriarchal ideas about women's roles and responsibilities in society. "Excitability" was always suspect, and he believed Zelda's breakdown had been caused by negative effects of overreaching, along with the fact that she had inherited an emotionally fragile disposition. He was unwavering in his conviction that nervous people not be overstimulated and considered her efforts to become a celebrated dancer an obsessive illness. His treatment plan called for neutralizing those tendencies with rest therapies, medication, and reeducation, with the goal of shifting her into a range of acceptable behavior. If she wanted to maintain peace in the marriage, Zelda needed to focus on her principal role as wife and mother.

However, once forces aligned to bring the diagnosis of madness into play, and Zelda was reduced to a psychiatric label, every aspect of her life got interpreted according to this illness. The hasty diagnosis became a straitjacket, condemning her to a life in asylums, where she was repeatedly traumatized with interventions that worsened preexisting disorders and precipitated new ones. Her medical record followed her everywhere. After accepting Bleuler's diagnosis of schizophrenia, Forel passed it on to Adolf Meyer at Phipps Clinic, who conveyed it to Charles Slocum at Craig House, who relayed it to William Worcester Elgin at Sheppard Pratt, who sent it to Robert Carroll at Highland Hospital. Although her diagnosis occasionally was questioned, medical loyalty trumped Zelda's needs, and physicians were reluctant to countermand earlier opinions. This was especially true in the budding field of psychiatry where many doctors had studied together in Europe. Zelda's psychiatrist at Phipps Clinic, Adolf Meyer, had spent his early career at Burgholzli, the psychiatric hospital of the University of Zurich, which Auguste-Henri Forel directed for twenty years, and it was Forel's son, Oscar, who headed Prangins. When Oscar Forel requested assistance in diagnosing Zelda, he asked none other than Eugen Bleuler, his father's successor at Burgholzli, who conferred the label of madness where there was no insanity, or only the most temporary kind, an infrequent but not unusual manifestation of the human condition.

Asylums disassemble people, seldom make them whole. Had Zelda returned to family and friends in Montgomery, she might have been able to grapple with her illness over time and achieve some measure of stability. Instead, her identity became invalidated at Prangins, as she battled for release with a justified sense of the wrong she was suffering. After fifteen months, she was discharged to Scott as an invalid, and he became a widower to her infirmity. Aware she would never recover her former self, Zelda told Sara Mayfield that she could never forgive Scott for institutionalizing her. Now each had something to hold against the other.

Like many women from her generation, Zelda was uncertain how to apply her many talents. Scott told their daughter that when her mother finally understood that work was the only dignity, it was too late. However, nothing could be further from the truth. From her mid-twenties, she worked steadily on stories, essays, and novels; created artwork; and trained in the most difficult dance aesthetic of the twentieth century, becoming an accomplished ballerina within five years. Although institutionalized, she continued to write and paint, and one of her most accomplished stories, "Miss Ella," was begun at Prangins. She wrote her first novel, *Save Me the Waltz*, at Phipps Clinic; completed an impressive body of paintings and watercolors at Craig House for an exhibition in Manhattan; and was creatively productive the entire time she remained at Highland Hospital. When she finally was released and returned to Montgomery, she spent her final years working on *Caesar's Things*, which initially incorporated Nijinsky's similar experience of being diagnosed as schizophrenic by Bleuler but later concentrated on her own breakdown and hospitalization. Ultimately the brilliance of her life rests on how much she was able to accomplish, despite the odds against her, the most formidable being, to use her own words, that she was Scott Fitzgerald's wife.

Acknowledgments

$\mathcal{R}$esearching and writing biography requires time and the assistance of many. Sometimes the work takes so long to complete, those crucial to the project do not survive to see the manuscript published. Upton Brady is one of those individuals, a man of singular intelligence who was my toughest and best critic, and whose astute editing and knowledgeable comments taught me much about writing. This book is better than it would have been otherwise, because of his suggestions.

I had not planned to write another study of the Fitzgeralds, but sometimes an author has no choice, and the subject chooses her, rather than the other way around. I am tempted to believe I was destined to write this story and followed where the subject took me. The topic could never have been broached without the assistance of Martine Jozan Work, who spoke to me over many years about her father and generously shared his papers, documents, and photos. After decades of innuendo about Edouard Jozan and Zelda Fitzgerald, the family desired a balanced view, and I intended to approach the subject in an unbiased manner, so it was an amicable match. I also benefited from insights offered by two of Jozan's countrymen: Louis Hourcade, son of Edouard's close friend, Jean Hourcade, and Robert Feuilloy, secretary general of the French Retired Naval Pilots' Association. To John Lomaki and Ann Spies goes my appreciation for assistance with translations of their correspondence.

In the course of research, I interviewed many people, some while I was a graduate student at Vanderbilt University, others during the 1980s and '90s, and most recently during this last decade. Many with whom I spoke are now deceased, and I have worked from notes of those conversations. The following people generously shared recollections: Scottie Fitzgerald Lanahan,

Rosalind Smith, Andrew Turnbull, Charles Angoff, Archibald MacLeish, Lawton Campbell, Helen Blackshear, Tom Johnson, Landon Ray, Dr. Basil T. Bennett, Dr. Otto Billig, Pierre Jozan, Robert Taft, Peyton Mathis III, and Anton Haardt. I am grateful to William T. Carpenter, Wendy S. Smith, and Larry Grace from the DuPont Edge Moor Plant outside Wilmington, Delaware, who provided access to what was Ellerslie, the estate on which the Fitzgeralds lived during 1927.

No biography based on original materials is possible without the help of archivists and librarians, and I have many to thank. The most comprehensive sources for my research were the personal papers and unpublished materials of F. Scott and Zelda Fitzgerald in the Special Collections Division of Firestone Library at Princeton University. I spent much time there, and the quality of their collection is comparable only to the professionalism of the staff. For assistance with images, special appreciation goes to Annalee Pauls and Margaret Rich in photo duplication.

Then, there are staff historians, curators, and archivists at research libraries and historical societies who provided valuable assistance: Norwood Kerr at the Alabama Department of Archives and History, Mark Wilson at the University of Auburn, Clarke E. Center Jr. with the W. S. Hoole Special Collections of the University of Alabama at Tuscaloosa, the Minnesota Historical Society, Duke University Medical Archives, Westport Historical Society, Association of French Retired Navy Pilots, Emil Buehler Naval Aviation Library, National Air and Space Museum, Smithsonian Institution, Wilmington Historical Society, Edgemoor Dupont Archives, Pyrantee Historical Library, Marine Nationale Service Historique, ARDHAN Aeronavale, *Asheville Citizen-Times*, *Montgomery Advertiser*, American Psychiatric Association Library, H. L. Mencken Collection at the Enoch Pratt Free Library, Sheppard Pratt Hospital Archives, George Jean Nathan Collection at Cornell University, and the Sara Haardt Collection at Goucher College. Of all locations where I did research and writing, the Saint Lawrence University Library deserves special thanks for providing me space to work on this book and two previous ones. I am particularly indebted to Michael Anzo, director of libraries; Theresa O'Reilly, administrative secretary; Julia Courtney from Interlibrary Loans; and Tish Munt, public services coordinator. If I have left anyone out, I offer apologies and the assurance that I valued their assistance.

I owe much gratitude to now retired literary agent, Betsy Nolan, who sold my previous Fitzgerald biography, *Sometimes Madness Is Wisdom: Zelda and Scott Fitzgerald: A Marriage* to Ballantine Books at Random House and provided unflagging support for this one. She spent years advocating my work, believed in it from the start, and never gave up on this project. All authors desire such a person in their corner, and I was fortunate to be among her clients. I am grateful for her introduction to my present agent, Kimberley Cameron, who was equally supportive and tenacious in placing my manuscript with the publishing house of Rowman & Littlefield. There, it has been a fortuitous experience to work with senior acquisitions editor Stephen Ryan, who skillfully shepherded this manuscript through several versions to present it to the reading public in the most effective way.

All along I have been supported by family and friends who bolstered my spirits and offered continual encouragement. They knew what I hoped to accomplish and understood it would take time. I thank Jacqueline Goodman, who never questioned when I would finish the book and was supportive throughout; Nelly Maude Case, who reminded me that Beethoven took thirty years to set Schiller's "Ode to Joy" to music; Donna H. Kennedy, Annemarie Bacon, and Will Recker, who reformatted this manuscript many times, transmitted photos, and were always there to be of assistance; my brother, Ronald Finne, who supported me spiritually and financially; fellow writers Marion Meade and Aileen Vincent-Barwood, who shared broad knowledge and experience; Barbara Brennan; Ann Ratner; Brenda Yarcag; Adam Jaffe; Zelig Pintow; Cypre Tannenbaum; Mary Burgess Avrakotos; Deede Tonelli Raylove; Sue Roughton; and Susan Scanlon.

A biographer has to go many places, and I was fortunate to have my daughter, Sophie (Dre), travel with me to southern France and take some of the photographs that appear in this book. Along the cobbled alleyways of Frejus, hilltop villages with sun-warmed medieval walls, and towering plane trees shading San Raphael's harbor, I was able to retrace Zelda and Jozan's steps to construct a narrative linked with the Riviera's romantic appeal.

It is gratifying when a manuscript reaches completion but also sorrowful, since the author must say farewell to someone she cares deeply about. So lastly, I thank this remarkable woman, Zelda Sayre Fitzgerald, with whom I have had an enduring interest over half a century, for the privilege of being able to write about her extraordinary life.

From *Tender Is the Night* by F. Scott Fitzgerald © 1933 by Charles Scribner's Sons, pp. 39, 300, 301, 323, 341.

From *The Last Tycoon; An Unfinished Novel* © 1941 by Charles Scribner's Sons, pp. 127, 136, 164.

From *The Last Tycoon* (*The Love of the Last Tycoon*) © 1995 by Charles Scribner's Sons, p. 73.

From *Save Me the Waltz* by Zelda Fitzgerald in *The Collected Writings of Zelda Fitzgerald*. Matthew J. Bruccoli, ed. © 1991 by Charles Scribner's Sons, pp. 33, 79, 81, 97, 92, 86, 84, 88, 89, 90, 91, 94, 95, 96, 285.

From "Show Mr. and Mrs. Fitzgerald to . . ." in *The Collected Writings of Zelda Fitzgerald*. Matthew J. Bruccoli, ed. © 1991 by Charles Scribner's Sons, p. 422.

From "Babylon Revisited" by F. Scott Fitzgerald in *Babylon Revisited and Other Stories* © 1960 by Charles Scribner's Sons.

From "Image on the Heart" by F. Scott Fitzgerald, originally published in *McCall's Magazine* 63, no. 7 (April 1936), pp. 8, 52. Republished by Alma Books as *Image on the Heart and Other Stories*, 2016, Alma Books, Castleyard, Richmond, Surrey, England. © 1936 by Charles Scribner's Sons.

Letters from F. Scott and Zelda Fitzgerald:

F. Scott Fitzgerald to Edmund Wilson, London, England, July, 1921, *F. Scott Fitzgerald: A Life in Letters*. Matthew J. Bruccoli, ed. © 1995 Simon and Schuster.

F. Scott Fitzgerald to Harold Ober, Capri, Italy, March, 1925, *F. Scott Fitzgerald: A Life in Letters*, Matthew J. Bruccoli, ed. © 1995 Simon and Schuster.

F. Scott Fitzgerald to Gerald and Sara Murphy, Encino, California, September 22, 1939, *F. Scott Fitzgerald: A Life in Letters*. Matthew J. Bruccoli, ed. © 1995 Simon and Schuster.

F. Scott Fitzgerald to Zelda Fitzgerald, Hollywood, California, December 6, 1940, *F. Scott Fitzgerald: A Life in Letters*. Matthew J. Bruccoli, ed. © 1995 Simon and Schuster.

Zelda Fitzgerald to F. Scott Fitzgerald, Baltimore, Maryland, April, 1932, *The Collected Writings of Zelda Fitzgerald*. Matthew J. Bruccoli, ed. © 1991 by Charles Scribner's Sons

Zelda Fitzgerald to F. Scott Fitzgerald, Baltimore, Maryland, after June 30, 1930, *The Collected Writings of Zelda Fitzgerald*. Matthew J. Bruccoli, ed. © 1991 by Charles Scribner's Sons

Illustration Credits:

Photos from the F. Scott Fitzgerald Archives at Princeton University Library: *Photo used by permission of Harold Ober Associates as agents for the Fitzgerald Trustees; reproductions arranged through the Princeton University Library.* Zelda on graduation from Sidney Lanier High School, Zelda with infant Scottie at White Bear Lake, Minnesota, Zelda, Scott, and Scottie in the Renault with the nanny, Southern France, 1924, Fitzgerald on the beach in southern France with Scottie, Zelda, Scott, and Scottie on steps at Villa Marie, Valescure, France, Zelda, Scott, and Scottie, shipboard, 1928.

Photos of Edouard Jozan *used by permission of Martine Jozan Work.*

Photos of hillside villages in southern France and other contemporary French photos *used by permission of Sophie Dre Garner.*

Chronology of Edouard Jozan
and the Fitzgeralds

September 24, 1896

Francis Scott Key Fitzgerald is born to Edward Fitzgerald and Mary McQuillan at 481 Laurel Avenue in St. Paul, Minnesota. Descended on his mother's side from Irish immigrants who came to America during Ireland's famine years (1840–1850) and established a successful grocery business in St. Paul. His father traced his family back to the colonial period and ancestors such as Francis Scott Key, author of "The Star-Spangled Banner" and brother of Scott's great-grandfather.

July 22, 1899

Albert-Edouard Jozan is born in Roi du Gault, a French fishing village twenty kilometers south of Nimes. The youngest of seven children, he was the son of Alexandre Jozan, a career army officer, and Louise Macours.

July 24, 1900

Zelda Sayre is born to Anthony Sayre and Minnie Machen in Montgomery, Alabama. Southern aristocracy, her fraternal grandmother was Musidora Morgan Sayre, sister of John Tyler Morgan, brigadier general in the Confederate Army and a United States senator. On her mother's side, her grandfather was also a United States senator and nominee for candidate of US vice president.

1905

Zelda enters Chilton Grammar School in Montgomery but resists attending and is allowed to remain home one additional year. At seven she reenrolls and starts elementary school.

1907
The Sayres move to 6 Pleasant Avenue, which remains Zelda's home until she marries in 1920.

September 1908
Scott enters St. Paul Academy in Minnesota.

1909
Zelda's father is appointed associate justice of the Alabama Supreme Court.

September 1911
Scott leaves Minnesota to attend Newman, a small Catholic boarding school in Hackensack, New Jersey, where he forms a strong attachment with Father Sigourney Fay and briefly considers becoming a priest.

1911
Edouard leaves Le Grau du Roi for Prytannee National Militaire, a prestigious French military school in La Fleche, near Anjou.

September 1913
Scott enters Princeton in the class of 1917 and establishes lasting friendships with Edmund "Bunny" Wilson (class of '16) and John Peale Bishop ('17), who share his literary interests. He is selected for Cottage, among the most prestigious eating clubs on campus, and becomes involved with the Triangle Club where he writes lyrics for "Fie, Fie, Fie."

June 1914
Zelda graduates from Sayre Street School and enters Sidney Lanier High School the following September.

January 4, 1915
Scott falls in love with Ginevra King, a sixteen-year-old Chicago debutante, and through her is introduced to the world of the wealthy.

November 8, 1915
Scott is forced to drop out of Princeton due to a poor academic record.

September 1916
Scott reenters Princeton as a member of the class of 1918. His relationship with Ginevra King ends.

October 26, 1917
Scott leaves Princeton for a second time without graduating. Upon America's entry into World War I, he enlists in the infantry and receives a commission as second lieutenant. He reports to Ft. Leavenworth, Kansas, on November 20 for Officers' Training Camp and works on his first novel, *The Romantic Egotist* later retitled *This Side of Paradise.*

March 15, 1918
Scott transfers to Camp Zachary Taylor near Louisville, Kentucky, and then to Camp Gordon in Georgia.

April 1918
Edouard Jozan enters the French Naval Academy at Brest.

May 31, 1918
Zelda graduates from Sidney Lanier High School.

June 1918
Scott transfers to Camp Sheridan near Montgomery, Alabama.

July 1918
Scott and Zelda meet at a Montgomery Country Club dance.

October 26, 1918
Scott leaves for Camp Mills, Long Island, to await transport to the front, but the war ends before embarkation.

November 1918
Scott returns to Camp Sheridan and becomes aide-de-camp to Brigadier General J. A. Ryan.

February 1919
Scott is discharged and leaves for New York City, where he rents a room at 200 Claremont Avenue. He continues work on his novel and writes advertising copy for the Barron-Collier agency. He and Zelda become unofficially engaged.

Spring 1919
Scott visits Montgomery during April, May, and June, but Zelda remains reluctant to set a marriage date.

June 1919
Zelda breaks the engagement.

August 1919
Scott returns to St. Paul and completes revisions on novel.

September 16, 1919
Scribner's accepts *This Side of Paradise*. He and Zelda become reengaged.

October 1919
Edouard graduates from the French Naval Academy and is commissioned Enseign de Vaisseau de premiere classe, then assigned to *Jeanne d'Arc*, the French Navy's training ship. After six months, he is reassigned to the tanker *Rhone*.

March 26, 1920
This Side of Paradise is published and becomes an overnight best seller.

April 3, 1920
Zelda and Scott marry in the rectory of St. Patrick's Cathedral in New York City, honeymooning at the Biltmore Hotel. They become luminaries in Manhattan's social scene.

May–September 1920
The Fitzgeralds summer in Westport, Connecticut, where Scott works on his second novel, *The Beautiful and Damned*. Four months into the marriage, Zelda has an affair with literary critic George Jean Nathan. In October, she and Scott return to Manhattan and rent an apartment at 38 West Fifty-Ninth Street near the Plaza Hotel.

1921
Edouard serves aboard the *Waldeck-Rousseau* as current deck officer.

March 1921
Zelda becomes pregnant.

May 3–July 1921
The Fitzgeralds embark on their first European trip to England, France, and Italy.

August 1921
Scott and Zelda travel to St. Paul, Minnesota, to await the birth of their child. They rent a cottage at Dellwood, White Bear Lake.

October 26, 1921
Their daughter is born and named Frances Scott Key Fitzgerald, nicknamed "Scottie."

November 21–June 1922
The Fitzgeralds rent a house at 626 Goodrich Avenue in St. Paul, Minnesota.

March 1922
Scott's second novel, *The Beautiful and Damned*, is published.

March 1922
Edouard begins his career as a naval aviator assigned first to Centre de Berre, then Saint Raphael on the Riviera where he is a test pilot.

Summer 1922
The Fitzgeralds stay at White Bear Yacht Club outside St. Paul.

October 1922
The Fitzgeralds return east and rent a house at 6 Gateway Drive in Great Neck, Long Island. Scott and Ring Lardner become friends.

1924
Edouard is the first pilot to complete a night landing aboard an aircraft carrier.

May 1924
The Fitzgeralds sail for France on the SS *Minnewaska*. After meeting Gerald and Sara Murphy in Paris, they leave for the French Riviera in June. En route they stop at Grimm's Park Hotel in Hyeres, the Ruhl in Nice, Hotel de Paris in Monte Carlo, and Continental in San Raphael. They sign a lease for Villa Marie in Valescure.

June 1924
Zelda meets Edouard Jozan, assigned to Frejus air field near San Raphael. She begins an affair with him while Scott is writing *The Great Gatsby*.

July 13, 1924
Scott learns of the affair. It ends abruptly, and Zelda is confined to Villa Marie. She does not see Edouard again.

August 1924
Gilbert Seldes and his bride, Amanda, visit the Fitzgeralds at Valescure. Zelda makes her first suicide attempt a month later at Cap d'Antibes Hotel.

November 1924–April 1925
The Fitzgeralds depart St. Raphael for Rome, where they stay at Hotel des Princes. After excursions to Tivoli, Frascati, and Naples, they depart for Capri and stay at the Hotel Tiberio. They return that spring to Paris and rent an apartment at 14 rue de Tilsitt.

April 10, 1925
The Great Gatsby is published.

May 1925
Scott meets Ernest Hemingway at the Dingo Bar in Paris.

August 1925
The Fitzgeralds spend a month in Antibes as part of the Murphys' circle, afterward leaving for Paris where Zelda begins ballet lessons with Lubov Egorova.

March–December, 1926
The Fitzgeralds return to the Riviera and rent Villa St. Louis at Juan-les-Pins.

January 1926
Zelda takes "cure" at Salies-de-Bearn.

March 1926
The Fitzgeralds depart for the Riviera and rent the Villa Paquita at Juan-les-Pins.

January 1927
Zelda, Scott, and their daughter return to America. They go to Hollywood, where Scott works on the script *Lipstick* for United Artists. In retaliation for Zelda's indiscretion with Edouard, Scott begins an affair with seventeen-year-old actress Lois Moran.

March 1927–March 1928
The Fitzgeralds sign a two-year lease on Ellerslie in Edgemoor, Delaware, near Wilmington. Lois Moran visits over the weekend of May 21, 1927.

1927–1928
Scott taunts Zelda with Lois's success. In response, she decides to become a professional ballerina and begins lessons with Catherine Littlefield in Philadelphia.

1928
Edouard Jozan marries Lucienne Gruss-Gallieni, granddaughter of General Joseph Gallieni, French minster of war and marshal of France. After leaving Frejus, he is assigned to sea duty aboard the aircraft carrier *Bearn*. He enters Officers Torpedo School.

April–August 1928
The Fitzgeralds return to Paris and rent an apartment at 58 rue de Vaugirard. Zelda returns to ballet lessons with Lubov Egorova.

October 7, 1928–March 1929
The Fitzgeralds return to Ellerslie in Delaware and remain until their lease expires.

March 1929
Scott and Zelda depart for Genova, Italy, aboard the *Conte Biancamano*. They continue to Nice, then Paris. In July they return to Cannes where they rent the Villa Fleur des Bois and remain until October when they return to Paris.

June 1929
The Fitzgeralds leave for Cannes where they rent Villa Fleur des Bois. Zelda continues studying ballet. She rejects an offer to perform with the Royal Ballet in Naples, Italy.

October 1929
The Fitzgeralds return to Paris by car. They rent an apartment at 10 rue Pergolese. Zelda resumes ballet classes with Egorova.

1929
Edouard is appointed to General Navy Staff.

February 1930
Zelda and Scott visit Algeria, leaving Scottie in Paris with her governess.

April 1930
Zelda experiences her first mental breakdown. She enters Malmaison Clinic outside Paris on April 23, transferring to Val-Mont Clinic in Glion, Switzerland, on May 22. On June 5 Scott drives her to Prangins Clinic near Nyon, on Lake Geneva in Switzerland.

Summer–Fall 1930
Scott moves to Switzerland.

January 26, 1931
Scott's father dies and he travels to Rockville, Maryland, for the funeral. Afterward, he visits Zelda's parents in Montgomery.

July 1931
The Fitzgeralds spend two weeks at Lake Annecy, France.

September 15, 1931
After fifteen months of treatment, Zelda is released from Prangins and the family returns to America on the *Aquitania*.

September 1931–Spring 1932
The Fitzgeralds live near Zelda's parents in Montgomery, renting a house at 819 Felder Avenue in the Cloverdale area.

November–December 1931
Scott departs for Hollywood alone to work on the *Red Headed Woman* script for Metro-Goldwyn-Mayer.

November 17, 1931
Zelda's father dies. She begins writing her novel *Save Me the Waltz*.

1931–1933
Edouard serves on torpedo boats and becomes secondary commander aboard the *Alcyon*.

February 12, 1932
Zelda suffers her second major breakdown and enters Phipps Psychiatric Clinic of Johns Hopkins University Hospital in Baltimore, Maryland.

March 1932
At Phipps Clinic, Zelda completes first draft of *Save Me the Waltz* and sends it directly to Maxwell Perkins at Scribner's.

May 20, 1932–November 1933
Scott rents La Paix on the Turnbull estate in Towson outside Baltimore. He befriends Andrew Turnbull, who becomes one of his early biographers.

June 26, 1932
Zelda is discharged from Phipps Clinic and joins Scott and Scottie at La Paix.

Summer 1932
Scott does not allow *Save Me the Waltz* to be published without his revisions.

October 7, 1932
Save Me the Waltz is published.

June 26–July 1933
Zelda's play *Scandalabra* is performed by the Vagabond Junior Players in Baltimore.

October 1933
Zelda enters the Independent Artists' Exhibition at the Baltimore Museum of Art.

November 1933–Summer 1934
Edouard receives his *brevete d'etat-major* from the Naval War College.

November–December 1933
Scott takes Zelda on vacation to Bermuda.

December 1933
Scott moves family to rental house at 1307 Park Avenue in Baltimore.

January–April 1934
Tender Is the Night is serialized in *Scribner's Magazine*.

February 12, 1934
Zelda has third major breakdown and returns to Phipps Clinic.

March 1934
Scott transfers Zelda to Craig House in Beacon, New York.

March 29–April 30, 1934
Zelda's art exhibition opens at Cary Ross's New York City studio at 525 East Eighty-Sixth Street. It is accompanied by a checklist Zelda designs with a swan depicted at top, bearing the words, in French, *Parfois la folie est la sagesse* (Sometimes madness is wisdom).

1934
Edouard stationed at Centre de Ballons Captifs de Toulon, then with French Air Ministry.

April 12, 1934
Scott's fourth novel, *Tender Is the Night*, is published by Scribner's.

May 19, 1934
Zelda is transferred from Craig House to Sheppard Pratt Hospital outside Baltimore.

June 1934
Scott suffers nervous collapse and remains for a week at New York Hospital.

February 1935
Scott stays at Oak Hall Hotel in Tryon, North Carolina.

May 1935
Scott spends summer at Grove Park Inn in Asheville, North Carolina.

September 1935
Scott rents a Baltimore apartment on Charles Street, where he lives with Scottie.

November 1935
Scott stays at Skyland Hotel in Hendersonville, North Carolina, and begins writing *The Crack-Up* essays.

January 1936
At Ministry of Aviation, Edouard Jozan becomes aide to the secretary of the navy. He crosses the Atlantic on the giant hydroplane *Lieutenant de Vasisseau-Paris*, copiloting the plane from Dakar, Senegal to Pensacola, Florida.

February–April 1936
Scott's *The Crack-Up* essays are published in *Esquire* magazine.

April 8, 1936
Zelda enters Highland Hospital in Asheville, North Carolina.

July–December 1936
Scott returns to Grove Park Inn.

September 1936
Scott's mother, Mollie, dies in Washington, DC.

September 1937
Edouard is promoted to lieutenant commander of naval patrol sea planes squadron, the Croix du Sud. He becomes captain de corvette.

January–June 1937
Scott stays at Oak Hall Hotel in Tryon, North Carolina, where he meets Nora and Lefty Flynn.

July 1937
Scott returns to Hollywood for the third time with a six-month MGM contract. On July 14, he meets gossip columnist Sheilah Graham with whom he begins a relationship. He moves five times: from the Garden of Allah Hotel on Sunset Boulevard to a bungalow in Malibu; then to Encino, where he lives in the cottage Belly Acres on the estate of Edgar Everett Horton; then to 1403 North Laurel Avenue in Hollywood; and finally to Sheilah Graham's nearby apartment at 1443 North Hayworth Avenue.

September 1937
Scott visits Zelda at Highland Hospital and takes her to Myrtle Beach and Charleston, South Carolina.

December 1937
Scott's MGM contract is renewed for one year.

March 1938
Zelda, Scott, and Scottie spend Easter week at the Cavalier Hotel in Virginia Beach, Virginia.

September 1938
Scottie enters Vassar College.

December 1938
Scott's MGM contract is not renewed.

1938–1939
Edouard appointed to the Special Staff of the minister for the colonies.

February 1939
Zelda takes course in costume design and life drawing at the Ringling School of Art in Sarasota, Florida, exhibiting her work later this year with the Asheville Artists' Guild.

March 1939–October 1940
Scott does freelance jobs with Paramount Pictures, Goldwyn Studios, Columbia Studios, Universal, and 20th Century Fox.

April 1939
Scott and Zelda go on a disastrous trip to Cuba. Scott is hospitalized when they return to New York.

March 1940
Edouard Jozan is assigned to Oran, Algeria, where he becomes commander of the French Naval Air Force.

May–June 1940
Edouard becomes commandant of the First Naval Chase Air Group at Calais. He distinguishes himself by shooting down numerous German planes during enemy attacks. He is promoted to commander in November 1940, then appointed to the General Naval Staff at Bizerte, Tunisia.

April 15, 1940
Zelda is discharged from Highland Hospital to live with her mother at 322 Sayre Street in Montgomery. For the rest of her life, she will return intermittently to Highland Hospital in Asheville, North Carolina.

November 1940
Edouard is appointed to captain de frigate.

December 21, 1940
Scott dies of a heart attack in Sheilah Graham's Hollywood apartment at 1443 North Hayworth Avenue. His body is taken by train to Maryland where he is buried in Rockville Union Cemetery on December 27.

1941
Edmund Wilson edits *The Last Tycoon* for posthumous publication. Zelda exhibits her paintings and watercolors at the Montgomery Museum of Fine Arts.

1942
Edouard joins French Resistance against the Nazi occupation of France.

March 1943
The German Gestapo captures Edouard at Luchon in the Pyrenees. He is taken to Eisenberg prisoner of war camp in Germany.

May 1943
Edouard escapes from Eisenberg but is recaptured and sent to Oranienburg concentration camp where he remains two and a half years.

August 1943–February 1944
Zelda is a patient at Highland Hospital.

April 21, 1945
Edouard is one of nine thousand prisoners on the death march from Sachenhausen toward Wistock and Schwarin in northern Germany. He survives and returns to Paris after the German defeat. Promoted to captain, he is assigned to the Navy General Staff, then to the cabinet of Edmond Michelet, minister for the armies.

January–May 1946
Zelda is a patient at Highland Hospital.

April 20, 1946
Edouard is promoted to contre-amiral.

1946–1948
Edouard becomes commander of the French Naval Forces in Morocco.

November 2, 1947
Zelda reenters Highland for insulin and electric shock treatments.

March 11, 1948
Zelda dies in a fire at Highland Hospital. She is buried with Scott at Rockville Union Cemetery in Rockville, Maryland.

1950–1953
Edouard heads up Mediterranean air and marine forces. He becomes *prefet* of the Marines in Tunisia.

1952–54
Edouard is appointed vice-admiral of France's Far Eastern Naval Force.

April 1954–1955
Assigned to Indochina, Edouard heads the French Navy in the Pacific Ocean and China Sea.

1956
Edouard is stationed on the ship *DeGrasse Escadre* in the Mediterranean.

1957
Edouard is promoted to vice-amiral descadre.

April 1959
Edouard becomes commandant in chief of the strategic zone of the Indian Ocean.

December 1959
Edouard retires as a full admiral and returns to Paris where he is appointed to the board of directors of ANECMA. He enters Navy Reserve with the rank of admiral. He purchases a country estate at Mezilles two hours northeast of Paris. Edouard and Lucienne move to Cannes in 1961.

1971
Edouard is awarded the Grand-Croix de la Legion of Honor. He becomes a member of the Conseil de l'Ordre.

November 7, 1975
Zelda and Scott are reburied in the Fitzgerald family plot at St. Mary's Church in Rockville, Maryland.

December 11, 1981
Edouard dies in Cannes at age eighty-two.

June 18, 1986
Scottie Fitzgerald Lanahan Smith dies in Montgomery, Alabama, and is buried with her parents at St. Mary's Church in Rockville, Maryland.

2006
Edouard's wife, Lucienne, dies in Cannes, France.

· 1 ·

Recklessness in the Making

$\mathcal{O}$ne sultry July night in 1918, First Lieutenant F. Scott Fitzgerald made his way into Montgomery from nearby Camp Sheridan and headed for the country club on Narrow Lane Road. Not a member, he had pulled strings to obtain an entry pass, and after presenting it at the door, headed for the sounds of Art Hickman's *Rose Room Fox Trot* coming from the ballroom. He found the crowd poised to watch seventeen-year-old Zelda Sayre perform Ponchielli's *Dance of the Hours* from *La Gioconda*. The operatic vignette portrayed time from morning through night, and before Zelda reached dusk, Scott was captivated, remembering how she glistened that evening, comparing that glow to the illumination Italian painters used to depict hovering angels.

She had started taking dance lessons at six and trained with several good teachers, the best being Professor Weisner, who was so exceptional, no one could understand why someone as talented should come to Montgomery. But there he was, and under his skillful tutelage, she appeared in numerous pageants and entertainments, receiving top billing in ballet recitals at the Grand Theater. Besides performing in classical ballet, Zelda knew the trendy dances, like the Blizzard Lop, Bunny Hug, and Tickle-Toe, and was the most popular girl in any ballroom. When her performance ended that Saturday night, Scott sauntered over to introduce himself and they began dancing, but it was impossible to sustain her attention. Boys lined the length of the ballroom and kept cutting in. To get her alone, Scott suggested a midnight date, to which Zelda laughingly responded that she never made late dates with fast workers. The demand for her was overwhelming, and frequently there were multiple dates during one evening: early dinner at six, a second engagement at nine, and a late date at eleven. Her strategy was to keep each suitor aching for more and it worked. In between, the Sayres'

1

phone rang incessantly, and deliverymen brought boxes of chocolates, long-stemmed roses, and fragrant gardenias.

Nonetheless, Scott's smartly tailored uniform made some impression, because he managed to get her phone number. When he rang the next day, though, he learned she was booked for weeks and devised a way to see her sooner by organizing a party in honor of her eighteenth birthday. It was a magical evening she never forgot, with Zelda playing the fragrant phantom and Scott the handsome lieutenant, caught up in a radiant light of soft conspiracy, in which even the pine trees agreed, it was all going to be for the best.

Voted the prettiest and most popular in her class, Zelda was noticeably different from other girls and the most sought after of Montgomery's young women. Scott was fascinated by the way she was so universally admired, a prize to be won against worthy competition. She was being pursued by not only local suitors but also soldiers from the nearby base. Two of them—Lieutenants Henry Watson of Douglasville, Georgia, and Lincoln Weaver of Wilkinsburg, Pennsylvania—were doing regular flybys over her house, until their airplane took a nose dive and crashed on a nearby racetrack. Zelda gave the article, "Aviators Crash to Earth Monday at the Speedway," a prominent place in her scrapbook.

With his blond hair parted down the middle and heavily lashed lavender eyes, and at five feet seven and 160 pounds, Scott was not overly masculine but was popular with women. Although he didn't have the two top things, animal magnetism or money, he was good looking and intelligent so remained in competition for the top girl. Dressed in his custom-tailored Brooks Brothers uniform, designed with side pockets to distinguish it from regulation issue, and wearing jodhpurs with knee-high leather boots, he exuded a jaunty confidence that suggested he belonged to the intellectual and social elite. The impression was not lost on Zelda, who thought he epitomized Ivy League fellows who smelled of Russian leather and seemed very used to being alive. In those days, it was still exceptional for young men from Montgomery to leave for law school or medical colleges, and most lived locally their entire life. As a Midwesterner from Minnesota, Scott was different from Southern men, and his tenure at Princeton had given him an urbanity against which fellows from Auburn and Tuscaloosa could not compete. Although Zelda was pursued by many men from better families with more money, none were superficially as impressive or possessed such lofty ambitions. She was awed by his certainty over becoming a famous author and flattered to hear that she resembled the heroine in his novel. Only secretly she wondered, if he had met her somewhere else, would he have been as interested?

Although Scott lacked financial security, he had the cache of being named after the composer of "The Star-Spangled Banner." Although he was only a distant second cousin, three times removed, it was something he mentioned immediately upon introduction. His mother, Mollie McQuillan, was the eldest daughter of an Irish immigrant who settled in Illinois during 1843 and established a thriving grocery business that grew into one of the Midwest's largest wholesale companies. When Mollie's father died prematurely, the estate was worth $300,000, which enabled his widow to raise their five children comfortably. Mollie was twenty-nine when she married Edward Fitzgerald, who managed a small wicker factory in St. Paul, Minnesota. Never adept at business, when that enterprise went bankrupt, he found employment as a salesman with Procter & Gamble in Syracuse, New York, but was soon fired. Scott's insecurities were heightened by his father's failures, and he never forgot the day his father had left the house full of confidence, then returned home a broken man.

After his dismissal, Edward never again found firm footing, and the family moved from one rented house to another, ultimately returning to St. Paul where McQuillan money became their primary support. With her dwindling inheritance, Mollie managed to educate her two children in private schools, but Scott always was embarrassed by his family's circumstances. At the core he felt ineffectual and believed he lacked the necessary qualities for success. The one area in which Edward was a positive influence involved refinement and manners. He taught his son a sense of decorum, and to acquire certain skills sent Scott to dancing school where he became a star pupil. Practicing steps in his parents' front parlor, he became adept with waltzes and fox-trots, as well as the trendy Maxie and aeroplane glide.

When Scott performed poorly at St. Paul Academy, he transferred to Newman, a Catholic boarding school in Hackensack, New Jersey, where his grades were equally unimpressive. Already drinking and smoking by fifteen, due to a genetic disposition or because the "idea" of consuming alcohol disoriented him, he became easily intoxicated. Consistently late for classes or skipping them entirely, his January 1912 grades revealed unsatisfactory results in most subjects. Newman should have prepared him for Ivy League colleges but did not. When he underwent entrance exams for Princeton, even after cheating on the multiple-choice part, Scott failed the essay section. Then, after studying all summer for the makeup test, he failed again. He had always fantasized about attending Princeton, where he saw success linked to his writing ability, and his remaining hope was an interview. A meeting with the board of appeals was scheduled for his seventeenth birthday, and impeccably attired in clothing from Brooks Brothers and Jacob Reed, he took the train to Princeton and, largely on the virtue of his charm, convinced admissions officers to accept him into the class of 1917.

Through his work with the campus literary magazine *Nassau Lit*, Scott got to know Edmund Wilson and John Peale Bishop, who introduced him to the poetry of John Keats and the French Symbolists, teaching him more about literature than his instructors. He also befriended John Biggs, who, like Scott, was the indulged son of a doting mother. John had a shaky relationship with his father, a prominent Delaware attorney, who considered his son lacking in intelligence. Actually, he was dyslexic, which made studies difficult and got him dismissed from several schools. Although he finished Princeton and entered Harvard Law, he was an equally poor student there, where he seldom attended classes and barely graduated with Cs. His father's contempt only deepened over the years, and John harbored deep resentment about that. Beneath his calm exterior, anger churned.

John wasn't alone in having difficulty making it through Princeton. By the end of Scott's sophomore year, he had failed so many classes, he became ineligible to remain an English major, and six weeks into his junior year was barred from all extracurricular activities. Since his real interests lay in writing for the dramatic club literary magazines and making social connections, he dropped out before the end of fall semester and was then told he would have to repeat it. A year of terrible disappointment brought upon himself, it marked the end of his college dreams.

Since many classmates already had left for war, Scott applied for a commission, having unearthed a federal statute authorizing officer status for those speaking French. It was a proficiency he didn't have, but details aside, he took examinations at Fort Snelling for a provisional regular army appointment as second lieutenant. When he returned to Princeton the following August and enrolled in John Biggs's class of 1918, temporarily moving into his room, he anticipated it would only be for a short time.

Scott was correct, since his commission arrived on October 26, 1917, when he left for St. Paul to say good-bye to his parents. From there it was on to Officers' Training School at Fort Leavenworth, Kansas, where the captain in charge was Dwight David Eisenhower. As poor a second lieutenant as a college student, instead of paying attention to lectures on trench warfare, he scribbled notes for a novel and worked on the manuscript during evenings and weekends at the Officers' Club and base library. In three months he finished a first draft. One of his Princeton professors suggested submitting it to Scribner's since Charles Scribner and his younger brother, Arthur, both were alumni. Unfortunately, the publishing house's chief editor, William Crary Brownell, disliked the manuscript, and it was only his apprentice, Maxwell Perkins, who thought it had potential. After graduating from Harvard, Max had joined Scribner's and was eager to shift its focus away from publishing established authors to bringing out the best new writers. They kept Scott waiting five months before announcing their decision, and the letter finally came from Max, who said the manuscript was original but needed more work.

His major criticism was that the story never advanced to any conclusion, and the hero drifted from one situation to another without any awareness or understanding. He encouraged Scott to revise and resubmit. Two months later, Scott sent an improved version that Charles Scribner III liked, but other editors again vetoed.

In February 1918, Scott was transferred with the Ninth Division of the Forty-Fifth Infantry from Fort Leavenworth to Camp Zachary Taylor near Louisville, Kentucky, and then to Camp Gordon in Georgia, where he got lucky and received an assignment as aide-de-camp to Brigadier General James A. Ryan, commandant of the Seventeenth Infantry Brigade at Camp Sheridan, outside Montgomery, Alabama. His Princeton credentials, although abbreviated, and Irish Catholic background won him an easy posting at Headquarters Detachment, where he functioned as Ryan's social secretary.

Montgomery had been chosen Alabama's state capital in 1846 and was a picturesque place with restaurants and shops occupying tree-lined streets that ran from its Victorian train station, smelling of bananas and marshmallows, to the town's center at Dexter and Commerce. Many of its roads were still unpaved, so people had to wash their feet before going to bed. On the surface Montgomery seemed genteel, but just below, passions simmered. As Zelda explains in her unpublished novel *Caesar's Things*, men had been shot for committing flagrante delicto (Latin for being caught in the midst of sexual activity) under the Confederate Monument and in most commercial hotels, and one blew his brains out in the main thoroughfare. As the way Zelda viewed it, people made mistakes because they were generous of spirit and not given to restraint.

Montgomery was neither as tranquil nor as accepting of outsiders as might first appear; the Civil War still lingered on peoples' minds. A generation of men had been massacred in the conflict, including Zelda's two uncles; the residence of another uncle was used as the first White House of the Confederacy. A quiet community of forty thousand until becoming an air depot for Southern training contingents, Montgomery had been selected because of already existing air fields and the base, Camp Sheridan, named after Union Army general Phil Sheridan. It was an affront Montgomery's residents strongly resented. Soldiers began arriving in the fall of 1917 when Zelda was a high school senior. Not since the Civil War had so many Northerners been seen and the place swirled with activity, the base housing half as many people as the town itself. The First World War brought swarms of men to the town, and Zelda remembered the jaunty aviation officers with sunburned noses and white around their eyes from where goggles had been, better dressed in their uniforms than ever before. The town smelled of khaki and army leather, telephone booths were never empty, and there were rendezvous everywhere.

That July, Scott was still recovering from being rejected by Ginevra King, daughter of the Chicago stockbroker Charles Garfield King. The third daughter over three generations to be named after Leonardo da Vinci's *Ginevra de Benci* and an equally enigmatic beauty, at sixteen she already was popular with Ivy League boys. The two were introduced in St. Paul during January 1915 when Ginevra was visiting her classmate, Marie Hersey, a neighbor of Scott's on Summit Avenue. Both were sophomores at Westover, an exclusive girls' school in Middlebury, Connecticut. Scott initially appealed to Ginevra, and she accepted his invitation to Princeton, but it was a one-sided romance that he fantasized out of proportion. Her younger sister, Marjorie, considered Scott a nonentity and never understood why she bothered with him. Ginevra generally dated wealthy boys with status, and Scott unquestionably was middle class. Once, at a party the two attended in Lake Forest, Scott overheard someone remark that poor boys shouldn't think of marrying rich girls, and knew the comment was directed at him. Ginevra's indifference toward their relationship finally registered after their breakup, when he asked for his letters back and discovered she had not kept them. Not only had he saved hers but had them typed and bound in a volume numbering three hundred pages.

Scott's feelings about the affluent being different from others stemmed from this rejection. He believed that possessing early made them soft where other people were hard and cynical rather than trusting. They simply considered themselves better than everyone else. Ginevra would always represent the golden girl who got away, and Scott was determined not to have that happen again. Just two weeks before meeting Zelda, his loss was reawakened when Ginevra wrote that she was marrying Ensign William Hamilton Mitchell, a Harvard grad and son of the president of the Illinois Trust and Savings Bank. The wedding was to occur on September 4, 1918, in Chicago at St. Chrysostom's Church, after which Mitchell would assume duties as a flight instructor in Florida at the Naval Air Station in Key West. To keep everything in the family, his younger brother, Clarence, would later wed Ginevra's sister, Marjorie.

When she met Scott, Zelda was days away from her eighteenth birthday, the last of Minnie Buckner Machen and Anthony Dickerson Sayre's six children. Her mother was almost forty when Zelda was born on July 24, 1900. The family was Episcopalian, and Zelda was baptized in the Church of the Holy Comforter where her three sisters were christened before her: Marjorie, the oldest, born in 1882; Rosalind, eleven years Zelda's elder, born in 1889; and Clothilde, nine years older, born in 1891. Her brother Daniel Morgan Sayre had died of spinal meningitis at eighteen months in 1885, leaving Anthony Jr., born in 1894, the remaining son.

Zelda was never close to her sisters but interacted with Rosalind more than the others. Considered exceptional for the period, Rosalind worked as a reporter and society editor for the *Montgomery Journal* before moving to Brussels with her banker husband, Newman Smith. Clothilde and Marjorie were attractive and popular in Montgomery long before Zelda. A classic beauty with creamy skin and large dark eyes, Clothilde (called Tilde) was the first girl from a respectable family to work in a job other than teaching. She raised eyebrows by becoming a teller for the First National Bank, where men lined up to stare at her through the front window, and she kept that position until marrying John M. Palmer. Marjorie (called Tootie) was considered the artistic one and created exquisite ink drawings and watercolors. A sickly child, she was prone to depression much of her life and worked as an elementary school teacher before marrying Minor Brinson. The only surviving boy, Anthony Jr., was an aimless and rebellious youth who dropped out of Auburn, suffered a nervous breakdown, and ultimately took his life, the third member in Zelda's immediate family to do so.

The Sayres were acknowledged Southern aristocracy. Already prominent in New Jersey and Ohio by the 1600s, the family moved to Alabama in 1819, where they became large landowners, prosperous merchants, and respected citizens. Anthony Sayre's mother, Musidora Morgan, was the sister of John Tyler Morgan, a general in the Confederate Army and six-term US senator from Alabama. He became a national figure who argued for the annexation of Hawaii and the Philippines, twice was presidential elector on the Democratic ticket, and died in office, his remaining term served out by John H. Bankhead, grandfather of Zelda's friend Tallulah.

On her mother's side, the family was equally prestigious. Minnie Machen came from a family of wealthy landowners, statesmen, and politicians. Descendants of early Maryland and Virginia settlers from the Scottish Mac Hen clan, they had emigrated to Virginia early in the seventeenth century when they changed their name to Machen. Minnie's father was an attorney and tobacco planter who owned three thousand acres on the Cumberland River, represented Virginia in the Confederate Congress, and after the Civil War served as a United States senator from that state. An artistic and talented young woman who sang and played the piano, after graduating from Montgomery Female College in 1878, Minnie traveled to Philadelphia for voice and diction lessons with aspirations of going on stage. However, when a role was offered, her father abruptly ordered her home. In the 1880s women from good families did not become stage performers.

Anthony Dickerson Sayre met Minnie in 1879 at a New Year's gala in Montgomery. Highly intelligent and valedictorian of his Roanoke College class, Anthony had taught math at Vanderbilt University for a year before returning to Montgomery to study law. The two married in 1884, but it was an unsuitable match. The spontaneous and expressive Minnie was not right for the taciturn and frugal Anthony, who desired an orderly home life and wished to live simply. He had a powerful aversion to debt and shunned the responsibility of owning property along with the attention it required. In short order, Minnie progressed from being a pretty and popular young woman to a housewife juggling household tasks. She was responsible for rearing the children with help from a colored nanny, organizing meals, seeing that laundry got done, and supervising the cook, laundress, and yardman, all former slaves. She tried to be a capable wife and mother but had no idea how to discipline her children. Zelda considered them two unhappy people, her mother dominated and oppressed by her father, who was forced to work for a large family in which he found little satisfaction. To compensate for her thwarted ambitions, Minnie wrote poetry for Montgomery newspapers, gave singing lessons, and produced plays and skits for community theater. She also taught her daughters to seek opportunities denied her and encouraged Zelda to shine in the spotlight.

In 1909, the family moved from one rental house to another, the first of which was a gray frame bungalow on Pleasant Avenue. Its large informal rooms were attractively papered and furniture positioned on pine floors centered with rugs. Tall bookcases lined hallways and a piano dominated the living room, on whose walls hung a painting of Minnie Sayre's mother and a hand-colored mezzotint of Napoleon bidding his wife and infant son goodbye. The house had a wide front porch covered with clematis vines, where a creaking swing occupied one corner, on which Zelda entertained suitors, the overflow of activity tumbling down onto front steps. Her room was directly above that porch on the second floor. The smallest and coziest, it was papered in a floral design that matched a chintz-covered dressing table. A straw mat covered the floor, and furnishings included a small white desk, slender rocking chair, and white painted iron bed. Zelda tells us the judge's room was upstairs and adjacent to hers and that her sisters also slept upstairs, but in the back on the other side. Her father may have positioned himself as a sentry to discourage suitors or desired proximity himself.

After being admitted to the Alabama Bar in 1880, Judge Sayre went on to become president of the state Senate and associate justice of the Alabama Supreme Court. In harmony with his colleagues, he was a white supremacist and during the 1890s introduced the Sayre Election Law into the Alabama legislature, which deprived Alabama's Negroes and poor whites of voting rights. Renowned for never having his legal opinions overturned, Judge Sayre was called "the brains of the Bar" and revered by the community. He neither smoked nor drank and was in bed by 8:30 p.m. Because his eyesight was poor, he never learned to drive and every morning walked to the corner and caught the tram to the capitol. So great a judge was he considered, Zelda tells us, that whenever it rained, the conductor of the street car he took to work would stop and walk two blocks with an umbrella to get him.

Not as successful in his personal life, Anthony was aloof with his family and a strict disciplinarian whom Zelda enjoyed defying. Behind his back she called him *old Dick*, a derisive reference to *Dickerson*, his middle name, and much of her youthful rebellion was in retaliation for his icy detachment. Although Judge Sayre disapproved of his daughter's behavior and was embarrassed by it, any attempts at discipline failed. When he locked her in her bedroom she crawled out the window, and if he called her a "hussy" she only laughed.

From him, Zelda inherited a razor-sharp mind and from her mother, a superb vocabulary and ability to use words imaginatively. Thoughtful and perceptive, Zelda possessed powers of observation recognized by everyone, but she showed little interest in school, and with the exception of literature and math, expended only enough effort to pass. Academics seemed useless to her, and she thought the education of children should be intuitive. Some of her difficulty completing assignments may have come from poor eyesight inherited from her father. Her sister, Rosalind, remembered, "The specialist to whom Mama took her for her sinus trouble discovered that she had no retina in one eye. He told mama about it, but I feel sure that mama did not tell Zelda, or that Zelda ever realized it." More likely, it was a detached retina. Nearsighted in one eye, she squinted whenever observing things closely, but scoffed at any suggestion of spectacles, suggesting that boys didn't make passes at girls who wore glasses. Along with eye problems, Zelda may have inherited her father's inclination toward depression. At the beginning of Zelda's senior year, the judge experienced what Minnie called "nervous prostration," an incapacitating depressive episode lasting nine months through which Minnie nursed him. Disorders of this type were common in her family, but Zelda's behavior may have aggravated the judge's condition. "As long as I can remember and long before that I have been told," one classmate remarked, "Montgomery always had at least one girl who either purposely or unintentionally stood out as the target of town talk. In the spring of that year, Zelda was the target."

None of this was evident that July night, when Scott became captivated by Zelda's abundant self-confidence and good looks. No photograph adequately captured that beauty. Chosen by her classmates as "the prettiest and most energetic girl with the most kissable mouth," she had gorgeous coloring, gray-green eyes, and masses of silky, honey-gold hair. At five foot five, she stood almost eye level with Scott, but appeared taller and seemed to float across the room with a dancer's grace. Scott greatly admired her slender, beautifully proportioned body, and Zelda put a premium on it. She never consumed large meals and was particular about what she ate, for a while practically living on tomato sandwiches, a peculiarity Scott wove into his second novel, *The Beautiful and Damned*. There was this strong conviction, he explained, that she had to have "a lemonade and a tomato sandwich late in the morning, then a light lunch with a stuffed tomato." Along with diet, a regimen of activity maintained the slimness she considered an important asset. Roller skating better than anyone else, she would race down Sayre Street toward the synagogue, turning only at the last moment to avoid traffic. Sara Mayfield recalled how she "skated at break-neck speed down the Perry Street hill with passing automobiles making the descent doubly hazardous, and urged more and more speed from her swains as they drove to and from parties, while the rest of us contented ourselves with a quieter pace." A natural athlete, Zelda was equally good at tennis and golf, and was a champion swimmer and diver. Swimming was her favorite activity, in those days quite a distinction for women, and in her Annette Kellerman suit, she would sneak into the Huntington College pool and practice strokes, her agile arms and legs propelling her effortlessly through the water. This was a vigorous effort with warm-up drills followed by a specific set of strokes, the aim of which was to propel through the water as efficiently as possible. The backstroke was then popular, having been introduced at the 1912 Olympics, and Zelda was very good at it, having also mastered the breaststroke and high dive. She loved plunging into the water from the crane others feared climbing at Roquemore's gravel pit, swam in jagged creeks, and jumped perilously from rotting trees, returning home smelling of dank loam. "She swam and dove as well as most of the boys and better than many," recalled one classmate. "She was absolutely fearless; there was a board rigged up at the swimming pool, from which everyone was afraid to dive, but Zelda did it without a thought." Knees together, she flexed her feet and up she went. Once, while swimming at the pool behind the chemical plant, while preparing for a dive from the high board, her arms got entangled in the straps of her suit, and without a thought, she stepped out of it, and posing like a water nymph, rose upon her toes and gracefully sprung from the board. Most women who swam wore a black serge bathing suit, made from tightly woven twill fabric, but Zelda's outfit was sheer, which startled people and turned men's heads.

From childhood, she was drawn to excitement and seldom encountered anyone she could not outdistance. With her mother allowing her free rein and father complaining to no avail, by sixteen her rebellious personality was firmly established. One friend recalled,

Zelda lived just around the corner from me on Pleasant Avenue. She went in our crowd and was my friend in high school days although she was different from us even then—not so different by nature, perhaps, as by the fact that she was unsupervised. The rest of us went directly home from school unless we had permission from home to do otherwise, but Zelda could go to town or home with someone without contacting her mother. The rest of us stayed home and studied on school nights, but Zelda went at will, often dropping in after supper to talk. She was smart but never studied regularly. Her grades were passing but seldom above average. She was amiable, kind, happy-go-lucky, uninhibited and undisciplined. She followed her own interests to the neglect of duties.

Zelda's antics were matched only by those of Tallulah Bankhead. Two years older, Tallulah was an athletic tomboy with daredevil courage who performed somersaults and handstands in front of the capitol building and cartwheeled before the circular staircase of its rotunda. Tallulah's mother had died three weeks after giving birth to her, and the newborn was shuffled between her grandmother's house in Jasper and aunt Marie Bankhead's home in Montgomery. A successful career woman, Bankhead directed the Department of Archives and History with her husband, Dr. Thomas Owens, a cousin of Sara Mayfield's. The Bankheads socialized with the Sayre family, and when Zelda was ten, Marie interviewed her for a newspaper article titled "Children of the Alabama Judiciary." In the piece, Marie described Zelda as an adventurous, imaginative, and gregarious girl who enjoyed energetic games like Robber and Indian because they involved running, and admired Indians because they were splendid swimmers and riders. Up and dressed before breakfast to greet the morning, she was prepared for the day's exploits yet to be revealed.

Tallulah's father, William Brockman Bankhead, was a United States congressman, and her uncle and grandfather both United States senators and influential politicians in Washington and Alabama. The Bankheads were better known than the Sayres, and their privileged status in Montgomery gave Tallulah, and her sister Eugenia, the same liberties accorded Zelda. The two did as they pleased, but Eugenia, older by one year and prettier of the two, was more exuberant and boisterous. They competed with Zelda for being the most talked about girls, and residents continually were amazed by their antics on Goat Hill, the grassy slope that cascaded down from the capitol dome. "Even in those days," recalled Sara Mayfield, "both of them had dash, a style and daring that left me wideeyed and open mouthed with admiration. For Zelda and Dutch, as we called Tallulah, were personalities and performers long before they became famous, routinely performing songs and dance numbers the Capitol steps. Tallulah was so limber she could do a back bend and pluck a scarf from the floor with her teeth." Her best routines were hilarious parodies of Miss Gussie Woodruff, the prim white-haired headmistress who oversaw one of the two private schools for girls in Montgomery, the other being operated by Margaret Booth. After dropping out of the Booth School, Bankhead endured several more educational trials before giving up and devoting herself to the antics her appreciative audience referred to as Tallulabaloos.

One generation earlier, women from good families were discouraged from performing in theaters, but the film industry changed all that, and females everywhere were obsessed with becoming actresses on stage or screen, envisioning themselves as the next Mary Pickford or Clara Bow. Tallulah was totally starstruck; at fifteen she answered an advertisement calling for photographs of aspiring actresses and won a trip to New York City. Her father opposed the idea, but finally relented, as long as she was chaperoned by her aunt Louise.

Young women from Tallulah and Zelda's social background generally attended Miss Booth's or Gussie Woodruff's School for Females, which prepared them for women's colleges and training as teachers. But, since Zelda's father served on the public school Board of Education, she attended the coeducational Sidney Lanier High School, where, with the exception of English and math, she found academics boring. Along with her friends, Eleanor Browder and Livye Hart, she readily admitted, "We played hooky almost every day from school, straggling along the streets in a kind of dare. We didn't know—or care—where we were going. . . . When we were tired, if we were near town, we would go in a picture show, and sit in the dark of the theater while the janitor swept around us and picked up peanut shells and tin foil we dropped in the aisles." At intervals when it came time for school report cards, Zelda thought it fine to cheat, and when others took grades home for parents' signatures, she signed those reports herself.

Sometimes, she would saunter downtown to slip into a drugstore drinking fountain and concoct a *dope* from Coca-Cola and aspirin, which people thought could make one high, or wander through the Negro section of town, taboo in an era of segregation. She had known black people since birth and was at ease with them. Her childhood nurse had been an African American woman the family called Aunt Julia, who occupied a small house in their backyard and was a bridge across races. As Zelda recalled, colored people lived separate lives and got smallpox instead of tuberculosis, grew sunflowers instead of hydrangeas, and had public baptisms instead of listening to radio sermons. They were characters to the white people with their own set of accomplishments and moved through life with grace and compatibility.

Carpe diem quam minimum credula postero—"Seize the day for tomorrow you may die"—was Zelda's motto, expressed under her yearbook photo by the query, "Why should all life be work, when we all can borrow? Let's only think of today and not worry about tomorrow." She might live in the conservative South, but she would not be confined by it. To behave outrageously amused her, like the time she drove a date's automobile to Boodler's Bend (*boodling* being the twenties expression for petting) and flashed its spotlight on couples necking in parked cars or turned that beam on boys leaving Madame Helen St. Claire's brothel. Nothing received forethought; it was all impulse, whether riding in cars with boys she hardly knew or hopping on motorbikes with soldiers from nearby camps.

One of her favorite pastimes was watching movies, and there were four theaters in Montgomery: the Strand, Empire, Plaza, and Orpheum. During her junior year, the film version of Owen Johnson's 1914 best seller *The Salamander* opened with Ruth Findlay re-creating her stage performance. When its heroine Dore Baxter exclaimed on screen, "I am in the world to do something unusual, extraordinary. I'm not like every other little woman. . . . I adore precipices. It's such fun to go dashing along the edges, leaning up against the wind that tries to throw you over," one can imagine Zelda's identification with the heroine. As Johnson defined his new woman: "She comes from somewhere out of the immense reaches of the nation, revolting against the commonplace of an inherited narrowness, eager and unafraid, neither sure of what she seeks, nor conscious of what forces impel or check her." His daring heroine would use any tactic to achieve her desires. The process was an elaborate game with the prize being the right man at the appropriate time. But as Dore makes clear, no ordinary man would do. "The man I marry has got to be able to give me everything I see other women have—dresses, jewels, automobiles—or I should be miserable. You see I don't spare myself. I tell you the truth; I've got to have money, and I've got to have New York." Zelda echoed Dore's feelings, professing she loved Scott but could not live a sordid existence, or it would make her despondent, and he would soon love her less. For salamanders—a metaphor in common usage during the twenties—all men were *props*, derived from the theatrical word *property*. "Each salamander of good standing counts from three to a dozen props," wrote Johnson, "waiting a summons to fetch and carry, purchase tickets of all descriptions, lead the way to theatre or opera and above all, to fill in those blank dates, or deferred engagements, which otherwise might become items of personal expense." To recognize and attract the right man was the plan, and Zelda considered marriage the most important decision of her life. Her determination to select carefully so impressed Scott that he incorporated whole sections from her diary on this subject into *The Beautiful and Damned*, in which his heroine asserts that women are grub worms to crawl through boring marriages, and that hers was "going to be outstanding. . . . I refuse to dedicate myself to posterity."

During summertime, the best way to meet eligible men in Montgomery was at Saturday night country club balls and weeknight script dances at the Oak Park pavilion. College boys would hire a band and a list of popular girls be posted on the door of Harry's Ice Cream Parlor. Men selected who they wanted to escort, and Zelda's name consistently was on top. Every week she could be seen dancing the fox-trot and one step on the pavilion's hardwood floor, sneaking out during intermissions to neck in parked cars. Once, when she became overheated, she asked her date to hold her panties and the episode became spicy town gossip. But Zelda remained oblivious to talk, and as the daughter of a respected judge, acquired the privilege of disregarding convention, which included ignoring the double standard that condoned promiscuity amongst men, but not in women. That people called her a "speed" didn't concern her, and she admitted never experiencing any embarrassment or doubt about her moral principles. Comfortable with her sexuality, she depicted the heroine of her novel *Save Me the Waltz* in a similar way: "'Alabama, you're positively indecent,' said the tall officer. 'You know what an awful reputation you've got and I offer to marry you anyway and—you'll be sorry,' he said unpleasantly. 'I hope so,' Alabama answered. 'I like paying for things I do— it makes me feel square with the world.'" During the winter, dances were held at the Old Exchange Hotel where Mrs. Jefferson Davis had been received as first lady of the Confederacy. On Friday evenings, as her friend Sara Haardt nimbly danced up and down the hotel's steps with her partner, Zelda circled the Old Exchange floor from midnight until dawn with scores of officers. Haardt recalled her friend's extraordinary appearance.

> I saw her as she had looked at that last Christmas dance we were together, wearing a flame dress and Gold-laced slippers, her eyes starry and mocking, flirting with an immense feather fan. Her bronze-gold hair was curled in a thousand ringlets, and as she whirled about, they twinkled enchantingly like little bells. Around her flashed hundreds of jellybeans—the Southern youth of the day—in formal black broadcloth and pearl-studded fronts and hundreds of other flappers in gold slippers and rainbow colored skirts, but they seemed somehow vain and inarticulate beside her. Beauty they had, and grace, and a certain reckless abandon—yet none of them could match the glance of gay derision that flickered beneath the black edge of her eyelashes—and none of them could dance as she did, like a flame or a wind.

There were endless cotillions and balls, college dances, benefit galas for the Red Cross and Liberty Loan drives, dances sponsored by officers at the Beauvoir and Jackson Clubs, and the annual Beauty and Folly Balls. Most exciting were enlisted men's dances that took place in the old city hall auditorium from nine at night until one in the morning. Zelda liked these best, rough affairs occasionally ending in scuffles that guaranteed a night of continual dancing to fabulous music with no intermissions, since there weren't enough girls to go around. After watching her one evening, a reporter for the *Montgomery Advertiser* observed, "Already she is in the crowd at the Country Club every Saturday night and at the script dances every other night of the week. She might dance like Pavlova, if her nimble feet were not so busy keeping up with the pace of a string of young, but ardent admirers set for her."

Filled with nervous excitement after an evening on the dance floor, early the next morning she would be up to volunteer for the Canteen Service League, which distributed coffee and donuts to soldiers at the train station. Other times, she and her friends rolled bandages for the Red Cross or sold tags to support the war effort. Because the young ladies talked so much, committee heads complained they would never get any work done, but they folded more bandages and sold more tags than anyone else. What fueled their frenzied activity was an understanding that many of these soldiers soon would die and their lives be extinguished in a moment.

Zelda set the pace and others followed. "She had superb courage, not so much defiance as a forgetfulness of danger, gossip or barriers," recalled Sara Haardt, who often became involved in Zelda's pranks along with Sara Mayfield, who was four years younger than Zelda and more easily swayed. The latter Sara's father, James Jefferson Mayfield, who served with Judge Sayre on the Alabama Supreme Court, considered Zelda wild and warned his daughter about becoming too involved. Both Saras shared Zelda's determination to escape the South. Mayfield would study at the Sorbonne in Paris, attend the University of Chicago, then graduate from Goucher College, where she majored in English. After getting her master's degree from the University of Alabama, she pursued a career in journalism, working as a correspondent for the *Baltimore Sun* and *New York Herald Tribune*. Haardt followed a similar path. Although she dated some of Zelda's suitors, including John Sellers and Peyton Mathis, she pursued a writing career and also attended Goucher as an English major. After graduation, she briefly returned to Montgomery to teach at Margaret Booth's School, became active in the local suffrage movement, then was hired by Goucher as one of the youngest individuals ever to serve on its faculty. During her first year there, she published essays and vignettes in *College Humor* and *Scribner's Magazine* and won a national story contest, the prize being dinner with literary critic and editor H. L. Mencken. The two shared much in common and a seven-year courtship commenced that evening, culminating in marriage, but it would be a brief union. Sickly from birth, having undergone the removal of her appendix and a kidney, Sara also battled smallpox and would die in her late thirties from a tubercular infection of the spine.

Haardt and Mayfield were introduced to Scott in September 1918 on the steps of Montgomery's capitol building. It was an impressive Greek Revival structure with Corinthian columns supporting a dome, and Zelda had taken him there to see the gold star by its entrance, where Jefferson Davis had been sworn in as president of the Confederacy. Mayfield recalled his eagerness to impress and how he introduced himself as the great-grandson of Francis Scott Key, who had written "The Star-Spangled Banner." She noticed how fascinated he was with the way Zelda spoke in a husky voice and Southern accent, using highly original figures of speech. He loved her verbal associations and tracked them easily, recognizing immediately her remarkable powers of observation.

Zelda possessed other characteristics about which he was not so enamored. She saw no guilt in rapture and possessed a natural sensuality upon which she often acted, never disguising her entanglements. Scott recalled when she openly admitted that she could sleep with others and it wouldn't affect her or make her unfaithful to him. He knew from the start, as he told the sister of a classmate, that any girl who gets drunk in public, enjoys telling shocking stories, and remarks she has kissed thousands of men and intends to kiss thousands more "cannot be considered above reproach, even if above it." Although Zelda's desirability to others was exciting, and Scott liked her being universally admired, just the idea of her being with another man made him insanely jealous. He was drawn to her independence and loved this type of flirtatious young woman who played along the danger line, but never reconciled that behavior with his conservative Catholic upbringing.

By the time she graduated from high school, Zelda had dated some of Montgomery's most eligible men: Lloyd Hooper, Dan Cody, Peyton Spottswood Mathis, and John Allen Sellers Jr. Hooper came from one of the most influential families in Montgomery. His father was a prominent businessman active in Democratic politics and mother, Anne Steele Coleman, was considered the "belle of her time." Lloyd attended Sewanee and the University of Alabama, where he pledged Phi Delta Theta, and later was state treasurer for several funding agencies. He was savvy about money and had enough to show Zelda a good time. Dan Cody, whose name Scott filched for *The Great Gatsby*, also attended the University of Alabama, and like Hooper, became a well-paid accountant, crunching numbers as chief financial manager for the Officers' Club at Maxwell Air Force Base. His father was president of the Union Bank and Trust, so he was comfortable around money and knew how to generate it. Solid bread winners, neither were dynamic enough to become serious contenders for Zelda's affection, unlike Peyton Spottswood Mathis and John Allen Sellers Jr. Ten years apart in age and called "the Gold Dust Twins" because of their close friendship and spending habits, Peyton, the older, and John, were drinking buddies and notorious womanizers. John had money, and Peyton owned one of the few automobiles in Montgomery, actually two: a Stutz Bearcat and Chrysler.

From the distinguished Spottswood clan, Peyton could trace his Virginian ancestry back to George Washington. He had come to Montgomery in 1908 from Pulaski, Tennessee, and lived near the Sayres on Haardt Drive, a street named for the Bavarian grandparents of Sara Haardt. Impeccably dressed and known for his flamboyance, Peyton possessed a commanding personality and could handle any circumstance. John Peter Kohn Jr., a contemporary and author of *The Cradle*, a collection of acerbic vignettes about Montgomery residents, portrayed Peyton as Dayton Bee, "built like an Olympic swimmer [with] large, appealing bright brown eyes and a face as if it had been marbled in ancient Greece. His muscles coordinated like a young leopard, and he could play tennis, dance and swim among the pros. With his charm, perfect diction, mellow voice and courteous manners, he was loved by all." Women flocked to him, and John Kohn fictionalized a courtroom interrogation involving one who had appeared nude on his doorstep:

> One night, the police were questioning him about a naked woman who rang his doorbell at one o'clock in the morning. Later, he was on the witness stand in this case, and on cross examination he was asked, "Now, Mr. Bee, didn't you think it was unusual for a woman in that condition to be ringing your doorbell at one o'clock in the morning while she was naked?"
>
> Dayton answered in his rich voice so all the courtroom could hear— "Not at all sir. It was not unusual. It frequently happened, although they usually were not 'pre-naked.'"

As proprietor of the Montgomery Marble Works, Peyton sold funerary objects like tombstones, porphyry slabs, and marble angels. His office was in an impressive stone building at Oakwood Cemetery, with the Egyptian wings of death sculptured in low relief above its front door. He fancied himself an artist and was particularly proud of two sepulchral memorials he had carved for Oakwood: *The Wings of Death* and *The Broken Column*. Sara Mayfield remembered one night following a dance, when Peyton drove Zelda and two suitors out to see the monuments. After one young man failed to be impressed, Peyton held a knife to his throat and demanded, "Say it's art." When he made the mistake of laughing, his neck received a nasty gash. "They dared not take him to a doctor," Sara recalled, "lest the doctor report them to the police and involve them all in a trial and scandal. Nor could they let him bleed to death while they rode around trying to think what to do. Finally, they decided to wake up a veterinarian who had once worked for Peyton. He stopped the bleeding and sewed up the gash with cat gut." Like many adventures Peyton and John perpetrated, this one got swept under the rug. Oakwood was a favorite haunt for Montgomery's teenagers who smoked cigarettes and chugged alcohol among the Confederate graves. Zelda wrote Scott of the time classmates had dared her to open an iron vault in the side of the hill, its broken columns and hovering angels evoking past romances. It made her ponder that "in a hundred years I think I shall like having young people speculate on whether my eyes were brown or blue." Scott would take her graveyard escapade and use it almost verbatim in *This Side of Paradise*.

Sara Haardt also dated Peyton and anticipated becoming his wife. While teaching at Goucher, she received a telegram from Peyton saying he was coming to marry her, only he never arrived. Alcohol was his downfall; either he was stone sober or dead drunk. After one too many on the train, Peyton wound up in Charleston, South Carolina, married to somebody else. That wife would commit suicide, but he would marry three more times, fathering two sons and two daughters, and dying at the home of Sara Haardt's brother, John, following a drinking binge. Sara never entirely got over him and remained single into her thirties.

John Allen Sellers Jr. was notorious for trying to outdo Peyton, and local papers reported the time he got shot in the hand by a guard at the country club. After a dance, he had returned and attempted a forced entry, crawling from the hood of his car to the clubhouse roof, only to be apprehended by the night watchman. When police arrived, he said he had left something in his locker, and no charges got filed; they seldom were. As the only son of John Sellers Sr., owner of Sellers-Orum, Montgomery's largest cotton brokerage, he came from a privileged upbringing. His family was one of the Twenty Twos, Montgomery's equivalent to Manhattan's Four Hundred roster of prestigious families. Like Peyton, he lived near the Sayres on South Perry Street and attended the Edgar School and University of Alabama, where he joined Phi Delta Theta. After graduating, he worked for Gordon Cotton in Houston, then returned to Montgomery and represented the cotton firm of Hall-Beale.

John Sellers began dating Zelda when both were fifteen, three years before Scott arrived in Montgomery, and the two were always perpetuating antics, like the time he dressed her as a beggar and pushed her through the train station in a wheelchair, exclaiming she hadn't walked in years and needed money. She loved recounting these adventures to Scott, who wasn't amused and felt threatened by the tall Southerner. On his part, John never considered Scott a serious contender for Zelda's affections, and after observing his drinking habits began calling him "Scotch Fitzgerald."

John posed a threat because he had two things Scott lacked—money and masculinity. On his army pay, Scott couldn't afford six-dollar dinners at the

Pickwick Café or a bottle of Sazarac, Zelda's favorite whiskey. The best he could offer was a movie with its seventeen-cent admission, the amusement arcade at Pickett Springs, or strolls in the wisteria-scented moonlight after a country club dance. She always recalled the night they carved their names into the club's doorpost, his much larger than hers. For transportation, Scott had to take the bus from Camp Sheridan into downtown Montgomery, then ride the streetcar to Zelda's house. At a dollar a mile, taxis were too costly. John had plenty of cash so could buy Zelda whatever she wanted, including a split of Pommery, her preferred champagne. He was also highly sexual, to which Sara Mayfield, who married him in 1924, would attest. She described John as tall, blond, and immaculate, to which Peyton wryly added, distinguished by maxillary regions similar to a Pontiac chief's; in simpler terms, broad, manly cheekbones. Looks aside, Mayfield divorced John three years into their marriage, citing as grounds alcoholism and sexual violence. Court records also indicate he violated the Mann Act, which made it a federal crime to transport underage girls across state lines for purposes of sex.

Zelda's earliest sexual experience may have been with John and Peyton and more traumatic than sensual. Scott always harbored anger against the Southerner, telling Zelda's sister, Marjorie, that their mother had taken such rotten care of Zelda that John had been able to seduce her at fifteen. "She was so drunk the first time I met her at the country club, that her partners were carrying her around in their arms." Over time, he became increasingly bitter over his wife's early promiscuity, complaining that the assumption she was some sort of prize package was a giant hoax. And later she openly admitted to having been seduced and provincially outcast years before meeting him. He sensed this the first night they slept together, feeling there was an elaborate self-consciousness about the seduction and that she was playing the role of an innocent but had been sexual long before him.

A scene in Zelda's unpublished novel *Caesar's Things* probably is the encounter to which he alludes. It begins on a porch one weekend afternoon where Janno, the female protagonist, is talking with four boys, Anton and Dan being the two named. Janno says they all subscribed to heavy petting and did not consider sex any outward expression of an inward emotion. Anton is described as having chestnut hair with the sensuous features of a star. Sophisticated and arrogant, he was a rich boy who knew how the world worked and one of those people in town who mattered. Janno is pleased they are paying her attention and tries to say clever things, but when they speak to her in superior tones, seems intimidated. The boys want her to follow them and go to the schoolyard, but she doesn't like the idea. She knows it would be unwise; "it's not right, I don't want to go," she tells Anton, then taking on Dan who asserts that girls usually follow where boys tell them to go, so why was she making such a fuss? They become exasperated, warning Janno that if she doesn't go, no one will have any more to do with her. Considering they are better dressed with nicer manners, she accepts their code of conduct and follows the four. "They went up to the haunted school-yard so deep in shadows and creaking with felicities of murder to the splintery old swing, and she was so miserable and trusting that her heart broke and for many years after she didn't want to live, but it was better to keep going."

While Zelda doesn't tell us precisely what happened, she suggests an assault by one or more of the boys. As to their identities, she offers clues. Dan is drawn as a "fair dark boy," implying light hair and darker skin, which describes John, and Anton is characterized as chestnut haired, debonair, and insouciant, suggesting Peyton. Zelda's reference to their casual attitude about sex defines both men's outlook. Later, we are told that Anton committed suicide, and though neither Peyton nor John took their own lives, both drank themselves to death. It was Sara Mayfield's brother, James, and his uncle, Burwell Mayfield, who were suicides. The other two boys on the porch may have been Dan Cody, whom Zelda also was seeing at the time, and Sara Haardt's brother, John, who was friends with Sellers and Mathis and whose father was Anton, an unusual name in those times. As for the aftermath, no girl in Zelda's position would have acknowledged what has the earmarks of rape. Instead, they would have remained silent and tried to expunge the incident from their mind. It would take another emotional trauma in France to resurrect the memory. Although there was some recompense, Zelda wrote, that God had not just left her out there under the oak tree, where she had tried as best she could, "there wasn't any more compensatory peace of human relationships, or any more solace of the evening meal, or any more pleasure of competitive effort. . . . The child never could quite remember what it was about life of which she was so heartbroken. Nor could she quite forget." That afternoon she experienced the brutal side of desire, and the traumatic episode would shroud her comprehensive view of things. Thereafter, the complaints of a sick sister or missed music lesson were robbed of their significance.

That afternoon's ordeal also may explain her obsession with cleanliness. Her friend Julia Garland recalled that Zelda was one of the cleanest people she'd known and always looked as if she had just taken a bath. Probably she had, since she took three or four daily, which, combined with her regimen of swimming, gave her the immaculate look she wanted, and may have compensated for her feeling dirty. Scott would portray Gloria in *The Beautiful and Damned* with Zelda's penchant for hygiene: "Always intensely skeptical about her sex, her judgments were now concerned with the question of whether women were or were not clean. By un-cleanliness she meant a variety of things, a lack of pride, a slackness in fibre, and most of all the unmistakable aura of promiscuity." As casual as she felt about sex, Zelda always took a bath immediately afterward, and like Scott, connected intercourse with some element of soiling. Common among assault victims, obsessive washing often is utilized to relieve stress and defray worrisome thoughts, especially those associated with being in a romantic relationship. After time, it simply becomes instinctual.

Scott was still recovering from being overthrown by Ginevra King when he wrote in his ledger that he fell in love with Zelda on September 7, 1918. He made no mention that three days earlier, Ginevra had celebrated her marriage to William Mitchell. Although Scott was prepared to commit, Zelda was reluctant until it was proven he could provide an extraordinary life, a hesitation he recalled with resentment. Except for the sexual recklessness, she was cagey about throwing in her lot with Scott and by temperament the most reckless of the women he had known.

When word arrived that Scott's regiment was preparing to depart for European battlefields, Zelda's farewell gift was predictable: a silver flask engraved with the date 9/13/18 and the sentiment *Forget Me Not*. Two weeks later, Scott's unit left for Hoboken, New Jersey, to await embarkation for France. He was ready to do battle, but at 5:00 a.m. Paris time on November 11, the Armistice was signed and guns put down in time for lunch. German troops retreated from France to Belgium; the Kaiser, empress, and crown prince fled to Holland; and the doughboys packed to go home. Scott was transferred back to Montgomery for demobilization and, being among the most expendable men in his regiment, was the second to be discharged. Gone were any illusions about becoming a war hero or winning Zelda's commitment without becoming a successful author. He had to prove himself—and fast.

After an emotional farewell with Zelda at the station, he boarded a train for New York and telegraphed several days later that he had rented an apartment in Morningside Heights. Unable to get work with a newspaper, he found a job writing advertising copy for the Barron-Collier agency, working alongside John Held Jr., who illustrated his slogans. He created one successful line promoting an Iowa steam laundry—"We Keep You Clean in Muscatine"—about which his boss was so pleased, he raised Scott's salary from twenty to thirty-five dollars a week, just enough to cover food and lodging.

In Montgomery, townspeople were welcoming home soldiers from the Rainbow Division of the 167th Infantry, and a radiant Zelda was there to greet them, as they paraded down Commerce Street from Union Station to the capitol building. In a newspaper photograph taken that day, she is clearly visible in the welcoming lineup. Still the most popular girl in town, she began seeing John Sellers again and was dating two football stars from

Auburn—Francis Stubbs and Pete Bonner, both of whom competed for her attention. Stubbs presented her with his gold football pendant, which she wore on a chain, and Bonner invited her to Auburn for the weekend of February 22, writing to remind her and warn his competition: "Have a date with you on Saturday p.m. Look out Stubbs." Zelda was so popular at Auburn that five members of their football team formed a fraternity in her honor, Zeta Sigma, membership limited only to those having at least one date with her. Three other Southern colleges crowned her prom queen, including Sewanee, where John Dearborn was her date. She told him that she didn't love Scott romantically but wanted to be his literary muse, and shared similar feelings with Scott's Princeton classmate and Montgomery resident Lawton Campbell. "Frankly, it all seemed such a gamble to her," he recalled. "I told her I was sure Scott could make money from his writing, and she told me about the interest some publisher had in his book and about his encouraging letters. As nearly as I can remember, my impression from what she said was, 'If Scott sells the book, I'll marry the man, because he is sweet. Don't you think so?'" Scott's concern over her involvement with others, particularly John Sellers, prompted him to ask his mother for her engagement ring, which he sent Zelda in March 1919. Although she accepted it, neither she nor her family took the proposal seriously, and after wearing it once to a country club dance, she put it away and began losing interest in the long-distance relationship. Although Scott's promise of celebrity piqued her interest, before making a commitment Zelda needed solid evidence of his success. She continued to collect military suitors along with their regimental insignia, filling her glovebox with silver and gold bars, flags, and castles, wearing a different one every night. When Scott chided that she really ought to marry him and be done with it, Zelda retorted that every girl should marry him, because he was an overture to romance no woman should be without.

In June 1919, she ended what always had been a trial engagement. Without financial stability, a wedding was out of the question. Scott shared his dilemma with John Biggs, who emphasized the impracticality of marrying without money. But Scott was determined, saying he'd had a terrible time getting Zelda away from Congressman Bankhead's son and had no intention of losing her now. With another Princeton classmate, Edmund Wilson, he expressed a similar sentiment, admitting he wouldn't care if she died, but couldn't bear to have her marry another. Soon after Edmund introduced him to George Jean Nathan, who coedited *The Smart Set* with H. L. Mencken, Scott learned they were going to publish his story *Babes in the Wood*. Although payment only amounted to thirty dollars, he was elated by this first success, and spent the money on a blue ostrich fan for Zelda and white flannel trousers for himself.

Each night after work, he returned to his cramped apartment and worked on his novel, and then arranged a meeting with Maxwell Perkins, who thought the manuscript much improved but suggested another rewrite in third person. That was all he needed. On July 4, 1919, he quit his job and left for St. Paul, where he moved into his parents' third-floor guest room and set about revising his novel, adding new segments and altering point of view. Set at Princeton, the narrative focused on the career hopes and love relationships of Amory Blaine, a thinly veiled version of himself. To develop the affair between Amory and his heroine, Rosalind, he wove Zelda's letters and diaries into the story, restructuring chapters to reflect his love for this remarkable young woman.

For relaxation he would walk to Mrs. Porterfield's boardinghouse on Summit Avenue and sit on the veranda discussing books with two of her roomers: John De Quedville Briggs, headmaster of St. Paul Academy, and Donald Ogden Stewart, a Yale graduate who was working for the American Telephone Company. Stewart later would become a popular humorist and friend of Ernest Hemingway's in Paris. The three sometimes would go to Frost's drugstore on Selby to buy Cokes and cigarettes, and occasionally play golf with Father Joe Baron, St. Paul's young dean of students. That summer, he also met St. Paul novelist Grace Flandrau, who introduced him to Harold Ober with the Paul Reynolds Literary Agency in Manhattan. Ober represented authors such as Catherine Drinker Bowen, Paul Gallico, and Philip Wylie, and specialized in placing fiction with high-paying, wide-circulation magazines. His taste and good judgment would make him the most celebrated literary agent of his time, although he preferred the title of author's representative, and he would become Scott's agent, banker, and steadfast supporter.

Scott's rewrite was completed on September 3, 1919, and given a new title: *This Side of Paradise*, taken from Rupert Brooke's poem "Tiare Tahiti." His boyhood friend Tom Daniels was taking the train east and offered to hand-deliver Scott's manuscript to Scribner's. He knew one of the editors, a former classmate at Yale, and offered to put in a good word. On September 3, Scott gave Tom the manuscript and several days later received word that he inadvertently had left it in a Manhattan taxi. Miraculously, Tom was able to track down the cab, retrieve the package, and deliver it to Scribner's. Shocked by that news, Scott was further surprised two weeks later, when a special delivery letter arrived from Maxwell Perkins, saying the book had been accepted. "I am very glad, personally, to be able to write to you that we are all for publishing your book, *This Side of Paradise*. I think you have improved it enormously. . . . The book is so different, that it is hard to prophesy how it will sell, but we are all for taking a chance and supporting it with vigor."

The *all* was an exaggeration, given that Charles Scribner II and several older editors considered the novel frivolous and opposed the decision. But Max pushed for its approval, and like Harold Ober, would become Scott's staunch backer. Scott immediately wired Zelda he was coming to Montgomery and arrived with the manuscript, a bottle of Sazerac rye whiskey, and the assurance he could persuade her to marry him. It took all his persuasive powers and several days to convince her, but she was still unwilling to choose a date until the novel was in bookstores.

Several weeks later, Ober announced that he had sold Scott's story "Head and Shoulders" to the *Saturday Evening Post* and movie rights to Metro-Goldwyn-Mayer, along with film options to three other stories not yet published. To celebrate this big success, Scott visited a Fifth Avenue jewelry store and purchased an exquisite platinum and diamond wristwatch. It either came from Cartier's, which opened its store on Fifth Avenue and Fifty-Second Street in 1917 and became renowned for watches modeled after the designs of Louis-Francois Cartier, or Tiffany's, which relocated its store in 1905 from Broadway to Fifty-Seventh Street and Fifth Avenue. Arrival of the luxury timepiece and news of Scott's literary success turned the tide. "'O, Scott, it's so be-au-ti-ful and the back's just as pretty as the front,'" she wrote him, having repeatedly turned it over to see, "From Scott to Zelda." The engagement was back on and Zelda apologized for past misgivings. "I am very proud of you—I hate to say this, but I don't think I had much confidence in you at first. It's so nice to know that you really can do things—anything—and I love to feel that maybe I can help just a little."

At nineteen, Zelda felt no need to establish a separate identity from Scott and made her lack of ambition so evident that Scott infused her dogged insistence into the character of Rosalind in *This Side of Paradise*. Although mature in many ways, in some aspects Zelda was just a girl who liked pretty things and dreaded responsibility. "I don't want to think about pots and kitchens and brooms. I want to worry about whether my legs will get slick and brown when I swim in the summer." That was fine with Scott, who openly admitted that any girl who made a living on her prettiness interested him enormously.

Galley proofs arrived from Scribner's in mid-December, and right after Christmas Scott left for New Orleans to escape the cold and be nearer Zelda. He rented a room in a boardinghouse on Prytania Street, where he made final corrections and worked on stories. He took two trips to Montgomery and on the second, resumed his sexual relationship with Zelda. She had slept with Scott early in their courtship but then held back. When her period was late that February and she feared being pregnant, Scott sent abortion pills, probably Chickester's Diamond Brand or Tansy and Pennyroyal Compound Pills, only she refused to take them, writing that she understood the mess she was making, but couldn't take the pills and had thrown them away. Whether she did or not, the pregnancy never continued.

Although Scott continued pressuring Zelda to tell her parents about their plans, because Judge Sayre opposed the union, she remained reluctant. Instead, she asked Scott to write and reassure her father. "Darling—Mama knows that we are going to be married someday—but she keeps leaving stories of young authors, turned out on a dark and stormy night, on my pillow—I wonder if you hadn't better write to my daddy. . . . I'm not exactly scared of 'em, but they could be so unpleasant about what we're going to do." Convinced their daughter needed a strong husband with sound character, her parents and sisters came out strongly against Scott and hoped she would change her mind. But the lure of Manhattan proved strong, and two days after *This Side of Paradise* appeared in the window of Scribner's bookstore on March 28, the *Montgomery Advertiser* announced Zelda's engagement, simply stating, "Judge and Mrs. A. D. Sayre announce the engagement of their daughter, Zelda, to Francis Scott Fitzgerald of New York, the marriage to take place at an early date." Several days later it further elaborated, "Mrs. M. W. Brinson, (Marjorie Sayre Brinson) accompanied by her sister, Miss Zelda Sayre, have gone to New York City, and while there will be the guests of Mrs. J. M. Palmer, formerly Miss Clothilde Sayre. Montgomery friends yield most reluctantly this beautiful and fascinating young girl to her new home in New York City, feeling assured she will soon be surrounded by the same admiring atmosphere as that left in this section of the picturesque South." The news shocked everyone, including two of Zelda's suitors, who expected to marry her themselves and refused to believe the story.

· 2 ·

Seeds of Discontent

$\int$cott was feeling satisfied with himself when he wrote Ruth Sturdevant, a classmate of his St. Paul friend, Aida Bigelow: "Next time you're in New York I want you to meet Zelda, because she's very beautiful and very wise and very brave as you can imagine, but she's a perfect baby and a more irresponsible pair than we'll be will be hard to imagine. You may laugh when I tell you I am getting married April Fools' Day but as a matter of fact I think I am." The nuptials actually took place two days later on Easter Sunday, April 3, in the rectory of Manhattan's St. Patrick's Cathedral. Instead of conventional white, Zelda wore a suit of midnight blue, with a matching hat trimmed in leather buckles and ribbons. She was holding the orchid corsage Scott had sent earlier with some white Swainsona to freshen it up. Neither Scott's parents nor hers attended, and the only witnesses were his Princeton classmate, Ludlow Fowler, who served as best man, and Zelda's sisters Marjorie and Rosalind, along with their husbands, Minor Brinson and Newman Smith. Her other sister, Clothilde, and spouse, John Palmer, were delayed driving down from Tarrytown and arrived late. To their annoyance, Scott began the ceremony without them, and they were dismayed to find he had not arranged for music, a photographer, or reception. "There was no luncheon after the wedding, because it appeared to us that it was not wanted," Rosalind recalled. "Scott did not communicate with us until the day before the wedding, when he phoned to say that it would take place at St. Patrick's the next morning, which made us feel that plans had been made, as he and Zelda wanted them, or he would have come to discuss them with us." The Sayres never excused Scott for his discourteous behavior, and it set the stage for what would become an acrimonious relationship. After Zelda's sisters and their husbands left to eat alone, the newlyweds strolled ten blocks up Fifth Avenue to peek in Scribner's window, where a large poster advertised Scott as "The youngest writer for whom Scribner's has ever published a novel."

Later that evening, Edmund Wilson and Princeton classmates John Peale Bishop, Alex McKaig, and Lawton Campbell helped celebrate by drinking orange blossom cocktails in their hotel room. Then, Ludlow Fowler invited them home for dinner, and it was the first time Zelda had seen an elevator in a private residence. The following week, Scott sent her shopping with his St. Paul friend, Marie Hersey, to purchase a new wardrobe; her Montgomery attire was simply not chic enough. It was then in vogue to copy the costumes of Ziegfeld Follies star Justine Johnstone, and Zelda returned with several sophisticated dresses and a smart Patou suit. It seemed strange to be charging clothing to F. Scott Fitzgerald, but she figured she would get used to it.

To Scribner's delight, Scott's novel about a young man's journey into adulthood became an instant best seller. Women identified with its liberated heroine, and men wanted to understand the era's independent females. Five thousand copies sold in its initial printing, three thousand within the first three days. Although Owen Johnson had foreshadowed Scott's flapper by six years in *The Salamander*, Scott more accurately portrayed the era's atmosphere of nervous stimulation. It was a cynical period fueled with illegal alcohol, in which youth rejected the previous generation's idealism and were more concerned with manners than morals. Scott got it right; the way people drove around in fashionable cars, talked the lingo, and opened accounts at Abercrombie and Fitch before they went mainstream. Everybody wanted instant sophistication and *smart* was the buzzword. You were *smart* if you owned a radio and refrigerator, smarter still if you had a car. There were plenty to choose from, some of the most popular with double names: the Franklin and Maxwell, Stutz-Bearcat, and Pierce-Arrow, many with rumble seats in the back where petting and kissing became epidemic. Floundering in a period of rapidly shifting values, the average man needed assistance in relating to this new woman, who, as columnist Dorothy Dix explained, "could play golf all day, dance all night, drive a motor car, and give first aid to the injured if anybody gets hurt." Old rules didn't apply and new ones had yet to be made.

The flapper movement was at its peak when Scott introduced Rosalind to American readers, making her the year's most widely known and imitated exemplar. A female exhibiting Ginevra King's cool reserve and his wife's audacious courage, as Zelda remarked, she flirted because it was fun to do, wore a one-piece bathing suit because it looked good, used makeup because she didn't need it, and refused to be bored when she wasn't boring. Delighted to be Rosalind's model, Zelda told the *Courier Journal*, "I love Scott's books and heroines. I like the ones that are like me. That's why I love Rosalind in *This Side of Paradise*. I like girls like that. I like their courage, their recklessness and spendthriftiness." Scott was writing about such women before meeting Zelda, but she more precisely embodied the heroine he hoped to define, a self-absorbed female who plucked everything she desired from life. H. L. Mencken had coined the term *flapper* fifteen years earlier, describing them as frivolous girls who spent their time partying and drove around in fancy cars. Never considering consequences, they did as they pleased. With callous observation Zelda described such a female, who would be yours for the evening if you had enough money to take her out. Were you rich, famous, or handsome, she would show you a good time and then hurt your feelings, but if circumstance had thrown her in your path, she would omit formalities and simply hurt you. As spokesman for the Jazz Age, Scott was considered an expert on such women but occasionally resisted the role, telling one audience that any notion he was interested in the number of knees on exhibition in the Biltmore lobby was wrong, and that none of his heroines ever cared enough to make an effort to shock anyone. Clearly, he was thinking about Zelda, who viewed life as a performance with herself the main attraction. He would portray that self-centeredness through the character of Gloria in *The Beautiful and Damned*, writing of how she took things from life as if she was selecting presents from an inexhaustible counter. When husband Anthony asks if she is interested in anything but herself, Gloria's smug response is "not much."

As hero and heroine of *This Side of Paradise*, the Fitzgeralds were catapulted into celebrity and made chief exponents of the Jazz Age. Manhattan's most sought-after couple, they were in demand at all the chic gatherings. Everyone wanted to meet the new author and his attractive wife, who embraced their obligations to keep things lively. One evening, they snuck into the kitchens of the old Waldorf Hotel to put on chef's headgear and dance on tables, only to be escorted out by house detectives. Another night on their way to a party, Scott rode on the taxi's roof, while Zelda perched on its hood. Soon, they were the most recognized couple in any audience. From the first row at *Enter Madam*, they antagonized cast members by laughing at all the wrong places, and the illustrator, Ralph Barton, caricaturized them in *Broadway Audience, 1921*, front row center—Scott with his hair slicked back, and Zelda dressed in a tuxedo, sporting a man's bow tie. There were jumps into city fountains, Zelda plunging into ones at Washington and Union Square, and Scott leaping into the Pulitzer outside the Plaza Hotel on Fifty-Ninth Street. Their antics captured the imagination of artist Reginald Marsh, who immortalized the couple on the overture curtain of the 1922 *Greenwich Village Follies*: Zelda at the center of the curtain, in a white bathing suit ready to dive into Union Square fountain, and Scott, in the company of Edmund Wilson, John Peale Bishop, Gilbert Seldes, and John Dos Passos, roaring down Seventh Avenue in a truck toward Washington Square. Zelda's plunge into Union Square fountain actually occurred after a dinner at John Williams's nearby apartment. To shock guests, she stripped naked and raced down the street toward the watering cascade with Williams and Scott in pursuit. After she plunged in, the three were confronted by policemen ready to book her, until one mistakenly mistook Scott for an Irish comedian and dropped charges. She had done similar things before, once disrobing in the middle of Grand Central Station on her way to meet George Jean Nathan.

So often were they in tabloids that William Randolph Hearst assigned a reporter solely to cover their activities. When friends warned of risks they were taking, the couple became more outrageous, wavering on the edge of precipices and skidding across tracks to the sound of warning bells. They spent huge sums of money on entertainment and, with their entourage of friends, watched Florenz Ziegfeld's *Follies* at the New Amsterdam Theatre; *Midnight Frolic* on its rooftop stage; spectacular performances at Stanford White's Madison Square Garden, then on Madison Avenue and Twenty-Sixth Street; and musical reviews at the Century Roof Theater on Sixty-Second. In an attempt to behave more outrageously than its scantily clad chorus, during one performance of George White's *Scandals*, Scott began removing his clothes, stripping to his underwear before getting evicted by ushers.

No couple drank more or seemed as intent on having a good time. In their hotel room, the tart smell of gin was everywhere, orchid corsages wilted in ice trays, and cigarettes disintegrated in spittoons. The Prohibition Act, which illegalized the sale of alcoholic beverages, although signed into effect three months earlier, had proved impossible to enforce. For every gallon confiscated, hundreds more reached consumers through illicit smuggling and bootlegging. It was exciting to break the law for a cocktail, and newspapers documented daily arrests. The *New York Times* reported on December 13, 1921, that police had raided the Little Club on West Forty-Fourth Street, later arresting ten guests at the Hotel Lafayette on University Place after discovering two cases of champagne in the basement. Zelda and Scott started drinking at lunchtime, joining the Princeton crowd at speakeasies like Matt Winkle's on Fifty-Third and Park, Fanelli's on Prince Street, or Jack Bleeck's Artists and Writers Café near the Herald Tribune Building. Their Greenwich Village favorite was Red Head, owned by cousins Jack Kriendler and Charlie Berns, who smuggled Ballantine Scotch and Roederer Cristal Brut Champagne by boat into Hampton Bay, Long Island. They made evasion a game during raids by triggering levers that overturned bar shelves and sent liquor bottles careening through a chute into the basement. The more expensive establishments were both restaurants and bars like Jack and Charlie's Puncheon Club at 21 West Fifty-Second, today known as 21. For those seeking something more casual, there was Tony's with its checkered tablecloths, and Petitpas in Greenwich Village, where Jack Yeats, younger brother of William Butler, held court.

Jack Shuttleworth, editor of the humorous magazine *Judge*, recalled running into Scott and John Held at the Bernaise. "He was tall, dark, and tweedy and I found him sitting with F. Scott Fitzgerald. I didn't know it then, but there I was smack in the middle of the Jazz Age with its two creators—Fitzgerald and Held." The two had worked together at Collier's Advertising, but after Held sold his first cover illustration to *Judge*, his illustrations became a mainstay of *Smart Set* and *Vanity Fair* covers. They immortalized the flapper with her bobbed hair and knee-length shingled skirts, petticoats, and brassieres replaced by an allinone flimsy piece of underwear called "stepins." These were young women who smooched with college boys in coonskin coats and pork pie hats, smoked incessantly, and drank bathtub gin.

Since alcohol at speakeasies was of questionable content and origin, and people could get poisoned drinking it, many concocted gin in their bathtubs. Scott had a favorite recipe using oils from juniper berries, coriander, and anise, to which he added distilled water, alcohol, and sweetening, but it was essential to locate a reliable alcohol source. Not only did Carl Van Vechten know where to obtain bootleggers' supplies, he even received advance notice of shipments. That October, George Jean Nathan introduced the tall Scandinavian to the Fitzgeralds, and he and his Russian-born wife, Fania Marinoff, a promising actress, took them to their favorite Harlem nightclubs above 125th Street. Carl was writing a novel about negro life called *Nigger Heaven*, a reference to theater balconies where blacks were required to sit. He introduced the couple to the newest gin concoctions at Harlem's "blind pigs," a twenties term for speakeasies. There was the Bronx Cocktail, which combined gin with red vermouth and orange juice; the French 75, a blend of gin with champagne, lemon juice, and sugar; and Gin Rickey mixed with lime juice and a dash of club soda. Zelda's favorite was an Orange Blossom that combined sweetened orange juice and gin. Carl had written several earlier novels and was a music and ballet critic for the *New York Times*. He enjoyed the unconventional, so evenings with him were unpredictable and exciting. Harlem nights blended into Manhattan mornings, and Carl immortalized these revelries in his novel *Parties: Scenes from Contemporary New York Life*, using Scott and Zelda as prototypes for David and Rilda Westlake who, "loved each other, desperately, passionately . . . they clung to each other like barnacles cling to rocks . . . but . . . wanted to hurt each other." Besides sharing an interest in dance, Zelda and Carl, whom she called Carlo, both had a distinctive way of expressing themselves. He loved her free association of ideas and unexpected comments, and she relished his sophisticated humor and clever barbs.

Scott recognized Zelda's conversational flair early, and Lawton Campbell and Edmund Wilson both recalled how he would hang on her words, jotting them down on bits of paper or backs of envelopes for future reference, his pockets often bulging with her clever observations. He encouraged her antics and enjoyed watching her unsettle people with outrageous questions. It was her way of gaining the upper hand, like the time she turned to John Biggs and asked if he regretted not being killed in the war. Drinking made that tactic easier, since a person could say anything when soused. Scott had boozed since prep school, but Zelda now drank as much from feeling overwhelmed as high spirits.

Being married to an author was all very exciting, but no one had warned Zelda it could be lonely. Scott needed solitude to write, and there was always a rush of preparation and admonition to be quiet while he was working. Told to amuse herself, she wandered around Manhattan, compared shoes on Forty-Second Street to those of upper Broadway, walked through Central Park, and smoked packs of Huyler cigarettes. When they went out for the evening, Scott gained assurance from having her on his arm. She became a symbol of his achievement, and "he danced her around the gilded edges of many fashionable hours . . . owned her, showed her off to an inclusive set of college friends, and made a big success of being an impresario." She remained ingratiating and adorable with no other purpose than to be possessed and wondered whether she had traded Southern bondage for some other type of prison.

Scott was finding it difficult to write in their cramped hotel room, and it became increasingly clear they needed larger accommodations. After guests in adjoining rooms complained about their partying, the decision was hastened when management insisted they leave. They decided to find someplace where Scott could work and Zelda occupy herself swimming. Again, he consulted Ruth Sturdevant, who suggested Lake Champlain. To get there, they purchased a secondhand Marmon sports coupé and drove north to Rye, New York, which they found boring, continuing on to Lake Champlain, which proved too cold. Turning southeast, they wound up in Westport, Connecticut, whose proximity to Manhattan, just fifty miles from Times Square, made it a popular retreat for writers and artists. That summer some of its celebrity residents included Ernest Boyd and his wife, Marguerite Van Voohis; Van Wyck Brooks; Dorothy and Lillian Gish; Eva Le Gallienne; and the Broadway producer John Williams, who often entertained theater people at his home on Long Island Sound.

A realtor found them a two-story saltbox of Revolutionary vintage, just outside the village on Compo Road, and on May 14 they signed a five-month lease. It had an extra room in which Scott could write and benches by the front door, where Zelda tanned in the afternoon sun. From the second-floor bedroom window, they could see the sound and it was a five-minute walk to Compo or Hendrick's Point beach, where John Held Jr. rented a summer cottage. While Scott worked on *The Beautiful and Damned*, based on their first year of marriage, Zelda swam in the sound or the pool at the Longshore Beach and Country Club.

That summer, female swimmers were competing in the Olympics for the first time, and the sport was becoming wildly popular. Most admired was Annette Kellerman, the first woman to swim the English Channel, who championed less restrictive swimming attire and was arrested in Boston for wearing a one-piece suit. Zelda still wore her flesh-colored, Kellerman suit, which from a distance made her appear nude, and swimming became the highlight of each day. It provided a sense of accomplishment and, before personal trainers and gyms came into vogue, was an enjoyable way to maintain a flexible body and stay slim. As swimming became popular so did tanning, with Coco Chanel credited for exploiting the fashion. On a cruise from Le Harve to Cannes, she inadvertently had gotten bronzed and designed sleeveless dresses to show off her color. To be tanned came to symbolize affluence, especially during winter months when only the wealthy could vacation in warm climes. To capitalize on this fad, *Vogue* carried its first advertisement for sunlamps in 1923, and shops began merchandising clothes for browned bodies, along with décolleté gowns that revealed much of it. Shoes started to be worn without stockings and beige-tinted powders got brushed on spots the sun had missed. To develop an even, glorious tan became top priority for Zelda, since it accentuated the fresh look she wanted to emphasize.

For amusement, the Fitzgeralds commuted to parties in Manhattan and invited friends to Westport, more from their fear of solitude than any desire to entertain. They filled the house with weekend guests who often overstayed their welcome, especially John Biggs who had roomed with Scott at Princeton. He frequently visited Westport that summer and stayed drunk much of the time. Zelda disliked him and felt physically threatened, taking caution to stay out of his way. She pleaded with Scott to make him leave, but he did nothing to intervene, instead transforming John into the derelict, Joe Hull, in *The Beautiful and Damned*, who approaches Gloria's bedroom with malevolence in mind, "standing regarding her, very quiet except for a slight swaying motion . . . the outline of his figure distinct against some indistinguishable light." Only after Zelda brought the situation to climax by saying either he was going or her did John get booted out.

With Scott maintaining a daily writing schedule no one could interrupt, Zelda eagerly anticipated weekends and kept an account of activities in her diary. Houseguests began arriving late on Friday afternoon, and after a round or two of drinks, everyone headed for dinner at the Miramar Club, which featured big bands and a gambling casino, or the Compo Inn, whose owners, Marion and Jake Levy, served decent meals. After that, it was on to the Rye Beach Country Club for more drinking and cavorting by the sound.

It was customary for Southern women to keep courtship diaries, on their wedding day presenting them to grooms, but Zelda's was noticeably different, chronicling her emotions and observations in a highly original way. From early on they proved inspirational for Scott, and he had incorporated excerpts into his first novel, *This Side of Paradise*, but now was using entire sections for *The Beautiful and Damned*. So original did he consider her diaries that he had them typed and mailed to Maxwell Perkins, who agreed that she possessed an original voice and natural talent. He also sent sections to Harold Ober, admitting he had used segments for his story "The Flight of the Rocket," for which *Metropolitan Magazine* had advanced $7,000. He made the mistake of showing her journals to George Jean Nathan, who expressed interest in publishing them under the title *A Young Girl's Diary*. When George wanted to meet her, Scott contrived some excuse, but George persevered and after a party in Westport, when guests had left or passed out, he wandered into the cellar and found Zelda's diaries in a storage box. After reading them, he approached her the next morning with a proposal to publish. "They interested me so greatly, that in my capacity as a magazine editor, I later made her an offer for them." Scott responded for Zelda with a resounding no. "He said he had gained a lot of inspiration from them, and wanted to use parts of them in his own novels and short stories." Zelda was flattered by George's interest and disappointed over Scott's outright rejection. But she had bigger plans for George. She wanted him to help her break into the theater. The most widely read drama critic of his time, George knew everyone in the theatrical world and was just the person to do that. As fellow critic Ernest Boyd observed about George, "His business is the theater, and his business is his pleasure, but of life itself, he has made a play, in which he is the leading character." Zelda had chosen the same role for herself and dreamed of becoming an actress or dancer on stage or in film. Now that she was in New York with George willing to help, she was determined to make that happen. Only Scott vehemently opposed the idea. Any celebrity she garnered was going to remain reflected glory.

As coeditors of the *Smart Set*, George Jean Nathan and Henry Lewis Mencken published authors generally ignored by more conservative magazines. In addition to Scott's "Babes in the Woods" (September 1919) and

"The Diamond as Big as the Ritz" (June 1922), the magazine published Sherwood Anderson's "I Want to Know Why," Stephen Vincent Benet's "Summer Thunder," and Willa Cather's "Coming, Eden Bower." The most influential social critic of his time, H. L. Mencken began his career as a newspaperman and lived in Baltimore but maintained a suite at the Algonquin Hotel for entertaining. Directly across the street from George's apartment hotel, the Algonquin catered to the literary and theater crowd and its mahogany paneled lobby became their unofficial clubhouse. Henry and George both were confirmed bachelors, until Henry surprised everyone at age fifty by marrying Zelda's Montgomery friend, Sara Haardt.

Zelda cavorted openly with George that summer, exchanging suggestive letters and openly showing her affection. Not to be outdone, Scott squired several women around Westport, among them the actress Miriam Hopkins and Tallulah Bankhead's older sister Eugenia, called Gene. In perpetual rivalry with her sibling, Gene drank heavily, took drugs, smoked 150 cigarettes a day, and was unabashedly promiscuous. Partly in response to Zelda's flirtation with George, Scott and Gene became sexually involved, though she was engaged to Morton Hoyt, brother of poet, Elinor (Hoyt) Wylie, who then was dating John Peale Bishop. Not that an engagement would have stopped Gene from being intimate with other men. That summer, Tallulah was performing on Broadway in *A Virtuous Vamp* and living at the Algonquin Hotel with her aunt Louise. Casting directors loved her quick wit, husky voice, and curvaceous body, expecting sexual favors in exchange for roles. Actresses who refused to sleep with agents and producers didn't get parts. Tallulah quickly learned the ropes and before long was staying out all night drinking and using cocaine; her chaperone aunt finally gave up and went back to Montgomery.

On one of her excursions into Manhattan, Zelda stopped to see Tallulah at the Klaw Theater and left convinced she was just as talented as her Montgomery friend. Afterward, she joined George at his Royalton suite. A hotel where people stayed long term, it was an undistinguished place with an uninviting lobby that functioned as a residence for bachelors seeking anonymity. George's apartment was decorated for dramatic effect; velvet draperies veiled windows and divans were strategically placed to encourage conversation and make it easy to serve drinks. When Zelda told Edmund Wilson that hotel rooms made her erotically charged, she probably was thinking of such a place. What intrigued George about Zelda was her youthful purity combined with the era's reckless spirit. He found the combination irresistible, and undoubtedly the two became sexually involved. "Most alluring to man is that woman," George wrote, "whose wickedness has to it, a touch of the angelic, and whose virtue a touch of the devil." Chauvinistic, he liked women beautiful but not intellectually threatening, and at twenty,

Zelda was both. "To a man, the least interesting of women is the successful woman, whether successful in work, or in life, or on the mere general gaudy playground of life. A man wants a woman whose success is touched, however faintly, with failure. The woman who is sure, resolute and successful, he may want for an associate in business, a friend and a confidante, a nurse or a housekeeper, but never for a sweetheart." He claimed that his test of a woman's mental agility was to ask directions to Grand Central. If she was half right, she was intelligent enough for him. George and Scott felt similarly about women, and Zelda would later write of her protagonist Jacob (based on Scott) that women usually were evocateurs of his grace, charming only as long as they did not exercise authority.

George was careful to keep their affair quiet, until Zelda revealed she had shown his letters to Scott. To avoid problems, George cautioned, "The calling of a husband's attention to a love letter addressed to his wife, is but part of a sagacious technique. It completely disarms suspicion. I suggest that you hire a post office box for my future confidential communications. True enough, this is an obvious gesture, but what else can we do?" He tried to avoid a quarrel, but after Zelda cut her tailbone on a broken bottle near his tub, angry words erupted between the two men. As she wrote to Ludlow Fowler, the accident occurred during one of George's parties when she was "boiled" and required three stitches, and now she was hardly able to sit down. George denied any impropriety, vigorously affirming, "In his biography on Fitzgerald, Mizener alleges that I once tried to flirt with Zelda, and so enraged Scott that he engaged me in a furious fist fight. The facts are far different." But Scott's first biographer was convinced the relationship was sexual and scribbled on a letter received from George: "He also made love to Zelda. He carried it off with typical high spirits."

That year, George was dating Ruth Findlay, the blond, diminutive actress Zelda had watched play Dore in *The Salamander*. By the time she was twenty, Ruth already had starred in six silent films and was an established Broadway actress. George always was attracted to petite women, shorter than his five feet, seven and one half inches, and especially blond actresses. Although he preferred seeing Zelda alone, occasionally he asked both Fitzgeralds to join him and Ruth for drinks. Although she usually agreed to come, often as not, Zelda did not appear, which tantalized George and elicited a prompt response. "Sweet Souse: What happened to you? Ruth and I got to the Beaux Arts at eleven and sat sucking ginger ale until midnight. Were you and Scott arrested? Fair Zelda—Why didn't you telephone me, as you promised? I missed your telephone message at the Royalton by half an hour. I had a table for four at the Century dress rehearsal, and Ruth and I were compelled to occupy it alone. You missed a very good show."

Scott agonized over Zelda's flirtation with George, and the critic was on his mind so often, he got woven into *The Beautiful and Damned* as two minor characters: Maury Noble and Joseph Bloeckman, the Jewish vice president of Films Par Excellence. Joseph is attracted to Gloria Gilbert but loses her to Anthony Patch. After her marriage, she reignites his attentions and announces she wants to become a film sensation like Mary Pickford, who makes a million dollars annually. Joseph encourages her, but Gloria's husband squelches the idea, saying it's just her craving for excitement. Dismissing her ambitions, he insists marriage should provide ample contentment, and what does she expect him to do—follow her around the country? Although Gloria acquiesces, three years later she recontacts Joseph and announces she's ready to take the plunge. Now a powerful producer, he schedules a screen test, first taking Gloria on a long car ride, after which she wonders—was it wrong to make him love her, because that is what she did. This is Scott's reference to whatever happened on the journey, but Gloria appears better at romance than acting, because she tests poorly and Joseph determines a younger actress is necessary. Like his fictional counterpart, George could have channeled Zelda onto the stage, but given Scott's determination to keep her from the spotlight, made the decision not to interfere.

To put distance between the two, Scott organized a road trip to Montgomery, and in preparation for the journey, ordered matching knickers or "plus fours," a golf-inspired fashion taken up by drivers. They planned to surprise Zelda's parents and document the journey for *Motor Magazine*. Since neither were experienced drivers, they encountered numerous mishaps along the way. The car's axle broke and several tires got punctured, which delayed their arrival by several days. When they finally reached Montgomery, their white knickerbockers were coated with red dirt, and the Sayres away on a trip. To make the best of a disappointing situation, they spent two weeks visiting Zelda's friends and relatives, played golf, and went to Pickett Springs Amusement Park. When it was time to leave, the Marmon was in such bad shape, it had to be junked and they boarded a train back to New York.

The Sayres were disappointed to have missed their youngest daughter. Without her, the house seemed empty and the judge occasionally found himself peering nostalgically into her room. They scheduled a visit to Westport the following month, but when they arrived, were dismayed to find two of Scott's friends drunk on the lawn and the cottage a mess. Zelda maneuvered the men to a nearby roadhouse, but they soon returned and continued drinking. An argument then ensued between Scott and Zelda that ended with her slamming into a door and getting a bloody nose. The next morning the Sayres expressed their disgust by leaving for Clothilde's home in Tarrytown, where they voiced concern over Zelda's marital situation.

As leaves began falling, even with two fireplaces blazing, the Westport cottage remained chilly, so the Fitzgeralds returned to Manhattan and rented a brownstone apartment on West Fifty-Ninth Street, around the corner from the Plaza Hotel, which conveniently delivered meals. Six months later, they moved to larger accommodations on East Fifty-Ninth, but the additional space only made housekeeping more burdensome for Zelda. When Lawton Campbell arrived for lunch one afternoon, he found the place a wreck. "The room was bedlam. Breakfast dishes were all about, the bed unmade, books and papers scattered here and there, trays filled with cigarette butts, liquor glasses from the night before. Everything was untidy and helterskelter." Scott liked changing his shirts twice daily and wanted fresh ones available, but Zelda was accustomed to a laundress and tossed soiled clothes into a closet. What happened afterward was not her concern. Garments got dumped on the floor, and half-empty trunks became a convenient receptacle for dirty laundry. No matter what Scott said, she did not consider it her responsibility to supervise his clothing and keep the apartment in order. Irritated as he was over the situation, Scott promptly integrated the chaos into *The Beautiful and Damned*, writing of how the apartment quickly assumed the taint that polluted the Westport cottage: a wretched smell of stale wine, the odor of tobacco and revelry remembered in disgust. Guests broke things, got sick in the bathroom, and made an unbelievable mess of the place. Marriage was more complicated than Zelda had anticipated. People, she mused, needed to be taught about matrimony in school, what to expect as its rewards, and which responsibilities they could accept.

In the midst of this mayhem, Zelda began hiding money, not large bills but enough to provide some independence. She disliked continually asking for cash and with no bank account of her own, was dependent on Scott's generosity. The situation was complicated by the uncertainty of his income; either there was abundance or nothing at all. With no training in financial matters and never having earned an income, Zelda was inexperienced about finances. Rosalind remembered one luncheon at the Plaza Hotel, when her sister paid with a wad of bills the size of a tennis ball. When she asked why Zelda was carrying around so much money, she said Scott had just given it to her, and she had no idea what to do with it.

Although their lifestyle took its toll on their living quarters, it had not yet affected their appearance. Scott remained the perennial undergraduate, and Zelda emanated the glowing radiance of a teenager. She still captured the attention of everyone who saw her. One afternoon in the Biltmore lobby, as Scott waited with her mother for Zelda to arrive, he brought that magnetism to her attention. "You just watch that elevator because Zelda will be down in a minute, and then watch all the men here in the lobby. There will be fifty men here who will tell you exactly how beautiful Zelda is." When Zelda appeared, Scott stood there bursting with pride, and her mother was amazed to see that every man seemed to watch her as Zelda drew near. Only it was more than that, for as Zelda crossed the lobby with confidence, not only were male eyes upon her, but women's too, some more beautiful. Her appeal transcended perfection; it was the power of a wholly natural sensuality.

That she was so universally admired came with its usual detriment. Several of Scott's classmates were living in Manhattan that fall: John Peale Bishop, Ludlow Fowler, Lawton Campbell, Townsend Martin, Alex McKaig, and Bill Mackie. Not since Montgomery had Zelda been surrounded by so many handsome men, and when Scott was writing, she saw many of them, going to matinees with Alex McKaig, joining Ludlow Fowler for cocktails, or meeting Lawton Campbell at his club. At first Scott dismissed Zelda's habit of kissing them, saying they were due embraces since they hadn't attended the wedding. But when she began disappearing without any explanation of where she had been, he started giving her the third degree. "He is afraid of what she might do in a moment of caprice," observed Alex in his diary.

Although there was tacit agreement among Scott's friends not to sleep with a buddy's wife, Zelda tried seducing several. She was particularly attracted to Townsend Martin, nephew of the prominent philanthropist and author Frederick Townsend Martin. She found his Nordic features and blue eyes appealing, and when she looked into them, admitted feeling stirred. Martin encouraged her attentions, but only so far, and when she insisted he give her a bath, he quickly announced his departure for Tahiti. Months later, when he sent a photograph from Pago Pago, showing himself relaxed in a tie-dyed sarong, oxford cloth shirt, and sneakers without socks, she gave it an entire page in her scrapbook.

Disappointed over his sudden departure, Zelda refocused her attention on John Peale Bishop, whose taste and intelligence she admired. A Southerner like herself, John was from the Shenandoah Valley in West Virginia, and according to his English professor at Princeton had the self-possession and poise of a young English lord. She teased him by saying, "I like you better than anybody in the world. I never feel safe with you! I only like men who kiss as a means to an end. I never know how to treat the other kind." One evening, employing the same tactic she had used with Townsend, as John was preparing for bed, Zelda appeared and insisted on spending the night. In deference to Scott, he took her home, but John had something else in mind anyway, marrying a wealthy woman and living a life of ease. As a young man he had become ill and grown accustomed to being cared for by women. When Townsend was away, he let John use his apartment, and the exquisitely decorated residence, filled with Japanese screens and antique porcelains, was exactly the sort of ambiance John wished to create for himself. It became a gathering place for the Princeton group. Gilbert Seldes, then managing editor of the *Dial*, recalled one all-night party when he had fallen asleep on Townsend's Renaissance bed and awoken to see Scott and Zelda coming toward him. "Suddenly, this double apparition approached me. The two most beautiful people in the world were floating toward me smiling. I thought to myself, 'if there is anything I can do to keep them beautiful—I will do it.'" There wasn't, for less than four years later in France, he would witness their downturn only weeks before Zelda's first suicide attempt.

John worked with Edmund Wilson at *Vanity Fair*, which appealed to sophisticated audiences and reported on contemporary culture in its popular columns, "In and Around the Theater" and "On the World of Art." They had been at the magazine only eight months, having filled positions vacated by Dorothy Parker, Robert Benchley, and Robert Sherwood. As the magazine's drama critic, Parker had made the tactical error of writing a scathing review of Billie Burke's performance in *Caesar's Wife*. She was married to Flo Ziegfeld who advertised heavily in the publication, and Dorothy got axed for compromising magazine revenues. Benchley and Sherwood followed her out the door in protest, and their positions became available to John and Edmund.

Considered overly intellectual at Princeton, Edmund was a perfect fit for the magazine, and he and John made good editorial partners. Although they were worlds apart personally—Edmund, detached and absentminded, John, urbane with a core of sensuality—they got along well. They even shared the same girlfriend, Edna St. Vincent Millay, who lived in a cold water flat and bathed at Edmund's apartment. Edna shared some characteristics with Zelda, flouting convention by being sexually involved with both men at the same time. Comfortable with her body, she thought nothing of walking around nude in Edmund's apartment.

Besides working at *Vanity Fair*, John tutored the children of Manhattan's elite and was comfortable around the wealthy. Although still dating Elinor Wylie, who was becoming a well-known poet, he intended to marry someone who could support him, so when socialite Margaret Hutchins appeared, his relationship with Wylie ended. Margaret not only was rich but controlling, and John gladly let her take the reins. They moved to France where she purchased the Château de Tressancourt at Orgeval, Seine-et-Oise, forty minutes outside Paris, originally built as a hunting lodge by Henry of Navarre, then expanded into an elegant residence during the eighteenth century.

Alex McKaig was the least attractive of Scott's friends, short and baby faced with curly hair and a stubby nose. He had known Scott only casually at Princeton and was not particularly popular at college. To make a living he worked for an advertising agency but was an aspiring playwright who wrote at night and on weekends, when not attending theater or partying. After graduating, he briefly attended Annapolis to obtain his lieutenant junior grade commission, and while serving at sea, started keeping a diary in a small navy logbook. After arriving in Manhattan, he began recording the daily happenings, emotional attachments, and rivalries among his Princeton friends. One of his entries concerning Scott's uneasiness with Zelda's flirtatious behavior foretells the crisis that would unfold in France. "If she's there, Fitzgerald can't work—she bothers him; if she's not there, he can't work, worried of what she might do." Zelda could always count on Alex for a theater escort, and his intention to become a playwright made him a good companion. Once, returning from a matinee, she offered her lips to him in the back of a cab, which he noted in his diary. "In taxi Zelda asked me to kiss her, but I couldn't. I couldn't forget Scott—he's so damn pitiful. . . . She is without a doubt the most brilliant and most beautiful young woman I've ever known."

Scott allowed Zelda's flirtations to continue, since they occupied her and gave him time to write. They also provided material for *The Beautiful and Damned* in which the newlyweds, Anthony and Gloria, discuss her romantic past. "I suppose I ought to be furious because you've kissed so many men," he complains, only to have Gloria protest that those kisses left no taint of promiscuity, "even though a man once told me, in all seriousness, that he hated to think I'd been a public drinking glass." Married or not, Gloria, and by extension Zelda, intended to keep doing as she pleased.

New York's theater scene sizzled with activity in 1920, with almost two hundred plays and musicals opening, many with heroines like Gloria, who did as they pleased and damned the consequences. Theda Bara was performing in *The Blue Flame*, and Marilyn Miller, whom Zelda strongly resembled, was a hit in *Sally*, which also featured the Philadelphia dancer Catherine Littlefield. Besides seventy-five legitimate theaters, there were also burlesque houses that showcased variety acts, chorus lines, and topless shows. Among the most popular was Minsky's, which performed in the National Winter Garden on Houston Street, where George Jean Nathan and Robert Benchley regularly went to watch strippers.

With each new show, Zelda grew more determined to become an actress, so when Hollywood producers offered the Fitzgeralds starring roles in the film version of *This Side of Paradise*, she jumped at the opportunity. Initially intrigued with the idea, after speaking with Maxwell Perkins, who expressed concern it might confuse readers and damage his writing career, Scott changed his mind. No matter how much Zelda pleaded, he would not relent, and when she asked Alex's help, he cautioned that she "would have to make up her mind, whether she wanted to go into the movies, or get in with the young married set." Zelda understood that breaking into films without a ready-made vehicle was more difficult, and Alex doubted she would make the effort. The combination of an acting career with marriage was rare during the twenties, when women generally retired after marriage to raise families. One of Scott's notebook entries suggests that was what he expected of Zelda: "When I like men I want to be like them. When I like women, I want to own them, to dominate them, to have them admire me."

Scott's reaction was a crushing disappointment to Zelda, who saw the perfect opportunity being snatched away. Evenings now often ended in arguments, especially when a more accomplished woman came along. Alex was then writing *Dark Victory* for Tallulah and recalled a terrible battle one evening involving Bankhead, Ludlow Fowler, and Jack Dennison. The situation started deteriorating when Zelda noticed her Patou skirt feeling tight around the waist. Ten months into their marriage, she discovered she was pregnant. Earlier that year, Alex had mentioned that possibility in his diary: "Went up to Fitzgeralds to spend evening. They just recovering from awful party. Much taken with idea of having a baby." The news came as a surprise to others, and when Edmund Wilson told George Jean Nathan, he quipped the child probably would be a cross between the Ziegfeld Follies and Dinty Moore's restaurant, an Irish pub on West Forty-Sixth Street popular with the theater crowd. That Zelda was more interested in being a performer than mother was true. With Scribner's set to publish Scott's second novel, *The Beautiful and Damned*, and film rights sold to Warner Bros., she already began strategizing, after the baby's birth, how she would audition for the part of Gloria Gilbert, the character modeled after her.

With six months left before Zelda's delivery, the couple decided on a quick tour of Europe and boarded the *Aquitania* for Southampton, England, on May 21, 1921. Their hasty departure caught George off guard. He had not fully repaired his friendship with Scott, and Edmund Wilson told Scott that when George dropped by the *Smart Set* offices, he "seemed a little crestfallen, and I think he was sorry that you should have gotten off without patching up your quarrel."

In London they received a dinner invitation from John Galsworthy, met up with Tallulah who was there appearing in a play, and after visiting Cambridge and the Houses of Parliament, marveled at the White Cliffs of Dover while crossing the English Channel for France. A day later they were watching the Folies-Bergere in Paris. After a shopping spree on rue St. Honore, they toured Versailles, where Zelda was photographed on Empress Josephine's bench, then visited Josephine's last residence, Malmaison, where Zelda would be hospitalized nine years later. Then, it was on to Italy by train with stops in Venice, Florence, and Rome, where they checked into the Grand Hotel, which grew less grand when they discovered it was ridden with fleas. They were disappointed with Italy and returned early to Paris, hoping to locate Edmund Wilson and Edna St. Vincent Millay, who recently had arrived. They found Edna, but could not track down Edmund, who neglected to leave his address with American Express, which before cell phones was one way people located each other abroad. When they arrived back in London, they checked into Claridges, but were disappointed with their drab room away from important guests and decided to return home early. Before boarding the SS *Celtic* in Liverpool for New York, Scott shared his disappointment about the trip with Edmund Wilson, writing, "I think it's a shame that England and America didn't let the Germans conquer Europe. It's the only thing that would have saved the fleet of tottering old wrecks."

After disembarking in Manhattan, they headed for Alabama where they planned to remain for the baby's birth. But with Prohibition federal law, Judge Sayre insisted on no alcohol and the atmosphere proved too confining. Montgomery was unbearably hot, but when Zelda headed for the city pool, her baby bump caused a scandal. Pregnant women did not then swim in public. Had she remained on the pool's sidelines, there might only have been whispers, but when she dove into the artesian waters, she got ordered out. To escape the oppressive heat and Southern conservatism, they boarded a train for Scott's Minnesota home. Amazingly, it was the first time Zelda had met Scott's parents, and though they welcomed her warmly, she was not comfortable with them. Actually, she didn't want to be around anybody until the baby was born and had misgivings over the pregnancy and what it was doing to her body. Again, Scott channeled her feelings through Gloria in *The Beautiful and Damned*, who bemoans the child-bearing experience as a menace to her beauty and fears winding up with wide hips and lusterless hair.

With the help of Scott's friend Xandra Kalman, they rented a cottage in Dellwood, a resort community on White Bear Lake, where St. Paul's affluent retreated for the summer. In her story "The Girl the Prince Liked," Zelda characterizes those vacationers as people who loved golf or sailing on the lake, bachelors who enjoyed the cheerful clattering of plates at the Yacht Club, and sun-dried women who welcomed back husbands escaping town and the five o'clock heat. Xandra came from an influential Minnesota family but had Southern roots; her great-grandfather had been one of Tennessee's prominent lawyers and legislators. A year older than Zelda, she was married to Oscar Kalman, a wealthy banker twenty-five years her senior, and was the only person Zelda befriended in St. Paul, the two women often playing golf at the country club.

A month before the birth, the Fitzgeralds returned to St. Paul, where Zelda purchased baby necessities and arranged for a doctor and nurse. Upset over her weight gain, she felt wretched these final weeks and ready for the ordeal to end. On October 26 it was over. When their baby girl was born that day, Scott scribbled down Zelda's first words out of anesthesia, that she hoped their daughter would be beautiful, but a fool. Less than two years later, a slightly altered version of those words would get uttered by Daisy in *The Great Gatsby*, who, upon learning of her baby's sex says, "I'm glad it's a girl. And I hope she'll be a fool—that is the best thing a girl can be in this world, a beautiful little fool." Given the frustration Zelda was feeling at being thwarted in every direction, the sentiment was understandable. Smart was good, but too much sense could get a girl into trouble.

Zelda had chosen Patricia for a name, but Scott insisted on calling the baby Frances Scott Key Fitzgerald. Nicknamed "Scottie," five months later Zelda was still calling her "Pat." Scott had wanted a son and Zelda also preferred a boy, telling Ludlow Flower, "She *is* awfully cute, and I am very devoted to her, but quite disappointed over the sex." When George received photographs of Zelda with the baby, he wrote back cryptically, "The pictures prove to me that you are getting more beautiful every day, but whose baby is it? It looks very much like Mencken."

To someone from Alabama, the Minnesota winter was intolerable and Zelda eagerly anticipated returning East, writing Ludlow, "I certainly miss you + Townsend + Alec—in fact I am very lonesome. . . . This damned place is 18 below zero." Scribner's publication party for *The Beautiful and Damned* gave them the excuse to leave. As the most autobiographical of Scott's novels, it chronicled the failing marriage of Anthony Patch and Gloria Gilbert, a woman married to an insecure man who undermines her every ambition. After creating that exact scenario with Zelda, he now was dissecting it in fiction.

With Scribner's $5,600 advance safely banked, the Fitzgeralds deposited Scottie with a nanny and departed for New York, where they registered at the Plaza and began a monthlong celebration. They visited the new speakeasies; went to parties at George Jean Nathan's, with whom Scott had reconciled; and lunched with Edmund Wilson, John Peale Bishop, and Donald Ogden Stewart. On Scott's urging, Edmund had helped Stuart gain entry into the publishing world, and he repaid the favor by introducing Scott to Ernest Hemingway in Paris. It had only been a year, but Edmund observed how much the couple had changed. Scott looked weary and Zelda decidedly matronly. She had not shed the baby weight and worried her figure was permanently ruined. Then, she was pregnant again. The timing could not have been worse, and though abortion was illegal, doctors could be found. Either they performed a D and C with a curette, or used pills containing abortifacients like pennyroyal or angelica that caused abortive bleeding. Scott noted the procedure in his ledger for March 1922, as "Zelda and her abortionist," and "Pills and Dr. Lackin," lamenting that his son went down the toilet of the xxxx Hotel after Dr. X—pills." Although neither wanted another child so soon and considered the abortion expedient, Scott later would express anger and revulsion over what he termed, the "chill-mindedness of his wife."

After publication of *The Beautiful and Damned*, Burton Rascoe, literary editor of the *New York Herald Tribune*, asked Zelda to write a satiric review of Scott's new novel. Rereading it, she was surprised how much of her writing had been used verbatim. "It seems to me that on one page, I recognized a portion of an old diary of mine, which mysteriously disappeared shortly after my marriage, and also scraps of letters which, though considerably edited, sound to me vaguely familiar." Burton loved her piece but was slow paying until Scott chastised that he was "withholding from her the first money she has ever earned." Since the review had been so easy to write, Zelda considered doing more pieces, and when *McCall's* requested an article titled "Where Do Flappers Go," she seized the opportunity. A year earlier she was content to have Scott appropriate her words and ideas, but that started changing when she saw everything in their life being used for raw material. It was particularly annoying when Scott used her originalities to impress other women. Later, Zelda would write of when David, drawn from Scott, flattered one woman by saying he imagined she wore something startling and boyish under her clothes. Scott had stolen that notion from her. All summer *she* had worn silk BVDs, a one-piece garment of long underwear for men, with convenient front buttons and back flaps.

After celebrating their second anniversary at the Biltmore Hotel where they had honeymooned, they returned to St. Paul in time for Zelda to portray a southern flapper in the Junior League Frolic on April 17. She was improving her acting skills, when producers again expressed interest in the couple playing themselves, this time in the film version of *The Beautiful and Damned*. When H. L. Mencken heard about the film, he offered his services for a bit part: "Are you going to act in *The Beautiful and Damned*? If so, I bespeak the part of the taxi driver." Again, Scott rejected their offer and Warner Bros. chose Marie Prevost to play Gloria and Kenneth Harlan for the male lead. The film premiered at the Strand Theater in New York and was universally panned. A day after its opening, Scott told the Kalmans he was thoroughly ashamed of it and considered it the worst movie he had ever seen. Zelda was furious over the whole situation and would not discuss the movie with Scott, but loudly criticized the performances from her seat during the screening.

When summer arrived, they returned to White Bear Yacht Club, where Zelda competed in a golf tournament, and would have stayed the entire season, but guests complained about their raucous parties and they were asked to leave. The Kalmans found them another place on the lake, where they remained until returning east for the publication of Scott's first collection of short stories, *Tales of the Jazz Age*. This time, Scottie was left behind with Scott's parents.

They planned to rent a place on Long Island and found a house on Gateway Drive in Great Neck, across the inlet from Sands Point. They signed a lease for $300 monthly and hired a live-in couple to cook and clean for $160 a month, a governess for $90, and a part-time laundress for $36. Whatever it cost, Scott was going to have clean shirts. Zelda returned alone to St. Paul in time for Scottie's first birthday, and when the two took the train back to New York, Scott met them in his newly purchased, used Rolls Royce.

Still among Manhattan's sought-after couples, the Fitzgeralds were invited by Gloria Swanson for dinner and dancing at the Ritz Carlton, and they were given celebrity seats at the 1923 championship boxing matches and baseball games. When Scott signed with Hearst Syndicate and their photograph appeared on the cover of *Hearst's International* and was picked up by other American newspapers, their status became magnified. Although the caption exaggerated Zelda's exalted position, announcing "Mrs. Scott Fitzgerald started the flapper movement in this country—so says her husband," she had become its exemplar. When interviewed over this accolade, Zelda expounded about how flappers had become mainstream. "Three or four years ago girls of her type were pioneers. They did what they wanted to, were unconventional, perhaps, just because they wanted to fight for self-expression. Now they do it because it's the thing everyone does." Questioned over how she might earn her own living, Zelda responded with an answer that foretold her future: "I've studied ballet. I'd try to get a place in the follies or the movies. If I wasn't successful, I'd try to write."

The area around Great Neck was home to show business personalities and wealthy bootleggers who entertained lavishly and provided character material for Scott's next novel. Some of their neighbors included Leslie Howard, Groucho Marx, Basil Rathbone, producers Sam Harris and Arthur Hopkins, and songwriter Gene Buck, who was assistant to Florenz Ziegfeld. Gene and his wife, Helen, often accompanied the Fitzgeralds to Princeton football games, and she played golf with Zelda at the Soundview Club. Although the Bucks enjoyed socializing with the Fitzgeralds, they warned friends about inviting them over, unless they wanted to see their furniture ruined by spilled drinks and cigarette butts.

Scott got to know Tommy Hitchcock, recently returned from a year at Oxford on a scholarship offered officers after the Armistice. He heroically had served as a pilot, and after being shot down and captured by the Germans, escaped and walked eight days to the safety of Switzerland. Hitchcock was then America's best-known polo player with the rank of 10, the highest appraisal of skill. Scott would watch him play at Meadow Brook Polo Club in Westbury, marveling how he led his team to victory in a game fraught with danger, where horses were worth thousands and riders, millions. Further out on the Island at Southampton, Esther Murphy lived on her father, Patrick Murphy's, estate. He had built the Mark Cross leather goods brand into a thriving business, catering to more than the carriage trade, and his son, Gerald, recently had departed for Paris with his wife and three children.

Directly behind the Fitzgeralds, in a rambling house on two acres with a tennis court and baseball diamond, lived Ring Lardner with his wife, Ellis, and four sons. He was a successful sportswriter who sold baseball stories to the *Saturday Evening Post* and had achieved modest fame as a lyricist and writer of satiric poetry. However, his primary income came from the quick newspaper pieces he wrote between alcoholic binges. Ring and Scott were on similar drinking paths and saw themselves reflected in each other. Only, Scott was nine years younger and could still binge without feeling the debilitating effects Ring experienced. Although Zelda was cordial to Ring and Ellis, she considered Ring a negative influence, especially when Scott began copying Ring's habit of disappearing into Manhattan for three-day benders and returning home to fall asleep on the lawn. "He is a typical newspaperman whom I don't find very amusing," she told her sister, Rosalind. "He is six feet tall and goes on periodical sprees lasting from one to X weeks. He is on one now, which is probably the reason he calls on us. Ring is drinking himself into an embalmed state, so he'll be all ready for the grim reaper." Ring's son agreed with Zelda's assessment of the situation and remarked that what "fascinated Scott in the Great Neck days, was the image he saw of his own future. He probably felt satisfaction that he could sleep off a drunk and get back to work with much more ease than his older friend, but he must have known he was heading in the same direction. Even the pattern he came to, of setting a specific beginning and ending date for going on the wagon was Ring's."

Scott now had a drinking buddy, and the two would swig Bass Ale on Ring's side porch and watch the partying next door at Maggie and Herbert Swope's Victorian mansion. Their lawns were the site of marathon croquet matches that stretched into the night, as guests positioned cars on the course to provide light with high beams. The foremost news reporter of his generation, Herbert Swope in 1917 had received the first Pulitzer award for his work as a war correspondent, and afterward joined the *New York World* as executive director when it was owned by Ralph Pulitzer. This was the gestation period for *The Great Gatsby*, and Ring's house provided access to activities that would inform the novel. While the Swopes' house bore little resemblance to Gatsby's fictionalized mansion, its parties did. "There was a porch on the side of our house facing the Swopes," Ring's son recalled, "and

Ring and Scott sat there many a weekend afternoon, drinking ale or whisky, and watching, what Ring described as, 'an almost continuous house party next door.' Though their entertaining fell a whit short of Gatsby's, the location of the Swopes' house was just right for the view of Daisy's pier across the bay."

Besides alcohol, the two shared an interest in boxing, and Ring got Scott ringside seats for the Jack Dempsey–Luis Firpo 1923 championship fight on September 14 at the Polo Grounds. That afternoon, eighty thousand spectators watched Dempsey retain his title against the Argentine boxer, and when Firpo knocked Dempsey out of the ring in round 1, sending him onto the lap of Grantland Rice, who was seated next to Ring, the two sportswriters hoisted the brawler back into the fray. Scott and Zelda were also ringside to watch Dempsey's fourth-round victory over Georges Carpentier in Jersey City, and afterward joined Ring, Robert Benchley, and Robert Sherwood for a celebration at Tony Soma's on West Forty-Ninth Street. Although a successful journalist and sportswriter, Ring didn't become a literary figure until Scott convinced Perkins to publish Ring's stories. That year, Scott also helped another newspaperman, Tom Boyd, literary critic for the *St. Paul Daily News*, break into the world of book authorship, by convincing Scribner's to publish his first novel, *Through the Wheat*. Three years later, Scott would do the same thing for an obscure writer named Ernest Hemingway.

Great Neck was just thirty minutes away from Manhattan by train, and what happened in Westport got repeated there. Friends took advantage of the Fitzgeralds' hospitality and arrived on Friday to stay through Sunday, considering it a convenient way to escape the city on weekends. There were continual parties and endless drinking that increased expenses and left the house in disarray. Although there was a sign in the kitchen stating, "Weekend guests are respectfully notified that invitations to stay over Monday, issued by the host and hostess during the small hours of Sunday morning, must not be taken seriously," many ignored it and refused to go. It got so bad that when Scott invited people to visit, Zelda would interrupt and say they should reconsider coming, because the baby cried constantly and the place was small. Scott summarized the period as full of failure and miseries, drink and debt, the most terrible year since his disaster at Princeton, dangerous and deteriorating with no ground under their feet. One evening, Zelda became so intoxicated that she drove their Rolls Royce off the pier into Great Neck Bay, but since the tide was out, the car only got stuck up to its hubcaps in mud.

They disposed of the months by killing time with partying and endless arguments about drinking and disorder. Zelda generally could hold her liquor, but after two whiskeys, Scott became obnoxious and embarrassed everyone. He might crawl under a table and start barking, try to eat his soup with a fork, or intentionally drop an orange peel down his throat and start gagging. One evening he chewed a wad of twenty-dollar bills and made the arrogant display of lighting his cigarette with another. Drinking provided an excuse for outrageous behavior, and he had taken to proclaiming, "I'm an alcoholic." Zelda continually was apologizing for him, and when Rosalind visited that August, she observed the deteriorating situation firsthand. After the sisters were stuck at a party that dragged on until morning, they finally left without Scott, and Zelda admitted she felt powerless to change things and regretted marrying him. The circumstances were similar when her other sister, Tilde, and husband, John, came for a planned luncheon, only to find Zelda and Scott in bed nursing hangovers. It was the second time they had been treated poorly and ended any possibility of future reconciliation. Rosalind recalled, "Tilde and John did not forget Scott's rudeness to them at the wedding, which is understandable, nevertheless they accepted an invitation to lunch at the Fitzgeralds in Great Neck, and that too proved a fiasco, with the hosts in bed when the guests arrived, and the wet diapers staining the borrowed suitcase (it was Tilde's) and no further effort was made by either side to reestablish peace."

That spring, when Zelda's Montgomery friend Eleanor Browder came and they met Scott at the Plaza, they found him being escorted out of the Palm Court, drunk. After driving them back to Great Neck, he got into an argument with Zelda and ruined dinner by ripping off the tablecloth and sending food in every direction. Seemingly unruffled, Zelda rose calmly and suggested they have coffee in another room. Had Zelda been prepared for motherhood, Scottie might have provided comfort, but overshadowed now by both husband and daughter, she showed little maternal warmth. One houseguest recalled when Scottie was brought in for a greeting and Zelda ordered, "Kiss mother, dear," that the child vehemently shook her head, at which point, Zelda quipped that Scottie only loathed her but hated Scott.

Their marital situation further unraveled when Scott acknowledged the extent of their debt. Although the *Saturday Evening Post* was paying $4,000 a story and he had earned $29,000 that year (equivalent to $300,000 in today's money), the couple had overspent by $7,000. The couple continually were at the Bucks', Lardners', or Swopes' and attended so many social gatherings, they felt obliged to give their own, which turned into expensive affairs. During their first year at Great Neck, between household expenses, entertaining costs, and weekly excursions into Manhattan, they had spent Scott's entire income and then some, with nothing to show for it.

To get out of debt, Scott sequestered himself above the garage and over four months wrote eleven stories and one essay for the *Saturday Evening Post* entitled "How to Live on $36,000 a Year." He could not understand how it was that the more he earned, the more he sank into debt. Their financial crisis made it clear they could not remain in Great Neck. To economize, they decided to leave for Europe. Everyone bragged how inexpensive it was, Germany the biggest bargain, with a dollar worth four trillion Deutsche Marks. France was almost as good with the franc hovering at nineteen to the dollar, an all-time low. Aside from economic advantages, foreigners generally could do as they pleased, and news of this latitude spread quickly. Many of Scott's friends already were there: Malcolm Cowley learning French on a fellowship, John Dos Passos studying anthropology at the Sorbonne, e.e. cummings working on a book of poetry, and the poet and anthropologist Ramon Guthrie researching Provencal verse. The couple told only Edmund Wilson and Maxwell Perkins of their plans, then asked Ring to sublet their house on which six months of their lease remained. At midnight on May 3, 1924, they departed from Pier 58 in lower Manhattan aboard the SS *Minnewaska* traveling first class, C deck, cabins 35 and 37, destination—France.

· 3 ·

The French Lieutenant

$\mathcal{W}$ith the anticipation of two explorers bound for adventure, Scott and Zelda arrived in Cherbourg with seventeen pieces of luggage and a set of the *Encyclopedia Britannica*. They intended to stay briefly in Paris before continuing to the Riviera, where Scott could work on his novel and Zelda be near a beach. After checking into the Hotel des Deux Mondes, they interviewed English nannies and hired Lillian Maddock for twenty-six dollars a month, even though they disliked her Cockney accent and patronizing manner. That accomplished, they lunched with John Peale Bishop and his socialite wife, Margaret Hutchins. She had selected an elegant restaurant at Armenonville in the Bois de Boulogne, where it was hard to order satisfactorily for Scottie. To amuse her, Scott took off his shoestring and let her play with it and some coins under the tables.

While their château was being renovated outside Paris at Orgeval, the Bishops were staying at the Hotel Campbell on Avenue de Friedland, and Scott and Zelda made plans to visit, even though they disliked Margaret, whom they considered pretentious. Two years earlier, John Bishop and Edmund Wilson had coauthored *The Undertaker's Garland* and seemed destined for literary fame. But Edmund now told Scott that he considered John's writing career over. The poet Alan Tate agreed: "John is like a man lying in a warm bath who faintly hears the telephone ringing downstairs, but is too comfortable to really do anything about it."

Two people they were eager to find were Fred Murphy and his sister, Esther, to whom they had been introduced in Great Neck. Elegant and intelligent, after marrying and divorcing the British writer and theorist John Strachey, Esther had wed Chester A. Arthur III, grandson of the twenty-first president. She was easy to locate and invited the couple to her fashionable residence at 23 quai de Grand Augustins, introducing them to her other brother, Gerald, and his wife, Sara. They never did meet Fred, who was in a Parisian hospital with complications from war injuries. In no shape for company, he died that month from a perforated intestine.

The Fitzgeralds immediately hit it off with Gerald and Sara Murphy, already established figures on the Parisian art scene and admired for their taste and style. One of the attractive Wiborg sisters from Cincinnati and daughter of a wealthy ink manufacturer, Sara was five years older than Gerald and had known him since childhood, their families vacationing on adjoining estates in East Hampton. They had married in 1915, the year after Sara was presented as a debutante before the Court of St. James. Gerald's father expected him to take over Mark Cross, but he had no interest in merchandising, and after graduating from Yale in 1912, enrolled in a landscape architecture program at Harvard. Like Scott, he was a poor student, limping through Hotchkiss, and flunking Yale's entrance exams three times before getting accepted. Never finishing the coursework for his landscaping degree, after marrying Sara and promptly having three children—Honoria, Baoth, and Patrick Francis II—he transported the entire family to France.

Sara and Gerald wanted to study painting and began taking lessons from Natalia Gontcharova, the first female set designer with the Ballets Russes. Through her introduction, they became friendly with the company's talented dancers, as well as its director, Sergei Diaghilev; composer, Igor Stravinsky; and poet and artist, Jean Cocteau, who designed programs and wrote libretti for the troupe. Of all the Americans in Paris, only the Murphys had total access to Diaghilev's Russian ballet troupe, attending rehearsals and opening night performances and joining the company in their communal effort to repaint backdrops and sets.

The Murphys had arrived in Paris to find many friends already there. Gerald's classmate Cole Porter and wife, Linda, had come over the previous year, and Archibald MacLeish, four years behind Gerald at Hotchkiss and Yale, soon appeared with his wife, Ada. Cole owed much of his college success to Gerald, who was a member of its top fraternity DKE and also selected for Skull and Bones, its prestigious secret society. Gerald never spoke about his private club experience, even with MacLeish who also was tapped for it, but Monty Wooley, who graduated the year before Gerald, knew something unpleasant had happened there. Voted best dressed in his class, Gerald possessed a sophistication Cole did not yet have and helped him get into DKE and chosen for Scroll and Key, second only in importance to Skull and Bones. Gerald's style remained legendary at Yale long after he graduated, and when MacLeish left for Paris, he was advised that if he wanted to experience the European avant-garde, he should look up Gerald. As Hemingway later would say, the Murphys were celebrity collectors, surrounding themselves with the most talented artists and writers.

Gerald and Sara recently had redesigned their St. Cloud apartment on 1 rue Git-le-Coeur, a sixteenth-century building overlooking Paris that once belonged to the composer Gounod and still remained in his family. They were also beginning renovations on their newly acquired villa at Cap d'Antibes on the Riviera. The area was Cole Porter's discovery. He and his wife, Linda, along with their traveling companion, Howard Sturges, nephew of the philosopher George Santayana, had rented a château at Cap d'Antibes the previous summer and invited the Murphys to visit. The beaches were deserted then since the French considered it a winter resort, leaving in May for cooler climes of Normandy on the Atlantic. Gerald and Sara loved the area and convinced the owner of the Hotel du Cap, about to close for the season, to lease them a suite of rooms for July and August. For a little extra, the manager left the chef, one waiter, and a chambermaid. Although giving the appearance of great wealth, the Murphys really were not affluent, just clever about manipulating the French exchange rate against the dollar.

What was spectacular about their newly acquired villa was its view. From the terrace, one could see the Mediterranean stretching west toward Cannes, north to Juan-les-Pins, and south to Cap d'Antibes. Using part of Sara's annual trust, amounting to about 350,000 francs, they hired Ohio architects Hale Walker and Harold Heller to expand the original structure, replacing its roof with a second story of extra bedrooms, above which they constructed a sundeck. An unpretentious chalet was transformed into an elegant Moorish-style villa, surrounded by date palms and eucalyptus, buttressed by terraces filled with lemon trees and tangerine orchards. Beyond its garden, the lighthouse at Antibes beamed light in sweeping arcs across the seven acres of grounds that Gerald transformed into a horticultural marvel. Renovations continued from June of 1923 until 1925, and during these summers, the Murphys stayed at the Hotel du Cap, residing at their Paris apartment the rest of the year. Upon completion, the villa would include fourteen rooms, a guest house called the Bastide, a small farm named La Ferme des Oranges, Gerald's painting studio, a playhouse for the children, gardener's cottage, chauffeur's quarters, donkey stable, and a storehouse.

When Gerald and Sara invited the Fitzgeralds to visit, they immediately accepted, eager to develop a friendship and thinking the Riviera would be an ideal place for Scott to write. During the last week of May, they took the train south with Scottie and Miss Maddock. Their initial stop was Hyeres, the oldest resort on the Riviera, whose palm-lined streets projected a tropical atmosphere. They arrived in the midst of a blistering heat wave and checked into Grimm's Park Hotel, which was filled with convalescents. Zelda considered the food inedible, convinced they were being served goat nightly for dinner. To combat the heat and avoid hotel guests taking one cure or another, she and Scott cooled themselves late into the night at Cafe l'Universe in Place Massillon from where Scott wrote Maxwell Perkins that they were surrounded by invalids and all the locals had goiter. From here, they proceeded to the Ruhn Hotel in Nice, then to L' Hotel de Paris in Monte Carlo, and finally to San Raphael, a little town built close to the sea with pastel-colored houses cascading to the shoreline. Until they could find someplace to lease, they registered at the beachside Hotel Continental, then went house hunting with a local realtor who, they were pleased to learn, spoke perfect English.

He found them a spacious house called Villa Marie, nestled in the hillside outside Valescure, two kilometers above San Raphael, studded with balconies overlooking the azure Mediterranean. A gravel drive led to its entrance, and it was set back from the road amid olive trees and umbrella pines, secluded by a terraced rock garden. In the rear garden were lemon and orange groves with winding paths through deep pockets of shade, rows of red roses, and fig trees growing wildly at the end of the orchard. The owner obviously had intended it for more ambitious purposes than a summer rental, but here it was at the Fitzgeralds' disposal.

Their house in Great Neck had cost $300 a month, and Villa Marie's rent was only $79, which included a gardener, but the housemaid was an additional $13 and cook $16. It seemed everyone was related, and when other family members arrived to help, expenses doubled. Since French law required that everyone be insured, costs quickly skyrocketed. Food also was more expensive, and by the time everything was tallied, their weekly grocery and butcher's bills averaged $65, higher than in Great Neck. They had calculated on cutting costs in half, but that was not going to be the case.

It was a two-hour drive from Valescure to the Murphys' hotel at Cap d'Antibes, along the sometimes-treacherous Corniche, a winding road that fringed the sea. Its most beautiful section was between Eze and Nice, where pine trees and oaks covered the hills above Paillon Valley. To make the trip, Scott bought a six-horsepower Renault, which was small enough to be parked under the veranda at night. Each time he watched Zelda, Scottie, and Miss Maddock drive away for the afternoon, he embraced the solitude and got to work. As May turned into June, he grew a mustache and let the French barber have his way with his hair. On weekends there were occasional shopping excursions, and during one to the sailors' quarter in Cannes, everyone bought sunglasses, cotton bathing suits, and espadrilles, canvas tops with soles made from esparto grass, and settled down to enjoy the quiet days of summer.

Although introduced to French at prep school and Princeton, Scott could barely understand it, although he had proclaimed proficiency to obtain his military commission. Never interested in learning the language, he mastered only some basic phrases and, in an atrocious accent, found it amusing to say, "Je suis a stranger here. Je veux aller to the best hotel dans le town." By contrast, during their first week at Valescure, Zelda bought some French novels at a bookstore near the beach, and with the aid of a French/English dictionary began working her way through them. Before long she was using French sentences and haltingly conversing with the gardener, cook, and driver of the rickety bus who delivered the milk.

She was particularly intrigued by that summer's best seller, Raymond Radiguet's *Le Bal du Comte d'Orgel*. Radiguet was Jean Cocteau's twenty-year-old protégé who had died the previous year of typhoid fever. On the Murphys' little beach, while Scottie played with their three children and Miss Maddock knitted in the shade, Zelda became immersed in the novel's scandalous love triangle. Set in Paris after World War I, its main characters were Comte Anne d'Orgel and his wife, Mahaut, modeled after Comte Etienne de Beaumont, a long-faced French aristocrat, and his wife, Edith, who were frequent guests at the Murphys' parties. In the novel, Mahaut is devoted to her husband, but he appears indifferent until the youthful Francois de Seryeuse falls in love with Mahaut. Only then does the Comte appreciate his wife, requiring evidence of another man's desire to experience his own. The masked ball of the title never occurs, but during preparations for it, Mahaut tells her husband that she loves Francois. When he seems less disturbed by her confession than that she has shared her feelings with Francois's mother, Mahaut recognizes her husband's superficiality and the marriage is compromised. The ménage à trois struck a chord with Zelda and provided a blueprint for what would follow. It was all there; the motive for the affair, the husband permitting it to happen, and the wife's remorse. That the novel's main characters were based on the Murphys' friends made it more compelling. Zelda narrated the story to Scott, who promptly recommended the book to Maxwell Perkins, writing that he was halfway through it, unlikely since he couldn't read French.

Several times a week, Zelda drove the Renault to Antibes and joined the Murphys and their friends by the seaside. The couple loved entertaining and being entertained by the people they chose to surround them, and that summer Zelda and Scott were among the selected few. A typical day started at eleven on the *garoupe,* the beach area Gerald daily cleared of seaweed. In contrast to many Riviera beaches, it was covered with sand rather than stones, and though only forty yards long, had been transformed into a perfect sunbathing spot. Zelda shared the Murphys' passion for swimming and sunbathing, so the three enjoyed each other's company. On straw mats shaded by striped umbrellas, Gerald offered his favorite sherry and sweet biscuits to guests, while the children drank lemonade and played near the water. Each day was an event with boating trips, picnics, and musical entertainment. Gerald's gramophone played the latest songs, conversations were absorbing, and there was always wonderful food and drink. Daytime attire was casual; when not in swimming clothes, men usually wore workmen's pants and jockey caps, and women, linen trousers with blue-and-white-striped mariners' shirts designed for the French Navy. The bohemian crowd set their own style. That summer, Fernand Leger was a frequent guest, along with Jean Cocteau, Georges Braque, and Igor Stravinsky. Cole Porter showed up with the playwright Philip Barry, whose comedy *You and I* was a Broadway hit. The Barrys lived nearby in an exquisite villa that Phillip's wife, Helen, had inherited from her father. Dick and Alice Lee Myers, whose daughter, Fanny, was Scottie's age, also were regulars. Dick was an amateur musician who had studied piano with Nadia Boulanger. He had a fabulous sense of humor and livened up afternoons by telling wonderful stories. One day blended into the next, punctuated at noon by the two-car train passing on its way to Menton at the Italian border. That signaled lunchtime and everyone headed off, regrouping by late afternoon at Eden Rock, a swimming pavilion where the children took diving lessons as adults watched. The best swimmer in the group, Zelda would climb to the highest peak and effortlessly dive from its jagged cliffs, her body cutting an even swath through the water. Scott hated swimming from those rocks while she liked nothing better.

Finally having regained her figure, Zelda was again confident in her appearance, and on the beaches at Antibes and San Raphael, men stopped to flirt with her. Photos taken of her that summer in cotton dresses and espadrilles capture her fresh good looks. Honoria Murphy recalled that radiance, "tanned and beautiful, often wearing her favorite color, salmon pink . . . a strikingly beautiful woman—blonde and soft and tanned by the sun who usually dressed in pink and wore a peony in her hair or pinned to her dress." Peonies grew everywhere and Zelda wore them like a hat. "She was the only woman I've ever known," Gerald recalled, "who could wear a peony in her hair or on her shoulder and not look silly." Her hairdresser had created a style for her called a "peony cut," and she told Sara Mayfield, who was taking summer courses at the Sorbonne, that she loved its magnificent blooms. Peonies were her favorite flower, in contrast to violets, lily of the valley, and lilacs, which seemed tame and self-satisfied.

Zelda always was doing something original, and that June it was her hairstyle, which Scott wove into his first draft of *The Great Gatsby*, cut from its final version. At one of his parties, Gatsby tells Daisy that a celebrated actress had just complimented her haircut and wanted to know her stylist's name. "Here's a chance to become famous," Jay tells her, but she whispers back, "It's a secret." Her stylist was a man she had discovered herself, and she had no intention of telling anyone. When he counters that she'd probably have her hair done the same way and start a new vogue, Daisy lightly responds, "No thanks." Not needing others' approval was a characteristic the Murphys admired in Zelda, and they acknowledged they couldn't have tolerated Scott alone. The starched cotton dresses she wore, considered strictly *Americaine* and unknown in France at that time, epitomized what Gerald recognized as her individuality and flair. "She might dress like a flapper when it was appropriate to do so, but always with a difference. Actually her taste was never what one would speak of as *a la mode*—it was better, it was her own." Her penetrating gaze punctuated that uniqueness. "It was all in her eyes," Gerald recalled. "They were strange eyes, brooding but not sad, severe, almost masculine in their directness . . . perfectly level and head-on." She passed that gaze on to her daughter, who, like her mom, used it to stop people in their tracks. "Scottie comes up to people when she meets them," Scott recalled, "as if she is going to kiss them on the mouth, or walk right through them, looking them straight in the eye—then stops a bare foot away and says hello, in a very disarming understatement of a voice."

On June 23, Scott wrote Tom Boyd, whose first novel he had recommended to Maxwell Perkins: "I think St. Raphael (where we are) is the loveliest spot I've ever seen. . . . Frejus which has aqueducts + is both Roman + Romanesque is in sight of window. . . . I'm perfectly happy. I hope to God I don't see a soul for 6 months. I feel absolutely self-sufficient + I have a perfect hollow craving for loneliness, that has increased for three years in some arithmetrical progress + I'm going to satisfy it at last." More powerful than his craving for alcohol was a determination to complete his novel, and he wrote Maxwell Perkins that he planned on writing something simple but intricately patterned. To do this would require solitude without interruption, and he planned on erecting a barrier no one could penetrate. He was convinced that seminal fluids contained substances enhancing creativity and told Zelda there could be no sexual contact. But abstinence was furthermost from her mind, and in a letter to her Minnesota friend, Xandra Kalman, she mockingly alluded to Scott's sexual withdrawal: "Scott has started a new novel and retired into strict seclusion and celibacy. He's horribly intent on it." His prohibition was calculated to make two points: that he was serious about work and in control of their relationship. At some deep level, he needed Zelda out of his way, and with renewed vigor, he wrote Edmund Wilson, "I have begun life anew. . . . Zelda has gone into a nunnery on the Peloponnesus."

In a strange country with nothing particular to do, and only her daughter and new friends for company, Zelda felt increasingly isolated. Scott couldn't understand her complaint. There she was in southern France with everything being done for her. She had the baby, and him, and a pint of wine at meals. Why couldn't she just be content with that? As she later wrote in *Save Me the Waltz*, "Alabama was much alone. 'What'll we do . . .' she asked, 'with ourselves?' David said she couldn't always be a child and have things provided for her to do." The temperature hovered around 80 degrees Fahrenheit and remained pleasant until a northwesterly mistral blew in from the Alps. There was no rain and fires burned in the Massif d' Esterel. Haze clouded the sky, and the smell of scorched pine and eucalyptus was everywhere; then the wind shifted, cleansing the atmosphere and the sun began to shine.

When Zelda didn't feel like making the long drive to the Murphys, she would go into San Raphael and swim in the sea, afterward stopping at the Café de la Flotte by the beach. There, she would order sweet and aromatic Pastis, the most popular of Provencal aperitifs, an anise-flavored cordial served neat with a jug of cold water. You mixed it yourself, drizzling the water until the ratio was right. It remained clear and tasted harmless until combined; then came the kick. Before long, she was practicing her French with some naval pilots from a nearby base: Bobbe Croirer, a veteran of Verdun; Robert Montagne, older than the rest, who had fought in the War of the Riff and and was fluent in Arabic; Jacques Bellando, recently awarded his flight wings at the seaplane training school in Berre west of Marseille; and the handsomest of the group, a twenty-five-year-old lieutenant named Edouard Jozan, to whom Zelda instantly was attracted.

The pilots were part of L'Aviation d'escadre, an elite unit formed in 1919 to test launching aircraft from ships. Their single engine planes could be seen in the skies above San Raphael, as they zigzagged toward the *bouchon de champagne*, a landing zone shaped like a champagne cork, replicating the dimensions and shape of the aircraft carrier *Bearn*. Maneuvers between Frejus and Berre were frequent that summer, but flying hours were not, and the pilots had ample time to amuse themselves. Zelda became the center of their attention. "All the young men fell a little in love with her," Edouard recalled, including the civilian son of a Cannes attorney, Rene Silvy, who openly showed his feelings. A photo of Rene outside Villa Marie captures him gazing at Zelda, as she glances in another direction, probably toward Edouard. When Scott objected to Rene's behavior, he quickly departed, but not before Scott grumbled to Sara Mayfield, "She thinks I'm in love with every woman that I shake a cocktail for, and carried away with every man whose work I praise. Yet she flirts openly with George Jean Nathan, Rene Silvy, Edouard Jozan, or anyone else she chooses, and I'm supposed to get a kick out of watching her."

Charismatic and powerful, Edouard possessed what the French call *aplomb*, and a snapshot taken of him in his twenties shows that mix of elegance and cool reserve. Aware of the impression he is making, he leans nonchalantly against a palm tree, one leg bent slightly at the knee, left hand in pocket, the other holding back his jacket, exuding sophistication. He might have stepped from a fashion magazine, this Frenchman, and his unmistakable hauteur mirrored Zelda's own tantalizing reserve. "I don't think she liked many people," the Murphys recalled. "Her dignity was never lost in the midst of the wildest escapades. No one ever took liberty with Zelda." Nor with Edouard whose imposing presence commanded respect. Nonchalant, but keenly aware, he could handle any circumstance, was at ease with everybody, and impressed by no one. "The flying officer who looked like a Greek God was aloof," wrote Zelda. "He seemed not too content with the official purpose which had brought him there, and was not casually available." Neither was Zelda, which made her particularly appealing to the young officer. Throughout her life, she would fictionalize their initial encounter many times and in *Caesar's Things* places it on San Raphael's beach near the Café de la Flotte, where the couple stop the young Frenchman on the windswept path leading to the pavilion. When the husband encourages his wife to speak to the officer, she demurs saying, "I don't somehow feel I ought," to which he responds, "Oh, go on, he's just a young Frenchman looking for a good time." "What's that got to do with it—I don't know French," she objects, to which he retorts, "Never mind; he does." They seem surprised when the pilot declines their invitation for a cocktail: "He was charmed; he didn't want a drink. Ingratiatingly, apologetically, some other time they would all drink together."

In *Save Me the Waltz*, Zelda portrays it somewhat differently, having the café's owner invite the Americans in for a drink, explaining there is food and dancing in the evenings: "My establishment would be honored if you would accept an American cocktail after your bath." After entering, the woman sees the pilot's face reflected in the mirror and is immediately attracted, as the French say, *un coup de foudre*—a flash of lightning, or passion at first glance. Once their gaze connected, it was all decided. "As her eyes met those of the officer, Alabama experienced the emotion of a burglar unexpectedly presented with the combination of a difficult safe by the master of the house. . . . She felt as if she had been caught red-handed in some outrageous act." From the moment his golden eyes gazed at Alabama, she did not look away. Instantly and without artifice, the connection was made; he was prepared to love and she, a willing accomplice.

Edouard was exactly one year older than Zelda and celebrating his twenty-fifth birthday that summer. Both were born on Leo's cusp, the astrological sign beginning on July 24. His birthday was one day before on the 23rd—hers, one day after on the 25th. Births on the cusp, five days before or after the beginning of a new sign, merge astrological traits, and for Leos and

Cancers, this meant passionate natures. Reflections of each other, they were dual flames burning brightly, tempting havoc others sought to avoid.

With the expectation sparks would fly, Scott maneuvers Zelda in Edouard's direction, and in *Save Me the Waltz*, she implies this is the husband's motivation: "My work's getting stale. I need new emotional stimulus; maybe something will happen . . . maybe it would refresh us." Wary of the officers, Alabama is uncertain if the Frenchmen are nice or not, unclear about their motivations as they lounged in the garden talking about Indochina and fin de siècle writers who sought inspiration in human emotion. "The French officer had quite a coterie of friends who followed the prescriptions of the decadent poets. . . . They drank Verveine and Champagne and thought in the tempo of Verlaine." To enjoy each other and love without inhibition was their credo; right or wrong, it made no difference. Zelda had heard this before when she followed the boys to the shadowy schoolyard. And now, maybe with Rimbaud in mind, she conjectured there's no such thing as a mistake, only what you do or don't do. Despite her headstrong ways, given the choice between right and wrong, Zelda preferred right. Only now what contradicted that premise is that wrong suddenly felt right.

The officers enjoyed visiting, and Scott welcomed their company. Close to his age, they made him feel part of the culture. One evening, as he awaited their arrival, he mused, "It is twilight as I write this. . . . In half an hour Rene and Bobbe, officers of aviation, are coming to dinner in their white ducks. Afterwards, in the garden, their white uniforms will grow dimmer as the more liquid dark comes down, until they, like the heavy roses and the nightingale in the pines, will seem to take an essential and invisible part of the beauty of this proud gay land." The aviators soon became part of the Fitzgeralds' circle, invited to formal dinners and casual suppers, where bouillabaisse was served with toasted bread cubes in a rust-colored sauce of garlic, peppers, and saffron. The ritual Provencal dish, as Zelda noted on her recipe card, must be served under special conditions according to the custom of Marseilles with at least seven or eight convivial people. It required a variety of rock fish and needed to be made in large quantities, so as to use as many fish as possible. The Frenchmen came to supper most weekends, curious meals Zelda recalled, served on large porcelain plates with tricolored ribbons and culminating with strangely fluorescent desserts. Only nobody cared what they ate or what went into their drinks. Victrola music drifted into the garden as French mingled with English amid clinking toasts of Cristal Brut. Some of the officers expressed regret over not making it to World War I battlefields, a disappointment Scott shared, and he wrote in his notebook, "Rene, who is twenty-three, and has never recovered from having missed the war, will tell us romantically how he wants to smoke Opium in Peking."

The French Navy was smoking opium much closer to home, in Mediterranean ports like Marseilles and Nice, where it was readily available and openly sold. In places like Brest, prostitutes established private dens offering opium, morphine, and cocaine, preferred narcotics of the day. The *New York Times* reported that Toulon had more than 150 opium dens, and a correspondent for *Le Matin* professed he had seen officers in these types of places smoking as many as eighty or a hundred pipes in one evening. Some sailors had acquired the habit in Indochina, which France occupied as a federation of colonies from 1887 to 1954, and when disembarking in Mediterranean ports, were as likely to head for opium dens as visit brothels. Reports circulated that officers from *Jeanne d'Arc*, the naval ship on which Edouard trained, repeatedly were carried out from such places. But drugs held little interest for the French lieutenant, who intended to make admiral by fifty and was cautious not to misstep, or at least not be judged badly for doing so. As those who knew him could attest, he always had an eye for the future.

Edouard initially may have questioned the Fitzgeralds' invitation into their circle, since they represented a life more worldly than his own. "Rich and free," he recalled, "they brought into our little provincial circle, brilliance, imagination and familiarity with a Parisian and international world to which we had no access." Unfamiliar with Zelda's celebrity in America, he considered her a beautiful woman who enjoyed simple pleasures. Scott was three years older than Edouard and initially seemed worldly, but that impression didn't last, and the Frenchman soon determined that Scott wasn't more sophisticated, just had more money. He quickly dismissed him, telling Sara Mayfield that he considered Scott "a bit of an intellectual, who seemed more concerned with commercial success—a proud, domineering man, who was sometimes tender and sometimes cruel." That cruelness amplified with each drinking round as Scott seized upon opportunities to demean and denigrate. Edouard's English wasn't good enough to pick up the subtleness of his remarks, but Scott provided ample other opportunities for disdain, and one entry in his notebook entitled "Situations in France" suggests the pilot may have revealed distaste for his host. Scott frequently launched into diatribes against Negroes and Jews, and Edouard may have witnessed such an outburst, since Scott mentions one scene at dinner, when the Frenchman, pretending to criticize American life in general, "really is criticizing Francis, who repeats experiences of race." Scott infused his prejudices into Tom Buchanan's character in *The Great Gatsby*, who warns that if the white race isn't careful, it will become completely submerged. Although Edouard may have shared Scott's opinions, he never openly would have expressed them, reticence about one's feelings being the prerequisite for an officer and a gentleman.

Try as he might, the Frenchman could not understand how Scott, aside from his literary reputation, could have attracted someone as exquisite as Zelda. He observed that he drank too much and was preoccupied with status and money. Scott later would imbue his censure into Tommy Barban's character in *Tender Is the Night*, who chides Nicole over her husband's drinking, only to have her tepidly defend him. Some men can drink, others can't, and Dick obviously was the latter. In contrast, Edouard drank sparingly and always kept his companions a little afraid of him.

As dismissive as Edouard was of Scott, he admired his accomplished friends. Someone prominent might drop by at any moment: Donald Ogden Stewart, John Dos Passos, or Archibald MacLeish and his wife, Ada. She was an accomplished soprano promoted by Nadia Boulanger, and he had graduated from Yale, where he was Phi Beta Kappa before continuing on to Harvard Law and graduating first in his 1919 class. Afterward, MacLeish applied his exceptional intelligence to one of Boston's best legal firms, Charles F. Choate Jr., and lectured at Harvard Law School, but abandoned the profession in 1923 to write poetry. Money was never a concern since his father was a prosperous manager who ran Carson, Pirie and Scott, Chicago's largest department store. For her second trip down the aisle, Ginevra King would marry John T. Pirie Jr., son of the store's founder.

Some of the French officers took advantage of Scott's celebrity and sought favors. "What chance does a smart young Frenchman with an intimate knowledge of French literature have in the bookselling business in New York," Scott wrote Maxwell Perkins. "Do tell me as there's a young friend of mine here just out of the Army who is anxious to know." Edouard's singular interest was Zelda. To be free during days, he arranged to fly at night, a hazardous endeavor when familiar landmarks were hidden and landings more difficult.

Scott usually worked until dinner was served around seven, and afterward he and Zelda often drove into San Raphael, where moonlight cast shadows over the plane trees by the harbor and a band played waltzes in the pavilion. Sometimes, they met the French officers at waterside bistros, and Zelda portrays one such evening in *Save Me the Waltz*, in which the men are drinking beers and portos because David is paying. She makes a point of saying that Jacques, based on Edouard, hated David to pay and always objected. Scott generally ordered Two Fingers, an inch and a half of straight gin in a bar glass, and Zelda a Stinger, brandy and crème de menthe. Zelda describes the café as being decorated in a North African motif with scimitars on the walls, brass trays on drum heads, and tiny mother of pearl tables. It smelled of brine and incense. As the music grows deafening, the attraction between Jacques and Alabama intensifies until the husband warns that if he catches her making eyes at the Frenchman, he'll wring his neck. No danger, she replies, since she can't even speak intelligently to him.

But language posed no problem. That Edouard spoke little English and Zelda rudimentary French seemed irrelevant. They communicated without fully understanding each other's words. The pilot had no difficulty expressing emotions through the cadence of his voice and timing of his breaths, and his limited vocabulary may even have accelerated the affair. Open to Zelda's presence, he intuited her feelings. Although English was required for officers at the Naval Academy, with few opportunities to speak the language, Edouard was not fluent. But, French being the idiom of love, he exploited its romantic nuances: *Je te bois des yeux* (I drink you with my eyes); *Je t'embrasse partout* (I kiss you all over); *nous sommes faits pour entendre* (we are meant to get along). As Zelda writes in *Caesar's Things*, "His English was more adequate about love than about anything else. He pronounced the word *lahve* and emphasized it roundly as if he were afraid of its escaping him. . . . 'You like France?' he inquired. 'I love France,' she replied. 'You cannot love France,' he replied arrogantly. 'To love France, you must love a Frenchman.'" As a chase pilot, Edouard was accustomed to pursuit and used to getting his way with women. He aimed to conquer. "It didn't seem to make any difference what she wanted to do, or intended either," Zelda wrote of the affair. "Life suddenly offered possibilities to a reckless extravagance which she didn't like. She had premonitions of wanton adventure." Just starting his career, the Frenchman had little money but Zelda didn't care; she only wanted to be in his presence.

The relationship began innocently enough. The two were seen basking in the sun and swimming in the sea, unafraid of strong currents near the shoreline. Scott seldom came to the beach, having learned to swim late and knowing only basic strokes. He hated sitting on the sand in a wet bathing suit, and when he did venture down rarely removed his shoes and socks, embarrassed over his feet. The second and third toes on his right foot were so bunched at the joint that he did not want them exposed. Once, when Zelda playfully photographed them and pasted the snapshot in her scrapbook, he ripped the offending portion away. An article in the *Smart Set* mentioned Scott's hammertoes, the journalist calling it a "pedentia complex" and explaining how Scott hated the sight of his feet, which caused him deep embarrassment. The reporter revealed that until Scott was twelve, he would not allow anyone to see his feet, refused to swim or go into the water, and pleaded to wear his socks.

When Zelda was seen with Edouard at a waterside bistro, people assumed an affair, but if Scott noticed, he did nothing. With attention focused on work, he ignored what was happening around him. Flirtations had always figured in the couple's relationship, employed to keep attraction at peak intensity. Scott strongly identified with the voyeuristic premise Raymond Radiguet had exploited in *Le Bal du Comte Orgel*. Jealousy titillated him, and he admitted being excited by another man's interest in Zelda. Early in their relationship he discovered the best way to hold on to one another was to torture each other through jealousy. He even had written an article on that subject entitled "Making Monogamy Work: Utilizing Jealousy as the Greatest Prop." Insecure about Zelda's devotion, he was always alert to the fact that she preferred a more powerful male. "I am half feminine, that is, my mind is," he admitted. "In the last analysis, she is a stronger person than I am. I have creative fire, but am a weak individual. She knows this and really looks upon me as a woman."

· 4 ·

A Mistress Not a Wife

$\mathcal{E}$douard Jozan was the type of man about whom Zelda always had fantasized. He was born near the fishing village of Le Grau du Roi in the Camargue, a few miles from the walled city of Aigyes-Mortes, where two branches of the Rhone flow into the Mediterranean. Along its marshy delta, rice was planted and on higher ground was farmland. Fishermen sold their catch by the harbor, where flamingos fed on plankton and strutted along beaches toward Sete in one direction and Sainte Maries de la Mer in the other, a pilgrimage site for the Gypsies' crowing of their queen. Brought up near the water, where the coming and going of boats gave rhythm to daily life, Edouard developed a love and respect for the sea. Like Zelda, he learned to swim early and was good at it, trained as a naval pilot to swim long distances and face the hazards of sea crashes, like navigating through burning oil or fending off sharks.

Raised Catholic, he was the youngest of seven children. He had an older brother, Amedee; one younger than himself, Etienne; and four sisters: Marie, Marthe, Madeleine, and Jeanne. The family lived in a traditional stone farmhouse or *mas*, a squat and massive building set against hillsides of cypress and asparagus beds, its north side left windowless to shield against Alpine winds. The family descended from a long military tradition. Edouard's father, Alexandre, was a career army officer, and his older brother, Amedee, would also become an officer in the French Army.

As landowners, the family was considered middle class. Edouard's father married twice, to women from prominent families who had wealth and owned property. After his first wife died, Alexandre wed Edouard's mother, Louise Macors, who had inherited a *mas* from her family. When she also died prematurely, it was willed to Alexandre. Motherless at four, Edouard was raised by his half sister, Marguerite, nicknamed "Grande," whom he adored, and her caring ways taught him to appreciate women. Class lines in France were clearly marked by ancestry, and mobility between them was difficult unless one married into the right bloodlines. At the top of the social structure were the aristocrats with titles and land. Then followed the nouveau riche, who recently had acquired wealth, and under them the middle and working classes. The military was a world unto itself, offering opportunities many could not find elsewhere and the best chance for upward mobility. Officers enjoyed considerable power and prestige, and whenever possible, fathers enrolled sons in military schools to secure officer commissions.

Edouard went to the most prestigious, Prytanée National Militaire in La Fleche. Located in the Sartre region of western France outside Anjou, it was a picturesque place where townsfolk fished along the Loire, and cadets caught frogs in the moats encircling the city. Founded as a Jesuit college in 1604, the school sought "to select and train the best minds of the time," and it was exceptionally good at this. The quality of its curriculum is reflected in its notable graduates, the most famous being the philosopher Rene Descartes, a contemporary of Galileo, who studied there for eight years. By the time Edouard arrived in 1910, it was renowned for training students to enter France's best military academies: the Ecole Navale and army's Ecole de St Cyr.

Austere and Spartan, Prytanée was organized around five courtyards, each housing a different academic division. Along with rigorous coursework, cadets participated in endless drills and did what students do best—got into trouble. Edouard was no exception; from the age of ten, he kept a journal detailing his pranks and escapades, in two entries describing how he and five classmates broke into a burial crypt underneath the choir stalls:

> Monday, 22 March 1915. One of us took out a candle and lit it. We lifted the trap door that was near the altar, and there we were descending into the black and damp crypt. It was said that there were skeletons of Jesuits, and I was ready to meet their fleshless bodies. I went into the chamber and at the very back, I saw a large white skeleton lying on a pile of rubble. I pulled back a little startled, but when we approached I realized it was only an old statue no longer in use. . . . In another corner was a skull . . . irreverently we grabbed it in a careless way, and to see the effect—put a candle under the skull. It was a little startling to see its red eyes and the shining mouth grimacing in the darkness. We thought we should leave a record of our visit. . . . There we were, scratching our names around the chamber. We finally decided to leave the place, and the two strongest lifted the trap door and we were once again in the church.

Apprehended and reprimanded, he could not understand the furor and in the handwriting of a fifteen-year-old, complained,

> Clearly I think fate is not smiling on me. We just got caught last night for going on our little jaunt. What I find the dumbest about this whole thing is having been caught. The authorities are making a colossal affair of this little escapade, and they interrogated us like real criminals. In the morning Lieutenant M . . . who commands the company will no doubt give me a dressing down that I will remember for a long time. . . . In the end the situation will complicate things to our detriment. The stupidest thing that I did was allowing myself to get caught.

Indifferent about school regulations and choosing the word *peripeties* (an event or happening) to describe the mishap, he considered it an innocent adventure and was annoyed over being punished: "You'll realize that it's nothing serious, to avoid being seen on a stroll, especially if one arrives at the same time as the others." After a reprimand from the company commander, his punishment was to sleep in the *pleu* for a week. Each night he carried his mattress down to the prison, returning every morning for inspection in his dormitory. Like Zelda, he enjoyed breaking rules and taking risks. At the same age, she was doing something similar in Montgomery's Oakland cemetery, prying open a mausoleum and describing its overgrowth as "weepy, watery flowers that might have grown from dead eyes—sticky to touch with a sickening odor"; cut from the same cloth, these two.

When Edouard was twelve, General Joseph Gallieni, military governor of Paris and a Prytanée graduate himself, visited the school and presented awards to cadets. Formerly the French minister of war, he was an impressive leader and idol to the French populace with a reputation equaled by few military officers. His powerful presence and dignified stature is evident in the ceremonial photograph taken that day. To the far right of the image, a youthful Edouard peers out at the camera. Fourteen years later, he would marry General Joseph Gallieni's granddaughter, Lucienne Gruss-Gallieni, and his naval career would benefit through association with this renowned military hero.

To select an appropriate wife was vitally important for advancement in the French military, and regulations once required that officers receive authorization to wed, accompanied by an investigation and proof of the bride's dowry. Although rules were bent and less affluent officers sometimes remained bachelors, many sought wives among the bourgeoisie and wealthy class. This provided some assurance that sons might follow in fathers' footsteps, which, given the professional hereditary of the military, often was the case. A wealthy or well-placed wife became a valuable asset to an officer's career. The formalized social life of more prestigious posts was not easily accomplished on military pay. Ambitious officers kept this in mind; love was good, and a beautiful woman desirable, but marrying someone with money and family prestige was best.

From his early days at Prytanée, Edouard demonstrated leadership abilities. He possessed a heroic vision, believed courage could change the world, and wanted to become involved with a worthy cause. Comfortable commanding and being obeyed, Edouard was not interested in ordinary battles, only those demanding skill and imagination. "I wouldn't go to war unless it was in Morocco or the Khyber Pass," reads one of Scott's notebook entries, probably emanating from Edouard's mouth. Idealistic and single-minded, he stirred Zelda's emotions with his patriotic ideals that reminded her of Confederate soldiers, but irritated Scott who considered him an anachronistic throwback to earlier times. Nonetheless, Scott was fascinated by his presence and channeled those feelings into the character of McKisco in *Tender Is the Night*. When confronting Tommy, McKisco has no idea what he is up against, neither the nature of Tommy's ideas nor complexity of his training. Faced by someone he did not fully comprehend, he nevertheless felt superior to the soldier he considered the end product of an archaic world.

After graduating from Prytanée with his baccalaureate, Edouard left for Paris to take entrance exams for the Naval Academy at Brest. The French Navy was considered more prestigious than its army and the Academy similar to Annapolis, accepting only the most qualified. Antoine de St. Exupery, author of *The Little Prince*, tried three times to get in but never succeeded. Seated next to Edouard at the examination was Jean Hourcade, son of a high-ranking official in the prosecutor's office. The two became friends, and when both learned of their acceptance, met in Paris to celebrate and promptly got themselves arrested. After Jean's father bailed them out, Edouard was invited back to their residence at 195 rue de l'Universite and received by their prominent family. His natural assurance and good looks made him a welcome addition to their circle, and he was introduced to the Parisian elite by the Marquis of Andreis, an influential relative.

That autumn, the escalators at the Grande Markets in Paris were the newest sensation, and on leave from the Naval Academy, Edouard and fellow midshipmen would meet there and watch the women "fall like flies." Accustomed to female attention, Edouard was conscious of his appeal and joked about the adulation; "What do you expect," he told Jean, "we are so handsome." With his ramrod posture and unflinching confidence, he was the powerful type women adored, but sensitive at the same time, and naval photographs show that captivating appeal.

As World War I drew to a close, Edouard received word that his brother, Amedee, had been killed in one of its final battles. For many nights he was inconsolable, and Jean Hourcade remained by his side. The loss brought a new pensiveness to his character, and in a picture taken soon after the tragic news, that change is evident. Seated in a damask chair and wearing formal navy blues, the grief in his eyes is unmistakable. A new quietude merged with his purposeful nature to give him an overwhelming presence. Now, when he entered a room, it was as if he altered the energy field. All attention shifted to him and the air got sucked out of the space.

After receiving his diploma from the Naval Academy in October 1919, Edouard was commissioned enseigne de vaisseau de premiere classe and assigned to the training ship *Jeanne d'Arc*, where he learned to avoid hazards and chart a safe course. On ship as in the air, multiple events happen simultaneously, each demanding attention. To remain sangfroid—cool in this midst of uncertainty—was paramount. Naval officers had to process information quickly, make sound assessments and take immediate action. Edouard's intelligence and clear thinking placed him at the head of his class, and on completion of training, he was given the coveted assignment to Berre, where he trained to fly seaplanes. He approached life as an engineer, carefully evaluating each situation and paying methodical attention to outcomes. He applied his mathematical skills to designing new landing gear for water approaches to aircraft carriers and became the first pilot to make successful night landings. On the glamour scale during the twenties, being a test pilot was right up there, and among the aviators in his squadron, Edouard was the best.

Pilots in the flying squadron at Frejus possessed a unique set of skills and a special camaraderie existed between them. As they waited for their flights in the ready room, where schedules got posted and aeronautical maps covered the walls, they were alert to dangers they faced. After the daily weather hop went up to report on conditions, it was time to climb and glide. As a flight instructor, Edouard occasionally accepted civilian students, and Antoine de Saint-Exupery became one of them. Turned down by the Naval Academy, he was still determined to become a pilot, and during one of his flights with Edouard, the two got reprimanded for taking off without permission and landing on an inland waterway. Edouard was placed under house arrest, but as a civilian, Saint-Exupery received only a verbal reprimand. After obtaining his pilot's license, Antoine went on to manage the Moroccan Field Station for the French express company Lignes Aeriennes Latecoere, later renamed Aeropostale, which developed the hydroplane Edouard later piloted.

Every airplane had its own characteristics, as air flowed over its surface and responded to commands. But engines were not always cooperative, and loss of control meant a plunge from the sky. Making life-and-death decisions was customary for Edouard. From youth, he had learned to confront danger and had no need to manufacture excitement. Every time he climbed into a cockpit, he faced threats more substantial than anything the Fitzgeralds could envision. With unreliable instruments and few navigational aids, flying required courage and daring—just man and machine. Buffeted by wind in open cockpits, aviators guided their planes by intuition and feel with engine failures and crashes common. "Flying by the seat of their pants" accurately described the situation. With seats the contact point, pilots could sense engine vibrations through their jodhpurs, and variations in gravity indicated whether they were going up or down. A pilot was pressed into his seat when climbing and felt heavier, but when diving felt lighter. In steep glides, their weight was thrown forward as the engine bucked in acceleration. To the north of Frejus there was constant danger from L'Esterel, a range porphyry cliffs extending into the sky, particularly treacherous when thick mist crept in from the sea. Flying at eight thousand feet against a steady stream of cold air, marginally protected against the elements, was beyond the realm of ordinary men. In his leather cap and goggles, a white silk scarf tied around his neck to prevent chafing, Edouard seemed larger than life, and if Zelda had any reservations about entering into the affair, they were quickly put aside.

Edouard flirted as naturally as others breathed and approached Zelda with confidence. She was the first American woman he had met and different from French girls, soft where they were hard, liberated and more accessible. Her vitality was a breath of fresh air, yet mystery enveloped her and she appeared elusive and sensual, more intangible than pretty with an undercurrent of necessity. Her eyes were full of secrets and body so assertively adequate that someone once remarked she often looked as if she had nothing on underneath her dress. Often she didn't, which may also have been true for Edouard, given her sensual description of the pilot in *Save Me the Waltz.* "He drew her body against him till she felt the blades of his bones carving her own. He was bronze and smelled of the sand and the sun; she felt him naked underneath the starched linen. She didn't think of David. She hoped he hadn't seen; she didn't care."

There was a clean scent about him she adored, something to do with his starched white uniform. Maybe, she thought, they added bouquet to the misting water while ironing. That fresh smell lingered, and she couldn't eliminate it from her mind. Nor did she want to; she felt intoxicated by it. With heightened expectations, she made excuses to drive into San Raphael and look for him by the harbor. Sometimes she went with Miss Maddock, more often alone. "It was an improbable affair full of passion," writes Zelda in *Caesar's Things.* "Janno often went into town after supper with Nanny. Sometimes they went to the tin-pan picture show, and sometimes they wandered around under the plane trees. Jacques met them one night at the movies. They kissed again—a long time before his friends." The Frenchman knew how to love Zelda, and she opened to him with an ardor not previously experienced.

At least once, Edouard appears to have flown his plane over Villa Marie, Zelda and Scott both fictionalizing his romantic gesture. In *Save Me the Waltz*, she describes how the pilot looped and barrel-rolled his plane, then dropped a note in French. "It was so low they could see the gold of Jacques' hair. . . . As the plane straightened itself, they saw Jacques wave with one hand and drop a small package in the garden." The dispatch box held a note with his regards: "Toutes mes amities du haut de mon avion." Surely it reminded Zelda of those pilots who had flown over her parents' house in Montgomery. Such risks excited her, so when Alabama asks Jacques in *Save Me the Waltz*, "Aren't you afraid when you do stunts?" and he replies, "I am afraid whenever I go in my aeroplane. That is why I like it," one can appreciate the pilot's appeal.

The flyover is characterized more menacingly in Scott's story "Image on the Heart" in which the couple duck and run to avoid the aircraft. "The plane had come out of its dive, straightened out and was headed straight for them. Tom caught at Tudy's hand, trying to pull her from the car, but he had misjudged the time and the plane was already upon them, with a roaring din—then suddenly it was over them and away." Edouard's pursuit was *ubermasculine* and ignoring the single seat in his cockpit, Zelda was smitten and determined to go along for the ride.

That she was married only added to her allure. It was accepted that a young officer, unprepared to wed, would take a mistress. Wives held particular appeal, rivaling single women, by offering pleasure without responsibility. Already chosen by another, a wife could return to her husband, no strings attached. Brief affairs and *relations suivies* (extramarital relationships) were acceptable in France and seldom merited a trip to divorce courts. For Edouard, the interlude was a *petite aventure*, a brief affair with a willing partner, and Scott the proverbial *mari trompe*, or cuckolded husband. Zelda may have entered the relationship to test her attractiveness, never considering she might be unable to extradite herself, but that is what happened. As her heroine in *Caesar's Things* rationalizes, "If things didn't work out, there would always be the memory. . . . She preferred to consider that she was merely feeling her way, and that at any moment she could withdraw. . . . One day she met Jacques and he told her to come to his apartment. She said she would; she was horrified. She could not possibly *not* do so."

Zelda's emotions propelled her in a direction reasoning could not comprehend, her actions generating memories that would haunt her forever. Like the salamanders in Owen Johnson's novel, she wanted to experience life with an adventurous soul mate, and Scott always worried she would find one. In a letter to Dr. Thomas Rennie, he later admitted, "All our lives, since the days of our engagement, we have spent hunting for some man Zelda considers strong enough to lean on. I am not." Johnson's title alluded to the Greek legend about lizards surviving fire. Watching them crawl from burning logs, the ancients called them "fire lizards" or salamanders, but their belief was wrong on two counts. Unlike toads, salamanders aren't lizards but moist-skinned amphibians that crave damp areas, and by fleeing flaming logs, they were running for their lives. Had Zelda been thinking clearly, she also might have taken flight. Although lizards and salamanders resemble each other, they are very different. Unlike salamanders, lizards and crocodiles are reptiles, formidable creatures that eat mammals and easily can knock a larger creature off its feet. Ironically, crocodiles were emblematic of Edouard's ancestral city, Nimes, adorning everything from road signs to public sculpture. Zelda's dealings with men had not prepared her for Edouard, and in retrospect she acknowledged, "I believed I was a salamander and it seems that I am nothing but an impediment."

Occasionally, Edouard would take Zelda back to Frejus, where he shared an apartment with a fellow pilot. The oldest Roman city in Gaul, now comprising Belgium, France, and Holland, Frejus was established during the Julius Caesar era and still contained remnants of a first-century amphitheater. In nearby woods, there was a brightly painted Buddhist pagoda honoring Vietnamese soldiers who fought alongside French forces during World War I. Edouard liked going there because it brought him closer to the Orient. Never interested in observing history from the sidelines, he was determined to become part of it. In *Tender Is the Night*, Scott would draw upon Edouard's heroic personality for Tommy Barban, a professional soldier itching for battle: "I haven't seen a paper lately, but I suppose there's a war—there always is. . . . My business is to kill people. I fought against the Riff because I am a European, and I have fought the Communists because they want to take my property from me." Edouard's friend and fellow officer Robert Montagne had battled the Riff in North Africa during the War of Melilla. Mountain warriors from northern Morocco, they struggled fiercely against the French during the 1920s, fighting in a region without roads or communication. It was the type of contest Edouard desired, leading men in battle and watching them grow under his command. "You must believe what you do is worth your time and energy. You do it, so at day's end, you can look back and say you contributed to something greater than yourself."

But Morocco was not where history was being made; China and Russia were the place. In 1924, Sun Yat-sen, aided by his young wife, Soong

Ching-ling, twenty-six years his junior and college educated in America, was organizing Chinese peasants and workers into the "Great Revolution." After establishing the Chinese National Peoples' Party, they were elevated to cult figures, along with John Reed and Louise Bryant, whose eyewitness account of the Russian revolution, *Ten Days That Shook the World*, became an international best seller. Scott would exploit Edouard's fascination with the Orient in "Image on the Heart," modeling Tudy and Lieutenant Riccard's affair on Zelda's relationship with Edouard, and describing him as being dark blond, handsome, with eyes that flashed brilliantly. He even went so far as to filch the names of Edouard's friends—Silvy and Croirer—for minor characters, altering their spelling to Silve and Croirier. Lieutenant Riccard tells Tudy that he would resign his commission if she would go to China and fight with him in the war. But Tudy chooses the wealthier suitor who proposes a quiet Sicilian honeymoon and security, not adventure.

It was a picturesque drive from Frejus to Le Massif de Esterel, a mountainous range of porphyry cliffs two thousand feet above sea level that jutted down ravines to secluded coves. Edouard and Zelda drove to its highest point, Mount Vinaigre, and walked through heather and broom to a watchtower offering an unobstructed view of Monte Carlo. Zelda's espadrilles, purchased only weeks before, now were shredded from much roving off the paths. Built for horse and wagon, the road wove through curtains of heliotrope, banks of rosemary, and cascades of scarlet geraniums. Flowers were harvested year-round, roses boiled, jasmine crushed, and orange blossoms macerated to create perfumed oils for which Provence was famous.

The hills were dotted with village perches encircled by ramparts, which earlier had offered protection from Saracen invaders. Proud of his heritage, Edouard was familiar with them all: St. Andre with its seventeenth-century château; La Trinite-Victor, where the Roman road wound down from Laghet; and above St. Andre at a thousand feet, beautiful Falicon with its silver-gray olive trees leaning toward the sea. Birdsong filled the air, along with the clang of a blacksmith's hammer and tolling of distant church bells. "Long roads wound implacably up and over into pine fragrant depths," Zelda recalled, "and gardens dropped into the sea. The baritone of tired medieval bells proclaimed disinterestedly a holiday from time to time. Lavender bloomed silently over the rocks. It was hard to see the vibrancy of the sun." They wandered through alleys as narrow as trenches, dipping under vaulted passageways, where windows and doors popped up in unexpected places. Some villages celebrated weekly festivals, Saint John's observed on June 24, the longest day of the year and the start of summer. To re-create rites of ancient sun worshippers, townsfolk decorated their houses with plants thought to possess magical powers and danced around bonfires to guarantee a year of happiness. Down cobblestoned steps lined with flowerpots, they followed a lane exiting at the base of a church tower and entered a sunbaked square to find the smallest bistro imaginable. Under a chestnut tree, the proprietor's dog dozed in the shade, and bourride was served, only neither was hungry, filled with exhilaration of being together. Edouard recalled Zelda's loveliness during those days, "a shining beauty, a creature who overflowed with activity, radiant with desire to take from life every chance her charm, youth and intelligence provided so abundantly."

From Callian to St. Paul de Vence, cresting a hill above Nice, the Renault wound through cypress groves and fields of rosemary. By July, violets already had passed, along with hyacinths and jonquils, but orange blossoms and mimosa were everywhere. It was only a short distance from there to the sea, where smells of cheese and wine mingled with salted fish. Along the quay, fishermen patched and painted their boats, while women sat on low stools repairing nets. Waterside cafes advertised the daily catch: *langoustes*, *huitres*, and *moules coquillages*—lobster, oysters, and mussels. At twilight the shoreline came alive with *pianola* playing that summer's American hit about a nonexistent yellow fruit: 'There's a fruit store on our street. It's run by a Greek. And he keeps good things to eat, but you should hear him speak. When you ask him anything, he never says 'no.' He just 'yes'es' you to death, and as he takes your dough he tells you' Yes, we have no bananas, we have no bananas today! We have string beans and onions and cabbages and scallions, and all kinds of fruit, and an old fashioned tomato, a Long Island potato, but yes, we have no bananas, we have no bananas today!" Silly words, but the French thought it wildly amusing.

When the Murphys saw Edouard and Zelda by the seaside, they weren't surprised, since they felt everyone knew of the affair, except Scott. No doubt he had suspicions as one scene in Zelda's *Save Me the Waltz* suggests: "David walked to the beach to join Alabama for a quick plunge before lunch. He found her and Jacques sitting on the sand like a couple of—'well a couple of something,' he said to himself distastefully. They were as wet and smooth as two cats who had been licking themselves." Perhaps to better understand their relationship, Scott may have joined Zelda and Edouard on a trip to Agay, five miles east of San Raphael. Zelda narrates such an excursion: "Alabama and David and Jacques drove in the copper dawn to Agay. . . . 'Those are the caves of the Neanderthal man,' David said, pointing to the purple hollows in the hills. 'No,' said Jacques, 'It was at Grenoble that they found the remains.'" Having demonstrated superior knowledge about Paleolithic cavern dwellers, the Frenchman then displays his physical strength—"Jacques drove the Renault . . . like an aeroplane with much speed and grinding and protesting tensions"—arrogantly declaring that if the car were his, he would drive it into the ocean. Only it wasn't, and David worried about how much it would cost to fix. Nervousness pervades the trip back to San Raphael through Boulouris and Cap du Drammont, as David recognizes how gravely his marriage is threatened.

As Zelda had done with George Jean Nathan, she may have caused the Frenchman concern by suggesting they tell Scott about the affair. When Jacques asks Alabama in *Save Me the Waltz*, "'What will you say to your husband' and she answers, 'I'll have to tell him,' Jacques replies, 'It would be unwise. We must hang on to our benefits.'" Edouard had in mind a *passade*, or summer romance, and may have implied that, only Zelda wasn't listening. That appears the case in *Caesar's Things* when Janno opens a conversation with the pilot by saying, "'When we are married' and he quickly refutes, 'that's absurd.' Janno loved him so that she never questioned his good faith. If he was unable to marry she thought, they could make other arrangements." But alternatives were unlikely and running off with another man's wife out of the question.

Scott notes the affair's climax in his ledger on July 13, 1924, calling it "The big crisis." That day, Zelda confessed her love for Edouard and asked Scott for a divorce. There are several versions as to how he responded. One suggests that he made a formal complaint to Edouard's commanding officer and demanded he be transferred. Edouard's daughter recalls her father acknowledging there was a scandal and that he was transferred, but military documents do not reflect this. According to naval records, Edouard remained a flight instructor at Berre until April 1925, overseeing seaplane trials at Marignane Airfield. He then returned to St. Raphael for a month before L'Aviation d'escadre relocated to Hyeres in May 1925, where he assumed duties as commanding officer of Fighter Squadron 7C1. Scott told some relatives that he bought a pistol and challenged Edouard to a duel, and that each fired one shot but missed. To others, he said that he demanded Zelda and Edouard declare their love before him, but that confrontation never took place. In another recounting, Scott bragged that he tried to engage Edouard in a fight but the Frenchman refused. He boasted, "I could have annihilated him in two minutes. . . . This kid didn't know his left hand from his right." Actually, Scott was only an average boxer and Edouard more powerful and in better condition. Probably closest to the truth is what Zelda writes in *Save Me the Waltz*: "Jacques spoke steadily into Alabama's face. 'I cannot fight,' he said gently. 'I am much stronger than he.' Alabama tried to see him. The tears in her eyes smeared his image. His golden face and the white linen standing off from him exhaling the gold glow of his body ran together in a golden blur." That Zelda literally or figuratively expected Edouard to fight for her shows her misreading of his intentions.

She believed he loved her, but that he avoided any confrontation shows how casually he viewed the romance and how seriously his career. To create a scandal was one thing, but to assume responsibility for someone else's spouse was something else entirely. He wanted a mistress, not a wife; best let her go, which is what he did.

From July 13 until early August when guests arrived, Zelda was confined to Villa Marie. As she writes in *Caesar's Things*, life's possibilities suddenly vanished. "It was inexpedient, unexpected and miserable that she should be in love. Janno told her husband that she loved the French officer and her husband locked her in the villa." Interior doors in French villas secured from inside and out, so all Scott most likely did was shut Zelda in a bedroom and pocket the key. During their courtship, he repeatedly had written her that he understood why princesses were locked in towers. Now, in some bizarre manifestation of that fantasy, Scott was actualizing what he always anticipated might happen. She would have to wait for Edouard to claim her, if he would.

The morning after her confession, fireworks could be heard everywhere. It was Bastille Day, July 14, the founding of the Republic, and in San Raphael a brass band played in the pavilion and there was dancing in the streets. Zelda saw none of it. She spent the day in her bedroom, her link with the world confined to a half-open window. As she writes in *Save Me the Waltz*, "How could she remain with her husband when she loved another? If she loved him, she could not possibly love him and live with another; she wouldn't be able. If she loved him, there wasn't any answer. . . . Adultery is adultery and it would have been impossible for her to love two men at once, to give herself to simultaneous intimacies." In the confines of that room, Zelda listened for Edouard's walk on the gravel driveway but those footsteps never came.

After Scott grasped he might lose Zelda, he reversed course and played the righteous cuckold. Yet, twice in his notebooks, he acknowledges culpability in the affair, calling his role "proxy in passion," then rewording the admission as "Feeling of proxy in passion, strange encouragement—he was sorry knowing how she would pay." Later, he would discount all responsibility, accusing Zelda of becoming involved with Edouard to sabotage his writing and blaming their marital problems on her betrayal. "Her affair with Eduard Josanne [he could never spell his name correctly] and mine with Lois Moran, which was a sort of revenge, shook something out of us."

That Scott encouraged Zelda's affair, then stood back and watched it develop, he considered his entitlement as a writer. If she got hurt in the process, call it artistic license. William Faulkner provided the creative justification, emphasizing this point by saying the writer's only responsibility was to his art, and that if he had to rob his mother in the process, that was fine. "The Ode on a Grecian Urn" was worth any number of casualties. That July, Zelda became one of them. "San Raphael was dead," she wrote. "The lush promenade under the trees, so rich and full of life and summer seemed swept of all its content. There was nothing but a cheap café and the leaves in the gutter and a dog prowling about."

Edouard never saw Zelda again after July 13. He recalled only that "one day the Fitzgeralds left and their friends scattered, each to his own destiny." Aware of the pain he had caused, he may have written Zelda, sending the letter through the wife of another pilot. She suggests this in *Save Me the Waltz*: "Alabama could not read the letter. It was in French. She tore it in a hundred little pieces and scattered it over the black water of the harbor. . . . Though it broke her heart, she tore the picture, too. It was the most beautiful thing she'd ever owned in her life, that photograph. What was the use of keeping it? Whatever it was that she wanted from Jacques, Jacques took it with him to squander on the Chinese." However, Edouard did not leave for China, at least not then. And no letters between the Frenchman and Zelda presently exist but may have. His daughter recalls her mother questioning Edouard about Zelda's mail, asking, "Why do you keep those letters?" That she may have written is understandable, but that he saved her correspondence suggests he cared more than he was willing to admit.

Zelda misinterpreted Edouard's intentions, but how did she get it so wrong? Language and culture played a part. She was accustomed to American men and used to wielding power over them. Edouard's responses were unfamiliar and left ample room for misunderstanding. As Janno admits in *Caesar's Things*, "She so hardly spoke the language and was never quite sure about what she was saying." Equally important was Zelda's sexual awakening. She was more attracted to the Frenchman than to anyone previously. When she met Scott, by no means was she so carried away. Sex between the two had never been satisfactory. Connected temperamentally, they were physically incompatible. Scott lacked a powerful sexual urge, and his Catholic upbringing and Midwestern Puritanism contributed to him being a poor lover. Inexperienced and prudish in bed, as his friend, Oscar Kalman, recalled, "He was not very interested in sex . . . not a very lively male animal. Scott liked the idea of sex for its romance and daring, but was not strongly sexed (and) inclined to feel the actual act of sex was messy." Even as an adult, he considered intercourse dirty, almost sinful, and his Catholicism operated as a moral chastity belt. His sexual inadequacies were compounded by occasional impotence caused by overdrinking, a tendency toward premature ejaculations, and what only could be described as a modestly sized penis. In her kiss-and-tell exposé, a North Carolina prostitute who knew Scott in Asheville recalled a conversation about his hurried manner in bed. When she asked if that was his usual way and he answered yes, Scott revealed that he thought the reason for his hasty climax was fear and guilt, going back to years of masturbating.

Anyone to whom things matter is susceptible to being misled by enthusiasm. Edouard's abrupt departure took an immediate toll on Zelda's health, and she began feeling ill soon after, a physical manifestation of psychic disruption. When Gilbert Seldes and his bride, Alice Wadhams Hall, stopped at Valescure on their honeymoon that August, they noticed something was wrong. One only had to observe Zelda's haggard face to recognize her anguish. "Love is a funny thing," she wrote. "It says so in the advertisements, in the popular songs, on the radio and in the moving pictures. Though it seldom says what to do about it, it always shows what havoc is wrought." Worn out from sleepless nights and highly agitated, she was also experiencing relentless discomfort in her abdomen. For that, she took Luminal and Atropine, and as a sedative, Dial, a white, crystalline barbiturate in tablet form, prescribed as a sleeping aid but also an effective means of suicide. One afternoon, as the Fitzgeralds were driving the Seldes from Valescure into St. Raphael, they became alarmed watching Zelda ask Scott for a Chesterfield, exactly where the road made a hairpin turn. As he rummaged in his pocket with one hand, the car almost veered over the embankment. Zelda laughed hysterically and seemed to get some bizarre pleasure from this moment of control, justice-making in its own way.

After the newlyweds departed, Ring Lardner arrived, but instead of staying at Villa Marie, he registered at the Hotel Continental in San Raphael. When he came for dinner, he brought a bottle of Johnny Walker and the two writers spent the night talking and getting drunk. Their conversation probably touched on Ernest Hemingway, since Edmund Wilson's review of his short stories, *In Our Time*, had just been published in the *Dial*, which Seldes edited. Scott would not meet Ernest until fall of the following year, but that October he wrote Maxwell Perkins, "This is to tell you about a young man named Ernest Hemingway who lives in Paris. . . . I'd look him up right away. He's the real thing."

During Ring's visit, Zelda tried to appear normal, but after he left, she made her first suicide attempt. It happened during a visit to the Murphys at the Hotel du Cap in Antibes, where they were staying until renovations on their villa were completed. At three in the morning, Scott burst into their suite, saying that Zelda had overdosed on Dial. They rushed back to his room, and after inducing Zelda to vomit, walked her through the corridors to keep her awake. Honoria Murphy recalled how, the next morning, Scott and Zelda abruptly left for Valescure, leaving Scottie and Miss Maddock behind with the Murphys, as rumors circulated in the hotel that Zelda had tried to kill herself. Scott never recorded the episode in his ledger, nor was it ever mentioned, but memory lingered, and Gerald and Sara revealed the incident to Calvin Tompkins, who shared it with Nancy Milford. By September, Zelda's abdominal pains had worsened, accompanied by a breathing paralysis she called asthma, more likely anxiety-induced panic attacks. The relationship with Edouard had only lasted five weeks, but it was five years before she could say she was over it, and exactly then, when she suffered her first breakdown.

Emotional upsets can derail reason and amplify life's traumas, and the affair's wrenching conclusion may have triggered memories of Zelda's schoolyard assault. As she writes in *Caesar's Things*, "She had forgotten all about this year of her life, until she was grown and married and tragedy had revived its traces, as she then saw, carved from the beginning. That's the kind of thing one forgets. The will to live and the right of self-respect relegate that sort of thing to the ash can until years later." Consigned to the unconscious mind, earlier traumas often can be awakened and amplified by another emotional upset. What Zelda perceived as Edouard's abandonment became a tipping point, releasing catastrophic forces and causing an emotional tailspin.

Old wounds also opened for Scott. He had not forgotten Zelda's reluctance to marry and her involvement with the aviator replicated Ginevra King's selection of a naval pilot over him. For the second time, he was matched against a more powerful suitor and found lacking. When Zelda admitted her love for Edouard and asked for a divorce, Scott's failed courtship of Ginevra merged with Zelda's betrayal. Gerald Murphy recalled how upset Scott was over Zelda's affair, but questioned whether it was of his own making. Responsibility aside, the crisis infused the writing of *The Great Gatsby* with a new tension; "I feel old too this summer," he wrote Ludlow Fowler, "that's the whole burden of this novel . . . the loss of those illusions that give such color to the world, so that you don't care whether things are true or false, as long as they partake of the magical glory."

Edouard could never have imagined how his affair with Zelda would affect Scott's classic novel, creating the emotional triangle between its main characters. What began as Gatsby's quest for vanished love evolved into something deeper, the wonderment Daisy had inspired and disillusionment over its demise. Scott's recollection of his broken engagement with Zelda merged with her betrayal, and the confrontation that never took place between himself and the French pilot got dramatized at the Plaza Hotel, when Gatsby announces to Tom Buchanan, "Your wife doesn't love you. She's never loved you. She loves me." Scott later would replay that scene between Tommy Barban and Dick Diver in *Tender Is the Night* with similar words but a different outcome. Here, Tommy steals Diver's wife. "Your wife does not love you,' Tommy said suddenly. 'She loves me.' 'I think Nicole wants a divorce. I suppose you'll make no obstacles?'"

When one compares Scott's first draft of *The Great Gatsby* with its final version, the influence of the Jozan affair becomes evident. Both have nine chapters with the first two almost identical. The differences occur in chapters 6 and 7, where Scott deleted two conversations, the first between Gatsby and Nick Carraway, in which the bewildered hero rejects any notion of running away with Daisy. "I'm very sad, old sport. . . . Daisy wants us to run off together. . . . But we mustn't just run away . . . that won't do at all . . . it's all so sad because I can't make her understand." The second deleted conversation, also involving Nick, occurs between Nick and Daisy, in which her ambivalence over leaving Tom Buchanan for Gatsby is strikingly clear. "'Do you think I'm making a mistake?' asked Daisy, leaning back and looking up into my face. . . . 'You know if you've never gone through a thing like this it's not so easy. In fact—I want to just go, and not tell Tom anything.'"

Scott sent *The Great Gatsby* manuscript to Maxwell Perkins on October 27, 1924, initially titled *Trimalchio in West Egg*, alluding to a freed slave during Nero's reign who grew wealthy and became notorious for hosting ostentatious banquets. The Roman courtier Gaius Petronius describes one of these parties in *The Satyricon*, during which guests berate Trimalchio after he leaves a room. Max warned Scott about the title's obscurity, saying various editors were objecting to the title, and he should consider another. As an alternative, Scott suggested *The Great Gatsby*, which gained immediate approval. Max then sent suggestions for revisions, his major concern being Gatsby's blurred character. "I would know Tom Buchanan if I met him on the street and would avoid him," wrote Max. "Gatsby is somewhat vague. The reader's eyes can never quite focus on him; his outlines are dim." Scott admitted that his hero's blended origins had created a blurred figure. Initially, he had based the character on Edouard, using Jay (J) to represent his last name, but later merged the pilot's personality with his own: "Gatsby was never quite real to me. His original served for a good enough exterior until about the middle of the book. He grew then and I began to fill him in with my own emotional life. So, he's a synthetic—and that's one of the flaws in this book." Tom Buchanan also was a fused character combining Edouard with Tommy Hitchcock, both the masculine types Scott envied. Each shared the distinction of being awarded the French Croix de Guerre. Hitchcock received his accolade during World War I serving with Lafayette Escadrille Squadron, an arm of the French Aviation Service predominantly composed of American volunteers, and Edouard was awarded his for heroism during World War II.

With late October came the rainy season, but there were few changes of color except for tints among highland fruit trees. Another mistral blew in

Zelda's graduation photo from Sidney Lanier High School, June 1918. *F. Scott Fitzgerald Archives at Princeton University; The Fitzgerald Literary Trust care of Harold Ober Associates*

Zelda Sayre and Scott Fitzgerald circa 1918. *Photofest*

Zelda with infant Scottie at White Bear Yacht Club, Minnesota, summer 1922. *F. Scott Fitzgerald Archives at Princeton University; The Fitzgerald Literary Trust care of Harold Ober Associates*

Zelda and Scott (front seat), Scottie and nanny (backseat) in a Renault, southern France, 1924. *F. Scott Fitzgerald Archives at Princeton University; The Fitzgerald Literary Trust care of Harold Ober Associates*

Scott on the beach in southern France with Scottie. *F. Scott Fitzgerald Archives at Princeton University; The Fitzgerald Literary Trust care of Harold Ober Associates*

Edouard Jozan with his father, Alexandre, and two brothers, Amedee, standing to the left with his legs crossed, and Etienne, seated. *Photo used by permission of Martine Jozan Work*

Jozan (top row, second from left) upon graduation from the French Naval Academy at Brest, 1917. *Photo used by permission of Martine Jozan Work*

Edouard Jozan's pilot's license. *Photo used by permission of Martine Jozan Work*

Edouard at his ancestral home, Nimes, 1922. *Photo used by permission of Martine Jozan Work*

Jozan and pilots under a hydroplane. *Photo used by permission of French Retired Pilots Association, Robert Feuilloy, Secretary*

Edouard Jozan, the summer before he met Zelda, 1923. *Photo used by permission of Martine Jozan Work*

Jozan's plane heading from Frejus toward San Raphael. *Photo used by permission of French Retired Pilots Association, Robert Feuilloy, Secretary*

Zelda, Scott, and Scottie at Villa Marie, Valescure, France, soon after Zelda met Jozan. *F. Scott Fitzgerald Archives at Princeton University; The Fitzgerald Literary Trust care of Harold Ober Associates*

Two vintage postcards, circa 1924: A plane flying over San Raphael and San Raphael beachfront scene. *Courtesy of the author*

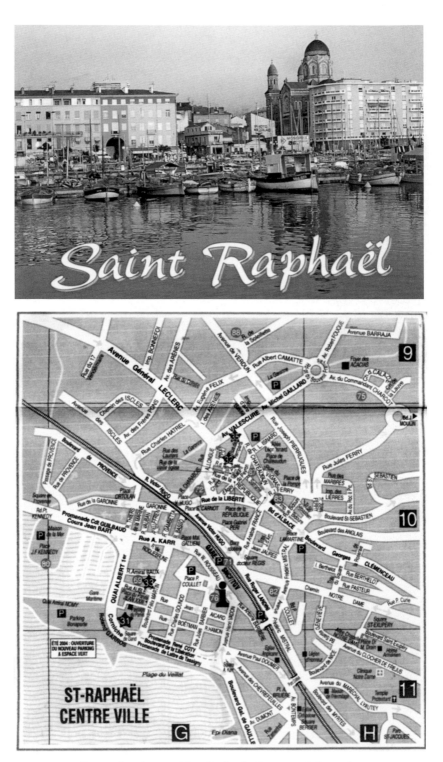

Postcard and map of San Raphael. *Courtesy of the author*

Hilltop walkways in L'esterel that Zelda and Edouard wandered. *Photos courtesy of Sophie Dre Garner*

The Fitzgeralds shipboard on their way to Europe, 1928. *F. Scott Fitzgerald Archives at Princeton University; The Fitzgerald Literary Trust care of Harold Ober Associates*

from the north, casting a pall over Valescure and filling the air with a smell of rotting leaves. Each week household expenses multiplied, and it became increasingly difficult to support a large staff who jokingly referred to themselves as the couple's servants. When the lease on Villa Marie expired, they moved back to the Hotel Continental on San Raphael's beach, but Scott soon announced they were leaving for Italy where the dollar was stronger against the lira. While writing *Gatsby*, he had earned practically nothing, and the $7,000 advance they had brought to France was practically gone. He wrote Harold Ober that he was almost broke, and as soon as the novel was off, would return to writing stories for quick money.

The decision to leave San Raphael was as much about Edouard as finances. As the couple drove toward Menton on the Italian border, they knew their marriage had suffered irreparable damage. Any romantic illusions were gone. Although both had engaged in casual affairs before, this was different. That Zelda was prepared to abandon her family, as if it meant nothing, was a devastating betrayal. She had lived by her own rules in America; by doing that in France, what befell her was so damaging, it could not be dispelled by all the confidence that had characterized her youth.

· 5 ·

Truly a Sad Story

After a dismal drive through Italy, with stops in San Remo, Savona, and Pisa, the Fitzgeralds arrived in Rome and checked into the fashionable Hotel Quirinal on Via Nazionale. A nineteenth-century building with old-world feel, it had a private entrance to the adjoining opera house and a charming restaurant in its interior courtyard. November happened to be flea season, and the insects were catapulting everywhere, from the gilded filigree of the hotel's chandeliers onto its draperies and tablecloths. However, when they crawled from the bed sheets, it was time to leave for the more accommodating Hotel des Princes within view of John Keats's house by the Spanish Steps. Although their rooms were smaller and nights perforated by snores from people next door, three meals with wine and service only cost $525 monthly, which they considered a bargain. They drank Corvo wine with Bel Paese cheese and made friends with a spinster reading her way through a three-volume history of the Borgias. To meet expenses, Scott wired Maxwell Perkins for another $750 advance, increasing his Scribner's debt to $5,000.

They planned on staying all winter, but from the moment they arrived, Zelda's abdominal pain worsened and she entered a Rome hospital, where Italian doctors performed a surgical procedure to determine its cause. Their diagnosis was colitis, a general term for inflammation of the colon. Caused by a virus or parasitic infection sometimes in the form of gonorrhea, it can infect the uterus or ovaries, causing infertility by preventing ovulation. During the operation, to aid future conception, physicians removed scar tissue from Zelda's earlier abortion. Rather than lessen her abdominal discomfort, the operation only worsened a lingering infection. She remained ill from an ailment nobody could cure, recovering slowly and with great difficulty, not what one would expect of a normally healthy twenty-four-year-old.

While Scott worked on galley proofs for *Gatsby*, rearranging sections to balance chapters and sketching in details, Zelda explored the area around Piazza di Spagna, then as now, a gathering place for locals and tourists. The monumental stairway near their hotel led to Piazza Trinita da Monti, where an imposing French Renaissance church dominated the plaza. Inside, chapels flickering with candles offered a place to reflect, and Zelda stopped there many afternoons. Four months had passed since Edouard's departure, but he still dominated her mind, and whatever it was she wanted from the Frenchman had vanished with him.

Since their hotel room was not optimal for writing, Scott began searching for an apartment, but it was a Holy Year and the Eternal City crowded with pilgrims. Rental prices were exorbitant for marginal accommodations, and landlords, as Scott recalled, a motley bunch of characters who rounded up every possible space that might pass for an apartment and offered them to Americans at inflated prices. They were forced to stay where they were, and cramped quarters only accelerated their quarreling, Scott noting in his ledger that he still harbored ill feeling towards Zelda.

It rained continually, dampening any enthusiasm for sightseeing, but they did manage to tour some historic sites and made excursions to Tivoli, Frascati, and Naples. Circumstances improved when they were invited to watch the production of *Ben-Hur* being filmed in the Quadro section of Rome along Appian Way. The project had started earlier that year and already run through one director and several leading men, with costs escalating past $4 million. Ramon Novarro was now the star, with Carmel Myers, a protégé of D. W. Griffith, featured as Iras the Egyptian, a vamp in the tradition of Cleopatra. Carmel had costarred opposite screen idol Rudolph Valentino in the comedy *All Night*, and Scott was impressed with her, telling a friend that she was the most exquisite woman he had met in years, and as nice as she was beautiful. Only a year older than Zelda, Carmel was untypical for Hollywood actresses, described by her friend, Mary Pickford, as someone of rare intelligence and character. She was the daughter of a rabbi who had advised D. W. Griffith on biblical scenes for his movie *Intolerance*, and through that connection was given a screen test and hired as a contract player. Her brother, Zion, also was in the film industry and a successful screenwriter.

When the Fitzgeralds met Carmel, she recently had divorced her lawyer husband and was glad to socialize with them. She dined with the Fitzgeralds several times at Scott's favorite restaurant with its spectacular views, the Castello dei Caesari on Monte Aventino, where in broken Italian he would try and convince the waiter that what he wanted was partridge with current jelly or duck with orange sauce, and not meatballs. Carmel may have introduced them to Lois Moran, who was filming near the Coliseum and invited Scott and Zelda to the cast Christmas party, honoring the film's new director, Fred Niblo and wife, Enid Bennett. It was the Fitzgeralds' introduction to the film industry, and along with other guests, they signed the dinner menu, which Carmel kept as a souvenir. As the evening progressed, Zelda began feeling ill, and Scott asked Howard Cox to drive her back to the hotel. Howard had graduated from Princeton in 1920 and published a novel, *Passage to the Sky*, the following year, but was a minor author compared to Scott. In the car, he made advances to Zelda, something she later mentioned in a letter, calling him "Hungary Cox," but given her poor health, it's unlikely she responded. Edmund Wilson later recalled one evening when he and Scott were drinking with Howard, and Howard bragged, "I could sleep with Zelda anytime I wanted." Edmund's response was that "Zelda was not so loose, nor Howard so dangerous, as this implied." The filming of *Ben-Hur* limped along, until Irving Thalberg, recently named head of production at MGM, called a halt to the disaster and transferred the film back to California and Culver Studios.

When Scott sent *Gatsby* proofs to Maxwell Perkins on February 18, 1925, he announced they were leaving for a better climate. "We're moving to Capri. We hate Rome. I'm behind financially and have to write three stories." After an easy drive to Naples, they boarded a ferry for the two-hour passage to Capri, where their accommodations were much improved. They rented a top-floor suite at the Tiberio Palace Hotel with an airy balcony overlooking the sea, "a high white hotel," Zelda recalled, "scalloped about the base by the rounded roofs of Capri, cupped to catch rain which never falls." While Scott continued working on stories begun in Rome, Zelda taught herself to paint, and received weekly punctures from doctors, but the injections only bruised her thighs, providing little relief. Scott wrote Ober that work was progressing, but not without difficulty. "We've had a hell of a time here. My wife's been sick in bed three weeks, and there isn't a typist nearer than Naples."

That February, the couple looked up the Scottish novelist Compton Mackenzie, who had been Scott's idol while at Princeton. Known for his sumptuous lifestyle, he owned a magnificent house perched on a cliff above the Tyrrhenian Sea. His first novel, *Sinister Street*, had impressed Scott, and his second, *Carnival*, reaped high praise from critics, but financial obligations now compelled him to produce a steady stream of popular novels, which Scott considered amateurish and uneven. What he secretly feared was getting into that situation himself.

Capri's uninhibited mores revolved around gossip and parties. Scott was equally repelled and fascinated by its homosexual milieu and told Max the place was "full of fairies," but Zelda liked its permissive environment and enjoyed meeting the heroines of Compton's novel *Extraordinary Women*, which portrayed Capri's lesbian intrigues. While on the Island she met Romaine

Brooks, who recently had ended her affair with the concert pianist Renatta Borgatti, a striking woman with luminous pale skin and lush black hair who resembled Franz Liszt.

On the day *The Great Gatsby* was published, Scott wrote Max that he was nervous over sales, and Max cabled back that early reviews were positive and Edwin Clarke at the *New York Times* had lauded the novel as sensitive and mystical, filled with keen psychological interpretations. Only, the mystical part had Max concerned since orders from bookstores were low. When first and second printings did not sell out, Scott responded with muted optimism, hoping that by some miracle, the book would sell twenty-five thousand copies and wipe out his Scribner's debt.

After reading the novel twice, John Peale Bishop wrote Scott about the book's characterization flaws.

> I feel this lack of complete realization also in the broader aspects of the book, in the character of Gatsby and his relation to the girl. What you have got is all right as far as it goes, but, it does not, to my mind, go far enough. . . . Gatsby should remain a vague, mysterious person to the end, but though he is seen through a mist, always, one should feel his solidarity behind that mist. And it's because you don't entirely "get" him, that the violent end seems abrupt. Everything of Gatsby is specified, but it's as though you saw him in patches instead of getting casual glimpses of— what is, after all, a complete man.

Scott repeated what he had told Max. "You are right about Gatsby being blurred and patchy. I never at any one time saw him clear myself, for he started as one man I knew and then changed into myself—the amalgam was never complete in my mind." He told something similar to Charles Scott, saying Gatsby was never real to him and that his original served as a good exterior only until the middle of the book. By trying to blend Edouard with himself and Tommy Hitchcock, he had created a blurred composite, rather than a deeply rich character, and the synthesis was never complete. Not until Gilbert Seldes gave the novel a glowing review and T. S. Eliot and Gertrude Stein heaped abundant praise did he begin to feel better about it. Nonetheless, it remained a commercial failure.

With income from *Gatsby* now uncertain, Scott concentrated on finishing three stories about compromised marriages. He attributed Edouard's disdain for him, to William Driscoll in "Not in the Guidebook." In the narrative, newlyweds Millie and Jim Cooley have just arrived in France, where he is to oversee an American military cemetery. En route by train from Cherbourg to Paris, Jim gets off, leaving Millie to continue on to Paris alone, where she is helped by Driscoll, who operates a touring service. After Cooley resurfaces,

Driscoll tells Millie her husband isn't any good and that she is ruining her life with him. He quickly wins her affections, and she divorces Cooley to marry Driscoll, the two honeymooning on his excursion bus, bound for Avignon, Bordeaux, and places not in the guidebook. Scott's second story, "Love in the Night," draws upon Edouard as the model for Val Rostoff, who has a chance encounter with a young American woman on the Riviera. When she acknowledges having made a poor choice in husbands, he asks if it's repairable, and she coyly responds, she isn't sure. Although they spend only one evening together, three years later she returns as a widow to renew the relationship. Scott's third story, titled "The Adjuster," models the character of Luella Hemple on Zelda, unsuited for marriage or motherhood. She hates ordering groceries, seeing if the fridge is clean, or pretending to be interested in the household. When their infant son dies and her husband breaks down, the psychoanalyst admonishes Luella that it's her turn to be at the center of things, to give others what she has been given for so long. It was Scott telling his wife to grow up.

Ober placed all three stories for publication that year, and with money in the bank, the Fitzgeralds headed back to Naples. They planned on driving to Paris, but when Zelda didn't feel up to the journey, boarded the SS *President Garfield* for Marseilles. Scott wrote Roger Burlingame on April 19, "Zelda has been too sick for a long overland trip to Paris in our French Ford, so we had to catch a boat on a day's notice to get the car back to France within the 6 mos. period of the international touring agreement." While being unloaded from the ship, the car's roof got damaged, and rather than pay for costly repairs, Zelda convinced a mechanic to remove it entirely. Along with its missing roof, the Renault's engine also was compromised, having been run without sufficient oil or water, and the mechanic showed Scott where the motor had overheated and burned paint off its casing. It was now irrevocably a convertible, and torrential rains on the way to Paris forced a stop in Lyon, where they garaged the vehicle and continued on by train. Two months later, Scott and his new friend, Ernest Hemingway, would return to retrieve it, and the episode would become literary history in Ernest's memoir, *A Movable Feast*.

It was Donald Ogden Stewart who introduced the two writers at the Dingo bar on rue Delambre, a payback to Scott for shepherding him into the publishing business. Stewart had been advised by John Peale Bishop to find Ernest in Paris, and on his first night there met him by chance at the Rendezvous des Mariners. Equally passionate about the outdoors, he had accompanied Ernest and wife, Hadley, to the bull ring in Pamplona, then fishing in Burgette, a mountain village near the French border. Ernest was then twenty-three and Hadley eight years his senior. As a result of briefly being invalided by a childhood accident, she grew up feeling fragile and was powerfully drawn to Ernest's robustness. She supported his writing wholeheartedly and backed him in everything. With no personal ambitions, Hadley was content to remain in the background and became a sitting duck for women attracted to her husband.

Scott was apprehensive about meeting Ernest and made a terrible first impression. After asking if he had slept with Hadley before marriage, Scott ordered champagne, then turned sweaty and passed out after one glass. The query revealed his ambivalence over Zelda's promiscuity but Ernest brushed it off, more annoyed about Scott's inability to hold his liquor than any evasion of his private life. He judged men by certain standards, and Scott failed an important test. There was also something "girly" about him. Along with Scott's puny legs, which if not undersized would have added inches to his height, there was his delicate face that Ernest described as something between handsome and pretty. Then, there were his delicate lips, which on a girl would have been a mark of beauty, but on a man something else. It was the mouth he thought, that worried you, until you knew him and then it worried you more.

Zelda initially charmed Ernest as she did most men, and his first notes to Scott included greetings and inquiries about her health. Although she seemed frivolous, he admitted to being attracted and noticed her golden hair, lovely legs, and beautiful skin. However, his overall impression was negative. He did not like Zelda, but that didn't keep him from having an erotic dream about her. When he told her about this, she seemed pleased, making the observation that it was the last time they shared anything in common. Untrue, since both shared a family history of depression and suicide; Ernest's father, Clarence, would take his own life, as would Ernest and his siblings, Leicester and Ursula, a yearning for peace finally achieved in the sleep of death.

Ernest and Zelda got along until he decided she interfered with Scott's writing. He warned Scott that, more than most people, he needed discipline in his life and chastised him for marrying someone who was jealous of his creativity and felt competitive. That he loved her made it even more complicated. Ernest felt Zelda intentionally encouraged Scott to drink beyond his capacity and told Maxwell Perkins that Scott could only be saved by her death or a stomach ailment that made it impossible to consume alcohol. She, in turn, blamed Scott's excesses on Ernest, who could drink with little effect, whereas Scott became intoxicated after two drinks, humiliating himself before heaving in a toilet. It wasn't unusual now for Scott to occupy his regular spot at the Ritz Hotel bar and consume gin, whiskey, wine, and liqueur in one night, his favorites being Pouilly, Mersault, Arbois, and Pilsner. Ernest and Zelda remained convinced the other was responsible for Scott's drunkenness, unaware he probably had some condition that hampered his body from metabolizing alcohol.

When Scott and Ernest met that spring, the divergence between the two could not have been greater. Scott was successful publishing mass market stories but wanted to write serious novels that made money, and Ernest was appreciated by the avant-garde but desired a broader audience. He barely scraped by with his writing, whereas Scott's lucrative advances generally afforded a comfortable life style. The Fitzgeralds' fifth-floor apartment on rue de Tilsitt was one notable exception. The building's clanking elevator usually was broken, forcing family and guests to trudge up five flights of stairs. Although in a fashionable neighborhood on a street circling Place d'Etoile on the Right Bank, it was a gloomy flat that always smelled musty, its walls badly in need of paint. Decorated hideously with purple and gold wallpaper, its living room was furnished with fake Louis XV furniture from Galleries Lafayette. Heavy drapes blocked sunlight, and it was impossible to heat or ventilate adequately, a perfect breeding ground for the bitterness they had brought with them from San Raphael.

Ernest's accommodations were far worse. Ernest and Hadley lived in a working-class neighborhood at 74 rue du Cardinal-Lemoine on the left bank, occupying a two-room flat, four flights up, with no running water and a Turkish-style toilet on each landing. To avoid the rancid hallway at night, they used a chamber pot and slept on a mattress covering the floor. When Hadley became pregnant they left for Toronto, since they wanted their baby born in North America, and when they returned, their new apartment was only slightly better. This one was without electricity and only had cold water. There was a narrow kitchen with a stone sink and small gas burner, a tiny bedroom for the baby, a slighter bigger one for them, and a dining room large enough to hold their massive table and chairs. Not that Ernest spent much time there. Most mornings he wrote at Cloiserie des Lilas, a café near his apartment, after lunch walking to a room he rented in an old hotel on rue Mouffetard where Verlaine once had lived. When he needed a break, he headed for his favorite bistros, Café des Arts and La Chape. The couple lived like paupers, scrimping by on Ernest's penny-a-word salary from the *Toronto Star Weekly* along with interest from Hadley's trust fund that netted them $5,000 annually.

At the beginning, the two writers saw each other often, but Ernest quickly tired of Scott dropping by when he felt like it. Ernest was becoming increasingly disciplined, retiring at nine and getting up by six. No author in Paris wanted more to succeed, and Scott's inability to focus on writing made their friendship untenable. Their relationship faltered when Ernest got reprimanded by his concierge after Scott tried to break down his door at three in the morning and urinated on the overhang.

Unlike Scott and his friends, Ernest had no college education and began his career as a sportswriter for his high school newspaper, modeling his style after Ring Lardner's columns in the *Chicago Tribune*. With that modest experience, he convinced the *Kansas City Star* to hire him as a reporter. Along with many of his contemporaries, he was determined to reach European battlefields before World War I ended, and after volunteering as an ambulance driver for the Red Cross, got assigned to Italy where he experienced his first big test of manhood. His heroics, especially on the Italian front, were greatly exaggerated, since he was not above embellishing his résumé. He once told a reporter from the *Chicago Tribune* that he had gone to Princeton, later admitting having lied. He envied Scott's education there, unaware he had only completed three semesters. While others discussed authors, Ernest more often sang praises of prizefighters, and his drive to excel at sports and project manliness covered a deep insecurity. His passion was boxing and he made extra money by sparing at the American Gym, putting on gloves against Harold Loeb from the Guggenheim family, who had published a novel, *Doodab*, and coedited the literary journal *Broom*.

Zelda loathed Ernest's bravado, which she considered a cover for weakness, and told him that nobody was as masculine as he pretended to be. Honoria Murphy recalled how much that irritated him but thought Zelda had gotten it right. Once, after the two writers had been out drinking and Scott returned home and passed out murmuring, "no more baby," she accused him of being sexually involved with Ernest. Only, "baby" was a Jazz Age endearment that could go either way. Disgusted by their constant sexual bantering, she told Sara Mayfield that she detested Ernest's preoccupation with sex and sadism, but whether he acted on those fantasies with Scott is anybody's guess.

Scott was eager for Ernest to meet the Murphys and arranged an introduction before Christmas. Ernest wrote Scott on December 15 that he found the couple "so damned nice," especially Sara, whom he preferred over Gerald. The Murphys were involved with the Ballets Russes that season, and Zelda eagerly joined them, attending rehearsals and performances and going backstage to meet the dancers and choreographers. Two new ballets by Massine and one by Balanchine opened that season: *Zephire and Flore*, for which George Braque did costumes and decor, and *Les Matelots* and *Barabau*, with set designs by Maurice Utrillo. The Ballets Russes had come to Paris in 1909 with Sergei Diaghilev as director, Michel Fokine its choreographer, and premiere dancers from the Bolshoi and Maryinsky Ballets like Anna Pavlova, Vaslav Nijinsky, and Sofia Fedorova. Sergei Diaghilev was a great organizer and discoverer of new talent with a broad knowledge of music, art, and dance. He wanted to integrate painting, music, and poetry into ballet, blending diverse artistic styles into new avenues of expression. His collaborations attracted the greatest visual artists of the twentieth century: Picasso, Braque, Matisse, and Miro. To provide original scores, he hired Debussy and Prokofiev, Stravinsky and Ravel, along with supremely talented choreographers Fokine, Massine, and Balanchine. The sets of Mikhail Larionov and costume designs of Leon Bakst generated as much attention as the ballets themselves. Bakst uniquely understood the function of costume and interpreted the body as a kinetic force, accentuating dancers' movements by attaching feathers and veils to their garments. His visions of the exotic evoked a fantastic world of sensations and sensual pleasures that captivated Parisian audiences. Scott could tolerate ballet in small doses but preferred parties and dragged Zelda to endless ones that often started on Wednesday and continued through the weekend. "Nobody knew whose party it was. It had been going on for weeks," she wrote, "and when you couldn't sustain another night, you rested and returned to find a new group committed to keeping it alive."

Seizing any excuse to escape their dismal apartment, the Fitzgeralds regarded cafés as an extension of their living quarters. Their favorite was the Dingo American Bar and Restaurant, which stayed open all night and featured as bartender the amiable Jimmie Charters, a former lightweight boxer from Liverpool. It was owned by an American whose Dutch wife, Jopie, befriended many of the female patrons, including Zelda and Lady Duff Twysden. Duff had been engaged at twenty-one, married to someone else the following year, and when that ended, wed to Sir Roger Twysden, a tenth baronet and naval officer, whom she met volunteering for the British Royal Service. Through him she acquired her title and son. After leaving both in Britain, she arrived in Paris with Patrick Guthrie, with whom she had an open relationship and slept with anyone she pleased. Ernest based the character of Lady Brett Ashley in *The Sun Also Rises* on Duff. As he described, she was good-looking in a unique way, her hair brushed back like a boy's, but voluptuous with curves like the hull of a racing yacht, accentuated by the wool sweaters she wore. The Fitzgeralds often met Duff at the Dingo with the Hemingways, and Ernest became infatuated with her. But, either from loyalty to Hadley or her lack of interest, she did not sleep with him. Instead, she became involved with his sparring partner, Harold Loeb, who had graduated from Princeton and had lots of money.

Zelda initially was the better known of the two women, but after *The Sun Also Rises* was published, Twysden became the most controversial and discussed woman in Paris. Everyone wanted to meet Ernest, and everyone was talking about Duff. Based on real people and events, the roman à clef concerned a group of friends traveling to Pamplona for the bullfights and a love triangle between Jake Barnes, Lady Brett Ashley, and Robert Cohn.

The three were thinly disguised characters based on Ernest, Duff, and Harold, who was portrayed in a blatantly anti-Semitic way. Harold never put the characterization to rest, and Duff was furious at being reduced to an alcoholic nymphomaniac, especially after Vassar and Smith undergraduates began adopting her opinions and emulating her actions. Well known in Paris before the novel's publication, afterward she became legendary. Jake Barnes became the decade's most popular antihero and Brett a cult figure, replacing Zelda as the quintessential liberated woman. With dizzying alacrity, Scott's prominence was eclipsed by Ernest's best-selling novel, which he had written in eight short weeks.

Although pleased for his friend's success, Scott was unhappy over his own inability to work, but rather than dwell on the situation, he joined other expatriates consuming quantities of alcohol, as drunkenness with its accompanying stomach disorders became endemic in Paris. Parties were feverish affairs at sophisticated places like Maxim's, which attracted the most charming people who by night's end lost much of their appeal. As Scottie later recalled, "It was a constant merry-go-round for them. (My Father) devoted six or seven years of his life from about 1924 to 1931, to having a good time in Paris. He wrote a few short stories just to keep the family alive." Now, after a night of drinking, it was customary for him to wake up someplace with no idea how he had gotten there. Scott would simply pass out, but for Zelda it meant delirium. In *Save Me the Waltz*, she fictionalizes a typical incident from the period: "They went to Bourget and hired an aeroplane. David drank so much brandy before they left, that by the time they were over the Porte St. Denis, he was trying to get the pilot to take them to Marseilles." When they returned to Paris, he tried to get Alabama to have dinner with him at Cafe Lila's, but she refused, pleading, "David, I can't honestly. I get so sick when I drink. I'll have to have morphine if I do—like the last time." Their friends were frank to say, that, if you got involved with them these days, you did so at your own risk.

Given the circumstances, it seemed prudent to accept the Murphys' repeat invitation to Antibes. Renovations on their villa were completed and they wanted everyone to see it. That June, the Fitzgeralds boarded Le Train Bleu departing Paris in the evening, first class only to Marseille, making three stops before arriving the next morning. From there, it was a short ride on local trains to the popular resort towns along the coast. Scott wrote John Peale Bishop that Paris had been a mad house with them in the thick of it, and he wasn't sure if they were going back. Archibald MacLeish and Ada already were in Antibes, and he confided he was starting a new novel with the Riviera as its setting. Some of the Murphys' friends were staying at the Hotel du Cap with the Fitzgeralds, while others were housed on their property in the Bastide or Ferme des Oranges, a donkey stable converted into a housekeeping cottage. Scott noted who was lodging where and realized they were just two more names on a list of illustrious visitors. Others coming that summer included the cabaret singer Mistinguet; John Dos Passos; Esther Murphy; Floyd Dell; Rex Ingram; Pablo Picasso and his Russian wife, Olga Khokhlova; Anita Loos; Igor Stravinsky; and Jean Cocteau. The silent film idol Rudolph Valentino and wife, Natasha Rambova, were staying in Juan-les-Pins with her stepfather, the cosmetics millionaire Richard Hudnut. Natasha was three years older than Zelda, born Winifred Kimball Shaughnessy in Salt Lake City, Utah. Her mother, Winifred Kimball, was granddaughter of Heber Chase Kimball, a leader in the early Mormon movement and one of the church's original twelve apostles. After being adopted by Richard Hudnut, Winifred Shaughnessy briefly took his last name, but after studying ballet with Russian choreographer Theodore Kosloff, changed it to Natasha Rambova and married Valentino in 1923.

The Fitzgeralds registered at the Hotel du Cap and made the daily drive to the Murphys' pristine beach, transformed into a perfect place to sun and swim. Scott was happy to be included but recognized a change from the previous year. A typical day began around eleven with a late morning swim, and for the rest of the afternoon, the three Murphy children and Scottie swam or played on straw mats, while adults chatted nearby. Evenings commenced with cocktails for six or eight of the Murphys' friends, Gerald mixing his special concoction of brandy, liqueur, and lemon juice, served in long-stemmed glasses rimmed with lemon and dipped in coarse sugar. Afterward, there was a sit-down dinner, animated conversation, and a song or dance by the children.

To be back on the Riviera was painful for Zelda, since Edouard was still in Frejus, preparing to leave with his squadron for Hyeres. Now part of the Parisian social scene, he was engaged to Lucienne Gruss-Gallieni, granddaughter of the general, whose prominent family owned a fashionable Parisian apartment and country estate outside Fontainebleau. Wealthy and well connected as well as attractive, she was exactly the wife he wanted. The Gallienis were less sure about him. Although there was no great excitement over the relationship, Edouard's charismatic personality and good looks won them over. Excluding something unforeseen, his military future was assured.

The Picassos were living in Juan-les-Pins that summer at a villa called Haie Blanche and came to the Murphys' with their four-year-old son, Paolo. When Olga met Picasso in Rome during 1917, she was a featured ballerina with the Ballets Russes, and he there to design scenery and costumes for *Parade*, a ballet based on a libretto by Jean Cocteau and choreographed by Leonid Massine. By then, she had danced in more than thirty ballet productions, including fifteen premieres, but after marrying Picasso the following year and giving birth to their son, never returned to the stage. Zelda enjoyed talking with Olga, who was full of stories about backstage intrigues, but the two shared more than a love for ballet. Olga also was suffering from a debilitating gynecological condition, for which she had undergone several surgeries and hospitalizations. Picasso had no patience with her illness, believing women brought sickness upon themselves, and never connected his continual encounters with prostitutes to her disease. The following year, he would leave Olga for seventeen-year-old Marie-Therese Walter, whom he met outside Galleries Lafayette. After announcing to the young girl that he was "Picasso," he proclaimed she had an interesting face he would like to paint, and a week later was sleeping with the teenager.

Zelda's conversations with Khoklova reawakened her interest in ballet, and upon returning to Paris, she asked Scott to write Gerald for the name of his daughter's dance coach. He promptly replied, "Honoria's teacher is Madame Egorova (Princess Troubetzkoy) top floor over the Olympia Music Hall on the Boulevard. The stage entrance is on the side street, 8 or 10 Rue Caumartin. You walk up thro' the wings while the performance is going on, and there's her studio . . . a big, bare room just for learning to dance in." After the Russian Revolution, Paris had blossomed into the ballet capital of the world, with exiled dancers opening private studios and Lubov Egorova among the most sought after and demanding of teachers. She had undergone rigorous training at the Maryinsky Imperial Theatre in St. Petersburg, becoming Princess Trubetzkoy after her marriage to Prince Nikita Sergeievich Trubetzkoy. In 1917 she left Russia for Paris and on Sergei Diaghilev's suggestion opened a school to train replacements for his dance corps. Besides being a gifted instructor, she was a talented dancer with a lyrical style characterized by softness and cantilena more than virtuosity. She accepted students only through introduction, so Gerald spoke to Madame Egorova on Zelda's behalf. With the idea that she was resuming a regimen started in youth, Zelda immersed herself in classical Russian ballet, the most difficult dance aesthetic of the twentieth century.

That Christmas, the MacLeishes joined the Fitzgeralds to open presents around their tree decorated with glass balls, snowy houses, and spun-glass birds of paradise, and Archibald photographed the family in front of it, the image becoming one of Scottie's keepsakes. "There are dozens of pictures of my mother, my father and me. . . . My favorite is the one of us dancing in front of the heavily tinseled tree in Paris. . . . Christmas was the time I was at my most useful. That is when I allowed my parents to give full vent to their romantic imaginations and throw themselves wholeheartedly into fantasy." Scott bought Scottie gifts at Nain Bleu, which sold exquisite dolls, choosing one named Monique that came with a wardrobe trunk filled with outfits for different seasons. The following week, Pulitzer prize–winner Louis Bromfield and his socialite wife, Mary Appleton Wood, arrived to celebrate New Year's Eve. As champagne corks popped, Bromfield noticed that drinking was now a serious problem for the couple. A little alcohol made Zelda terribly agitated, and Scott simply couldn't drink; one cocktail and he was off.

Although Zelda tried to be at her best for the holidays, the dampness of the Parisian winter aggravated her abdominal infection, and she felt miserable throughout the Christmas season. After welcoming in 1926, they followed the advice of her doctor and left for Salies-de-Bearn, a mineral spa in the Pyrenees near the Spanish border, whose salt springs and curative waters were famous throughout Europe. It was off-season and most of the buildings were boarded up. The only place open was the Hotel Bellevue, with just seven other registered guests, and the empty town with its almost vacant hotel became etched in Zelda's memory. Henry IV's mother had been born there, and on the mantle of their white pine room was a small bronze statue of the king, alongside her row of medicine bottles. Before the development of antibiotics, "taking the waters" was standard treatment for inflammatory diseases, and Zelda's gynecologist was confident those medicinal springs, containing potassium bromides and sulfur, could help her lingering ovarian infection. While she immersed herself in mineral baths and drank foul-smelling water from glasses etched with the spa's crest, Scott worked on several stories, writing Ober, "We have come to a little, lost village called Salies-de-Bearn in the Pyrenees, where my wife is to take a special treatment of baths for eleven months, for an illness that has run now for almost a year." To pass time they wandered through cobblestoned streets and bought souvenirs, took carriage rides to Basque towns, and made weekend excursions to Biarritz, Lourdes, and San Sebastian.

Eleven months got shortened to six weeks, since they returned to Paris in March and joined Robert Benchley and Dorothy Parker for dinner at Closerie des Lilas. The two had just arrived in Cherbourg aboard the SS *President Roosevelt*, crossing the Atlantic with Ernest Hemingway with whom they played cards and shared stories. Good friends since their working days at *Vanity Fair*, Parker and Benchley were on their way to see the Murphys in Antibes, so the Fitzgeralds decided to follow. They hired a limousine to take them to Nice, driving through Cote d'Azur to Toulouse, where they stopped at the Hotel Tivollier before continuing to the coast. Gerald found them a rental in Juan-les-Pins, a short drive to their place across the narrow width of the peninsula. Called Villa Paquinta, it turned out to be damp and uncomfortable, so they immediately searched for a replacement. Antibes had noticeably changed. Tranquil before, with only one restaurant and a cinema, it now was a tourist attraction overrun by Americans, with new establishments opening daily.

They anticipated socializing with the Murphys, but competition for the couple's attention was fierce, and everyone wanted to meet the Hemingways, who were invited to stay in the Murphys' guest cottage. Since Ernest was still at the Spanish bullfights, Hadley arrived alone with their son, Bumby. Both had planned to go, but when Bumby became ill, Hadley remained behind. After their arrival, the Murphy's English doctor diagnosed the boy with whopping cough and quarantined mother and son. To protect her own children, Sara asked Hadley to stay elsewhere. The Fitzgeralds had just located a wonderful house to lease called Villa St. Louis that had a private beach and was located on an inlet facing Lerins Island. Since they were leaving Villa Paquinta, on which six weeks of their lease remained, they invited Hadley and Bumby to stay there.

Hadley was an attractive woman, more handsome than beautiful, whose childhood had been disrupted when her father, an executive in the family's pharmaceutical business, committed suicide. Sent to boarding school at twelve, she became close friends with Katy Smith, who would marry John Dos Passos. Throughout her marriage, she considered Ernest's writing her primary concern and wanted to be his helper, not a hinderer. When Zelda criticized Hadley for being too accommodating, saying that Ernest made all the decisions and she just went along, Hadley insisted that was how she wanted it. Zelda disagreed with her approach and couldn't understand how she could just be a servant for him. Hadley also had blundered in her relationship and was paying for it. Four years earlier, Ernest had asked her to bring his manuscripts to Lausanne, where he was reporting on territorial negotiations between Greece and Turkey. Lincoln Steffens was there and wanted to see his writing, so Hadley collected his stories, poems, and a novel about his war experiences; packed them in a valise; and boarded a train for Switzerland. After placing the suitcase in an overhead rack, she momentarily left to get water and returned to find it gone. For Ernest, the loss was a betrayal, since he felt Hadley should have understood his works' importance and safeguarded their value. Like Scott, who held tightly to his anger over Edouard, Ernest was never able to forgive Hadley, and it provided an excuse for infidelity.

When Ernest finally arrived, the Murphys hosted a welcoming party in his honor and invited the Fitzgeralds, MacLeishes, Charles and Elizabeth Brackett, Philip and Ellen Barr, Donald Ogden Stewart, and the Princess de Poix and Princess Caraman-Chimay. The highlight of the evening was to be Ernest reading from his new novel before the assembled guests. Zelda refused to go until Sara insisted, but regretted changing her mind. Annoyed at Ernest being the center of attention and already drunk when he arrived, after making sarcastic remarks about the champagne and caviar, Scott grabbed some ashtrays and flung them at a nearby table. Then he lobbed a fresh fig down the décolletage of the Princess de Poix's gown, who plucked it out as if nothing had happened. Zelda got up to leave, but not before Gerald already had excused himself. Once home, she started a heated argument with Scott, but nothing got resolved. Sara Mayfield recalled how, "Whenever they fought, Zelda threatened to pack up and leave. She threw everything she owned into her trunk, and dragged it out to the street. There she would wait—one never knew what for. When she got sleepy she'd go back to bed, but the trunk was left behind."

Relegated to the sidelines, Scott determined to beat Ernest at his own game, and Archibald MacLeish recalled one incident that placed everyone's life in danger.

> We were swimming at the beach in front of the villa, Ada and I, Scott, Zelda and Ernest Hemingway. The villa lay above the beach on the cliff and in front of it was a circular section of gravel, not really very large, I suppose fifty feet or so across, so that a large car could just barely turn around in it. Scott got out of the water and went over to his car, and beckoned for Ernest and me to come over and get in with him. We couldn't understand what he could possibly want, but he stayed there waving at us and insisting we come, until finally we got up and went over to him. His car was a small one with a rumble seat in back, and Ernest and I got in the back, though it was a very tight squeeze. Scott drove up the road to the villa, and as he approached it, he began to put on speed; when he reached the circle he turned the car around very suddenly, so that we were afraid in that small area it would overturn, and then headed for the cliff with as much speed as he could get. He drove as fast as he could towards the edge of that cliff, and applied the brake at the very last minute, the last second, so that we came to rest on the very edge of the cliff. Then he jumped out of the car and looked round at us; his face was very flushed and red, and he laughed like a mad-man, almost uncontrollably, for several minutes. I was petrified; I still couldn't believe that it had happened; it had all taken place so quickly, and Ernest, beside me, was white as a sheet. Ernest was a very brave man, but he hated stupid risks such as Scott had taken, and it was probably well for Scott that he was so shocked and pale; he said nothing and did not get out of the car for awhile. When Zelda found out about it (she knew because she had seen it from below) when she saw him, she was very angry with him for doing something so ridiculous and let him know it.

Although she may have smiled seeing Ernest tremble, Zelda was very upset at Archie being placed in that position. They were good friends and nobody better understood the difficulty she faced living with Scott. "Zelda was a finer wife to Scott than anyone else could have been," Archie recalled. "I don't think there was anyone else in the world, no other woman I have known, who could have put up with Scott the way he was."

Scott's behavior only exacerbated Zelda's anxiety and she reacted by becoming moody or provoking Scott with her own dangerous behavior. "One particular night we had driven over through the mountains," Archie remembered,

> and spent an evening there at sort of a Swiss nightclub, and Scott and Zelda, who were particularly gay, had finished off the evening dancing on one of the tables, which the proprietor seemed to think was very gay and very romantic, but which was the sort of thing they were always doing. As we were driving home that night, Ada and I were riding with the Murphys, and Scott and Zelda were driving ahead. About halfway home, there was a place where the road veered off to the left, and we were all surprised to see Scott drive straight ahead into a little dirt road which went on, and as we went around the curve, we looked back to see that he had driven out on to a large railroad trestle which crossed a pass in the mountains there, and it must have been two or three hundred feet down from where he stopped his car right in the middle of it. Ada and I were worried and thought we should go back for them, but Gerald Murphy laughed and said that Scott had probably found out that the trains did not run at night or something, and was trying to give us all a scare, and that we would probably see them in the morning. The next morning, while we were at breakfast, Scott and Zelda came in and told us that they had spent the night on the trestle, and upon waking in the morning had driven home. I really have no reason to doubt it, because it seemed like just the kind of thing Scott would do.

When Sara warned against doing such crazy things, Zelda laughed saying they didn't believe in conservation.

However, it was evident something needed to change. By June, Zelda was increasingly unsettled and her abdomen pain so constant, they returned to Paris where she entered the American Hospital at Neuilly to undergo an appendectomy. Doctors also may have removed one of her ovaries or fallopian tubes, since she wrote about how ill she was trying to have a baby, and that Dr. Gross had concluded, there was little use trying to save her ovaries. A subsequent medical report mentions the Neuilly admission but gives contradictory information: "At twenty-four in Europe, patient has a near peritonitis caused by an inflammation of the right ovary and is practically disabled for a year. The matter is cleared up by an operation for appendix. [Dr. Gross and Dr.] Martel find appendix in bad shape but ovary fundamentally healthy." Worried over her sister's condition, Rosalind contacted the hospital asking why Zelda had been admitted but received no reply. After two years of ineffective treatments, the Neuilly procedure cleared up an infection that had plagued Zelda since the Jozan affair. Following this, there is no mention of pregnancy; at twenty-six, it seems her childbearing years were over.

When they returned to Juan-les-Pins, she needed to avoid strenuous exercise until her stitches were removed, so while others gathered at Villa America, Zelda remained at Villa St. Louis. She wanted Scott to spend time with her there, but he preferred the *garoupe* with Marise Hamilton, the Murphys, and the MacLeishes, where the atmosphere was gayer. That August, beach talk centered around Gertrude Ederle, who on her second try, was the first woman to swim the English Channel, crossing in two hours less than the fastest man. Zelda admired her determination and when her stitches came out and strength returned, she resumed swimming and began looking for a ballet coach, selecting one just over the French border in Switzerland. Archibald recalled her phenomenal effort:

> Zelda was a very extraordinary woman. She had an intense urge to create, to do something, and it was that summer she decided to take up ballet dancing. She would drive for two hours into Switzerland, practice for seven, and then drive back every night. . . . She had convinced herself that she could be great at ballet, and she had always wanted to do it, so that was what she set out to do. At this time she was twenty-eight, I believe, and you must know, for a woman of that age to seriously try to take up ballet, to work that hard on all that strenuous exercise, well it was just ridiculous. The physical strain to which she subjected herself and her inability to conquer the art were what greatly contributed to the nervous breakdown that ruined her.

MacLeish and Zelda were the best swimmers among the Murphys' friends and often met at Eden Roc Pavilion to dive from its highest peaks into the Mediterranean. The Hotel du Cap had built a swimming pavilion four hundred yards from their main building, blasting a pool into massive rocks and leaving its uppermost ledges perched over the sea. "There were notches cut in the rock at five, ten, up to thirty feet," recalled Sara Murphy.

> Now, that's a high dive at any time, but especially at night, and one had to be a superb diver in order to make it, have a perfect sense of timing, or one would have been smashed on the rocks below. Zelda would strip to her slip, and very quietly ask Scott if he cared for a swim. I remember one evening when he was absolutely trembling when she challenged him, but he followed her. They took each a dive, returning from the sea all shivering and white, until the last, the one at thirty feet. Scott hesitated and watched Zelda until she surfaced; I didn't think he could go through with it, but he did.

After this episode, Zelda became increasingly withdrawn and though occasionally swimming with the Murphys, began distancing herself from her surroundings and retreating to an inward life nobody could touch.

Her turmoil became apparent during a dinner with the Murphys on the terrace of Colombe d'Or in St. Paul de Vence. Midway through the meal, Gerald drew Scott's attention to Isadora Duncan, who was seated nearby with three men. Scott walked over to introduce himself and crouching by her table praised her innovative artistry. She confided that she had received an advance to write her memoir and was being pressured for the manuscript. After Scott offered to help, she wrote down her hotel and room number, affectionately tousling his hair and calling him a centurion—her protective soldier. Upon observing this, Zelda stood on her chair and scaled the retaining wall of the terrace, then flung herself down the steps of its entrance. Probably, she intended only to recapture Scott's attention but easily could have killed herself. When Sara reached her, she was bloodied and bruised, but otherwise unhurt. As a girl, she had tried to perform like Pavlova and now was struggling to dance like Isadora, so when she saw Scott kneeling at the great dancer's feet, interpreted it a sign she had failed.

Soon after, the relationship between the couples unraveled, when Scott again behaved contemptuously at one of Sara's elegant dinners, tossing three of her favorite Venetian glasses over the terrace. Gerald immediately ordered him to leave, and Sara made clear in a note sent the next day, that at this stage in their lives, they could not be bothered with sophomoric behavior.

The Hemingways then surprised everyone by announcing they were separating and promptly left for Paris. Ernest had gotten involved with Hadley's friend, Pauline Pfieffer, an editorial assistant with the French edition of *Vogue*. Initially, he had been attracted to her sister, Jinny, who was amused by the attention but more interested in women. Four years older than Ernest, rather than Hadley's eight, Pauline was ultra-chic and possessed a larger trust fund. Clever and entertaining, she lived in a fancy apartment on rue Picot, had plenty of money for expensive restaurants and barhopping, and had come to Paris searching for a husband. Her father, Paul, had made a fortune on the St. Louis grain exchange and owned huge tracts of Arkansas farmland. He and his brothers, Henry and Gustav, also had a large drugstore chain and controlling shares in Warner Pharmaceuticals, which acquired the Richard Hudnut Company in 1916. Family money allowed Pauline to do as she pleased, in this case to commandeer Hadley's husband. In part, Hadley attributed the breakup to her loss of Ernest's manuscripts but admitted she could not compete with Pauline's sophistication, wealth, and determination to steal her mate. Although Ernest seemed content having two women in love with him, he felt conflicted over the situation and asked friends for advice, including the Murphys, Gertrude Stein, Sylvia Beach, and Scott. Everyone warned him against it except Gerald, who encouraged Ernest to leave Hadley, whose self-effacing manner seemed provincial to him. So he would have somewhere to stay, he gave Ernest the keys to his sixth-floor Parisian studio at 69 rue Froidevaux and deposited $400 into his Morgan Guaranty bank account. Meanwhile, Hadley moved to a small flat on rue de Fleurus. Appreciative then, Ernest later would rebuke the couple for supporting his decision to abandon his wife and son, complaining they were bad luck for people and collected them like others collected paintings or racehorses, and had backed him in every selfish decision he'd ever made. Hadley felt deeply betrayed, and when Donald Ogden Stewart brought her home from a Parisian party, she cried the entire way back to her apartment. In September of that year, Ernest wrote Scott that in no time short his life had gone to hell, which was the one thing you could count on life to do.

Scott felt allegiance toward Hadley and disliked Pauline, warning Ernest that she was shopping for a husband and had enough money to buy one; if he succumbed to her, he was courting irreparable tragedy from which he might never recover. Pauline, however, was accustomed to getting what she wanted and was making a relationship sound increasingly attractive. She told Ernest they could live on her money and that Uncle Gus was prepared to buy them a house, car, and his own fishing boat, and pay for a $25,000 first-class African safari. Although Scott felt like writing, "don't marry her, you'll regret it," when answering Ernest's letter, he only asked if they had broken up for good and took the opportunity to share his own marital difficulties. He confessed he had been unable to satisfy Zelda since the Jozan affair and that she constantly complained about his small penis and unimaginative lovemaking, saying that the way he was built, he could never make a woman happy. Ernest dismissed her carping by saying she was only trying to undermine his masculinity. In some detail, Scott also told Ernest about Zelda's affair with Edouard in San Raphael, and how the pilot's plane had buzzed their diving raft and swooped over the pontoons that cast shadows across the sea. Ernest did not ask the question that was on his mind, of how, if the story was true, he could have slept each night in the same bed with Zelda? He wondered how Scott could have forgiven her. The answer, of course, was he couldn't.

Rather than return to Paris that fall, the Fitzgeralds remained at Villa St. Louis until their lease expired, then traveled to Genoa and boarded the *Conte Biancamano* on December 26 for New York. Miss Maddock, who had witnessed the Jozan affair, still was overseeing Scottie, and by the time they had been on the boat half an hour, had everyone running errands and making their cabins comfortable. Also aboard was Ludlow Fowler, best man at their wedding, and his bride, Elsie Blatchford. The four shared a table for meals, and one evening over dinner, Zelda leaned over and warned Fowler not to let drinking overtake his life and ruin the marriage.

They had fled Great Neck three years earlier to save money and put their lives in order, but their time abroad only had created more problems. And while *The Great Gatsby* received impressive reviews, it sold poorly and was a financial disappointment. Scott had hoped sales would match the forty thousand of his first novel, but they never reached twenty thousand. Given what Scribner's had advanced, they were returning home more in debt than before.

Since publishing *Gatsby*, Scott had written little of consequence, churning out stories for quick money, whereas Ernest's reputation was firmly established with *The Sun Also Rises*. Eclipsed by his fellow author, Scott still considered their friendship the only positive outcome of his time abroad, and on shipboard stationery wrote Ernest about how much he valued their friendship. By contrast, toward Zelda all he felt was anger and resentment. Everywhere he looked, nothing seemed left of happiness, and in his ledger he summarized the period as shameless and futile, except for the $30,000 in revenue from his 1924 work. To celebrate his thirtieth birthday, which for him commenced middle age, Scott celebrated by getting tight for a week.

· 6 ·

Retribution and Remorse

$\mathcal{T}$o be back on American soil was somehow reassuring. After visiting friends in Manhattan, the family departed for the nation's capital to see Scott's parents, who were living at the Hotel Roosevelt. Then it was on to Montgomery for Christmas with Zelda's family. They planned on returning to Manhattan for New Year's, but plans changed on December 30, when a telegram arrived from John Considine Jr., head of Feature Productions in Hollywood, offering Scott a contract to write a flapper comedy for the comedic actress, Constance Talmadge. It was a three-month commitment with an advance salary of $3,500, followed by an additional $12,500 upon the script's acceptance. Scott needed the money, so it was back to Washington, where they deposited Scottie and Miss Maddock with Scott's parents, then boarded the Twentieth Century Limited for Los Angeles, arriving in time to experience their first earthquake.

They registered at the Hotel Ambassador on Wilshire Boulevard and checked into suite 17, a cozy apartment bungalow nestled amongst palm groves, where white roses climbed a trellis outside their living room window. It had two bedrooms, one of which Scott commandeered as an office, hoping he could avoid showing up daily at MGM Studios. Celebrity occupants of the other bungalows included Carmel Myers, their Rome acquaintance; John Barrymore; and Carl Van Vechten, who described the luxurious accommodations in a letter to his wife, Fania: "This hotel is extraordinary. It is like living in London. You need a guide. I am in one of the cottages on the grounds and Scott Fitzgerald is in another just opposite me. The Fitzgeralds are here because he is writing a scenario for Constance Talmadge. I had great fun with them yesterday afternoon." Carl took the couple to the most fashionable Hollywood parties and introduced them to its A-list of producers, film stars, and directors. They went on set with Lillian Gish—who later said the couple didn't exemplify the twenties; they *were* the twenties—and Gish's husband, actor James Reny, who became Scott's drinking buddy. The best gatherings occurred on Sundays when actors had the day off, and the Fitzgeralds arrived at one in nightgown and pajamas, parodying the habit of performers who came in set costumes. At one occasion hosted by Samuel Goldwyn for the Talmadge sisters, they arrived uninvited, barking like puppies at the door to be let in. Guests were uncertain what to make of it, and when Zelda wandered upstairs with Colleen Moore to take a bath, nobody seemed amused. Life became a swirl of activity, with Zelda telling one interviewer from *Motion Picture* that Carl had come to Hollywood for peace and quiet, but with their assistance was disrupting the entire movie colony.

At MGM Studios, they were introduced to King Vidor and went to dinner with him and his wife, actress Eleanor Boardman. He was just starting production on his film *Hallelujah* about Southern sharecroppers after Emancipation and wanted to create an authentic film with an all-Negro cast using genuine plantation songs and spirituals. Scott told King about Gerald Murphy, who was knowledgeable about that subject and owned a large collection of jazz and blues records, hoping the recommendation might restore him to the Murphys' good graces. In the MGM commissary, Scott briefly met with twenty-seven-year-old studio head Irving Thalberg, already a legend in the film industry. With youthful egotism, he told Scott a long-winded parable about the challenges of leadership, which Scott took seriously, unaware the discourse was one he routinely gave scriptwriters.

John Barrymore invited them for dinner, they had afternoon tea at Ronald Coleman's, and attended a luncheon in their honor at Pickfair, the palatial home of "America's Sweethearts" Mary Pickford and Douglas Fairbanks, who, after a fairy-tale romance, had married the same year as the Fitzgeralds. During the event, Scott met Lois Moran, the blond, blue-eyed protégé of Samuel Goldwyn. Just seventeen but cultured for her young years, she was managed by her twice-widowed mother, Gladys, who was about Scott's age. After the death of her first husband by an automobile accident and her second in the influenza pandemic of 1918, Gladys moved to Paris with her twelve-year-old daughter Lois, who quickly learned French, joined the Paris Opera as a ballerina, and performed in her first film. When the Fitzgeralds were in Rome during Christmas of 1924, Lois was there filming Pirandello's *Feu Mathias Pascal*, and they initially may have met then. The following year she was catapulted to fame as the daughter in Samuel Goldwyn's *Stella Dallas*, singled out by the *Chicago Tribune* as one of the brightest up-and-coming stars and compared to Clara Bow and Gloria

Swanson. Although many found her innocence appealing, others, including Henry Pringle from *Collier's Magazine*, dismissed her as a shade too sweet in appearance, and Zelda always thought she resembled "a breakfast food that so many men identified with whatever they missed from life, with no definite characteristics of her own save a slight ebullient hysteria about romance." That she was still a virgin probably contributed to that.

Aside from her Irish beauty and unaffected manner, what appealed to Scott about Lois was her passion for literature and dedication to acting. She was totally committed to her work, and like him kept a journal, in one entry expressing her commitment to self-expression, asserting the only emotion that authentically moved her was the desire to create. Although she was still a teenager, and Scott, thirty-one, he made no effort to hide his feelings for Lois, and in the courtyard of the Ambassador Hotel, the two often were observed in deep conversation. "I can't remember a thing he said," she told Arthur Mizener, "but everything was right and everything was beautiful."

Scott seemed intelligent and worldly to Lois, who informed one reporter that, along with Rupert Brooke and Romaine Rolland, he was among her favorite authors. "My worship for him was based on admiration for his talent. I thought he was perfect." She recently had read *The Great Gatsby* and auditioned for a role in Paramount's film of the novel. When rejected for the part, she suggested to studio heads that Scott play leading man in her next picture, about which he seemed enthusiastic. She even arranged for a screen test, but when bosses saw it, they were unimpressed by his acting.

Soon after, Famous Players Studio renewed their interest in having Scott portray Amory, and Zelda play Rosalind, in *This Side of Paradise*. Whether he still believed it could diminish his literary reputation or simply did not want to do it, Scott rejected their offer. That he would perform opposite Lois but not her was unfathomable to Zelda. Although she had reassured Scott during their courtship that she would never become ambitious enough to try anything, she was now held to that promise, while being criticized for not measuring up. The contradiction was deeply unsettling. In a city filled with attractive and talented people, where Scott observed, "The girls who mop the floor are beautiful, the waitresses, the shop ladies. You never want to see any more beauty," he provoked Zelda by comparing them to her and praising their loveliness and ambition.

If Scott's interest in Lois was calculated to wound Zelda, it did. Miserable in Hollywood, she wrote Scottie of how she yearned for France: "The weather here makes me think of Paris in the spring, and I am very homesick for the pink lights and the gay streets." What she couldn't say was how much she missed Edouard. As Scott worked on the Talmadge script, she swam in the hotel pool and learned syncopated steps for the newest dance craze—the Black Bottom—remaining alert for other movie roles. However, when matched against more beautiful and talented actresses, she felt inadequate. "Everybody here is very clever and can nearly all dance and sing and play," she wrote Scottie, "and I feel very stupid. If we ever get out of here I will never go near another moving picture theatre or actor again."

She tried to ignore what was happening between Scott and Lois, knowing it was "tit for tat," equal punishment for like offense, only the matrix was excruciatingly painful. By seducing Lois, nine years Zelda's junior and a trained dancer who had performed in Paris, Scott was creating a charged situation. One evening, after he returned from taking Lois and her mother to dinner, Zelda vented her resentment, only to have him belittle her for doing nothing with her life. The next day, she gathered the clothes she had designed and been sewing and set them aflame in the bathtub. She was expressing that she also created things, and that by ignoring her talents, Scott was destroying them. The message was as lost on him, as it was obscure to her.

Scott also was facing conflict at the studio. Scriptwriters were expected to work eight-hour days, including Saturdays, and most occupied cell-like offices, on average earning $4,000 a year. Scott behaved arrogantly to co-workers, which turned them against him, especially after he stopped coming in, using the excuse that he worked better at home. Also in Hollywood at the time, Sara Haardt defended him, telling writers that Scott basically was a sensitive man who wanted people to like him, and his arrogance only a defense mechanism. At least one colleague remained unconvinced, retorting that, underneath it all, Scott really was a son of a bitch. After placing a "Do Not Disturb" sign on his office in their hotel suite, he told Zelda to amuse herself, but when Carl Van Vechten suggested an afternoon outing with him and Betty Compson, she was not allowed to go. Compson was one of the busiest actresses in Hollywood and about to receive an Academy Award for her performance in *The Barker*. Zelda wanted the star's advice about seeking film roles and also planned to ask Carmel Myers for assistance. But Scott discouraged any interaction and forbade Zelda to leave the hotel without him. She later reproached him for this, writing, "In California, though, you would not allow me to go anywhere without you, you yourself engaged in flagrantly sentimental relations with a child." Conveniently for him, Scott's involvement with Lois preceded California's Statutory Rape Law, Penal Code Section 281-289.6.

Lois and her mother had a home in Beverly Hills, but to be nearer downtown studios and perhaps closer to Scott, they rented an apartment on Mariposa Street alongside the Hotel Ambassador. One of their first social occasions was a tea for Carmel Myers, to which Zelda and Scott were invited. On the pretense of doing a magic trick, Scott gathered everyone's jewelry and headed for the kitchen, where he proceeded to boil the items in a pot of to-mato sauce. That he considered this amusing seems incredulous, and Ronald Coleman became so outraged over his ruined watch, he would have nothing more to do with the couple; neither would Constance Talmadge, who had lost one of her rings.

In March, when Scott submitted his screenplay entitled *Lipstick,* a re-working of his story "Head and Shoulders," studio bosses criticized its weak premise and rejected it outright. Scott's incessant quarreling with Talmadge over the script had not helped matters. The project was assigned to another writer, and Feature Productions refused to pay the remaining $12,500 on Scott's contract. Since his advance already was spent, there was nothing to do but go home. On the train east, Zelda and Scott got into a heated argument when he announced that Lois would be visiting them once they were settled. Infuriated, she opened their compartment window and onto the tracks hurled the engagement gift Scott had given her in Montgomery. Her most precious possession, it was a diamond and platinum watch worth more than $15,000 in today's money.

A telegram from Lois to both of them was delivered on the train the following afternoon. Wired from Los Angeles on March 14 at 11:40 a.m., it read, "Hollywood completely disrupted since you left. Bootleggers gone out of business." When they reached New York, letters addressed only to Scott were waiting. "Darling Scott—I miss you enormously—life is exceedingly dull out here now. Have just been bumming around the studios and seeing people I am not the least interested in. . . . Darling, dumbbell, upsetting ador-able Scott—I keep remembering and forgetting, remembering and thinking you are forgetting—then forgetting again, then a word from you—. You're outrageously upsetting."

Although Lois never acknowledged a sexual relationship with Scott, her son, Tim, thought otherwise.

> When you asked mother about Fitzgerald, you always sensed there was something she was hiding. . . . She would always shy away from mention of a physical encounter with Fitzgerald. . . . She, of course, would not have wanted to admit having an affair with a married man in the Twenties, es-pecially when she built a career on being the perpetual vestal virgin, but the facts are there. By today's standards, it isn't a disgrace. She had premarital sex with a man she loved. . . . I believe Fitzgerald took her virginity. . . . It was the end of her innocence.

Lois's journal entries, which surfaced after her death, especially those dated between May 1927, when she and Scott met, until April 1929, imply a sexual relationship. In several entries, she addresses her comments to an older writer, saying: "Will you like me as a woman? Dear—dear—dear! I love you so and miss you so—Here I am again, feeling that little ache once more. It has grown so sadly faint and gentle. I want to make it strong again. . . . I'm upset tonight—It makes me think of you, dear. You started it all. . . . I'm so happy—feel so grown up, complete."

That Scott and Lois were lovers explains Zelda's hostility toward the young actress. To aggravate matters, Scott used Lois as his heroine in four stories about older men who become infatuated with young women: "Jacob's Ladder," "Magnetism," "The Rough Crossing," and "The Swimmers." In this last story, he portrays his protagonist as a thirty-year-old man who breaks down after finding his wife with another man. At the seaside, he meets a seventeen-year-old girl who teaches him how to swim and reconnects him to life. Lois would also appear in two of Scott's novels, serving as the model for Rosemary Hoyt in *Tender Is the Night* and Cecilia in *The Last Tycoon*.

After arriving in Washington and retrieving Scottie, the Fitzgeralds headed for Wilmington, Delaware, to find somewhere to live. Scott wanted to be near *Saturday Evening Post* offices in Philadelphia, and Maxwell Perkins thought the area would be a good location to work. John Biggs Jr. was practicing law in Wilmington, and his family was well connected to the area. The senior Biggs had served as state attorney general and grandfather, Benjamin Biggs, was Delaware's governor from 1887 to 1891. John Jr. knew the region well and found the Fitzgeralds an elegant home north of Wilmington in Edgemoor. A Greek Revival mansion called Ellerslie, set on the west bank of the Delaware River, it was built in 1843 and owned by founders of the Edgemoor Iron Company, which manufactured steel girders for the Brooklyn Bridge. Family members had occupied it until 1923, when it began being rented as a vacation home. Its imposing structure was flanked by a pillared portico, two and a half stories high over its central portion and three stories over its wing. A circular stairwell plumbed its depth, recalled Zelda, and its rooms were high and filled with the immensity of beautiful proportions. Built on the crest of a hill and shaded by white pines, chestnut trees, and ancient oaks, its lawns sloped down to a rocky beach on the Delaware River. Violets grew among yellow rose bushes, and farther up the riverbank, a red buoy station jutted out from behind the sandbars. The mansion's thirty rooms with high ceilings and broad windows was too much space for them, but a wonderful place in which to entertain. In March 1927, they signed a two-year lease for the modest sum of $150 monthly, and two housekeepers were hired to cook and clean: Ella, who sang gospel songs all day, and Marie, who found everything funny and laughed incessantly.

Scottie was glad to be somewhere she temporarily could call home, and in conjunction with the Calvert School, was tutored at home by Miss

Maddock. "My earliest formal education," she remembered, "took place at Ellerslie . . . where, every week, a packet would arrive from the Calvert School in Baltimore, complete with wonderful stickers to be pasted in workbooks and red and gold stars to be dispensed when a poem was memorized or a dictation properly taken down."

H. L. Mencken welcomed back the Fitzgeralds and suggested they meet. "Thank God you escaped alive! I was full of fears for you. If Los Angeles is not the one authentic rectum of civilization, then I am no anatomist. Anytime you want to go out again and burn it down, count me in. Can you and Zelda come to lunch on Sat. of this week? I'll ask Sara Haardt to come along; she will be eager to hear the latest Montgomery scandals." They had a lot to catch up on, these women who had thrown in their lot with writers.

Six weeks after settling in, their first guests arrived on Saturday, May 21, 1927, the day Charles Lindbergh crossed the Atlantic. At 4:24 that afternoon, 10:24 p.m. Paris time, a toast was proposed to Lindbergh's monoplane, *The Spirit of Saint Louis*, as it slipped from the air and landed at Le Bouget field. The sandy-haired twenty-three-year-old, having used no navigational tools except a compass, crawled out of his cockpit with a toothy smile, and became America's hero. That weekend's guests included Lois Moran and her mother, Gladys; Scott's parents; Ernest Boyd; Theodore Chanler; Helen Hayes and Charlie MacArthur; Ben Hecht; Carl Van Vechten; Catherine Littlefield; and Tommy Hitchcock. Ben and Charlie had been reporters for the *Chicago Examiner* and created a hit Broadway play, *The Front Page*, based on their newspaper experiences. Charlie had come to New York in 1920, leaving behind an estranged wife, and moved into Robert Benchley's apartment on Madison Avenue. Through Robert, Charlie met Dorothy Parker and the two had a tumultuous affair, culminating in her aborted pregnancy and wrist-slashing attempt at suicide. By then, Charlie already was involved with Helen Hayes, whom he would later marry.

John Biggs recalled the weekend's festivities.

> We used to have riotous parties at Ellerslie. We used to do all kinds of crazy things, like playing polo using croquet mallets and balls, on huge Percherons borrowed from the nearby Edgemoor Iron Works. It was a bright moonlit night. I was feeling very cocky, I remember, because my first son had just been born. Lois Moran, to show how strong she was, picked up her stage mother; Charlie MacArthur then picked up the mothers of both Helen Hayes and Lois Moran, and I, to show how strong I was, picked all of them up, but I couldn't hold them and dropped one of them into the river. Catherine Littlefield was doing *jetes,* and her partner dropped her and she nearly broke her neck.

Zelda disliked John and barely concealed her feelings. If she disapproved of someone, Xandra Kalman recalled, she made it quite clear, and there were not many people she liked. Nevertheless, she tried to remain cordial and played gracious hostess at a picnic on the shaded lawn. Photographs from the festivities show Lois in a prim white dress, looking dewy-eyed and innocent, hair pulled back above her head, smiling at the camera or looking adoringly at Scott. As evening approached and she and Scott drew away from others to stroll in the moonlight, Zelda started a nasty argument that left guests only slightly less embarrassed than she would be upon reflection. Later, she apologized to Carl: "From the depths of my polluted soul, I am sorry that the weekend was such a mess. Do forgive my iniquities and my putrid drunkenness. This was such a nice place, and it should have been a good party, if I had not explored my abysses in public." The following day, Lois and her mother took the train back to New York with Charlie MacArthur, who talked about Helen Hayes the entire way.

Although Wilmington was a commercial center, after the excitement of Paris and New York, it felt excruciatingly dull. There were the occasional dinner cruises up the Delaware River on the Wilson Line to Philadelphia, and band concerts at Longwood Gardens where John Philip Sousa's band played, and Sunday brunches at the Hotel du Pont in Wilmington. Decorated by Italian and French craftsmen, the du Pont's elegant rooms were complemented with rich woodwork and terrazzo floors, and off its lobby was the duPont Theatre, a venue for shows heading to Broadway. *Funny Face* arrived that year, starring Fred and Adele Astaire, with music by George and Ira Gershwin. Zelda and Scott drove in to see it and returned singing, "S'wonderful, marvelous, that you should care for me"—almost as if they meant it. Hollywood's first feature-length sound movie, *The Jazz Singer*, starring Al Jolson opened at Wilmington's Media Theater, and the Fitzgeralds attended its premiere. Soon, Zelda was querying people if they considered Al Jolson as important as Jesus. She posed that question to the Murphys, John Biggs, and Ernest Hemingway; Gerald and Sara laughed it off, John was shocked, and Ernest ascribed the comment to madness, entirely missing the point. It was her original way of making an observation about celebrity.

Scott wanted his friends to see Ellerslie, and it quickly became a literary Mecca, where any Friday afternoon, a taxi might deposit Thornton Wilder, John Marquand, Carl Van Vechten, Ring Lardner, or Edmund Wilson. Nothing was ever organized, and when Scott held a polo match for his Princeton friends, and John Peale Bishop and Edmund Wilson arrived to join Ludlow Fowler and Townsend Martin, they were alarmed by the delirium that had overtaken guests. On the front lawn, Charlie MacArthur was using dinner plates for target practice and ruining the flower beds by riding plow horses over them. When John Dos Passos arrived late to one party, he found nothing to eat: "Those delirious parties of theirs; one dreaded going. Dinner was never served. Oh, a complete mess. I remember going into Wilmington; they lived some miles out, trying to find a sandwich." Although food was scarce, alcohol was in abundance and John Biggs recognized Scott was in trouble. "His drinking and frustration while at Ellerslie worried me, and one day we had a long, serious talk. I told him that if he kept it up, he was going to get into serious trouble. . . . I asked him to please try and tell me why he had to drink so heavily, often pure gin. His answer encapsulated the problem: 'I drink because I'm the top of the "second rates,"' he told me."

Although Scott continued seeing Lois in New York, he prohibited Zelda from entertaining male guests while he was away. The New York attorney, Richard Knight, who attended their party for French diplomat Paul Morand, especially was off-limits. Richard was unpredictable; one never knew what he would do or say. He enjoyed shocking people, like the time he arrived at a party announcing he had just come from identifying his brother at the morgue. Zelda and he often spoke on the phone, even after Scott insisted they stop. She confided in him and one weekend, when Scott was in New York with Lois, she appeared at Richard's apartment in a black lace dress and, as she put it, "spent one lost afternoon with him. They had cocktails and afterwards, she sat a long time on the stairway, oblivious with a kind of happy desperation."

Scott's affair with Lois and dismissive attitude quickened Zelda's resolve to achieve something independently. Progressively separated from Scott's world, she felt life moving over her in a vast black shadow and compared herself to those little fish swimming about under a shark, indelicately feeding on its offal, swallowing what it drops with relish.

On a visit to Ellerslie that fall, Amy Thomas, married to John Biggs's brother, noticed Zelda had placed by her dressing table gold and silver stars leading to the ceiling, ten feet high like a milky way. They symbolized her determination to excel, and when news arrived of Isadora Duncan's accidental death, the direction presented itself. Zelda had always considered Isadora a role model and became obsessed with the notion that she might replace her as America's premier dancer. The goal was not as fanciful as might first appear. In her youth, Zelda had received accolades for dancing and now was determined to prove people right. Eleanor Boardman, who had met the Fitzgeralds in California, associated her ballet aspirations with Lois, believing Zelda developed an obsession about becoming a ballet dancer because she believed Scott was in love with the actress who had danced in Paris. While not entirely true, Scott's admiration for the young star's ambition certainly accelerated Zelda's determination to succeed. It had taken time, but she now was convinced that only by establishing a life apart from Scott's would she find contentment and some basis upon which to build compatibility.

After inquiring about ballet teachers, she selected Catherine Littlefield, who trained with Lubov Egorova in Paris. Five years younger than Zelda, she had performed on Broadway with the Ziegfeld Follies at fifteen and was selected for Florenz Ziegfeld's 1921 production of *Sally*. Littlefield had a fresh approach, had high technical standards, and used classical ballet techniques to generate unhampered expression. She and her two siblings had grown up in the world of dance. Her mother, Caroline, was ballet director of the Philadelphia Opera Company and operated the Littlefield School of Ballet off Rittenhouse Square in Philadelphia where Catherine gave lessons.

When Sara Haardt interviewed her friend for an article she was writing on wives of famous authors, Zelda shared her ambitious goals. "Zelda Fitzgerald is studying ballet dancing with an absorption and seriousness that is very apt to make it her career. All of her life she has danced and adored dancing. As a child in Montgomery she took lessons and danced the sole parts at all the closing balls." And while Zelda acknowledged that dancing required the resilience of youth, she declared she felt younger now than when she was sixteen or any other age.

Although parties continued at Ellerslie, Zelda removed herself from the frenzy and wrote Carl Van Vechten on October 10, "I joined the Philadelphia Opera Ballet . . . and everybody has been so drunk in this country lately, that I am just finding enough chaos to pursue my own ends in, undisturbed again." To pay for lessons, she wrote stories about debutantes and young married couples for *College Humor* but was told they had to be published under both her name and Scott's. Although written entirely by her, five appeared "by F. Scott and Zelda Fitzgerald," and the sixth, "A Millionaire's Girl," was published in the *Saturday Evening Post* under Scott's name alone. Ober felt uncomfortable over this, writing Scott, "I really felt a little guilty about dropping Zelda's name from that story, but I think she understands that, using the two names would have tied the story up with the *College Humor* series, and might have gotten us into trouble." Practicality outweighed fairness, and understanding her pieces would not command high fees without Scott's reputation, she allowed her work to be published in this way.

Several times a week, she commuted to Philadelphia for lessons, afterward practicing for hours in the living room that been fitted with a ballet bar and now contained an enormous mirror that once hung in a brothel. Anna Biggs remembered when Zelda had discovered it in an antique store. "One of the objects that caught her fancy was a gigantic gilt mirror, nineteenth century, I think. It was surrounded by scrollwork and cherubs and wreaths in the best heavily decorated style. She loved it. At Ellerslie, when I next saw it, it was hung in the front room beside her Victrola. She had run a ballet bar in front of it and practiced there all day." Anna's husband, John, recalled how Zelda would "start at six or seven o'clock in the morning, and she had one tune she used to play constantly, *The Parade of the Wooden Soldiers*. She would keep it up until ten o'clock at night, when she would drop from sheer exhaustion." Along with the repetitious music were resonating sounds from *ballonnes, jetés,* and *pas de basque,* and endless thumping on a wooden floor—*schstay, schstay; brise, brise.* It grew so distracting that Scott moved his desk from the ground floor library to an upstairs room. Not that he took her efforts seriously. From the start he considered her dancing amateurish and resented her trips into Philadelphia, which he considered a complete disregard for the household.

When Rosalind and Newman visited in February 1928, they recognized tension in the household and an agitation in Zelda not there before. One evening at dinner, after Scott began arguing and knocked over some chairs, he slapped Zelda hard enough to cause a nosebleed. Although Newman tried calming everyone down, Rosalind insisted her sister leave. She had previously witnessed Scott growing confrontational when drunk and knew Zelda was afraid of him in that state. By now, seven-year-old Scottie was accustomed to such outbursts: "I knew there was only one way for me to survive my parents' tragedy, and that was for me to ignore it."

Maxwell Perkins arrived the following week to find both in terrible shape. Scott was drinking continuously and unable to work, and Zelda either practicing routines or in bed. To flee Delaware seemed the only solution, an escape to somewhere more promising than where they were. She wrote Carl in March that they were sailing for Europe. "We want to go in May because Wilmington has turned out to be the black hole of Calcutta. . . . I want to feel a sense of intrigue which is only in Paris." If, by intrigue, she was recalling Edouard, what she didn't know was that he was celebrating his marriage to Lucienne Gruss-Gallieni. That April, with ten months remaining on their lease, the Fitzgeralds closed up Elleslie and departed for France aboard the SS *Paris*. After disembarking at Le Harve, they continued to Paris by train and rented another expensive but dismal apartment on the corner of rue Bonaparte near the Luxembourg Gardens.

Now there were so many foreigners flooding Montparnasse bars, its bohemian atmosphere was gone. Duff Twysden was still there, but when her divorce from Lord Twysden finalized that October, she married the American artist Clinton King, nine years her junior, and put her partying years to rest. The change of scene did little to reduce tensions in the Fitzgeralds' household, and when Robert Penn Warren visited, he witnessed their quarreling laced with obscenities. Richard Knight was a continual source of conflict with repeated arguments over his visits to Paris that spring and fall. Sara Mayfield was back at the Sorbonne, and Zelda confided over lunch that her marriage was a sham. "Scott and I had a row last week, and I haven't spoken to him since. . . . When we meet in the hall, we walk around each other like a pair of stiff-legged terriers spoiling for a fight." Scott summarized the deteriorating situation in his ledger as "First trip to jail, and dive in Lido" then "second trip to jail . . . being carried home from the Ritz . . . drinking and general unpleasantness."

Zelda returned to Lubov's studio, taking group classes each morning and private sessions every afternoon. She was the oldest student and in competition with younger and more agile dancers. In *Save Me the Waltz*, she describes some of those ballerinas as Marguerite dressed in white, and Fania in rubber undergarments, and Anise and Anna, who lived with wealthy men and wore velvet tunics, and Ceza in scarlet, who people surmised was a Jew, and three almost identical Russian Tanyas. What might have daunted others, Zelda took in stride, although Scott continually emphasized that she was competing with dancers who had trained their whole lives. "There's no use killing yourself," David tells Alabama in Zelda's novel. "I hope you realize that the biggest difference in the world is between the amateur and the professional in the arts." True, but sometimes that demarcation is shockingly thin.

To keep up with others, Zelda spent long hours daily in concentrated practice, retiring early to prepare for the next lesson, eating practically nothing to achieve the emaciated look Lubov demanded. Never would Scott have predicted her ferocious dedication and the strain soon showed. When Sara met her at Prunier's, although dressed fashionably, Zelda appeared haggard and unkempt, her hair straggly and the sparkle gone from her eyes. Self-conscious about her appearance, she lamented, "I'm twenty-eight years old and I've already got sweetbreads under my eyes and calipers around my mouth. . . . All I do is dance and sweat—and drink to keep from getting dehydrated." Along with water she was talking about alcohol, which she consumed to boost energy, but it was making her feel edgy, and it was difficult for her to engage even in ordinary conversations.

Scott also was drinking to get through each day, but increasing amounts were necessary to make him feel good, and a few drinks had the opposite effect. Earlier in the decade, he recalled a softness about intoxication and the gloss it gave, but the opposite was now true, and Zelda told Mayfield, "Two drinks puts him in a manic state, absolutely manic—he wants to fight everybody, including me." If she complained he consumed more, and when she ignored things they simply persisted. In Great Neck, Scott had considered Lardner his alcoholic, but now he had become Ernest's. "Am going on the water wagon," he wrote Maxwell Perkins, "but don't tell Ernest, because he has long convinced himself, that I am an incurable alcoholic. . . . I am his alcoholic, just like Ring is mine, and do not want to disillusion him." Concerned over Scott's downturn, the Murphys tried to help, and with that in mind, Gerald reconciled with Scott in April 1928, writing of how fond they were of them both and that arguments were a natural part of life.

With five months remaining on their Ellerslie lease, the Fitzgeralds returned there on October 1, 1928, to put things in order, traveling aboard the SS *Carmania* with Scottie's new French nanny and Philippe, a taxi driver and boxer Scott had met at the rue de Vaugirard gym. Hired as a general handyman, chauffeur, and drinking companion, Philippe always seemed startled, as Zelda recalled, perhaps in the uncertainty of his new role. Nobody had bothered to check if Philippe had a valid passport, so upon docking in Manhattan, the Fitzgeralds spent several days addressing that problem with immigration before continuing on to Wilmington.

Three weeks later, the Murphys also arrived in New York, headed for Hollywood where Gerald had been hired as music consultant on King Vidor's production of *Hallelujah*. Scott had mentioned Gerald to King the previous year, and King later visited the couple at Villa America where the family performed a medley of Negro spirituals and plantation songs. With money from a generous contract, the Murphys rented a bungalow in Beverly Hills, where their children roller skated on the driveway, learned to ride horses in the countryside, and were driven to parties and movie studios by the black chauffeur. King's wife, Eleanor Boardman, was starring in a war film, and invited the children to the set, where they watched her admirably expire in a death scene. As a preventative measure, a California doctor recommended that the three children undergo tonsillectomies, so with the promise of ice cream, Honoria, Baoth, and Patrick spent an overnight at the hospital and were picked up the next day by the chauffeur, who carried each into the house.

At Ellerslie, Zelda settled back into her dance routine and resumed lessons in Philadelphia, this time with Alexandre Gavrilov, a Nijinsky protégé who performed with the Ballet Moderne in New York City. Like Lubov Egorova, he had trained at the Mariinsky School in St. Petersburg and danced with the Imperial Ballet, later joining Diaghilev's Ballets Russes, where he understudied for Nijinsky and was introduced to new artistic expressions under the influence of Fokine. Zelda approached her lessons with a religious fervor, dressing entirely in white for classes and training with a feverish intensity that excited the Russian dancer. One afternoon, after taking her to lunch at Reuben's, Alexandre brought her back to the apartment he shared with his mistress on Chestnut Street. It was an icy day and she recalled the strange tension between them. "There was nothing in the commercial flat except the white spitz of his mistress and a beautiful collection of Leon Bakst.

It was a cold afternoon. He asked me if I wanted him to kill me and said I would cry and left me there. I ran to my lesson through the cold streets." Alexandre spoke French and, rather than murder, probably was referring to the French euphemism for orgasm, *la petite mort*—the small death.

In his role of chauffeur, Philippe met guests at the Wilmington train station on Friday afternoons and returned them on Sunday. Aside from this, he spent most of his time drinking with Scott, winding up in bar brawls, and getting arrested. John Biggs regularly had to bail them out. Scott now felt good only when belting one down and had symptoms of an advanced alcoholic— little appetite, cold sweats, and trouble sleeping. After a night of boozing, morning jitters often were so bad he needed a drink just to get going.

On November 17, Ernest and Pauline Hemingway met the Fitzgeralds at Princeton's Palmer stadium for the Yale–Princeton football game. They had married the previous May in Paris at the fashionable L'eglise Saint-Honore-d'Eylau church in Place Victor Hugo. To commemorate her prize catch, Pauline ordered gold-embossed wedding announcements from Cartier and wore a dress designed for her by Lanvin. On a more subdued scale, Ernest chose Edouard's birthplace of Le Grau du Roi for their honeymoon, but celebrating got curtailed after the accident-prone Ernest cut his foot on rocks while swimming and they were forced back to Paris, where he rested in bed to let his festering wound heal. He would use Le Grau du Roi as the setting for his novel *The Garden of Eden*, in which deeply rooted tensions in a couple's marriage rise to the surface. After Princeton trounced Yale 10–2, Ernest and Pauline boarded the train with the Fitzgeralds for Philadelphia's Thirtieth Street Station, where Philippe picked them up in Scott's Buick. As they drove to Ellerslie, Ernest noticed the engine was overheating. When he questioned Philippe over that, the chauffer explained that Scott would not allow oil to be put in the car. The situation quickly irritated Scott, who chastised Philippe to quit jabbering about oil, convinced the American car did not regularly require a dose of lubricant.

After Scott uncorked too many wine bottles and baited the maid, demanding she tell Ernest what a good piece of pussy she was, Pauline hastened the couple's departure the next morning. Three weeks later, Scott unexpectedly saw Ernest again. He had been in New York to meet his son, Bumby, who had come from France to spend Christmas, and was on the train back to Florida, when he received a telegram saying his father had shot himself. With only forty dollars on him, Ernest wired Maxwell Perkins for money to catch the night train to Chicago but received no reply. He then telegrammed Scott, who brought cash to Philadelphia's Thirtieth Street Station. Upon reaching Key West, Ernest wrote Max about his father's suicide and said he was feeling like hell; twenty years later, he would end his life in the same way.

That Christmas, Zelda surprised Scottie with a magnificent dollhouse she had designed and built, papering and painting all the rooms and then decorating it with exquisite pieces of furniture. They spent all morning playing with it, but the afternoon got ruined when some of Scott's drinking buddies intruded on their holiday dinner. By now, Scottie was accustomed to such interruptions and, self-preservation being the strongest of human instincts, continued to ignore what was swirling around her.

When their lease finally expired in March 1929, they headed for Italy aboard the *Conte Biancamano*. They realized people took troubles with them and did not think locale change could cure spiritual ills. But, Zelda felt there were worse things to live with than one's mistakes and hoped a new place might offer a different evaluation. After arriving in Genova, Philippe said his farewells and the couple, along with Scottie and her governess, continued to Nice, which was experiencing a mistral. The windy weather kept them indoors much of the time, so while Scott played baccarat and chemin de fer at the casino, Zelda searched for a Russian dance teacher. Her address book lists three: Ourousoff at 16 Avenue Shakespeare, Carpova at 7 bis Avenue des Orangers, and Nevelskaya, who gave lessons in the Hotel Polonia, upon whom she settled.

In July they left for Cannes where they rented Villa Fleurdes Bois in Cannes, and Zelda met the Scottish dancer Margaret Morris, who ran a summer dance school in Juan-les-Pins with her student, Helene Vanel, and Scottish gymnast Lois Hutto. Scott began frequenting Café des Alles, where besides drinking he would order their specialty, mushroom soup. The Murphys were back at Villa America after a disappointing experience in Hollywood. Irving Thalberg continually had interfered with King's production, asserting authority over every aspect of production. After hearing the sound track, he thought the music sounded too depressing and added two Irving Berlin songs to liven things up. Appalled by this intervention, Gerald quit. Now it was irrelevant, since he and Sara had more important things to consider. Their youngest son, Patrick, had become ill that May, initially diagnosed with an intestinal virus. When it didn't improve, doctors thought he might have bronchitis, but after the Murphys brought him to a specialist in Paris, the alarming diagnosis was tuberculosis. To catch TB requires continual daily contact for several hours with someone who has an active infection, since tubercular bacteria spreads through the air in close quarters, usually when somebody sneezes or coughs. Gerald and Sara traced Patrick's infection to their Hollywood chauffeur, who had a persistent cough and was in daily proximity to the children. They were particularly vulnerable because of their tonsillectomies, but Patrick, the most delicate of the three, was the only one infected. Scott was distraught over the boy's situation and remorseful about having brought Gerald to King's attention.

Zelda's summer was filled with creative bursts of energy followed by bouts of intense fatigue. Nevelskaya gave her minor roles to perform with the Nice Opera chorus, and Zelda choreographed a ballet called *Evolution* for which she also designed the scenery and costumes. It was an allegory of her dance aspirations and audiences enthusiastically responded. Lubov Egorova was so impressed by Zelda's progress that she contacted her colleague, Julie Sedova, director of the San Carlo Opera Ballet Company in Naples to say Zelda was ready to perform. Lubov and Julie both had trained at the Mariinsky Ballet Theatre in St. Petersburg, where Sedova performed alongside Pavlova in *Chopiniana* and danced with Nijinsky in his first public appearance in *La Source*. On her strong recommendation, Sedova invited Zelda to join the Italian company and offered her a solo role in *Aida*. Her efforts had paid off. Sedova emphasized how important the opportunity was and assured Zelda that if she remained the entire season, she would be given other roles and an adequate salary. She stressed that living costs in Naples were inexpensive: "La vie de Naples n'est past trés chere et on peutavoir le pension complet a 35 lires par personne par jour." (Life in Naples is not very expensive, and one can have room and board for 35 lire per person, per day.) Zelda delayed responding until Sedova sent a second handwritten offer, which arrived on September 29, 1929. She pleaded with Zelda to accept, explaining that Theatro di San Carlo was a magnificent performing space: "Notre theatre est magnifique et il vous seraittres utile de danser sur la scene." (Our theater is magnificent, and you will find it valuable to dance there.) Europe's oldest, continuously active opera house, Theatro di San Carlo was founded in 1727 by King Charles VII of Naples, and its opulent, six-tiered arena could seat a thousand. Sedova's company was part of the opera with dancers providing incidental pieces for operatic performances, but also staged independent ballets. It had an excellent reputation, because Sedova was not only a capable director, but a strong dancer herself.

This was Zelda's big chance to become a professional ballerina. Along with *Aida*, Sedova was offering additional roles to provide valuable stage experience. Given Zelda's efforts to warrant such an offer, why did she delay responding and ultimately turn Sedova down? Two primary reasons: mistakenly, she considered the San Carlo Opera inferior to companies in London and Paris, and believed that performing with such a venue, where ballets often were short performances presented as interludes, would mean relinquishing more ambitious goals. She also felt insecure about moving to Naples. With no practical life experience, and having never lived on her own, she could not envision going alone. And it would be solo, because Scott made it clear that he was not following her. Nor was he giving her permission to go. Rosalind recalled her sister's ambivalence and Scott's disapproval. "I have always felt that this frantic effort on Zelda's part, towards a professional career in the thing she did best, was motivated by the uncertainty of their situation at this time, perhaps also by unhappiness, which she refused to admit, but which nevertheless I thought I saw beneath an always brave front, and by her desire to put herself on her own. She told me that she received an offer from one of the Italian opera companies as a premiere ballerina, but that Scott would not allow her to accept it." Zelda's determination to succeed stemmed from her conviction that only in proving herself would she gain the confidence that came with accomplishment. But accepting Sedova's offer required a reversal of behavior followed since childhood, and relinquishing comforts she had come to expect. It also meant incurring Scott's disapproval, leaving Scottie in his custody, and in all likelihood, divorce. Paralyzed by fear, she agonized over whether she was adequately trained and whether she could live on a meager salary without Scott's backing.

When she rejected the Naples offer, Zelda knew she was jeopardizing future prospects but believed there would be other opportunities. Her optimism became remorse when she heard of Diaghilev's death in Venice. Any dreams of dancing with his company now were gone. "Diaghilev died," she wrote, "the stuff of the great movement of the Ballets Russes lay rotting in a French law court. . . . What's the use?" Her anguish over the dismantling of Diaghilev's ballet corps and ambivalence over rejecting Sedova's offer propelled Zelda into a deep depression.

Although Scott purchased a month's pass to the casino in Juan-les-Pins, she had no interest in going, and when they were invited to parties she made excuses. "We went (to) sophisticated places with charming people, but I was grubby and didn't care." Things suddenly appeared odd to her with everything out of proportion. One evening when they joined the Murphys to watch a film about underwater life, Zelda became hysterical. "There were all sorts and varieties of strange fish swimming by the camera," recalled Gerald. "Quite nonchalantly, an octopus using his tentacles to propel himself, moved diagonally across the screen (and) Zelda, who had been sitting on my right, shrieked and threw herself all the way across my lap, on to my left shoulder, and, burying her head against my neck and chest, screamed, 'What is it? What is it?' Now, we had all seen it and it moved very slowly—it was perfectly obvious that it was an octopus—but it nevertheless frightened her to death." Sara cautioned Scott not to ignore her worsening condition, and on the return trip to Paris that October he was forced to confront it. As he drove along treacherous roads through Pont du Gard and the château country, Zelda grabbed the steering wheel from his hand and shouting, "God's will," attempted to force the vehicle off the cliff. After grabbing the wheel back, he brought the car to a halt at the dropoff. Scottie was stunned in the backseat, and the three sat in shock. Zelda had no explanation for why she had done it, but Scott was sure she had wanted to kill them all.

When they finally got back to Paris, they rented an apartment on rue Pergolese and Zelda tried to repair her relationship with Lubov, who felt she had thrown away an important opportunity. Treated with an unfamiliar coolness by her teacher, she was determined to turn things around, and became even more dedicated to her lessons. "I worked constantly and was terribly superstitious and moody about my work, full of presentiments. I lived in a quiet, ghostly, hyper-sensitized world of my own." What free time she allowed herself, she spent with her daughter, avoiding Scott, who ridiculed her dancing as a neurotic obsession. "I found myself saying hateful things to her. I couldn't stop. I was at war with myself," he wrote. "We quarreled, poked in the ashes of the past, and flung words that raised a wall of indifference between us. We became hostile strangers and went our separate ways while living a hell under the same roof."

To camouflage a progressively deteriorating situation, Scott followed up on a suggestion the Murphys had made earlier: "We might all four take that Compagnie General trip to Tunisia. Just three weeks. Very cheap. High powered cars with Arab chauffeurs meet you at the boat, and you course through the country, staying as long as you want in each town. More like being a guest than a tourist." Scott bought two tickets for a Compagnie Transatlantique tour of Algeria, and on February 7, 1930, their ship sailed from Port-Vendres near the Spanish border with scheduled stops in Biskra, Constantine, and Algiers. Given Zelda had been ill with fever and bronchitis for two weeks prior and was in no condition to travel, it was an unwise decision. She already had missed several ballet lessons and could not put Lubov from her mind. No sooner had they arrived in Algiers than she begged to return home. Photographs of the trip show her on the verge of collapse, awkwardly perched on a camel in Biskra and appearing mute and distressed at the Gorge of Constantine. She counted the days until they reboarded the ship, but the return voyage was turbulent and she stayed in bed the entire time.

Convinced she had barely escaped disaster, Zelda resumed lessons with heightened fervor, but as Easter approached she feared danger at every turn. She wanted to buy Scottie a present but was afraid to go out alone and needed the housekeeper to accompany her. For days, she went without sleeping or eating, and when she did rest, disturbing dreams woke her, leaving her bewildered the following day. She began hearing threatening voices and during class jumped higher to quiet them, but would have terrible headaches the next day and feel sick. She found it difficult to function in any normal way, and Rosalind and Newman came from Brussels to monitor the worsening situation. She had long condemned Scott for putting her sister in an intolerable living situation and told him, "I would almost rather she die now, than escape only to go back to the mad world you and she have created for yourself." Xandra and Oscar Kalman visited after Easter, and during a luncheon for them at their apartment, Zelda became so anxious over being late for class that midway through the meal announced she was leaving. Oscar recognized something was terribly wrong and accompanied her, but when their cab got delayed in traffic, Zelda changed into her dancing clothes and jumped out, running between cars toward the studio. She arrived in such an agitated condition that Lubov contacted Scott to take her home. It was clear she needed to be evaluated and quickly.

· 7 ·

Locked Away

On April 23, 1929, Scott took Zelda to Le Sanitarium de la Malmaison, a private hospital ten kilometers outside Paris at Rueil that occupied a nineteenth-century mansion in which Empress Josephine Bonaparte had lived, and now was a sanitarium specializing in nervous disorders. Five years earlier, T. S. Eliot's first wife, Vivienne Haigh-Wood, also had arrived there exhibiting erratic behavior. One of the "river girls" who punted on the Cherwell to meet Oxford boys, Vivienne encountered T. S. in March of 1915 and married him three months later. She always suffered from "nerve storms," as she called them, which worsened after marriage, and besides being confined to the same hospital, shared some other commonalities with Zelda. Also an excellent swimmer, she entered the dance world late, studying with Isadora Duncan's older brother, Raymond, and was foisted by her husband onto another man, T. S.'s Harvard professor, Bertrand Russell.

Like Vivienne, Zelda appeared in a highly agitated state, not having slept for days. She paced the room and insisted that Scott was involved in a sexual relationship with Ernest Hemingway. Concerned that the attending physician, Dr. Claude, might believe her, Scott insisted that Zelda was delusional and nervous disorders were endemic in her family. To support this, he explained that her father, along with two of her sisters, had experienced breakdowns, and another suffered from a nervous affliction of the neck. Her maternal grandmother had committed suicide, as had her mother's sister. The family was certifiably crazy; it was all quite evident. In his admission report, Professor Claude diagnosed her symptoms as a case of nervous exhaustion: "It is a question of a *petite anxieuse*, worn out by her work in a milieu of professional dancers. Violent reactions, several suicide attempts never pushed to the limit." After being kept under observation for ten days, she discharged herself, explaining to Scott, "I went of my own free will. . . . You also know that I left (with the consent of Professor Claude) knowing that I was not entirely well, because I could see no use in jumping out of the frying pan into the fire." To put herself under control of the nerve doctors seemed a dangerous proposition.

When Zelda returned to their Paris apartment she found it in disarray, with Scott celebrating the impending marriage of Ludlow Fowler's brother, Thomas, to Virginia Megeur. Many of his Princeton classmates had arrived for the festivities, and days leading to the May 10 nuptials were occupied with bachelor dinners, receptions, and parties. Ludlow had been Scott's model for *The Rich Boy* and again would be portrayed in a story about these wedding festivities called "The Bridal Party" published that August by the *Saturday Evening Post*. The commotion at home only aggravated Zelda's fragile state, and after experiencing a week of terrifying nightmares, she attempted suicide with an overdose of barbiturates. It was the second time she had tried to end her life. On May 22, Scott brought her to Valmont Clinic in Glion, Switzerland, outside Montreux, known for treating gastrointestinal problems but familiar with the correlation of physical ailments to nervous conditions. She told doctors she was unable to eat or sleep, became hysterical without warning, and heard menacing voices, in itself not symptomatic of mental disease, but something that caught their attention. Placed under observation, she was sedated with Garderal and given Medinale to sleep. After several meetings, the attending physician, Dr. H. A. Trutman, wrote a detailed report describing her symptoms and evaluating their causes.

Two sisters have nervous break-downs, a third suffers from a nervous affliction of the neck. At twenty-four in Europe, has a near peritonitis caused by inflammation of the right ovary and is practically disabled for a year. The matter is cleared up by an operation for appendix. (Dr. Gross and Dr. Martell) Dr. Martell finds appendix in bad shape but ovary fundamentally healthy. Morphine taken for two weeks during peritonitis attack.

Becomes depressed in Hollywood by the fact that younger girls than herself have attained a position of their own, and a relative importance. At twenty-seven takes up an old ambition, ballet dancing—her first really serious effort. Three hours a day, six days a week. Stops drinking. Till the time of taking up ballet work, she has been a heavy but intermittent drinker, and inclined to hysteria when drunk. Violent hysteria—occasionally even suicidal, occurred perhaps four to seven times a year, when she could only be calmed by a minimum dose of morphine. Capacity to hold liquor diminishing; while dancing, drinks half a pint of wine at meals and either an aperitif or a nightcap. During times of enforced idleness on shipboard, it becomes more and more obvious—that all capacity to use liquor has departed. Hysteria almost sure after two days of, what would usually be considered the most moderate drink. Never in danger of dipsomania, because after two days, she collapses. Understands this herself, and avoids alcohol except when circumstances force it on her.

Previously a heavy smoker, but has reduced consumption to a minimum. Drinks 4–5 cups of coffee a day. Last Autumn made enormous progress. Two substantial offers to appear as ballet dancer, La Scala in Naples and as premiere dancer at Follies Bergeres. Writing only with a fixed obsession to pay, quite unnecessarily, for her dancing lessons herself and make her own career. Writing has never been a pleasure because one eye is practically blind and the other strained and she pays for it in agonizing headaches. Once a great reader, has given up reading.

Sequence of symptoms: no appetite, depression, quarrelsome, rude to old friends in curious ways, quarrels with Egorova and quits school, then on Egorova's urgent request returns to school, drinks heavily and collapses, develops a curious horror of people—this produces a violent timidity in her, a horror and shrinking away from people, becomes silent with friends, pale and shaken in stores, becomes abnormally quiet with sudden outbursts of despair, hums to herself all the time, wants to be alone, music her only pleasure. Resents African trip husband forces on her; hysteria lasting 6 days, hears voices, imagines people are criticizing her and makes scenes about it, unable to face shopkeepers, servants etc., seems to live in some horrible, subconscious dream, more real to her than the real world, sleeps a good deal, honestly wants to die, hysteria breaks out without warning, can't let Scott out of her sight, complete lack of control—picking at fingers.

After being observed for two weeks, no neurological or organic diseases were discovered, but Trutman felt an expert opinion was necessary. He contacted Dr. Oscar Forel, head of Prangins Clinic near Nyon on Lake Geneva and a member of the medical faculty at the University of Geneva. His father, Auguste Forel, had directed Burgholzli, the psychiatric hospital of the University of Zurich, and was a pioneer in the field of psychiatry. The specialty had only been formalized in the 1890s and was still poorly defined, in part because overlapping symptoms made emotional disorders difficult to diagnose.

The Swiss psychiatrist Emil Kraepelin advanced knowledge in the specialty by clarifying the general term *hysteria* in his authoritative textbook published in 1907, and while admitting its cause was still unknown, defined it as a neurosis linked with nervous exhaustion. He theorized that women were predisposed to hysteria because they experienced greater emotional fluctuations, were more susceptible to sentiment, and had weaker powers of resistance. Kraepelin identified twenty separate psychoses in his textbook, the most common being manic depression and dementia praecox, then divided them into four classifications: hebephrenic schizophrenia, in which patients experience language disorders and smile inappropriately or make grotesque gestures; catatonic, in which a patient is mute and rigid; simple schizoid, in which the patient shows lack of interest or drive; and paranoiac, characterized by delusions. Although he believed mental disease ran in families and a predisposition to it was inherited, he thought life crises or persistent negative situations were a major determinant. People susceptible to stress were at greater risk and more easily could become unstable. While his new classifications more precisely defined symptoms, they only made it easier for doctors to position indicators within a prevailing diagnosis. What had been labeled hysteria was now called schizophrenia as women became pathologized in a new way.

Although auditory hallucinations sometimes are indicative of schizophrenia, hearing voices is not always symptomatic of that disease, and Dr. Forel was uncertain if that was Zelda's condition. Of one thing he was sure: a simple rest cure would not be sufficient. He agreed to accept her as a patient, and though she initially consented, after quarreling with Scott in Lausanne, Zelda changed her mind. Exasperated over what to do, Scott summoned her brother-in-law from Brussels. A pragmatic man, Newman considered all options before making a decision and came as a representative of the Sayre family. With her best interests at heart, he believed she would be safer in Montgomery surrounded by comfort of family and friends. However, doctors were against her traveling, having warned Scott that, even with a full-time nurse, making the journey to America would be risky. Although Prangins had only been open a year, it was considered among the most advanced psychiatric clinics in Europe, so Newman assumed she would be in good hands. Had he known of alternatives, he might have decided differently. The Quakers, for example, were promoting gentle care sanitariums and building retreats around the British countryside, where they treated mental patients with consideration and compassion. Although they didn't know what caused madness, they reasoned that the afflicted needed to be treated with simple kindness. In such an environment or under the watch of family and friends, Zelda's distress might slowly have dissipated over time without intervention.

But that was not the case, and whatever Newman said to her that afternoon convinced Zelda to become Forel's patient, and the three left Valmont for Prangins early on June 5, arriving late in the day. Disheartened and exhausted, she considered that drive the end of life as she had known it. When Scott and Newman drove off, she was taken to her room and became so frightened she could hardly breathe. Her symptoms only worsened after she was incarcerated with others in emotional distress, and rather than being treated caringly, she was manhandled by attendants and forcibly restrained.

Les Rives de Prangins, more commonly referred to as Prangins, was situated by a lake in a hundred-acre park between Geneva and Lausanne. The main building had once been the château of another Bonaparte, Joseph, elder brother of Napoleon. The grounds contained tennis courts, a riding stable, golf course, and bathing beach, and its exorbitant fees reflected those amenities. Annual charges were 70,561 Swiss francs or $13,000, which in today's money would amount to approximately $174,000.

Despite its services and facilities, Prangins was a dangerous place for Zelda. Most doctors and nurses spoke little English, and even those fluent had difficulty understanding her Southern accent and manner of speaking. Fearful of anyone's help, she believed harm would come if she revealed anything, so kept to herself and schemed how to escape. During the first month, she made several attempts. Once, out walking with a nurse, she managed to break away, and only with the assistance of several attendants, was apprehended and dragged back to the clinic. Until she became compliant, she was placed in solitary confinement at Eglantine, the building used for disruptive patients. Restraint and isolation were standard procedures for reducing agitation and injury, and Dr. Forel had precise directives for dealing with unruly patients. Two or three large orderlies would grab the person, cover her hands with leather mitts to avoid being scratched, and forcibly carry her into a darkened room, where she would be straitjacketed and confined by leather straps, then given bromides and morphine. Without seclusion rooms and restraints, most sanitariums would have found it impossible to operate a program for severely symptomatic patients, and Prangins was prepared for such incidents. If Zelda needed taming, Eglantine would provide the way.

Like most doctors of his generation, Forel wielded complete autonomy over patients and believed authority immediately needed to be established. He used an authoritarian approach that was punctuated by his dictatorial way of speaking English with a heavy German accent. From a markedly different culture, he considered Zelda's challenges to authority intolerable. Discipline was used when gentleness failed, and whenever she misbehaved, privileges were taken away and she was threatened with solitary. Obedience rebuffed in Montgomery was extracted here. Compared to many of his contemporaries, Forel was considered a modernist and highly respected in psychiatric circles. He had coauthored two books that pioneered the reform of asylums and transformed Switzerland's mental health system. His publications also revolutionized the training of nursing personnel, altering their role from custodians to active members of the health care team. Besides supervising patients, their mandate was to observe them carefully and report back to doctors. Continuously watched, Zelda quickly learned to conceal her feelings and tell doctors only what they wanted to hear. She never cried when anyone could see her, since weeping was reported as a sign of depression, and saved tears for her pillow. Bereft of everything meaningful and outraged over her confinement, she wrote Scott, "You must try to understand how dreary and drastic is my present position . . . alone in a strange part of Switzerland with hardly a soul to speak English with. . . . For a month and two weeks, I have been three times outside my room, and for five months I have lived with my sole desire that of death."

Before neuroleptic drugs were developed, sedatives were the primary way of treating psychiatric disorders, and most patients at Prangins regularly were given synthesized derivatives of barbiturates. Never regarded as therapeutic, and despite limited effectiveness and dangerous side effects, they served as medical restraints. Bromides and opium were prescribed to control behavior and reestablish calm, but at varying dosages could be used for insomnia and as a general anesthetic. Sleep medications like chloral hydrate and the highly addictive Bella Donna routinely were given to keep patients from causing disturbances at night, when there was less staff supervision. Bella Donna later was curtailed when it was found to *cause* psychiatric disorders. In spite of detrimental side effects, morphine and the powerful narcotic hyoscine routinely were injected, along with phenobarbital, which made patients lethargic and depressed. Dosages varied, with no standardized regulation and little knowledge about contraindications. Doctors were unaware that morphine could be fatal if administered with sleep medicines and that some drugs made patients more vulnerable to relapses. By the time Zelda entered Prangins, she already was addicted to sleeping pills, and the barbiturates she was given only exacerbated her symptoms of agitation and depression.

Prangins regularly employed hydrotherapy to counteract bouts of mania, and the use of hot and cold water at varying temperatures became their medical specialty. It was considered the best intervention for agitation, and entire hospital wings were devoted to it. Continuous tub immersions routinely were prescribed to promote calm by causing a diminution or increase in circulation. Very different from the mineral baths Zelda had undergone at Salies des Bearn, these were ordeals patients sought to avoid, where they were submerged in water temperatures ranging from 90 to 100 degrees for an entire day. More dreaded were ice water soaks intended to revitalize organic functions and restore equilibrium. To subdue uncooperative or severely agitated patients, water jackets also were used, which involved attendants dipping sheets in hot or cold water, then tightly binding patients, first in a rubber blanket; followed by a cold, wet sheet; then another wool blanket; and finally a second iced sheet. Kept wrapped this way for several hours, the procedure caused a contraction of the small arteries, capillaries, and veins. As water evaporated from the soaked sheets, patients initially felt cold, but as their body generated heat, the pack would warm and they would become drowsy.

When Zelda arrived, Prangins already was famous for its Swiss sleeping cures, popularized in the 1920s by Swiss psychiatrist Jacob Klasi, who instituted the Dauerschlaf while working with Eugen Bleuler at Burgholzli. The procedure resembled those rest cures developed by the American neurologist Weir Mitchell, a preeminent specialist in nervous diseases, who used them to treat depression and hysteria. He blamed worn-out nerves for psychoses, believing bad signals got transmitted to the brain and that relaxation healed a sick mind like inactivity cured a diseased lung. His rest cure involved total isolation and a fatty, milk-based diet that usually produced a weight gain of fifty pounds over six weeks. Patients remained in bed twenty-four hours a day for weeks at a time, supervised by a private nurse who cleaned and fed them. Most of Mitchell's patients were female, and he attributed their neuroses to the mistake of entering a male sphere of intellectual labor. From his viewpoint, women needed to avoid overstimulation in order to remain stable.

Once the hypnotic properties of barbiturates were discovered, rest cures became easier to administer. After a shot of morphine and scopolamine, patients were injected with a mixture of diethyl and dipropylbarbituric acid that produced a prolonged narcosis, during which they slept for one or two weeks, roused only to eat and relieve bladder and bowel functions. This procedure was thought to relax a patient's mind and some woke calmer, but this was not Zelda's experience. She came out of the narcosis covered with eczema and in excruciating pain. Transferred from the sleeping ward to the main house, she was bathed in Fleming's solution and swathed in bandages of grease and powder, neither of which had any therapeutic effect.

Intended to serve a physical purpose, rest cures also crushed a patient's will and Zelda recognized this, writing Scott, "I am thoroughly humiliated and broken if that was what you wanted." Her eczema persisted until Dr. Forel placed her in a thirteen-hour hypnotic trance, from which she woke improved, but with a fierce pounding in her head. Three days later the rash returned in a milder form. Forel had learned hypnotism from his father, Auguste, who trained with the renowned French doctor, Hippolyte Bernheim. His book on somatic techniques was popular with the European medical community early in the twentieth century, especially after Freud translated it into German. Forel soon observed that whenever Scott visited, Zelda's eczema flared and she experienced severe mood swings, vacillating from warmth to bitterness in less than an hour. With this in mind and given Zelda's fragile condition, Forel suggested Scott not visit until fall.

Sick as she was, Zelda remained convinced her recovery depended on personal achievement. She begged Scott to ask Lubov Egorova if she was talented enough to become a great dancer. Forel opposed the communication, feeling her obsession with ballet had contributed to her collapse, but to his credit, Scott wrote Lubov on July 9. Her response was more positive than he expected. In assessing Zelda's ability, Lubov emphasized that she might become a very good dancer, performing important roles in repertory companies and smaller ballet groups, as well as secondary roles with larger companies. However, because she had started late, she would never become a prima ballerina like Vera Nemtchinova, Alice Nikitina, or Maria Danilova, among the greatest Russian dancers of the nineteenth century. Although generally positive, Lubov's evaluation came as a crushing blow, since Zelda aspired to perform with a premiere group and abhorred the prospect of becoming a second-rate dancer in an inferior company. With despairing finality, she put away her ballet paraphernalia and declared that if she couldn't be great, it wasn't worth doing at all.

Shortly thereafter, she again was transferred to Eglantine because of her disregard for hospital rules and refusal to stop masturbating. Doctors then considered masturbation one cause of psychosis and blamed it for everything from cancer to epilepsy. Mental institutions imposed brutal punishments on female patients for masturbating, including the application of pure carbolic acid (Phenol) to the clitoris, which burned and caused numbness. Some institutions went so far as to remove the inner labia of the vulva. Interventions at Prangins were less severe but included laxatives with a cold enema and cool sitz baths (from the German word *sitzen,* meaning to sit). Chair-shaped tubs were filled with cold or hot water to which salts, vinegar, or baking soda were added, and women were forced to sit for hours with water covering their hips and buttocks. If that didn't remedy the problem, it was off to Eglantine and reformative opiates, particularly a soluble form of morphine. Dr. Forel warned Scott that if nurses could not stop Zelda from masturbating, they were prepared to tie her hands to the bed. "For too long, your wife has taken advantage of our patience," he wrote Scott. "For her health, for her treatment, L'Eglantine is, from our point of view, indispensable. She must see that there are limits and that she must give in." There seemed no alternative; under control of the mind doctors, the mark of insanity was scattered abundantly over her every action. It became clear that only through compliancy would she gain release, and as long as Scott paid the bills, doctors would keep her there. She immediately assumed the role of good patient and began writing Scott conciliatory letters.

Rosalind wanted Zelda's parents involved in her treatment, but Scott warned against that, saying it would slow progress. "I beg you to think twice, before you say more to them. . . . Zelda at this moment is in no immediate danger. I have promised to let you know if anything crucial is in the air." Eager to determine when her sister's difficulties started, she wrote Scott,

You say you place the beginning of the change in her, at about ten months before our visit to Ellerslie. That would be just about three years ago. You think the change began at Hollywood? Did anything happen out there to particularly disturb her? Were there any unhappy incidents? I seem to remember, also having heard something about Zelda throwing from the window of the train, en route to Hollywood, a wristwatch that you had given her as her Christmas present. Is that true, and if so, why did she do it, and wouldn't it signify the trouble had already begun?

Although Rosalind placed the watch incident out of sequence, she did accurately recall that Zelda's unstable behavior had started at Ellerslie. It was evident to her then that Zelda's personality had greatly changed, and she was in need of medical attention.

With Zelda institutionalized indefinitely, Rosalind believed Scott was in no position to supervise Scottie's needs and suggested she live with them in Brussels. "It was at this point that her smoldering quarrel with my father broke out into the open," Scottie recalled, "because she deemed him too unreliable to be in charge of me while my mother was in the hospital and demanded that he let her adopt me." Scott angrily responded to Rosalind's accusations, writing, "I know your ineradicable impression of the life that Zelda and I led, and evident your dismissal of any of the effort, and struggle success or happiness in it . . . but I have got Zelda and Scottie to take care of now as ever, and I simply cannot be upset and harrowed still further." Shortly thereafter, he composed a harsher response, never sent: "Do me a single favor. Never communicate with me again in any form, and I will try to resist the temptation to pass you down to posterity for what you are." Scottie was placed under the care of an Alsatian governess named Mademoiselle Serze, and Scott rented an apartment for the two at 21 rue de Marioniere in Paris. Besides being privately tutored, Scottie attended school twice weekly at Cours Dieterle, with coursework equivalent to the third and fourth grades, and made weekend visits with her governess to her family in the Alsatian countryside.

One of Scott's best stories, "Babylon Revisited," stemmed from this controversy with Rosalind. In the narrative, Lincoln and Marion Peters, drawn from Rosalind and Newman, are guardians of Charlie Wale's daughter, Honoria. Charlie's wife, Helen, is dead, and after three years of separation from his daughter, he returns to Paris to convince Marion he can adequately care for her. Although Marion initially agrees, after two of Charlie's drunken friends come to her apartment, she changes her mind. "He would come back some day; they couldn't make him pay forever," Charlie declares. "But, he wanted his child, and nothing was much good now, besides that fact." Scottie loved her father but felt safer with Uncle Newman and Aunt Rosalind, and admitted "at one point, when things were not going well with my father, wishing that they had adopted me!" Her feelings over her mother's hospitalization were a mix of sadness, anger, and embarrassment, with Zelda slowly becoming a distant idea. Whatever relationship they had shared was fading fast.

To guarantee that Rosalind never would gain custody of his daughter, Scott wrote his cousin, Ceci, that if something happened to him while Zelda was institutionalized, she was to bring Scottie to maturity. Cecelia Delihant Taylor, "Ceci," was the daughter of his father's sister and raising her four daughters alone in Norfolk, Virginia, having been widowed as a young woman. To eight-year-old Scottie, Aunt Rosalind's motivations seemed entirely reasonable. "She was concerned, quite simply, that my father had driven my mother crazy. . . . It was all his fault because of his drinking and his terrible temper. . . . I can't think of a worse life style for someone who was unstable to begin with than my father."

And while Scott rejected Rosalind's accusations, he felt partially responsible for Zelda's breakdown and shared those feelings with her. Only, she cared nothing about fault: "Please don't write to me about blame. Blame doesn't matter. The thing that counts is to apply the few resources available to turning life into a tenable, orderly affair." Hardly the words of a mad woman, what concerned Zelda was getting free and she continually pleaded for release. "I am a woman of thirty and it seems to me, entitled to some voice in decisions covering me. I have had enough. . . . Will you make the necessary arrangements that I leave here and seek some satisfactory life for myself?" She insisted on the right to live as she wished. When Scott ignored her appeals, she asked to be transferred to another hospital. "I demand that I be allowed to go immediately to a hospital in France, where there is enough human kindness to prevent the present slow butchery." After he didn't answer, she threatened to get her parents involved. "Shall I write to daddy that he should come over? They know what's the matter with me, so do not think that I feel the slightest hesitancy in communicating with them." As she vacillated between periods of lucidity and bouts of despair, she moved to have Newman intervene and wrote Scott, "If you think you are preparing me for a return to Alabama, you are mistaken, and also if you think that I am going to spend the rest of my life roaming about without happiness or rest, from one sanatorium to another—you are wrong." She then wrote a fragmentary letter to Newman, begging him to take her back to France, saying that Scott was ignoring her requests and implying he hadn't time because of all his drinking and tennis, so there was no point in asking him for help or pity.

Since Zelda's condition did not present as a pure neurosis or psychosis, and there had not been a formal diagnosis, Forel asked the assistance of Paul Eugen Bleuler, professor of psychiatry at the University of Zurich and then head of Burgholzli. Oscar's father, Auguste, had spent twenty years as director there, with the young Sigmund Freud as his assistant, and upon retiring had selected Bleuler as his successor. Under Bleuler's leadership many exceptional psychiatrists were hired, including Abraham Brill, Adolf Meyer, and Carl Jung. Bleuler was an authority on psychoses and schizophrenia, having differentiated that disorder from what previously was called dementia praecox or paranoia. The term meant "split mind" and described someone with shifting affective states, not so much the popularized notion of a person hearing voices, as a lack of emotional affect. Its essential characteristic was emotional deterioration, evidenced by people becoming indifferent to their surroundings and unable to make reasonable associations. New diagnostic categories separated patients into groups so that doctors could more easily discuss them. Bleuler's designation of schizophrenia quickly merged with more general definitions of psychoses, and by 1930 was the commonest diagnosis on admission papers. To the twentieth century, it became what hysteria had been to the nineteenth.

Freud added new dimensions to Bleuler's categorizations, hypothesizing that early traumatic incidents contributed to the pathology of mental illness. He believed psychotic symptoms in women frequently could be traced back to a premature sexual trauma with another child or adult, and that auditory hallucinations usually were connected to these episodes. Difficult to integrate at the time, these ordeals remained buried until reawakened by another emotional disturbance, and this construct precisely mirrored Zelda's situation.

Eugen Bleuler spent the afternoon of November 22 talking with Zelda, then met with Forel and Scott to present his diagnosis of *schizophrenie*. He identified three reoccurring states in her condition: a depressed but calm stage, a hysteric period when she blamed others for everything, and a desperate phase where her situation seemed hopeless. Like his predecessor, Krapelin, Bleuler felt schizophrenia ran in families, with a predisposition to it inherited, but believed traumatic events and negative situations could trigger the illness. Based on what Zelda had shared, he told Scott that her breakdown was connected to an occurrence five years earlier, placing it near the aftermath of the Jozan affair, and that an emotional trauma had generated the psychosis causing a downward turn. Although the breakdown might have been delayed, he assured Scott it could not have been prevented. Zelda took an instant dislike to Bleuler—who charged Scott $500 for the consult, about $7,000 in today's money—and always referred to him as "that great imbecile."

Although Forel told Scott it was a great help to discuss Zelda's case with Bleuler, he was not entirely comfortable with the diagnosis, given its specificity and the speed with which it was delivered. He felt Zelda did not exhibit enough characteristics to be diagnosed in this way, given the relatively late onset of symptoms and alternation between psychosis and normality. Yet, he was reluctant to countermand his colleague's verdict, and on the basis of one afternoon's observation, Bleuler's diagnosis became a conclusive straitjacket. Forel would later acknowledge that the identifying process was filled with error, an inexact and precarious science, and for many patients the process was risky, with the number of diagnoses made equaling the number of institutions to which they were sent.

In an effort to understand Zelda's situation, Scott chose to rely on this expert opinion and hoped the specific diagnosis would offer a basis for effective treatment. On December 1, 1930, he wrote Zelda's parents summarizing Bleuler's evaluation and responded to their request about bringing her home. "He said it wasn't even a question. That even with a day and night nurse and the best suite on the Bremen, I would be taking a chance not justified by the situation—that a crisis, a strain, at this moment might make a difference between the recovery and insanity."

Although psychotherapy for the treatment of schizophrenia was relatively new at mental hospitals, Forel had known Sigmund Freud at Burgholzi and believed in its benefits, but whenever he tried to engage Zelda, she grew evasive. Nevertheless, he continued observing her and kept detailed notes on her condition. One afternoon, he asked her to summarize the pivotal emotional events in her life, and when she agreed, it was the breakthrough he needed.

> My marriage, after which I was in another world, one for which I was not qualified or prepared because of my inadequate education. A love affair with a French aviator in St. Raphael. I was locked in my villa for one month to prevent me from seeing him. This lasted for five years. When I knew my husband had another woman in California I was upset because the life over there appeared to me so superficial, but finally I was not hurt because I knew I had done the same thing when I was younger. . . . I determined to find an impersonal escape, a world in which I could express myself and walk without the help of somebody who was always far from me. . . . One day the world between me and the others stopped—I was dragged like by a magnet—I had headaches and I could jump higher than ever, but the day after I was sick. . . . My husband forced me to go to Valmont—and now I am here, with you, in a situation where I cannot be anybody, full of vertigo, with an increasing noise in my ears, fearing the vibrations of everyone I meet. Broken down.

Forel concluded that effects of overreaching had made Zelda vulnerable to stress and exhausted her nervous system. If she wanted to recover, he advised, she must surrender ambition to avoid conflict in the marriage. She dismissed his opinion, complaining, "Why do I have to go backward, when everyone else who can—goes on? Why does my husband and other people find, that, what was so satisfactory for them, is not the thing for me—and if you do cure me, what's going to happen to all the bitterness and unhappiness in my heart I am neither young enough to think that you can manufacture out of nothing something to replace the song I had." Although Forel believed Zelda's dance aspirations were fueled by her illness, Rosalind disagreed, considering her ambition a clear-eyed realization of her marital situation and uncertainties in life. She and the entire Sayre family agreed with Zelda, that doctors would never be able to restore what they were stealing from her.

By fall Zelda's condition had turned into a continual flattened depression, and she told Scott that "panic seems to have settled into a persistent gloom punctuated by moments of bombastic hysteria." By Christmas she felt well enough to see Scott, and he brought Scottie along to help trim her tree. Only, the excitement of seeing them proved too stressful, and after Zelda broke some ornaments and started acting oddly, attendants suggested they leave. Presents were deposited under the half-decorated tree, and father and daughter left for Gstaad, where Scottie took skiing lessons while Scott drank at the Alpine lodge.

Soon after New Year's, Scott learned that his father had died of a heart attack, and he booked passage aboard the SS *New York* to attend the funeral in Maryland. Afterward, he headed to Alabama and steeled himself for a visit with Zelda's parents. He anticipated hostility and got it, some relatives accusing him of institutionalizing Zelda to rid himself of a problem. As calmly as possible, he explained the situation and left. When he got back to Switzerland, Zelda had improved to where she was acting more normally and emerging from her shell. She had even attended a hospital dance. "I had a very nice time," she told Scott, "and got myself stepped on a sufficient number of times to make it quite worthwhile."

Forel allowed her to write for an hour or two most afternoons, and she began working on a story about a woman she had known in Montgomery. She also was reading again, selecting a novel by James Joyce to see if she could master it. The Fitzgeralds had met Nora and James Joyce in Paris and invited the couple to dinner at their rue Vaugirard apartment. Their daughter, Lucia, would arrive at Prangins two years later, similarly diagnosed as schizophrenic. During 1929 she also trained with Lubov, taking six hours of daily classes, so Zelda undoubtedly saw her at the studio. They may already have known one another, since Lucia taught dance classes for children on the beach at Juan-les-Pins during the summer of 1926. Like Zelda, she inherited eye problems from her father and experienced heartbreak. After falling in love with James's writing disciple, Samuel Beckett, who rejected her, she was spurned again, this time by the American sculptor Alexander Calder. Carl

Jung briefly treated her but considered the case too complex, believing her neurosis was tied to her father's. As Jung put it, they were like two people heading to the bottom of a river, James diving and Lucia falling. The psychiatrist, Adolf Meyer, later made a similar observation about the Fitzgeralds, saying theirs was a folie a deux, or mutual madness, and that Scott was as much in need of treatment as Zelda.

Forel's approach was to wean patients gradually from Prangins, initially allowing them short trips with a nurse, then with other patients or family members. If they did well, they could take longer trips, visit with family members in a hotel, and finally be allowed an extended holiday. Scott could now take Zelda on short outings to a café or museum, or on excursions into surrounding towns. From the terrace of the Restaurant du Parc des Eaux-Vives in Geneva, she wrote her mother a postcard filled with optimism. "Here is where Scott and I lunched yesterday in the soft Spring air—and I thought you would be proud to know: without a nurse—much progress." Once they drove to Montreux and saw a performance featuring Serge Lifar, who had studied under Lubov and danced with the Ballets Russes. For Zelda's thirty-first birthday, the family visited Annecy in the Haute-Savoie, where they sailed on the azure lake and picnicked in the gardens of the Hotel Palace. After traversing the countryside in an open car, Zelda wrote her father that the sky was so blue, it felt as if they were living in an aquarium. It was a welcome taste of freedom, and she described every detail. "We played tennis on the baked clay courts and fished tentatively from a low brick wall. . . . We walked at night toward a cafe blooming with Japanese lanterns, white shoes gleaming like radium in the damp darkness," swirling to the same Viennese waltzes they had danced to a decade earlier in Montgomery.

The Annecy trip was followed by one to Munich, visits to Vienna and Caux, then an excursion to the Murphys' mountain retreat in the Austrian Tyol at Montana-Vermale. No cure then was available for tuberculosis, and their son's life could only be prolonged by exposure to mountain air, so they had gone to an Alpine resort near Sierre. A funicular brought the Fitzgeralds to the sanitarium perched on the mountainside, and it was a contemplative time for both couples upon whom fortune had turned its back.

Zelda dreaded returning to Prangins and wrote Scott about how much she missed Paris: "Was the Madeleine pink at five o'clock, and did the fountains fall with hollow delicacy into the framing of space in the Place de la Concorde, and did the blue creep out from behind the Colonnades in the rue de Rivoli?" Before long she would know firsthand, since she was pronounced well enough to leave Prangins on September 15, 1931. After fifteen months of being hospitalized, she said good-bye to doctors and nurses, and drove with Scott to Lake Geneva, where they rested before continuing on to Paris and retrieving Scottie. They sailed for America aboard Cunard's *Aquitania*, the same liner that had brought them to Europe ten years earlier. The ship held many memories and the couple grew nostalgic over dinner in the Palladian Lounge, under the architectural motifs of Christopher Wren. They had crossed the Atlantic often during the previous decade, but this would be their final farewell to Europe.

As the photo on Zelda's reissued passport shows, the illness had taken its toll. Gone was her youthful beauty, the softness of her expression replaced by severity and coarseness. Poorly cut, her once stylish hair now was pulled back with a simple barrette, accentuating the angularity of her face. But, the alteration was more than skin deep. Asylums dismantle people, rarely assemble them, and Zelda's internment only worsened preexisting conditions, leaving deep psychic scars. Any relief came at a steep price. The diagnosis of schizophrenia dehumanized her in a way that was impossible to correct, and she told Sara Mayfield, she could never forgive Scott for putting her there. Never could she be sure if he had called upon psychiatrists to assist her or protect himself.

Zelda needed help, but schizophrenic she was not, and the interventions prescribed for that disorder precipitated many of the symptoms associated with it. Had Freud done her consultation instead of Bleuler, and Scott initially considered using him, she might have been diagnosed with an alcohol-induced anxiety psychosis. The distinguishing of it from schizophrenia is particularly difficult, especially when mood disorders coexist. Its symptoms include later onset, higher anxiety levels, and better insight, all of which Zelda exhibited. Most importantly, an alcohol-related psychosis, unlike schizophrenia, remits with abstinence and resumes with exposure. Forel must have considered this a possibility, since he warned Zelda against drinking even the smallest amount of alcohol, saying it could trigger another episode.

However, once Bleuler's hasty diagnosis was made and doctors closed ranks, every aspect of Zelda's life got construed according to that disease. Instead of her breakdown being viewed as an extreme response to stress, sometimes the mind's bizarre mechanism of coping, her sanity got brought into play and sealed her fate as a crazy person. From then on, her life took a downward turn, with relief sought but never found. But she did not know this then, and upon leaving Switzerland, assured Dr. Forel that in America, she was determined to create a life in which to breathe freely. She would have little time to inhale that blissful air.

· 8 ·

No Hope Salvaged

*W*hen the *Aquitania* pulled beside pier 90 and the Fitzgeralds disembarked in lower Manhattan, the alteration in American society was visibly evident. The stock market crash had catapulted America into economic crisis, and fifteen million people were out of work. Bread lines encircled street corners, shanty towns overtook the Bowery, and the mood was grim. The year 1930 became one of nervous breakdowns, and while most professions lost clients, psychiatrists and social workers were overbooked, their waiting rooms flooded with patients. Several of Scott's classmates had crashed with the market, like Zelda winding up in asylums or jumping from office windows on Wall Street. Their roster of friends was getting depleted by a general disability to prevail.

Instead of checking into the Plaza, they registered at the New Yorker opposite Pennsylvania Station on Thirty-Fourth Street and looked up Townsend Martin and Alex McKaig. After Scott met with Harold Ober and Maxwell Perkins, he shared a brief lunch with Ernest Hemingway, whose career was on the ascent. *A Farewell to Arms* had just been published and was being made into a film, and *Death in the Afternoon* was awaiting release. By contrast, it had been six years since the publication of *The Great Gatsby* and two since Scott had put any solid work into another novel.

Zelda wasn't feeling well enough to socialize, so after ten days the family left for Montgomery, where doctors thought she might benefit from being around relatives. Initially, they stayed at the Greystone Hotel, later moving to the more modest Jefferson Davis, where a suite of rooms with private baths cost nine dollars a day. After house hunting for a week, they signed a six-month lease on a brown-shingled bungalow at 819 Felder Avenue in the fashionable Cloverdale section. The street was abloom with camellia trees, and there was a thriving magnolia in their front yard. Scottie entered Miss

Booth's School for Girls and was tutored by the French governess who had accompanied them from Paris.

In an effort to reconnect with her daughter, for Scottie's tenth birthday Zelda organized an elaborate party, concocting a huge spiderweb in the front yard with yards of strings leading to presents. The family acquired a Persian cat named Chopin and a bloodhound called Trouble, who proceeded to dig up the flower beds. The Sayres behaved cordially to Scott, but he had to modify his drinking around them, which set him on edge. For transportation, he purchased a blue, secondhand Stutz costing $400, and joined the nearby country club, ostensibly to play golf, but really to throw down a few drinks in the locker room.

In New York, Harold Ober was becoming increasingly concerned over Scott's mounting debt to Scribner's in the form of advances and began soliciting another Hollywood assignment. At the end of October, Harold secured a six-month contract for Scott to revise the screenplay of *Red Headed Woman*, Katherine Bush's best-selling novel about a secretary who marries a French aristocrat. The weekly salary was $1,200 and the production provided an opportunity to work with Irving Thalberg, Hollywood's wunderkind, whom Scott had briefly met in 1927. Only twenty-one when put in charge of Universal's production studio, at thirty-two, Irving was running MGM and renowned for selecting the best scripts, hiring talented actors, and making profitable films. Scott later would model Monroe Stahr after him in *The Last Tycoon*.

This time there was no question about Zelda going. Her condition was still precarious and her father seriously ill, having contracted influenza the previous April. Not yet adjusted to autonomy so soon after being released from Prangins, she was upset over being left behind and apprehensive about Scott being in Hollywood alone with all those glamorous movie people. When he boarded the train in early November, they quarreled at the station, after which Zelda telegraphed apologies and followed up by writing thirty-two letters during his eight-week absence. She had expected Montgomery to provide security and comfort, but it only felt oppressive and unsettling.

In the time leading to Scott's departure, Zelda had convinced him to let her take ballet lessons with a local teacher, Amalia Harper Rosenberg. Only, the skill level between Amalia and Lubov was too great and the arrangement quickly soured. "I had a violent quarrel with Amalia this morning. She called me a cow, because I told her I couldn't do the steps that neither fit the time nor the spirit of the music." Instead, Zelda poured her energies into writing a one act play for Scottie and her friends; composed a fugue and nocturne; played tennis with her niece, Noonie; and swam in the Huntington College pool. She also spent time with her parents, taking morning walks with her mother and sitting by her father's bedside during the afternoon.

One day, the judge brought up the question of divorce and shared his feelings about Scott, saying she could not make a life with a man like that. After considering his admonition, she sought the opinion of Peyton Mathis, who recently had convinced a friend's husband to accept an uncontested divorce. When Zelda explained her situation, Peyton wasn't optimistic. Without family money or the means of earning an income, he warned, Zelda would find it difficult to survive alone, and Scott would demand custody, claiming she was mentally unfit to supervise Scottie. Whichever way she considered her situation, she was trapped.

Out in Hollywood Scott also was feeling bound. Talkies were the rage and writers an interchangeable and replaceable component of the dream factory. Studios recruited an assortment of writers to satisfy production needs, and eight or nine might be employed on one screenplay with the final result bearing little resemblance to the original story. Scott's MGM contract called for a Christmas deadline, but things got off to a bad start when he and another screenwriter, Dwight Taylor, were invited to a party at the Malibu beach house of Irving Thalberg and Norma Shearer. Irving knew about Scott's drinking problem and already held a negative opinion of him, but when Scott headed for the piano after too many cocktails and began reciting "Dog, Dog, I like a good dog," a Princeton party song, he created an embarrassing situation and Irving wrote him off. He hated drunks, whom he labeled "rummies," and observing Scott from the back of the room, made a mental note to ditch him.

Zelda's Christmas surprise was to be the play she had written for Scottie and her friends to perform in, and she had rented the Little Theatre for the occasion. Those plans were abandoned when her father suddenly died. On November 17 she telegraphed Scott about his passing, but he could not come east, so she faced the funeral alone. An American flag was flown at half-mast above the capitol building and black crepe draped over the entryway to Supreme Court chambers. The judge was buried beneath an ancient oak in Oakwood Cemetery, not far from Peyton's *Broken Column* memorial. The judge had always been Zelda's invulnerable fortress, and his death triggered another emotional turmoil. Within days after the burial, her eyes ached and patches of eczema appeared on her neck. Then, after a week of continual rain, her asthma flared and she wrote Scott that she was feeling light-headed and having difficulty understanding conversations. "I feel like a person lost in some Gregorian but feminine service here. . . . I have come in on the middle, and did not get the beginning, and cannot stay for the end, but must somehow seize the meaning." His death could not have come at a worse time. Just when she was putting her feet on firm ground, the earth was swept from under her.

In an attempt at distraction, she began working simultaneously on three stories, one started at Prangins. A story of lost love, it was inspired by her feelings for Edouard, initially called "Miss Bessie" but later retitled "Miss Ella." The main character was modeled on Bessie Walker, whom Zelda had known during her youth, a spinster who lived on Montgomery's outskirts in a pre–Civil War mansion surrounded by stone walls covered with night-blooming Cereus. Bessie was in her fifties; nobody knew why she had remained single, but there were rumors. Like many love stories, Miss Ella's had taken place in the past. While engaged to Mr. Hendrix, she had become attracted to Andy Bronson and jilted her fiancé for him. But minutes before her wedding, the spurned suitor entered Miss Ella's property and shot himself in the head, his brains covering the earth in a bloody mess. The festivities were canceled and Miss Ella's future irrevocably changed, true love being as elusive, Zelda mused, as jam in *Alice in Wonderland*—jam yesterday, jam tomorrow, but no jam today. *Scribner's Magazine* published the story in its December 1931 issue, and Zelda proudly mailed a copy to Dr. Forel at Prangins and to Richard Knight, who wired a complimentary telegram. The story was among her best writing efforts, and its publication bolstered Zelda's confidence so much so that, with the intention of writing a best-selling novel, she began drafting a thinly veiled narrative about her years in Europe. With the single-mindedness of which she was so capable, Zelda had the book's outline completed within three weeks.

Things in Hollywood were not going as smoothly. Scott found the screenwriters' collaborative system unworkable, and two weeks before script deadline, he was yanked off *Red Headed Woman* and the project reassigned to Anita Loos, who understood the formula for these movies. Her revision got Irving's instant approval, and the film became wildly popular, placing Loos on top of the screenwriting ranks and making Jean Harlow a star. For a second time, Scott had failed in the movie industry, and he returned to Montgomery in a miserable frame of mind.

When he learned that Zelda was working on a psychological novel drawn from their experiences in Europe, Scott insisted she stop, saying he planned to tap that same resource. Given that he was the professional author, he considered Zelda's writing a creative intrusion. Only, she felt entitled to that story and protested: "The . . . material which I will elect to write about, is nevertheless legitimate stuff, which has cost me a pretty emotional penny to amass and which I intend to use."

Since Rosalind was about to arrive from Brussels, and Scott wanted to avoid seeing her, he organized a trip to Florida's Gulf Coast and took off with Zelda by car, leaving Scottie with Zelda's sister Marjorie. After driving the Stutz to Biloxi, then St. Petersburg, they checked into the Don Ce-Sar Hotel and spent the first day on the almost deserted beach. By day two they were again quarreling over her desire to write, and as Zelda became increasingly anxious, biting the inside of her mouth and picking at her fingers, her eczema returned. Forel had cautioned her not to consume even the smallest amount of alcohol, but on their drive back to Montgomery, as Scott slept in their hotel room, she became so nervous that she drank the entire contents of his whiskey flask. Within hours she was hallucinating, and after arriving back in Montgomery experienced four prolonged psychotic episodes that only could be calmed by morphine injections. When they contacted Forel for advice, he suggested Zelda immediately return to Prangins, but she was adamant about never going back to what she labeled a "Swiss nut farm." As an alternative, Scott took her to Phipps Psychiatric Clinic at Johns Hopkins University in Baltimore, Maryland.

Dr. Forel probably recommended the place since his Swiss colleague, Adolf Meyer, was director there. Named for its benefactor, Henry Phipps, a partner of Andrew Carnegie, the clinic had opened in 1913 and was the first psychiatric hospital to promote a scientific approach in treating mental illness. Meyer believed science ultimately would discover the biological underpinnings of mental disorders, but until it did, he employed a psychobiological approach in treating patients, considering psychological and social factors along with biological determinants. He encouraged staff members to consider their patients' behavior and life experiences when establishing a treatment protocol and not to proceed before examining these carefully.

On February 12, 1932, when Zelda arrived at Phipps, her mouth was frozen in a permanent grimace and she was actively hallucinating. The relapse caught her off guard, and she urged Scott to maintain his distance as doctors did their work: "I do not seem to be strong enough to stand much strain at present," she told him. "I'd rather just stay here until I'm quite well." After talking with medical staff and determining she was in capable hands, Scott returned to Montgomery where he had left Scottie, and rather than interrupt her school year, stayed there until their lease on the Cloverdale house expired.

During the first half of the twentieth century, Phipps' director Adolf Meyer was considered the most influential psychiatrist in America. Born in Zurich, he had studied psychiatry at the University of Zurich with Oscar's Forel's father, Auguste, and after finishing medical school, began his professional career at Burgholzli under Eugen Bleuler. When he failed to obtain a tenured position at the University of Zurich, he decided career opportunities were better in America, and in 1892 left for Chicago. Despite impressive credentials, he was unable to secure a position at the University of Chicago and lowered his expectations by accepting an appointment ninety miles south at Eastern Illinois Hospital for the Insane in Kankakee. Two years later, he moved to the State Lunatic Hospital in Worcester, Massachusetts, and in 1902 became head of the Pathological Institute of the New York State Hospital System. There he shaped much of America's psychiatric terminology by introducing Emil Kraepelin's classification system along with Sigmund Freud's psychological theories. He also established what seems elementary today, a system for keeping detailed patient records.

Meyer was asked in 1908 to head the newly established Phipps Clinic at Johns Hopkins and remained there for thirty-one years. In all that time, although his treatment of mental disorders considered psychological and social factors, along with biological determinants, he never developed a theory about the cause of mental illness, and his therapeutic approach remained broad enough to accommodate diverse treatments, including art and play therapies. Unlike many of his contemporaries, he employed psychiatric social workers and encouraged psychotherapy, since he believed the few treatments available should be offered to patients, regardless of diagnosis or results. Considered an authority on the treatment of schizophrenia, Meyer believed Zelda's condition was a joint problem with her husband, a folie a deux in which two closely associated people develop similar obsessions, the weaker and more submissive yielding to the stronger. Whenever separated from the dominant person, the disturbed individual generally relinquishes their delusions and improves. He recognized that Scott was able to function in the world, whereas Zelda could not, but insisted Scott also needed to undergo treatment if his wife was to improve. He saw no positive prognosis unless Scott relinquished alcohol and joined the therapeutic process, telling Zelda's sister, Rosalind, that he considered Scott equally in need of treatment. When Meyer suggested this, Scott adamantly refused, as he previously had with Dr. Forel, insisting alcohol enhanced his creativity and that any treatment might get publicized and damage his literary career. Dr. Meyer never was able to convince Scott that his alcoholism and controlling behavior always would impede his wife's recovery, and the two men never communicated effectively. Nor did Meyer get along particularly well with Zelda, since his European formality impressed her as autocratic and lacking of humanity.

Rather, it was Dr. Mildred Taylor Squires, an assistant resident psychiatrist at Phipps, who gained her trust and with whom Zelda developed a good relationship. Only four years older than Zelda, Squires had undergone medical training at the University of Pennsylvania, and though not a specialist in psychiatry, was particularly interested in Zelda's case. Within the first week of Zelda being here, Squires wrote Scott about the case, saying Zelda appeared preoccupied, had scattered thoughts, and often stopped speaking in the middle of sentences. She refused to discuss her feelings or symptoms, and Squires emphasized the difficulty of treating someone who did not wish to be treated. "At no time have I been able to get any statement of the suspicious, paranoid ideas which apparently led up to her coming to the clinic. She has told both Dr. Meyer and me, that she will not talk about any of her illness, and of course we cannot force her to do so." Furthermore, Squires related, "Mrs. Fitzgerald does not accept any of the nurses' suggestions unless they are labeled as my orders. These she has accepted but in a reluctant, though very friendly spirit, trying to avoid them but usually giving in rather gracefully."

To clarify personal information Zelda may have shared, Squires questioned Scott about the couple's sexual compatibility. Emphatically, he assured the female doctor, "Our sexual relations have been good. . . . She had her first orgasm about ten days after we were married, and from that time to this, there haven't been a dozen times in twelve years, when she hasn't had an orgasm." It was the opposite of what he confided to Ernest, admitting he had not been able to satisfy Zelda sexually since the Jozan affair. Finally, he told Squires that Zelda's betrayal with the pilot was at the root of their problems, but that they couldn't keep paying for it forever.

Mental hospitals were then separated from the mainstream of American medicine, and their staffs received little specialized training. Medical schools offered no regular instruction in psychiatry, and untrained physicians often supervised wards. Their choice of treatment was a matter of personal preference. Zelda recognized the advantage of having Dr. Squires on her case, since female doctors were a rarity in psychiatric hospitals. Although a powerless minority, they often were more intuitive and interested in their patients than male colleagues, who frequently were described as patronizing and hurried. Squires put aside the standard protocol of detachment between psychiatrist and patient and engaged with Zelda, asking numerous questions and helping her acquire insights into her marriage. To express appreciation, Zelda designed a Christmas card for the doctor, showing a female figure holding a wreath and lighted candle, printing them in black ink and adding white gouache by hand. Squires made the mistake of sending one to Frederick Wertham, consulting physician on Zelda's case, who had come from Europe to work with Meyer in 1922 and specialized in art therapy. He questioned the appropriateness of using a patient's design and shared the card with a colleague writing, "This card was designed and printed by Mrs. Fitzgerald. I knew nothing of them until they arrived. I thought you might be interested in seeing them." Any reservations Wertham had were later put aside, since he acquired eleven of Zelda's paintings, now in the Wertham Collection at Harvard's Fogg Art Museum.

Dr. Squires offered Zelda encouragement rather than drugs or psychoanalysis. Against the opinions of male colleagues, she felt Zelda could benefit from productive work, and allowed her to write for two hours each day. In a burst of creative energy throughout February and March she worked on her novel, and by her eighth week at Phipps, completed it. She titled it *Save Me the Waltz*, taking the phrase from an RCA Victor record catalog. After Squires read it and offered suggestions, Zelda sent the manuscript directly to Maxwell Perkins, who was impressed by its originality and immediately considered it for publication. Scott knew Zelda was writing something but anticipated seeing her work before submission, so when Max called to say he had the manuscript, Scott was furious and telegraphed: "PLEASE DO NOT JUDGE OR IF NOT ALREADY DONE EVEN CONSIDER ZELDA'S BOOK UNTIL YOU GET REVISED VERSION. LETTER FOLLOWS." Some of Phipps' medical staff apologized for letting the manuscript be sent without his permission, and Squires was reprimanded. Scott was as furious with her as with Zelda, complaining that he was unable to complete *his* novel because of having to pay for her confinement. Surprised by his fury, Squires suggested a legal separation, which Scott vehemently rejected saying, "It would be throwing her broken upon a world which she despises; I would be a ruined man for years." Whether he meant that he would become emotionally unstrung, or that his reputation would become tarnished, is unclear.

Before allowing Zelda's manuscript to be published, Scott insisted that major portions be deleted, selections to be determined by him, and that a clause be inserted into her contract, stipulating that half the book's royalties, up to the amount of $5,000, be credited against his debt to Scribner's. His rationalization was that she had been exploitive, writing on time paid for by him. Since Scribner's investment was in Scott, Max agreed. Throughout spring of 1932, Scott supervised Zelda's reshaping of the book, and demanded its entire middle section be redrafted. Almost a third was deleted, including most of the material about the Jozan affair, which Scott likened to something from *True Confessions*, a magazine notorious for romantic intrigues. He felt the character based on him was depicted in a demeaning way, so those sections were cut and replaced with passages of which he approved. Scott also insisted that the protagonist's name, Amory Blaine, identical to his hero in *This Side of Paradise*, be changed. Zelda's new choice of name, David Knight, a reference to Richard Knight, proved equally annoying, but Scott let it stand. Since Zelda's original manuscript and first draft revisions have been lost or destroyed, we cannot know what was deleted, only that large amounts were redrafted or edited out. However, one member of Scribner's promotion department who read the original recalled it as very provocative, containing vindictive attacks on Scott, scandalous material about their private life, and lurid details about Zelda's affair with Edouard.

Save Me the Waltz is separated into five parts: the heroine Alabama's upbringing in the South; marriage to David, a painter; departure for Manhattan and Europe; determination to become a ballerina; and return to her birthplace.

The narrative chronicles her unsatisfying marriage, the struggle to create an independent life, and her interlude with the French pilot. After her husband puts an end to it, he continues having affairs while demanding fidelity from his wife. With the realization that she must achieve something on her own, Alabama trains as a ballerina and becomes skilled enough to warrant an offer from an Italian dance company. Contrary to Zelda's decision, her heroine accepts the challenge and goes to Italy, leaving husband and daughter behind in Paris. Neapolitan audiences applaud her talent, but when glue from her ballet shoe seeps into a blister and causes a serious infection, her career is cut short. In the hospital she learns that her father has died, and the family returns to her Southern birthplace. The novel ends abruptly midst the stale remnants of a party as David reprimands Alabama for dumping ashtrays before guests leave. Although she utters the last words, they do not sound convincing as she proclaims, "It's very expressive of myself. I just lump everything in a great heap which I have labeled 'the past' and having just emptied this deep reservoir that was once myself, I am ready to continue."

Textured with innuendo, Zelda gives her French pilot the name of Jacques Chevre-Feuille, the French word *chevre* meaning goat and *feuille*—leaf. Together, *chevre-feuille* denotes honeysuckle or horny goat weed, an aphrodisiac used to promote potency, sort of a Medieval Viagra. The aviator's surname also is an oblique reference to "Chèvrefeuille," the narrative poem or lai by Marie de France, a twelfth-century poet. The first known female author to write in French, her lais frequently involve love triangles between a cuckolded husband, cheating wife, and lover, and "Chèvrefeuille" is one example.

Zelda's multilayered writing replicated her speech, and her lover's name alludes to an episode from *Tristan and Iseult*, a popular folk tale in the Middle Ages. It tells the story of Tristan, son of a Breton lord, who on a return voyage to Ireland with Iseult, prospective bride for his uncle, King Mark, commits a tragic error. He and Iseult drink a potion that attracts them to one another. In the courtly version its effects last a lifetime; in more common accounts, three years. Some tellings suggest they consumed the potion accidentally; in other accounts the potion's maker instructs Iseult to give the elixir to King Mark as an aphrodisiac, but instead she offers it to Tristan. Although Iseult marries King Mark, she and Tristan are hopelessly attracted to each other. Marie de France's lai describes the moment Tristan secretly returns to Cornwall, signaling his arrival on the road Iseult will travel, by writing his name on a hazelnut tree. The poet writes that, along with his name, Tristan carved the words, "Ni moi sans vous, ni vous sans moi" (Neither me without you, nor you without me). Equally improbable was Zelda's love for Edouard, and in choosing *Chevre-feuille* as her lover's surname, she was alluding to not only La France's lai, but also the symbiotic connection of hazel trees and honeysuckle in the botanical world. Honeysuckle clings to hazel trees by winding itself around its branches, and if any effort is made to separate the two, the hazel tree dies along with the honeysuckle.

Dans ces deux, il en fut ainsi	In these two it was so,
Comme du chèvrefeuille était	As honeysuckle was
Qui au coudrier s'attachait:	When attached to hazel:
Quand il s'estenlacé et pris	When he embraced and took her
Et tout autour du fût s'estmis,	all around was started,
Ensemble peuvent bien durer.	and together may survive.
Qui plus tard les veut détacher,	Who wants them off later,
Le coudrier tue vivement	The hazel will kill quickly
Et chèvrefeuille mêmement.	the honeysuckle.
Belle amie, ainsi est de nous:	Dear friend,
Ni vous sans moi,	Neither you without me,
ni moi sans vous!	nor I without you.

Zelda's novel *Save Me the Waltz* was published on October 7, 1932, and dedicated to Mildred Squires, something that irritated male colleagues and may have contributed to Squires's imminent departure. Anxiously, Zelda awaited the response from readers and critics, but it was not the best seller for which she hoped. Only 1,392 copies sold from a printing of 3,010, earning her the pitiful revenue of $120.73. Since Scott had not arranged for proofreading, much of the profit went to correcting a manuscript filled with spelling and typographical errors, many the result of Scott's revisions. Even with last minute corrections, the *New York Times* complained, "It is a pity that the publisher could not have had a more accurate proofreading, for it is inconceivable that the author should have undertaken to use as much of the French language as appears in this book, if she knew so little of it as this book indicates." In her review for the *Bookman*, Dorothy Brande agreed: "Mrs. Fitzgerald should have had whatever help she needed to save her book from the danger of becoming a laughing stock. . . . It is not only that her publishers have not seen fit to curb an almost ludicrous lushness of writing . . . but they have not given the book the elementary services of a literate proofreader." The most favorable review came from William McFee at the *New York Sun*, who assured readers they would devour the novel with dizzy delight.

Frustrated at seeing her manuscript so drastically altered and deflated over its poor sales, Zelda asked Maxwell Perkins to place an advertisement on the dance page of the *New York Times* or *Herald Tribune*, but after Scott voiced objections, none appeared. He had instructed Scribner's not to overdo publicity, so there was no promotional budget or distribution plan; he wanted

it to fail and it did. The book promptly fell into obscurity, but not before
Edouard read it, since he told Nancy Milford and Sara Mayfield that Zelda's
portrayal of their relationship was quite accurate. Unware of all that had been
deleted, he probably thought she was being decorous. As a cadet that year
at the Naval War College, France's training ground for future admirals, no
doubt he breathed a sigh of relief.

As Zelda started showing improvement at Phipps, she began socializing with other patients and described one of the dances to Scott: "We had
a madman's ball today. . . . We were dressed as George Washington and
Independence Hall and the Fall of Ticonderoga. Only I went as a Manet cour-
tesan." Now she was allowed day trips, and since the lease on the Cloverdale
house had expired, Scott enlisted the aid of Princeton classmate Edgar Allan
Poe Jr., a descendant of the famous writer, to find him someplace to live near
the hospital. He located a fifteen-room country house on the Bayard Turnbull
estate at Rodgers Forge near Towson, Maryland. Called La Paix because of its
peaceful setting, it was situated on twenty acres of rolling hillside, with a tennis
court and lake, so close to Phipps that part of its property abutted its grounds.
As usual it was too big for the Fitzgeralds. The Turnbulls lived nearby in a new
home Bayard had designed. Scott established a warm relationship with Mrs.
Turnbull, but was only mildly tolerated by her husband, a Baltimore architect who disapproved of his drinking habits. Their three children—Eleanor,
Frances, and eleven-year-old Andrew—were happy to have a new playmate in
Scottie, and she also made friends with Peaches Finney, daughter of another
of Scott's classmates, Eben Finney. After sixth grade, when Scottie's coursework at Calvert School finished, she and Peaches became day students at Bryn
Mawr, and when things grew tense at home, she would stay with the Finneys.
Scott treated Andrew like a son, and the two could be seen tossing a football
on the front lawn or boxing in a makeshift ring by the gravel driveway. As an
adult, Andrew would become one of Scott's biographers, and recall how Zelda
used to read under the majestic oak tree and swim to the raft in the middle
of the lake, her tawny hair water-slicked and skin very brown. It was a haven
compared to the hospital, and she wrote John Peale Bishop, "Scott likes it
better than France and I like it fine. We are more alone than ever before while
the psychiatres [*sic*] patch up my nervous system."

Zelda's friends Sara Mayfield and Sara Haardt visited one weekend, just
after the couple had quarreled over Richard Knight. He had irked Scott by
overpraising Zelda's novel and encouraging her to continue writing and dancing. In a rage, Scott accused Richard of attempting to draw Zelda back into
a world that had ruined her. The argument ended with Scott calling Richard
a "fairy," a slur that held particular resonance for him. Mayfield remembered how Zelda looked that afternoon, immaculate as always, dressed in a

yellow-linen dress and white espadrilles, but lacking her characteristic vitality. Her once lustrous hair had taken on a dull tint and once faultless skin was scarred from eczema. The corner of one eye twitched and her mouth twisted when she spoke. After the confrontation Scott wrote Richard an apology, explaining his irritation and emphasizing that if he could have seen Zelda during her breakdown, he would not be encouraging her to enter the fray again.

As Zelda's partial release from Phipps neared, Scott dreaded her return, and on May 17 wrote Austin Fox Riggs at Stockbridge Sanitarium in Massachusetts, inquiring if she could spend part of the summer there. Riggs responded that an evaluation of her condition from Dr. Meyer was needed and may have denied Scott's request since no further correspondence exists. Early in June Zelda learned that she could spend mornings at La Paix, then return to Phipps for afternoon therapy sessions. Whenever she visited, Scott insisted that she maintain a strict schedule that alternated exercise and rest. However, making her adhere to rules was difficult, because she wanted to paint and write far into the night. Scott feared another breakdown and asked Dr. Meyer to give him the option of returning Zelda whenever she became unmanageable, but he refused. To occupy her time with something other than work, Scott hired a professional tennis player named Crosley to give Scottie, Andrew, and Zelda lessons. But she easily became frustrated, often ending sessions by throwing her racquet at the coach. She memorialized such an episode in a watercolor over graphite entitled *Le Sport*, where she portrays two racquets flying over a man's head, writing in French on verso, "Il Etait un jeune American qui n'avait besoin de rien!" (He was a young American who didn't need anything.) This drawing also found its way into Frederick Wertham's collection.

Zelda wanted to start work on another novel, but because the genre required intense concentration and Scott strongly opposed the idea, Dr. Squires suggested she concentrate on shorter pieces. Scott resented the female physician's interference and requested Zelda's case be transferred to Dr. Thomas Cummings Rennie, but Zelda fought to keep Squires and was temporarily successful. Emotionally fragile, Zelda fluctuated between creative highs and suicidal lows, and walking on hospital grounds with Scott one afternoon, she suddenly threw herself on the tracks bordering its boundary. Only seconds before the engine passed was he able to pull her off. Until these impulses subsided, she was not allowed trips home, but it was a strain Scott only could endure briefly. John O'Hara recalled one Sunday when he offered to drive her back to Phipps: "I had Scott and Zelda in my car and I wanted to kill him. We were taking her back to her institution, and he kept making passes at her that could not possibly be consummated. . . . I wanted to kill him for what he was doing to that crazy woman."

Doctors cautioned Zelda against overconcentrating on writing, and for a time she complied, painting enough watercolors and oils to exhibit in the October 1933 Independent Artists Exhibition at the Baltimore Museum of Art. Simultaneously, however, she was outlining a novel called *Caesar's Things* in which she planned to depict the story of herself in conflict with herself. Scott reacted as he had earlier, insisting she not write about mental illness until he had completed *Tender Is the Night*. Although it was her breakdown at the core of his novel, Scott felt entitled to the material because he paid the bills: "I wish I had a whole lot of money," she told him bitterly. "I would give you every nickel you ever spent on me."

That May, Mildred Squires announced that she was leaving and transferred Zelda's case to Thomas Rennie. He had come to America from Scotland in 1911 and attended the University of Pittsburgh, then entered medical school at Harvard. To familiarize himself with the couple, he asked the Fitzgeralds to share personal reflections. Zelda summed it up by saying, she considered herself a shallow shell of what she had been, with no life of her own, and reactions inferior to those experienced when normal. As far as family relationships, she sadly admitted, "I am incapacitated for helping her (Scottie) by the constant ill humor in which I find myself in her presence. My relations with my husband are being robbed of all significance or happiness by intrusive and unprovoked irrelative thoughts."

Scott characterized their marital problems as a struggle between egos, linking Zelda's breakdown to his novel-in-progress. "In her subconscious, there is a deathly terror, that I may make something very fine in the use of this material of 'ours,' that I may preclude her making something very fine. This conflict is at the root of it. She feels that my success has got to be, otherwise we all collapse—she feels, also, that it is a menace to her, 'why should it be him—why shouldn't it be me? I'm as good or better than he is.'"

Rennie shared these observations with Dr. Meyer, who reiterated that he saw no positive outcome unless Scott relinquished alcohol and participated in the therapeutic process. Scott responded by writing Meyer a lengthy clarification questioning whether Zelda was more worth saving than himself. "She is working under a greenhouse, which is my money and my name and my love," he complained. "This is my fault—years ago I reproached her for doing nothing and she never got over it. So she is mixed up—she is willing to use the greenhouse to protect her in every way, to nourish every sprout of talent and to exhibit it—and at the same time, she feels no responsibility about the greenhouse, and feels she can reach up and knock a piece of glass out of the roof at any moment, yet she is shrewd to cringe when I open the door of the greenhouse and tell her to behave or go." Again, he asked for authority to send Zelda back to the sanitarium whenever she was stubborn or unmanageable, but Meyer rejected this request and reiterated the necessity for Scott to give up alcohol. He replied to Scott,

> Your complaint of futility of our conversation is as much my own as it is yours. It is a question of both of you and not only one. You also figure as a potential but unwilling patient. Since you refuse a closer understanding between ourselves, as if it would be a psychoanalytic, or I don't know what kind of surrender of yourself, I simply should say, I am sorry for the misunderstanding, avoiding any futilities. I wish I could reach a practical plan free of uncertainties. We can get on safer grounds I am sure; but it is difficult without a conjoint surrender of the alcohol.

During her sessions with Rennie, Zelda confided the core of her discontent: "It is the great humiliation of my life that I cannot support myself. . . . I have always felt some necessity for us to be on a more equal footing than we are now, because I cannot possibly—I cannot live in a world that is completely dependent on Scott." As for her daughter, she emphasized how frayed the relationship had become, and that she felt unable to provide her with anything.

Rennie tried to help Zelda develop strategies to live peacefully and recommended a dialogue between the couple with him as facilitator. That meeting took place in the living room of La Paix on Sunday, May 28, 1933, beginning at 2:30 p.m. and continuing until dark. The session was recorded on a Dictaphone by Scott's secretary, Isabel Owens, and when transcribed, filled 114 pages. Scott began the discussion by describing what he considered an unbearable situation at home. "The evenings are so terrible. Zelda will sit at the table, and stand over by Scottie, and draw her mouth together and make a little noise. She cannot stand it downstairs, and won't take a walk; nothing for anybody else, nothing. This whole household has got to be for her. She is used to that life in the clinics, where she feels that things are revolving around her."

Zelda then offered her version: "He made it impossible for me to communicate with my child, by refusing, first to take any of my judgments or opinions of people who were in charge of her, or anything else, and there was nothing in my life except my work, nothing. I was trying to achieve some kind of orderly life, when Scott was being brought in night after night by taxi drivers, at six o'clock in the morning. I just spent sleepless nights until I convinced myself that I did not give a damn and did not care." Scott interrupted to say that his behavior was a reaction to her mental state. "Zelda—had almost a hundred doctors, I figure, who gave her bromides, morphine; I can count six in St. Raphael. I can think of five in New York." When she objected to his arithmetic, Scott reduced the number: "I can think of—well, say fifty.

Maybe I have exaggerated; fifty doctors who had to give you morphine injections. Do you remember that?" Edouard was never far from their discussion. Scott accused Zelda of sabotaging his writing by getting involved with the Frenchman, to which she countered, "As far as destroying you is concerned, I have considered you first in everything I have tried to do in my life."

Of critical importance to Zelda was creative freedom, what she would be allowed to write. Scott insisted on approving her ideas and claimed their life experiences as his literary property. He dismissed her writing as amateurish, telling Rennie she had nothing to say and would never have gotten published but for his reputation. "Why do you think you met Leger? Why do you think you were in the Russian ballet? Why do you think the Johns Hopkins Clinic got us? And why do you think Dr. Forel kept you there? Do you think they did it because you have a pretty face? They did it for commercial reasons. It was part of their advertising and the money that was being paid for it." He demanded that she not write about mental illness or their experiences abroad until *Tender Is the Night* was published. "If you write a play, it cannot be a play about psychiatry, and it cannot be a play laid on the Riviera, and it cannot be a play laid in Switzerland, and whatever the idea is, it will have to be submitted to me." If she didn't agree it was back to the asylum: "Here are the alternatives. Either you be committed to a sanitarium, which is scandal, a trouble and an expense, or you do differently." Zelda argued that she had fueled Scott's work at her expense but would no longer. "I am so God-damned sick of your abuse. . . . I have considered you first in everything I have tried to do in my life. . . . I would rather *be* in an insane asylum, where you would like to put me." As the breadwinner, Scott remained adamant that Zelda not encroach on his territory. "A woman's place is with the man who supports her. I am the one to steer the course and the pilot. I am the captain of the ship. Everything we have done is mine. If we make a trip and you and I go around—I am the professional novelist and I am supporting you. That is all my material." He wanted her to pursue another direction and suggested she go to art school, become a cartoonist or designer, or write observations about things she could sell for money. As Dr. Forel had previously, Rennie concluded that Zelda needed to relinquish her literary ambitions or the marriage. She responded by telling Scott, "I don't want to live with you. . . . I think honestly the only thing is to get a divorce, because there is nothing except ill will on your part and suspicion." Ultimately, she gave in to his demands but with conditions. "I am perfectly willing to put aside the novel," she told Rennie, "but I will not have any agreement or agreements, because I will not submit to Scott's neurasthenic condition and be subjected to these tortures all the time. I cannot live in this world, and I would rather live in an insane asylum."

Shortly after, Scott contacted his classmate Edgar Allan Poe Jr., a partner in the Baltimore law firm of Bartlett, Poe, and Claggett, to ask which states allowed divorce on grounds of insanity. Under certain conditions, sixteen did. Nevada was the most lenient, requiring only a six-month residency with the patient needing a two-year confinement. Although Scott did not pursue this route, he outlined a divorce strategy and offensive tactic, to be employed if Zelda continued working on her novel: "Attack on all grounds. Play (suppress) Novel (delay) Pictures (suppress) Child (detach) Schedule (disorient to cause trouble) No typing. Probable result—new breakdown." He had figured it all out. And though Zelda installed a lock on her study door, ultimately she realized it was fruitless. She put the manuscript aside and told Dr. Rennie, "I am going to be a writer, but I am not going to do it at Scott's expense. . . . So, I agree not to do anything he doesn't want, a complete negation of myself, until the book [*Tender Is the Night*] is out of the way."

Several weeks later she vented her frustration by burning clothes in a second-floor fireplace at La Paix, replicating something she had done in Hollywood. Fire spread throughout several rooms, destroying her artwork and some of Scott's books. A photographer from the Baltimore paper captured the aftermath, Andrew Turnbull looking perplexed at the camera and Zelda sitting among things hastily thrown into cartons. Still in pajamas with a topcoat thrown over, Scott told reporters that faulty wiring had caused the fire. The next day he offered apologies to Bayard Turnbull, who was furious over the incident, especially when Scott asked that repairs be postponed until his novel was completed. Bayard agreed, thinking the smoke-damaged house might encourage the Fitzgeralds to leave.

Scottie also attracted media attention that summer when a reporter for the *New York Times* interviewed her about being the progeny of Jazz Age parents. The headline read, "Daughter of Fitzgerald, Aged 12, Criticizes Heroines of *This Side of Paradise*, Holds Flappers Fail as Parents." After saying they had become incompetent parents who expected children to be taught everything in school, and provided no solid foundation, she complained, "They don't seem to think a lot about their children . . . they don't see them very often, except when they come home from business, and say 'go upstairs and be quiet.'" That had been her experience and finally she was prepared to admit it.

The following month Zelda faced a greater calamity when her mother telegrammed that her brother, Anthony, had suffered a nervous breakdown. He had never been able to navigate through life, and distressed over the loss of his job and inability to pay bills, had started having nightmares about murdering their mother. He told doctors he would kill himself first. After being sent to a sanitarium for a rest cure, he was taken to a nerve specialist in Asheville, North Carolina, then to another in Mobile, Alabama, where he was admitted to a hospital. When Zelda spoke to him by phone, he asked to be transferred to Phipps Clinic, but the family said they could not afford it. Although nursing staff were advised to monitor Anthony carefully, he managed to leap from his hospital window and died on August 27, 1933. Obituaries in the Mobile and Montgomery papers provided few details, and the Sayres fabricated a story saying he had contracted malaria as a civil engineer and fallen through the window in a state of feverish delirium. Malaria may have contributed to Anthony's death but in a different way. When it was observed that symptoms in schizophrenics lessened after their temperatures rose dramatically, doctors employed Wagner-Jauregg's malarial fever treatments, inducing fevers in patients by injecting them with sulfur and oil of turpentine. From a chemical standpoint, there is no difference between depression caused by the end of an affair or the death of a family member, and replicating what had occurred after her father's passing, this became a tipping point. The whole episode was beyond Zelda's comprehension, and she began to question whether the entire family was doomed.

Although Scott's novel was still unfinished, abruptly he announced they were moving into Baltimore, where he rented a brick town house at 1307 Park Avenue in the Bolton Hill neighborhood. It was a narrow three-story row structure with high ceilings, shuttered windows, and white marble steps, six blocks from the Menckens and a short distance from the Maryland Institute College of Art where Zelda took lessons. The couple immediately made friends with John Work Garrett and Alice Warder Garrett, who were prominent in the Baltimore art scene and owned a magnificent forty-five-room estate called Evergreen on North Charles Street. Alice was the socialite daughter of an Ohio businessman who started the farm machinery business that became International Harvester, and John, grandson of the president of the B and O Railroad. Out of civic interest, John spent three decades with the State Department, being posted to various embassies, and was assigned to Paris in 1914, where Alice became involved with dancers and choreographers of the Ballets Russes. As a patron of classical dance, she co-funded the Ballet's 1917 season that debuted Jean Cocteau's *Parade*, featuring costumes and sets by Picasso with Olga Kolchova in a leading role. The artist and dancer were in a relationship then and would marry the following year. One of Alice's decorative projects at Evergreen was to turn John's boyhood gymnasium into a theater, and she commissioned Leon Bakst to create set designs. Zelda long had been captivated by Bakst's work and relished the opportunity to view it firsthand. The couple owned almost a hundred Bakst pieces, and Alice had convinced the artist to lecture at the Maryland Institute of Art. Although two decades older, she and Zelda developed a friendship and Zelda gave the couple several paintings she had completed in art class.

Before long, however, dwindling finances necessitated another move, this time to the Cambridge Arms Apartments in Charles Village opposite the campus of Johns Hopkins University. Scott now was drinking continuously, often frequenting the Owl Bar on Chase Street in the Belvedere Hotel, one of the city's notorious speakeasies. Starting early in the afternoon, he would throw some down with other writers and journalists, including Louis Azrael who then wrote for the *Baltimore Sun*. One afternoon Scott became so drunk, Louis had to take him home. This elicited a note of appreciation from Scott, saying that without his help, he might have wandered through the streets and met the fate of Edgar Allan Poe, who was found delirious outside a Baltimore bar and died soon afterward. Richard and Alice Lee Myers, neighbors of the Murphys at Cap d'Antibes, were then living in Baltimore and their daughter Fanny had renewed her friendship with Scottie. She recalled one noontime, when Scott rang their doorbell, stumbled in drunk, and staggered upstairs to fall asleep on her bed. For Zelda and Scott both, things were spiraling downhill—and fast.

· 9 ·

An Ailment No One Could Cure

*W*ith the repeal of the Volstead Act on December 6, 1933, Prohibition finally ended, and after celebrating for a week, Scott settled down to complete final revisions for *Tender Is the Night*. He had taken the title from Keats's "Ode to a Nightingale": "Already with Thee! Tender Is the Night; but here there is no light, save what from heaven is with the breezes blown through verdurous glooms and winding mossy ways." Set on the French Riviera, the novel's heroine, Nicole, is someone who gives little thought to consequences and enters recklessly into an affair. "Nicole did not want any vague spiritual romance; she wanted an affair; she wanted a change. . . . All summer she had been stimulated by watching people do exactly what they were tempted to do and pay no penalty for it." Her lover is Tommy Barban, a half-French/half-American soldier of fortune who embodies the characteristics of Edouard Jozan and Tommy Hitchcock, who Scott earlier had tapped as his model for Tom Buchanan in *The Great Gatsby*. Again, he employs Hitchcock's first name, selecting Barban as a surname to suggest barbarianism, fictionalizing what he imagined might have occurred between Zelda and the French pilot. "Barban came over behind her and laid his arms along hers, clasping her hands . . . their cheeks touched and then their lips, and she gasped half with passion for him, half with the sudden surprise of his force. . . . There was some scent in his hair, a faint aura of soap from his white clothes. . . . 'Do you like what you see?'" No need for an answer; his response said it all.

He patterned Dick Diver and Nicole Warren after himself and Zelda with certain characteristics drawn from Gerald and Sara Murphy. Since diving from heights was Zelda's favorite feat, Diver became the couple's last name. The young actress, Rosemary Hoyt, was based on Lois Moran, and Mrs. Hoyt, on her mother, Gladys. The novel opens when Rosemary encounters Nicole and her husband, Dick, along with Tommy Barban, Dick's exact opposite and a powerful opponent, portrayed as having ferocious courage, something between a lion and a drunken man. When Nicole asks if his heroics resemble anything from the movies, he responds, "I *only* know what I see in the cinema . . . now this Ronald Colman—have you seen his pictures about the *Corps d'Afrique du Nord*? They're not bad at all." When she chastises him for staying away too long, asking why he couldn't just slaughter a smaller number of men, he explains further that such is the way of courageous men. "Mais pour nous heros, il nous faut du temps, Nicole. Nous ne pouvons pas faire de petits exercises d'heroisme—il faut faire les grande compositions." (For us heroes, we cannot do small exercises of heroism; they must be the great compositions.) Barban takes what he desires without hesitation, what Zelda expected that July day, as she listened for Edouard's steps outside Villa Marie. "He was one of those men who had a charger," she wrote. "She always knew it was tethered outside, chafing at its bit, but now, for once, she didn't hear it, though she listened for the distant snort and fidgeting of hoofs."

Scribner's serialized Scott's novel several months before its publication on April 12, 1934. After reading excerpts, Ernest Hemingway told Maxwell Perkins that much of it was better than anything Scott had written previously. Zelda's response was markedly different. Not having seen the manuscript, she was shocked at how much he had pillaged her writing. Along with personal details of her breakdown, she recognized entire sections of her letters from Prangins. Although Scott had used her correspondence before, she considered this a callous exploitation of her psychological trauma. "What made me so mad," she told Rennie, "was that he made the girl so awful and kept reiterating how she had ruined his life, and I couldn't help identifying myself with her because she had so many of my experiences." After having been forced to put her book aside, only to see personal details of her breakdown now in his novel, Zelda became distressed to the point where outpatient sessions could not keep her stabilized. Still grieving over Anthony's suicide and struggling with her own depressive episodes, she suffered another relapse, and almost two years from the day of her initial hospitalization, was readmitted to Phipps and placed under the supervision of Drs. Rennie and Meyer.

What exacerbated Zelda's relapse was Scott's connection of Nicole's psychosis to a molestation by her father. As unlikely as it seems that Judge Sayre might have abused Zelda, after *Tender Is the Night* was published, rumors to that effect circulated in Montgomery. Virginia Foster Durr, a younger contemporary of Zelda's, revealed that Minnie Sayre told her the judge once had come to her bedroom, and she locked him out. The story went around town, that after this refusal, the judge might have turned to Zelda. More likely, Scott's connecting of Nicole's psychosis to a sexual encounter stemmed from his knowledge of Zelda's ordeal on the school playground. His character notes for Nicole suggest this: "Nicole is a portrait of Zelda—that is, a part of Zelda," and the rape took place when she was fifteen, "innocent, widely read, but with no experience and no orientation." However, Scott usurped not only her psychological trauma, but also sensitive information about her treatments and interactions with doctors. So informed was his narrative, that the *Journal of Nervous and Mental Diseases* called him an expert on adaptive responses to mental illness and lauded the novel as "an achievement which no student of psychobiological sources of human behavior, and of its particular social correlates extant today, can afford not to read."

Although Zelda and Dr. Rennie had developed a good relationship, after the publication of *Tender Is the Night*, she no longer wanted to remain at Phipps and asked to be transferred elsewhere, telling Adolf Meyer, "My reason for wanting to change is that I feel an environment in which I have not suffered so much unhappiness would be beneficial." Out of desperation she reached out to Oscar Forel at Prangins, but Scott would not let her leave the country and instead contacted Craig House, a private sanitarium in Beacon, New York. Forel probably recommended it, since his colleague, Jonathan Slocum, was supervisory physician there. Located on a large estate overlooking the Hudson River, with gardens and expansive views, its central building once had been called Tioronda, the mansion of Civil War general and philanthropist Joseph Howard. Upon his death, it was donated to the cause of mental health and acquired by Drs. Jonathan Slocom and Robert J. Lamb, who had worked together at Mattawan Hospital for the Criminally Insane. They named it Craig House after a Scottish sanitarium where patients walked around freely. As the first licensed, private psychiatric hospital in America, it soon became popular with celebrities, including John Kennedy's sister, Rosemary, institutionalized there in the 1940s after being rendered infantile by a lobotomy. During following decades, Jackie Gleason, Truman Capote, and Marilyn Monroe also were patients. Henry Fonda's second wife, Frances Seymour, mother of Jane and Peter Fonda, arrived there after their divorce and committed suicide in her room, slitting her throat with a razor. His first wife, actress Margaret Sullavan, who later starred in Scott's screenplay *Three Comrades*, would also take her life.

Craig House resembled a country club, with indoor and outdoor swimming pools, tennis and badminton courts, a golf course, and art studios. By selecting such a place, Scott may have been assuaging guilt, and Zelda initially appreciated its pleasant atmosphere. "It's so pretty here," she wrote him. "The ground is shivering with snowdrops and gentians. The curtains are like those in John Bishop's poem to Elsperth, and beyond, the lawn never ends." The sanitarium used the cottage system, in which patients lived with a private nurse and doors remained open. Patients could do as they pleased within certain limitations, and recreational activities were encouraged along with occupational therapies. However, when Zelda arrived on March 8, 1934, Dr. Slocum seemed perplexed by her symptoms, noting in his admissions report that "she suffered from fatigue, was mildly confused, and mentally retarded, with a degree of emotional instability." Ten days later, he wrote Scott that Zelda still appeared exceptionally fatigued, and they were prescribing a rest cure. "It has been our observation that she tires easily, and the matter of fatigue must be watched and cared for. I talked with her yesterday about the possibility of her having a week's rest in bed, getting up between three and four for outdoor exercise, and going back to bed." A week later Slocum sent a progress report: "We try to have her rest as much as possible; in this direction we insisted that she have her breakfast served in bed, and have her relax following it. She has massage at 11:00 o'clock, and in this way, she rests for a half hour after. She thinks this is not the way to make good, because she wants to be as active as possible in her work. However, I assured her that she requires this amount of rest and she looks much better." Given Zelda's proclivity for physical activity, Scott questioned Slocum's approach and requested a more precise diagnosis, but he was reluctant to provide one, writing Scott, "I would not like to make even a tentative diagnosis at this time. I think that therapy would be wrong at this particular time; many of her thoughts and feelings are simply a matter of fatigue." Although visits were discouraged during these initial weeks, Scott continued writing Slocum long letters about Zelda's condition. He sought clarity about intervals between her breakdowns and grasped at any theory that might explain their recurrence. Whatever life left to them was slipping away quickly.

During occupational therapy, Zelda worked on amassing a body of artwork, and that March, Scott contacted Cary Ross, a poet they had met in Paris, to arrange an exhibition of the work. Now involved in the New York art scene, Cary attempted to interest Manhattan galleries, even contacting Alfred Stieglitz and Georgia O'Keefe, but received only negative responses. He then suggested showing Zelda's thirteen paintings and fifteen drawings in the lobby of the Algonquin Hotel and his Manhattan studio. Scott believed recognition for Zelda's art could be recuperative and wanted preparations to go smoothly, but when he inserted his opinion into every detail, she grew frustrated and refused to continue. After Cary wrote her a pleading letter she finally relented, telling Scott he could proceed and apologizing for her rudeness. The exhibition went forward and Zelda came to the opening with a nurse, staying at the Algonquin with Scott. The show ran from March 29 to April 30, 1934, accompanied by a checklist she had designed, which bore the image of a swan and epigram, *Parfois la Folie est la Sagesse*—Sometimes

Madness Is Wisdom. The title worried Scott, but Cary assured him the public would interpret it symbolically, and never know the work was completed in a mental institution.

Zelda used her time in Manhattan to visit Georgia O'Keefe's show at Stieglitz's An American Place gallery. She felt connected to the artist in style and subject matter, particularly her close-up magnification of flowers. From her room at the Algonquin, she wrote Thomas Rennie about O'Keefe's work: "They are so lonely and magnificent and heartbreaking and they inspire a desire to communicate, which is perhaps the highest function of anything creative." Maxwell Perkins hosted a luncheon in her honor and friends came to the exhibition and bought works. Richard Myers, Muriel Draper, and Robert Lovett purchased drawings. The Murphys bought an oil painting titled *Chinese Theater Acrobats* portraying a gnarled mass of performers, and Gilbert Seldes selected two oils and a drawing called *Swimmer on a Ladder*. Maxwell Perkins chose *The Plaid Shirt* and *Spring in the Country*, and Tommy Hitchcock bought *Au Claire de la Lune*. Tom Daniels, who had carried Scott's manuscript of *This Side of Paradise* from St. Paul to New York, purchased *La Nature*. Zelda's two most accomplished works, a portrait of Lubov Egorova and one of Scott entitled *Portrait in Thorns*, showing him with a crown of thorns piercing his forehead, elicited multiple offers. The art patron and collector, Mabel Dodge Luhan, who often invited Scott to her Greenwich Village evening soirees in the twenties, wired a bid from New Mexico for his portrait, but when Zelda refused, instead purchased a drawing called *Red Death*. Zelda yearned for just one victory to propel her toward wellness, and while *Time* magazine called her work rhythmic and vividly painted, and the *New Yorker* and *New York Post* both ran complimentary articles, art critics considered her an inspired amateur and devoted more space to discussing her as a twenties icon than professional artist. It was a deflating experience that Scott described to Dr. Slocum by letter: "The exhibition, as she may have told you, was a weird affair of sizable and enthusiastic clusters of people, and of long blanks, where Zelda and the curator sat alone in the studio, waiting for someone to appear. I can't guess at her reaction, except she seemed sunk."

Critics treated *Tender Is the Night* only slightly better, with the *New York Times* saying the novel was brilliantly surfaced, but not the work of a mature novelist. Scott dismissed the article, writing Mabel Dodge Luhan that he no longer respected their opinion. "I get a pretty highly developed delirium tremens at the professional reviewers . . . the dumb men who regularly mistake your worst stuff for your best and your best for your worst." Nevertheless, he was aware their opinions influenced sales, and when the book sold poorly, it was a crushing disappointment.

With Scott's novel in bookstores, Zelda anticipated being able to resume work on *Caesar's Things* and reminded Scott of their agreement. "About my book, you and the doctors agreed that I might work on it. If you now prefer that I put it aside for the present, I wish you would be clear about saying so." Scott evaded the question and cautioned psychiatrists to discourage Zelda from undertaking such a project. When it became clear that she would not be allowed to write in the form or subject she desired, a veil dropped between her and the world. The hospital now seemed a pointless extravagance and she wrote Scott, "I cannot see why I should sit in luxury when you are having such a struggle. Since there seems to be no way in which I can hasten my recovery, maybe it would be wise to try a cheaper place. . . . I am not headstrong, and do not like existing entirely at other peoples' expense and being a constant care to others, any better than you like my being in such a situation." When Scott disregarded her suggestion, she grew insistent. "You must realize that to one as ill as I am, one place is not very different from another, and that I would appreciate you making whatever adjustments would render your life less difficult." She suggested being transferred to a state hospital, and wrote Scott, "I do not feel as you do about state institutions. Dr. Myers, and I suppose many excellent doctors, did their early training there." Scott knew differently, aware that conditions at state institutions often were so overcrowded that patients slept in hallways, and the more severely ill restrained in straitjackets. Many were filled with chronic schizophrenics who simply were warehoused. He dismissed that possibility and settled instead on Enoch and Sheppard Pratt Hospital in Towson, Maryland, outside Baltimore, one of America's oldest mental hospitals and private, but less expensive than Craig House. On May 18, 1934, Zelda boarded a train in Beacon accompanied by a nurse and arrived at Grand Central Station in Manhattan by noon. Scott met them at the information desk, and from there the couple continued on to Baltimore. Dr. Slocum wrote Scott the next day, acknowledging that Zelda's nine weeks at Craig House had largely been unproductive. "I hope Mrs. Fitzgerald reached Baltimore safely and comfortably, and that Chapman will be able to influence her in the right direction with reference to her progress and career. This, I very much regret to say, our group was quite unable to do."

Adolf Meyer was kept aware of Zelda's circumstances through Thomas Rennie and probably encouraged Scott to transfer her to Sheppard Pratt, since three of their doctors spent one day each week working in Phipps's outpatient clinic. Founded in 1853 as Sheppard Asylum by Quaker merchant Moses Sheppard, in 1929 it was renamed after railroad magnate and steamship owner Enoch Pratt, who designated it a beneficiary in his will.

By the time Zelda arrived, Harry Stack Sullivan, loved and hated with equal intensity, had been gone three years, but his influence was still being felt. Colleague Dexter Bullard considered him a genius and prophesized his work would outlast that of Adolf Meyer. Sullivan pioneered psychoanalytical treatment for patients, believing that mental health problems initiated in dysfunctional relationships and could be mediated by teaching patients to recognize recurring patterns. He trained staff members to become involved with patients as participant-observers, an approach with numerous detractors. William Worcester Elgin was one of them. After he completed his medical degree at Johns Hopkins, he replaced Sullivan and became Zelda's supervisory physician. Described by Dr. Ross McClure Chapman, who directed Sheppard Pratt from 1920 to 1948, as an excellent physician and able psychiatrist with a pleasant personality, he never impressed Zelda that way. She took an immediate dislike to Elgin, and he found her expressionless and inaccessible. Like many large hospitals Sheppard Pratt was overcrowded, and Zelda was assigned to a barren ward filled with patients in various stages of emotional upheaval, some violent, others suicidal. Within a short time, her symptoms worsened. As one of Elgin's thirty-one cases, it was easy to avoid contact, but when she began vacillating between violent outbursts and seclusiveness, he confined Zelda to a restricted area, instructing attendants to watch her closely. For comfort she turned to the Bible and riveted her attention on the scriptures, writing Sara Mayfield that it was her only solace, and to live she needed to pray. Her hallucinations returned, only this time it was Scott's terrifying voice shouting the message she had died.

Elgin accepted Zelda's label of schizophrenia at face value, and new drug interventions for that condition were being tested at the hospital: stramonium administered for mania, digitalis for depression, and the newly discovered barbiturate, sodium amytal, for sleep. Psychiatric treatments varied according to doctors' whims, and it was a period of unregulated experimentation. In 1934, Sheppard Pratt began administering convulsive treatments using the drug metrazol. The procedure first had been used by a Hungarian physician in 1933 but was perfected by Manfred Sakel at the University of Vienna. Between 1934 and 1935, he published thirteen papers on the benefits of metrazol shock therapy for treating schizophrenics, his most famous patient being the dancer Nijinsky, who improved slightly but suffered memory loss. Oscar Schwoerer trained with Sakel in Vienna and was hired to initiate these new procedures at Sheppard Pratt. Doctors were uncertain why metrazol shock relieved symptoms, so the intervention was never used with young patients during their first attack, or if the prognosis indicated that symptoms would be of a short duration. Generally, it was reserved for patients with a history of the condition who had enough strength to withstand the arduous treatment.

This was not taking a pill with a glass of milk, but a grueling ordeal. There was no control over which region of the brain was disabled or the degree to which it was traumatized. Twice each week, Zelda was injected with an aqueous solution of metrazol. After experiencing what felt like an explosion in her head, preliminary seizures followed for a minute, producing contractions violent enough to cause fractures and cerebral hemorrhaging. After initial confusion, there would be uncontrollable outbursts, drooling, bedwetting, and finally the convulsive seizures. These lasted for about an hour and usually ended in coma. Most patients appeared calmer afterward, but there was a dulling of intellect and memory loss. They could no longer recall what had caused them anguish, but their ability to think and feel was impaired. Gradually, the subtle distinctiveness of Zelda's personality was getting erased.

Terrified by what was being done to her, in a letter to Scott in February 1935, dictated to a fellow patient because her eyes were clotted with blood, Zelda articulated clearly—for one so out of her mind—that she saw no purpose in continuing the marriage. "You have always told me, that I have no right to complain, as long as I am materially cared for, so take whatever comfort you may find in whatever self-justification you can construct . . . since we have neither found help or satisfaction in each other, the best thing is to seek it separately. You might as well start whatever you start for a divorce immediately." She recognized everything was out of her control, and seeing no end to suffering, told Dr. Harry Murdoch who had joined the staff five years earlier that she wanted to do away with herself. Suicide was commonplace at Sheppard Pratt and patients found ingenious ways to carry it out. One smashed his head to a pulp on the walls of a seclusion room, another tore the door off a medicine cabinet and drank a bottle of carbolic acid, and a third drowned herself by sticking her head in a toilet. Although Zelda was carefully watched and permitted only occasional and closely monitored outings, she tried two times, once by strangulation with a bed sheet. Placed on suicide watch, she was transferred to a part of the hospital with twenty-four-hour observation. Scott's part-time secretary, Isabel Owens, kept him informed of her condition: "Mrs. Fitzgerald has been moved to a closed ward and has a special nurse. She is very confused again and rather depressed but offers no reason. I first noticed the beginning of a change two weeks before you left."

To seek clarification about the hospital's approach, Scott wrote Murdoch a lengthy letter about Adolf Meyer's largely unproductive treatment: "He gave back to me both times, a woman not one whit better than when she went in. . . . He encouraged Zelda's desire to express herself—knowing she had broken down over that twice before! . . . Once he had done what he could with Zelda, he shoved her back on me and refused to take her back." In fact, Meyer disapproved of continuing institutional care for Zelda, believing it did more harm than good. He recognized her need for freedom and warned Scott that prolonged confinement could render her passive and further disintegrate her personality. But Scott contradicted him and focused on Dr. Murdoch, asking what he was prepared to do. Scott also wrote Thomas Rennie at Phipps, inquiring if he should move Zelda again, obliquely trying to determine if Meyer would take her back. Dr. Rennie replied on May 27, "It is Dr. Meyer's feeling that this present condition is a true depressive reaction, from which she will recover, but the course may be protracted, and in her present state of suicidal intent, she needs the constant supervision that she is getting at Sheppard." Rennie recently had published an article in the *Archives of Neurology and Psychiatry* concerning improvement rates in schizoid patients, and told Scott that patients often faced unpredictable changes in their recovery. Although contact with a physician or hospital was helpful, the most critical element was the removal of stressors causing psychotic episodes, along with the person's ability to resynthesize their personality.

Besides Mrs. Owens's discouraging letter about Zelda, the mail brought more bad news when Mencken wrote on March 31 that Sara Haardt was in critical condition: "My dear Scott, Poor Sara, I fear, is now gravely ill—in fact, the chances that she will recover seem to be very remote. After all her long and gallant struggles, she has developed meningitis, and the doctors tell me that the outlook is virtually hopeless. You can imagine my state of mind." Loss and illness permeated Scott's world, the most incomprehensible being the death of Gerald and Sara's fifteen-year-old son, Baoth. A boarding student at St. George School in Rhode Island, he had been placed in the school infirmary after catching a severe cold, but then developed measles along with ear complications, which progressed into a double mastoid infection. His uncle Fred had undergone two mastoid operations in 1913 and the family was very concerned. They had reason to be; as a result of a procedure on his ear, bacteria entered his spinal fluid and triggered meningitis. Although immediately transferred to Massachusetts General Hospital, he soon died. Unlike his younger brother, Patrick, who had contracted tuberculosis in Hollywood, Baoth was always the healthier of the two boys, which made his death seem more tragic. The Murphys shared their grief about Baoth's death and apprehension over Patrick's lingering illness with Scott. "It occurs to me that you alone knew how we felt these days—still feel. You are the only person to whom I can ever tell the bleak truth of what I feel," Gerald wrote, "Sara's courage and the amazing job which she is doing for Patrick, make unbearably poignant the tragedy of what has happened—what life has tried to do to her. I know that what you said in *Tender Is the Night* is true. Only the invented part of our life, the unreal part—has had any scheme of beauty. Life itself has stepped in now and blundered, scarred and destroyed. In my heart I dreaded the moment when our youth and invention would be attacked in our only vulnerable spot—the children, their growth, their health, their future." Sara took time from her own grieving to bolster Scott's spirits: "You have been cheated (as we all have been in one way or another) but to have Zelda's wisdom taken away—which would have meant everything to you, is crueler even than death. She would have felt all the right things through the bad times— and found the right words to help. For you, and for her real friends—I miss her too—you have had a horrible time—worse than any of us, I think—and it has gone on for so long, that is what gets us, saps our vitality—your spirit and courage are an example to us all."

A continent away in France, Edouard Jozan's life could not have been more different. By 1936, he was rapidly advancing in his career and still the most impressive presence in any room. Earlier in the decade, he had been assigned to torpedo duty aboard the *Tempete, Fortune,* and *Alcyon,* afterward selected for the Naval War College in Toulon, and upon receiving his Brevet d'etat Major, assigned to Centre de Ballons Captifs de Toulon, the airbase for dirigibles employed in aerial observation. On schedule to make admiral by fifty, his next assignment as aide to the naval secretary at the French Ministry of Aviation would position him for that rank.

As Zelda deteriorated at Sheppard Pratt, Edouard was preparing to fly across the Atlantic in commemoration of one hundred years of French rule in the West Indies. In January 1936, he climbed into the cockpit of the *Lieutenant Vasseau-Paris* to copilot the giant seaplane from France to Senegal, then across the south Atlantic to Brazil and Martinique. Through fog and rain, it roared across the ocean, landing safely at Pensacola's Naval Air Station in Florida, which had welcomed foreign vessels since the nineteenth century. The following day as the seaplane was about to take off for Miami, it unceremoniously was overturned during a squall, then retrieved by a derrick, dismantled, and shipped back to France. Edouard and copilot Bonnot were feted for two weeks at the base, then flown to Washington, DC, on January 28 and entertained at the French Embassy. Zelda was only an hour away, but Edouard would never have recognized her. Her mind was washed clean, and as Scottie recalled, she exhibited that apologetic self-consciousness of people who feel distanced from others. "She began to look different as most people with mental illness do. I suppose you are under such a strain that you begin to show the intense fatigue in your face. Mother was not pretty anymore."

By spring, her absorption with religion had escalated to where she believed the end of the world was near. Rosalind grew increasingly concerned, and when she visited that May, recognized how desperate her sister's condition was. Doctors informed her that because Scott interfered so persistently with their care, there was little they could do for her. When Rosalind returned to New York she wrote Scott, "Her present condition was a great shock to me, and I feel discouraged about her. Zelda seemed to me to be very ill. She was dressed in white and seemed very ethereal somehow, like somebody not of this world. She begged all during the visit for me to take her for a ride." She and Newman took control of the situation, and after conferring with Adolf Meyer, arranged to get her transferred to Highland Hospital in Asheville, North Carolina. Rosalind was asked to collect her things and recalled how few items there were. "One of the saddest memories I have, is of going through her trunk in Baltimore at Scott's request, before her departure for Dr. Carroll's, to see what there was that she might want to take with her. What I found was a bit of old clothing, a brass candlestick, and a musical powder box with a Pierrot on top that turned with the tune." Most of her possessions had disappeared along the way, left in places no one could remember.

Zelda arrived at Highland Hospital for Nervous Disorders on April 8, 1936, somewhat hysterical, and in the midst of hallucinating about William the Conqueror and Apollo. She considered it a fittingly lonely setting for whatever grieving needed to be done but wondered if she could make it through dogwood season. By the time apple trees blossomed, she would learn much about minding the rules, and not only survive one year but four, the exact amount of time Scott had to live.

All in Disarray

Zelda's initial impression of Highland was positive. It seemed a welcoming place situated on fifteen acres of landscaped grounds with tennis courts, swimming pools, and flagstone walks winding through oak groves and pine forests. Compared to Craig House it was moderately priced with a quarterly fee of $1,200. Pleading hardship, Scott negotiated the lower monthly rate of $240. To that was added $100 for Zelda's personal expenses and costs of day trips. Female patients were housed in Old Central, which overlooked tennis courts and flower gardens, and men stayed at Oak Lodge with mountain views, a well-stocked library, and club room for billiards.

Dr. Robert Carroll had founded Highland Hospital in 1904 and lived on the grounds in an impressive Norman-style residence. His wife, Grace, had been a concert pianist and ran a music school in their home, giving lessons and holding performances in an assembly room that could seat two hundred. A forceful and demanding man with a large nose and even larger ears, Dr. Carroll ruled by moral authority and established discipline from the moment people arrived. Female patients could not wear makeup, mirrors were forbidden in their rooms, and Sunday vespers at 4:30 were obligatory. Everyone was expected to cooperate in the hospital's systematic routine, and even staff members were wary of Carroll's authoritarian rule. As one student nurse recalled, the class was a little frightened of Dr. Carroll and in awe of the dictatorial doctor. Carroll pursued his medical degree at Marion Sims College of Medicine, going on to complete psychiatric training at Chicago's Rush Medical College, where Ernest Hemingway's father had studied. Having begun his career as a pharmacist, he had a broad understanding of the body's response to drugs, and generally believed they did more harm than good. He theorized that mental disorders stemmed from toxic substances in the body, and that by restricting the diet to certain foods and having patients engage in rigorous exercise, enough poisons could be dispelled to keep nervous diseases under control. Zelda's daily regimen involved a five-mile tromp through nearby hills, where rustic seats dotted the countryside and pegboards strategically were placed to let patients keep track of progress. Everyone had a personal goal and was expected to work toward it. The aim was to develop endurance, and given Zelda's natural athleticism, this proved effective.

Along with required walks, camping trips, and climbing expeditions, there was competitive baseball, softball, and basketball as well as tennis tournaments. Landon Ray directed outdoor activities. He was eight years younger than Zelda, attractive, and full of energy. They often took walks together, gathering wood for camping excursions, and he recalled one hike across Sunset Mountain when it started to rain, and Zelda trudged off into the briers to gather dry kindling. When the two were alone, things remained calm, but Zelda resented the intrusion of others, especially if female. "She once became so possessive," Landon recalled, "that she slapped a cup of coffee out of the hand of another woman who approached us in conversation."

Unorthodox in his thinking, Dr. Carroll prepared a graphoanalysis of Zelda's handwriting to better understand her character, and it accurately captured the spirit of her personality and approach to life. It described her as

> an enthusiastic person with an active mind and with great firmness and determination of character, and the will to have her way recognized or there will be trouble; but all in an amiable and quiet and even tempered manner. While having a scientific mind, her ideas are often inspirational, her intuition even amounting to psychic power. Is earnest and conscientious. Has social gift which makes her companionable, but she is bored by too much concentration on any subject. She has very little reasoning power and does not think connectedly or logically. Has decided creative ability, and is interested in life in general, but does not attach herself deeply to any one love, and does not demonstrate affection, her head ruling her emotions. She is capable of great efficiency in any work she undertakes. She has a variety of interests and some gift as a teacher and can transfer her impressions and knowledge with ease, and acts impulsively and hastily on occasions. Has little talent for the waiting game. Most contradictory nature. In almost every trait she has touches of the opposite. One thing the matter is, that she cannot concentrate on anything very long. Has scattered her energies in every direction, and has unsettled her gifts.

That Carroll could construe this from Zelda's handwriting in a matter of days, whereas Craig House remained baffled by her personality after two months, is indicative of his nontraditional treatment approaches.

Highland's prospectus summarized its innovative interventions and advertised itself as "an institution employing all rational methods in the treatment of nervous, habit, and mental cases, especially emphasizing the natural curative agents—rest, climate, water, diet, work and play." Its restrictive dietary rules stressed natural juices, starches, and vegetables, but no meat, milk, or eggs. Sweets were kept to a minimum, and no alcohol or tobacco allowed. Diet laboratories were maintained in each building, where specially developed meals were prepared. Since Carroll had no faith in laboratory-produced vitamins, considering them of little value, he viewed regulated diets as the only remedy for digestive problems. His nutritional beliefs were influenced by Presbyterian minister, Sylvester Graham, who concluded in the nineteenth century that a diet of fruits, vegetables, starches, and limited dairy could help manage neuroses. The Grahamite movement waned after its founder's death, but one of his followers, John Harvey Kellogg, superintendent of Michigan's Battle Creek Sanitarium, required patients to follow a similar regimen, and while experimenting with dietary options, perfected the corn flake, which was served daily to good result. He pioneered the wellness movement promoting biologic living and published *Good Health* magazine, which advocated a grain and vegetable diet, no alcohol or coffee, and chaste living to avoid syphilis, which before antibiotics was a highly contagious and deadly disease. Dr. Carroll based much of his nutritional thinking on the magazine's articles, with current and past issues displayed in Highland's library and made available to patients.

No whims of palate were allowed at Highland, and Zelda followed its regimen with wry humor. "Now, the head doctor had devoted considerable research to proving his point, that people were noticeably stupid, but not to be blamed for it. He couldn't understand why everybody didn't subscribe to living forever on milk and green vegetables, with chicken for national holidays and ice-cream twice a year." The occasional treat was a peanut butter sandwich on whole wheat. After years in mental institutions, Zelda had learned to survive their arbitrary rules, accepting that manifestations of human spirit always were regarded as illness and subject to reprimand: "Knowing this, patients (mostly) suppress themselves as much as possible, endure, and hope to get out." Each day was like the former and followed a strict regimen: gym class every morning, then occupational therapy followed by a walk. Visitors were not allowed during the first phase of treatment, and unannounced guests never permitted into patients' rooms. Nurses kept close watch on patients, and Zelda quickly learned to be mindful of staff members who always were snooping around.

Conscious of the connection between body and mind, Highland encouraged individual and group therapy sessions, along with reeducation programs tailored to patients' needs. Within months, Zelda's suicidal tendencies eased, and she started showing interest in her surroundings. For the Highland's New Year's costume ball in 1936, she choreographed a ballet, but there was still a feverish tinge to her dancing, and if nurses forgot to monitor her, she would practice to the point of exhaustion and be unstable the following day. Patients had to select some type of occupational therapy and Zelda chose art, trudging into nearby hills to paint the landscape. After setting up the portable easel a fellow patient had made for her, she painted the hollyhocks and rhododendrons that abundantly grew there and filled her room with magnolias and angel's trumpets that bloomed at night.

Along with his regimen of nutrition and exercise, Dr. Carroll promoted hydrotherapy, which he believed cleansed the system of toxins and produced tonic reactions not otherwise obtainable. He installed a new bath department in Central Building with sitz tubs, Turkish and Russian steam baths, and needle showers. Patients often underwent hydrotherapy sessions there before starting rest cures, which he felt offered unparalleled results for tension and exhaustion. This individualized treatment of overfeeding and complete relaxation required a private nurse and was an expensive proposition few could afford. However, since Highland operated a training program associated with Duke University, offering postgraduate courses in psychiatric nursing, costs were reduced since student nurses could serve in this capacity.

Science at any time is a consensual reality, and by the time Zelda arrived, Highland already had begun experimenting with insulin and electroconvulsive therapies to shorten the duration of schizoid symptoms. Metrazol had been replaced by insulin because it brought patients to coma more easily, and Manfred Sakel had renamed the new procedure insulin shock *behandlung*. Both drugs relieved symptoms in a similar way by dimming brain function. In May 1936, Sakel reported to the Swiss Psychiatric Society that he had observed improvement in numerous patients, and his improved method entered the psychiatric arsenal as its latest intervention. Sakel even moved to New York where he promoted its use in American hospitals. Although there was no scientific evidence or understanding of how insulin shock therapy or electroshock therapy worked, the dramatic recoveries doctors witnessed were enough for them to promote the procedures. Adolf Meyer quickly instituted insulin shock procedures at Phipps Clinic and recommended the treatment to colleagues.

Dr. Carroll was one of his collaborators and enthusiastically supported the new intervention: "The benefits of scientific treatment have been strikingly enlarged these last years," he wrote, "through the introduction of insulin, drug, and electric shock treatment—each offering special helpfulness in various types of mental disorder. Such specific treatment, followed by an adequate period of physical and emotional re-education, accomplishes degrees of restoration previously unknown." What Carroll meant by *emotional reeducation* was interactive therapy that trained patients how to reduce anxiety by altering behavior.

Mildred Squires, now acting director of the Long Island Home for Nervous Invalids in Amityville, New York, also supported the use of insulin and metrazol therapies, and discussed their effectiveness in the *Psychiatric Quarterly*. Although she felt some schizophrenics had more on their mind than shock could divert, for others the treatment successfully interrupted the illness and broke apart frustrating states. She cautioned, however, that patients responded to convulsive therapies at different intensities, and advised doctors to approach treatments both quantitatively and qualitatively. Certain patients reacted more favorably to metrazol than insulin, or the reverse, and these differences appeared related to their prepsychotic personalities and hostilities underlying their psychoses. Squires believed success depended on whether the illness was still in flux and the patient fighting to get well, or if the person had given up. It was what her former boss, Adolf Meyer, had warned against, if Zelda remained institutionalized.

Since there were no standard guidelines for insulin treatments, doctors developed individual approaches. The preferred daily dosage was gradually increased until comas were produced, each lasting up to an hour and terminated by intravenous glucose. Seizures sometimes occurred before or during the coma, when there would be much moaning and thrashing about. All patients at Highland undergoing this treatment were kept together on the fifth floor of Central Building, where they were carefully watched, since there was always the danger of hypoglycemic aftershocks.

In addition to standard fees, specific treatments like insulin and electric shock therapy, incurred additional charges, and Scott was having difficulty paying the adjusted rate. All his books were out of print or going that way, and he was $40,000 in debt. He wrote Harold Ober that Craig House was suing him for nonpayment of fees, and that it was impossible to write under these conditions. "I realize that I am at the end of my resources physically + financially. After getting rid of this house next month + storing furniture, I am cutting expenses to the bone, taking Scottie to Carolina instead of camp + going to a boarding house for the summer."

He relocated to Tryon, North Carolina, about an hour north of Asheville, and immediately after arriving, was introduced to Nora and Maurice Flynn. Nora was the youngest of the five Langhorne sisters, Southern belles who became Northern debutantes, each exceptional in her own way. Phyllis wed a renowned British economist, Lizzie became the wife of a Southern gentleman farmer, and the most celebrated, Nancy, married Waldorf Astor, the richest man in England, later becoming a member of Parliament and championing women's rights. The most beautiful, Irene, became the wife of Charles Dana Gibson and was immortalized as the "Gibson girl," fashion icon of the twenties. Of the five, Nora was the most independent and high spirited, and like Zelda craved attention. Her affairs were not only about passion; she loved the "idea" of romance and one followed closely on another. Her first marriage to British architect Paul Phillips ended as a result of her infidelity and after divorcing him, she wed Maurice Bennett Flynn, nicknamed "Lefty" because he kicked with his left foot while playing football for Yale. Like Edouard and Tommy Hitchcock, the good-looking Flynn had been a fighter pilot, then went on to star in silent films. Predictably, Nora became involved with Scott in Tryon, and later he boasted she fell in love with him and wanted to run off, but he declined because of not wanting to be her last conquest. Scott found Nora and Lefty engaging narrative material and fictionalized their marriage in a story called "The Intimate Strangers," in which the couple, Sara and Killian, while loving one another, remain strangers scarred by past relationships. In notes for the story, summarized under the heading "Descriptions of girls: the fearlessness of women," Scott expressed his astonishment over the recklessness of females like Nora and Zelda, who entered perilous situations without thinking, spoiled babies, he thought, who never felt the economic struggle. He considered Zelda the most reckless of them all, someone who never planned, just let herself go and allowed the overwhelming life in her to do the rest.

When Zelda began showing improvement she was permitted weekend excursions and visited Rosalind in Manhattan, who noted her sister's progress. "At Asheville, where much of the institutional atmosphere was lost in pleasant lodgings, but where uncompromising strictness was the rule, and cooperation of the patient was demanded, Zelda bloomed again, and on several visits to me in New York during that period, was almost like her old self, beautiful once more, still interested in music, the theatre and art, but toned down to an almost normal rhythm." To see her more regularly, Scott moved from Tryon to Asheville during the summers of 1936–1937 and stayed at the Grove Park Inn. The massive granite structure had a long terrace lined with rocking chairs, from where one had a panoramic view of the Blue Ridge Mountains and across the valley, Highland Hospital. For Zelda's thirty-sixth birthday that July, Scott planned an excursion into those mountains, but the day got ruined after he injured himself diving into Grove Park's pool. "I left the hotel for the hospital that morning, fully intending to be back here in time to lunch with you," he wrote apologetically, "but the xray showed that there was a fracture in the joint of the shoulder, and a dislocation of the ball and socket." To compensate for the disappointment, he brought her to the

Grove Park Inn for lunch the following week, where they ate in the formal dining room and she ordered a cucumber salad. Although it was important for Zelda to remain calm, Scott was still capable of provoking a stressful situation. While they waited by the lobby's elevator to go upstairs, Scott approached a group of librarians meeting there and introduced himself as the author of a Ernest Hemingway novel. When one of them expressed doubts, he countered, "You don't believe me, do you? I'm Scott Fitzgerald. I wrote *Of Time and the River.*" The assertion made the librarian laugh:

> I assured him, that either he wasn't Fitzgerald, or he hadn't written *Of Time and the River.* This effrontery on my part only increased his indignation. It was unthinkable that a mere snippet of a librarian should doubt the word of a celebrated author. Meanwhile, the woman at his elbow kept muttering impatiently, "Come on, Scott! Come, on Scott!" "I'll prove to you that I'm Scott Fitzgerald. Come with me!" He was quite excited now, and my companion and I followed him through the crowd to the hotel registration desk. A dark haired little clerk on duty there saw us coming. The alleged Mr. Fitzgerald said to him indignantly, "You tell this young lady who I am!" The clerk took in the situation at a glance. In a quiet, even voice and looking directly at me, he said: "This is Mr. Scott Fitzgerald. He wrote *Of Time and the River.*" We walked over to the elevator after this, and the Fitzgeralds, as they proved to be, got out before we did. Mr. Fitzgerald turned and looking me straight in the eye, delivered his parting shot. "Any time you read a book about a river, remember I wrote it!"

Although Scott was having money problems and being hounded by Zelda's former hospitals for nonpayment, he still enrolled Scottie at Ethel Walker's School in Connecticut, one of the most expensive preparatory schools for young women. As she later recalled, "The choosing of what was then, one of the five or six best-known rich girls' schools in the country, illustrates once again that curious conflict of attitudes he had about money and society with a capital S. In one sense, I think he would have hated it, if I hadn't been at a 'chic' school, but no sooner was I there, than he started worrying about its bad influence on me." To pay its hefty fees, Scott borrowed additional funds from Maxwell Perkins and Harold Ober and approached Rosalind and Newman, who declined, saying it would be an inconvenience. Scott reminded Zelda that when he had loaned Newman $500 in 1925, it hadn't been any more convenient for him.

Awkward as it was, Scott had to request additional money from Harold in May 1937. "What I need is a substantial sum: 1st to pay a percentage on the bills, 2nd for a full month's security + 3rd to take Zelda for a three day trip to Myrtle Beach, which I've been promising for two months and which the sanitarium wants her to take. She hasn't been out of hospital for 3½ years + they feel that she's well enough for the trip." Harold sent the money, but two weeks later, when Scott requested another advance, he closed the tap and said no. Scott was incensed and appealed to Max Perkins, who wired $600, enough for Scottie's tuition and Zelda's hospital expenses. Weeks later, when the situation again became desperate, he telegraphed Oscar Kalman in St. Paul that he was deeply in debt to Scribner's and the insurance company, and no longer could pay the typist or buy medicine. He asked Oscar for an immediate $1,000 and $5,000 within the week. Oscar wired it immediately, and that was followed by a check from the Murphys. Scott wrote both his appreciation, saying their generosity was the only pleasant thing to surface in a world where he felt passed by.

Temporary relief came that summer, when Scott's mother died of a cerebral hemorrhage and there were funds from her estate. Now, when he visited Highland he could take Zelda shopping in Asheville and to dinner. She never missed an opportunity to plead with him for a normal life. "There are so many houses I'd like to live in with you. I don't know how you get one, but I think if we saved a great many things—stamps and cigar bands, soap wrappers and box tops we could have it some way."

That reality seemed increasingly unlikely. When he rented a cottage in the North Carolina countryside and brought everyone together, Zelda's fluctuating moods required constant supervision and allowed no time to concentrate on anything else. He summarized the experience to Dr. Carroll: "There would be episodes of great gravity that seemed to have no build up, outbursts of temper, violence, rashness, etc. that could neither be foreseen nor forestalled." When the couple met with a psychiatrist at Highland to discuss the situation, the doctor was struck by their shared intimacy. They understood each other so well and could shift from anger to amusement in seconds. In an effort to illustrate something unsettling, Scott referred to an incident that had occurred while they were out riding, but when Zelda denied it, Scott simply shrugged it off, saying perhaps it was a schizophrenic horse. Zelda thought that hysterical and burst into laughter, complimenting him on the joke.

Their sense of humor was still intact, but so were other things. Though more than a decade had passed since the Jozan episode, Scott still was replaying its drama, and that year *McCall's* published "Image on the Heart," his most detailed working out of Zelda's betrayal. Filled with predictable twists, the story opens in Rehoboth Beach, Delaware, where Scott's male protagonist, Tom, learns that Tudy's husband has drowned on their honeymoon. Barely knowing her, he convinces Tudy to let him fund a trip to France. "He fell in love with her helplessness, and after a few months he persuaded her to let him lend her the money to go abroad and study for a year." Soon afterward, he proposes and she accepts, but conflict emerges when Tom arrives in Provence for the wedding and discovers Tudy has become involved with a French pilot, Lieutenant Riccard. Aware things have changed, he asks, "Are you by any chance interested in this French boy? If you are, it's all right with me. We've been apart for a long time." Tudy denies any relationship, but later kisses Riccard in front of Tom. When he objects, complaining, "You didn't actually have to kiss him tonight," she counters in typical Zelda fashion, "You were there—you saw. There was nothing secret about it. It was in front of a lot of people." The two men later confront each other, and Riccard agrees not to see Tudy again, but upon leaving defiantly flies his plane over Tom's car, something Edouard may have done at Villa Marie. Then, when Tudy leaves for Paris to shop for the wedding, Riccard follows and takes the train back with her, getting off in Lyon so Tom will remain unaware. Only after the wedding does he discover that they have been together, and the seeds of doubt are planted: "He had to decide now, not upon what was the truth, for that, he would never know for certain, but upon the question, as to whether he could now and forever put the matter out of his mind, or whether it would haunt their marriage like a ghost." The heroine never reveals what occurred between herself and the French lieutenant, so Tom's torment is not put to rest, and their marriage begins under this cloud of suspicion. Like Zelda, who neither confirmed nor denied suspicions, Tudy allows her husband to imagine the worst. *Professio fundo vita*—art follows life.

After Scott celebrated New Year's Eve with Zelda, he returned to Tryon where he received word from the Murphys that their second son, Patrick, had died. He replied immediately: "The telegram came today, and the whole afternoon was sad with thoughts of you, and the past, and the happy times we had once. Another link binding you to life is broken, and with such insensate cruelty. . . . The golden bowl is broken indeed, but it was golden; nothing can ever take those boys away from you now."

Their telegram was followed by a letter from Harold Ober, asking if Scott felt well enough to make another attempt screenwriting in Hollywood. Scott was still angry over his begrudging response for a loan but replied in the affirmative. Harold then negotiated a six-month contract at MGM, beginning in July 1937 with an extension and raise in January 1938, if things went well. The weekly salary was $1,000, out of which Scott agreed to pay Harold $600 against what he owed, plus a commission for obtaining the job and money against his debt to Scribner's and Max. That left practically nothing for him.

He took a train from North Carolina to Manhattan to meet with Harold and attend the American Writers' Congress, where Ernest was presenting an anti-Fascist speech before the audience of 3,500 writers. Afterward, everyone was discussing it and Scott felt uncomfortable and deflated. When Carl Van Vechten ran into him at the Algonquin the following day, he was shocked how defeated he looked. "I was to have lunch with Edmund Wilson. We were to meet at the Algonquin. As I came into the room, my eyes had to readjust to the darkness, and I noticed a man with Wilson. I didn't recognize him and went forward to be introduced. It was a terrible moment; Scott had completely changed. He looked pale and haggard."

Scott arrived in Hollywood eager to work but with little energy. He budgeted thirty dollars a week for Zelda and a monthly allowance for Scottie, and when he sent his daughter the July check, emphasized his resolve to avoid studio politics. "I must be very tactful, but keep my hand on the wheel from the start, find out the key man among bosses and the most malleable among the collaborators, then fight the rest tooth and nail until, in fact or in effect, I'm alone on the picture." It sounded optimistic but wasn't the way Hollywood worked.

Assigned to a third-floor office in the Thalberg Building on the Culver City lot, he kept to himself, which was interpreted as arrogance. By now he was suffering from hypoglycemia, which gave him a tremendous craving for sugar. Generally, he would skip lunch in the studio commissary and eat chocolate bars at his desk, smoking filtered Raleighs and drinking Coca-Cola, sometimes thirty a day. If someone stopped by uninvited, he showed annoyance by acting rudely, which made others criticize him behind his back. On day one, he was asked to polish the script of *A Yank at Oxford* starring Robert Taylor, an easy assignment given all he had written about Princeton. Nevertheless, he had difficulty getting down to work because the whole endeavor seemed pointless.

Ernest then arrived to arrange studio distribution for the Spanish Civil War documentary he had cowritten with Lillian Hellman and Archibald MacLeish. Dorothy Parker and husband Alan Campbell also were in Hollywood and made sure Scott got invited to the screening of Ernest's film at the home of Frederick March and Florence Eldridge. Ernest was to ask for contributions, and on the day of the event, Robert Benchley invited both authors to lunch, neither knowing the other would attend. Afterward, Ernest sent Scott an autographed copy of *For Whom the Bell Tolls*, prompting him to write Zelda with apparent envy, that Ernest's novel was a Book of the Month Club selection, and had been sold to the movies for $100,000. It was a far cry from Paris, he reminded her, when Ernest used to deride him for discussing "mere" sales. The novel would sell half a million copies in its first six months and make Ernest a wealthy man.

Almost evangelical in his resolve to remain sober, Scott avoided heavy drinkers and declined an invitation from Robert Benchley and Dorothy

Parker to go bar hopping along Sunset Boulevard, where both were regulars at Mocambo and Trocadero. Robert lived at the Garden of Allah on the corner of Sunset Boulevard and Crescent Heights, a group of villas and cabins converted to a hotel and apartments in 1927. It formerly was the residence of actress Alla Nazimona, who co-founded United Artists Studio with Mary Pickford, Douglas Fairbanks, D. W. Griffith, and Charlie Chaplin. Of Russian Jewish parentage, she was born Adelaida Yakovlevna Leventon in the Crimea and immigrated to America in 1905, reinventing herself many times over and becoming a leading silent film star.

Convenient for transients in the movie industry, when Robert Benchley moved in, the property housed twenty-five two-story stucco bungalows surrounding a swimming pool and catered to producers, actors, and screenwriters, who often were seen typing away outside their apartments. Every afternoon, residents congregated in Robert's bungalow for tea martinis served in cups and saucers from a glass teapot. The regulars included Dorothy Parker, John O'Hara, Charlie Butterworth, John McClain, and Eddie Mayer. When Scott stopped by, he noticed how much Robert could throw down and warned, "Don't you know that drinking is slow death?" to which his host quipped, "So, who's in a hurry?" Robert had come to Hollywood as a writer, but RKO subsequently hired him as an actor, and in 1935 he won an Oscar for the short film *How to Sleep*. Usually cast as an urbane sophisticate and heavy drinker, he was credited with the line, "Let's get out of these wet clothes and into a dry martini," to which Dorothy Parker added the quatrain, "I like to drink a Martini, but only two at the most, three I'm under the table, four I'm under the host."

Before Scott arrived, Edwin Knopf had rented him a Santa Monica apartment with a nice ocean view, but it was too far from the studios. So, when Carmel Myers suggested the Garden of Allah, he relocated there and occupied Villa number 1. It really was two apartments, upper and lower, and Scott used the second floor, while screenwriter, Eddie Mayer, lived in the space below. What made the place so convenient were its maid and room service. Billy, the Schwab's Pharmacy boy, delivered alcohol and cigarettes to the bungalows, and Ben, the bellboy, ferried sandwiches from Greenblatt's delicatessen across the street. As one former guest recalled, you could wake up at 10 a.m., phone Schwab's, and be certain that a bottle of Jack Daniel's would be at your villa by the time you'd hung up.

On Bastille Day, July 14, Robert hosted a party to celebrate the engagement of his friend Sheilah Graham, which began at her place on Kings Road and then moved to his apartment. Robert called Scott to come over, and Sheilah saw him there for the first time. The two never spoke that evening, but Sheilah later asked Robert who he was. When he told her it was Scott

Fitzgerald, she was impressed. Not that she had read his books; she simply was aware of his reputation. Two weeks later, they met again at a dinner dance sponsored by the Writers Guild at the Coconut Grove and exchanged a few words. The next day Eddie Mayer telephoned Sheilah to say Scott wanted to be formally introduced. Eddie had his own history with Sheilah. Unattractive, he had a hard time charming women, but managed to seduce Sheilah during her first months in Hollywood.

There was something about the glow of Sheilah's complexion that reminded Scott of the youthful Zelda, and he would later describe it in *The Last Tycoon*: "The skin with its peculiar radiance, as if phosphorus had touched it, the mouth with its warm line that never counted costs." Like Zelda, chosen by classmates as the girl with the most kissable lips, Sheilah's mouth was her best asset, set off by straight white teeth and a seductive smile. Uninhibited sexually, she openly admitted that, if not always happy, from the time of first discovering sex, she used it to get what she wanted. The year before, she had been involved with King Vidor, divorced from Elizabeth Boardman, and he had mentioned marriage, but just before Christmas eloped with somebody else. With the resourcefulness to survive anything, she considered it a temporary setback and quickly recovered. As Zelda had done in Montgomery, Sheilah played one man off against another and had no reservations about lying to ensnare them. A self-invented woman, when Scott asked her age, she responded twenty-seven, although actually thirty-four, and when he inquired how many men she had slept with, Sheilah answered eight, adding that was only an approximate figure. It probably was closer to eighty. Since the film industry was fabricated from lies and those running it as shallow as she, Sheilah thrived in Hollywood.

Sheilah accentuated her English accent and masqueraded as British upper class, when actually she was the daughter of an impoverished Jewish couple who fled Ukrainian pogroms to settle in Leeds, England. Born to Rebecca and Louis Shael in 1904 and named Lily, she was the youngest of six children. Her father was a tailor who died of tuberculosis when she was three, and her mother, who was illiterate and could not speak English, was forced to clean public toilets and do laundry to survive. With too many mouths to feed, when Lily was six, her mother deposited her at the Jewish Hospital and Orphan Asylum in south London, which became her home for the next eight years. While there she figured out how things worked, and changed the spelling of her name from *Shael*, to the more refined German sounding *Shiel*. She never fully recovered from being abandoned or the feelings of unworthiness that followed her throughout life. After leaving the orphanage and working as a housemaid, she found a job demonstrating toothbrushes and was noticed by John Gilliam, twenty-five years her senior. When they married, she changed her name to Sheilah, took speech lessons, and began reinventing herself. Although still married to John, she came alone to America in 1935 and bluffed her way into a newspaper job in New York, then got transferred to Los Angeles where she evolved into a gossip columnist. Two years later, Sheilah divorced John and became engaged to the Marquess of Donegall, part of their unwritten marriage contract being that she would give him a male heir. Always looking for a better deal, when she met Scott, she calculated him a wiser choice, believing she stood less risk of being discovered a fraud.

No longer widely read, Scott was still considered a celebrated author and Sheilah viewed him as an intellectual. He seemed to inhabit a world of lofty ideas, and when he put her on a reading program, she fancied herself the heroine in Shaw's *Pygmalion*. She was flattered by his interest and legitimized by his presence, but according to her son, "not in his league at all. Perhaps she had been with too many men; told outrageous lies." Acknowledging this, Sheliah told Eddie Mayer that she never understood why he loved her, since he had always fallen for rich and confident girls.

Deception was rampant on both sides. Sheilah concealed her impoverished Jewish background, and Scott kept his alcoholism under wraps, initially at least. When he brought her east to meet Maxwell Perkins, Harold Ober, and the Murphys, the reviews were mixed. Some of his friends considered her shallow and materialistic, while others thought she was a steadying influence. Scott remained conflicted, and Helen Hayes thought he stayed because she provided emotional support and treated her badly because she represented the second rate into which he had fallen. Clearly he was ambivalent. He never spelled her first name correctly, inverting the *i* with the *e*, and appreciated the fabrication more than the woman. These were Scott's declining years, and Sheilah provided what he needed. She genuinely admired Scott and never considered him a failure, and he appreciated their relationship for what it was. "Better take it now. It is your chance, Stahr," he wrote in *The Last Tycoon*. "This is your girl. She can save you . . . she can worry you back to life."

Though she knew Scott was married, Sheilah was unaware how connected he was to Zelda. He never discussed his marriage, and when she suggested they wed and have children, he was astonished she could *think* he had the energy or interest for a second wife and offspring. There was much brooding by Sheilah over this, but she moved in with him anyway, locating a Malibu beach cottage rental, owned by Frank Case who managed the Algonquin Hotel in New York. Since Scott did not own a car, she used hers to move his things from the Garden of Allah. The entire time they lived in Malibu, he never went into the ocean or took his shoes off on the sand, still embarrassed by the sight of his feet. He even kept his socks on in bed, which was fine with Sheilah, who never took off her brassiere. That summer, when Scottie and Peaches Finney visited California, things became awkward when Scott asked Sheilah to remove her belongings temporarily from the house. That he considered her something to be hidden came as a shock.

To commute to the studios, Scott bought a 1937 Ford from S. J. Perelman, who was married to Laura Weinstein, sister of Nathanael West. It wasn't long before it got stolen, and with wry humor he wrote Scottie, "The police have just called telling me they've recovered my car. The thief ran out of gas and abandoned it in the middle of Hollywood Boulevard. I hope next time he gets a nice big producer's car with plenty of gas in it."

During their time together, Scott and Sheilah moved three times: from the Malibu beach cottage to a guest house on the estate of Edward Everett Horten in Encino, and when that drive proved too long for Sheilah, from the San Fernando Valley back into West Hollywood. For appearances, she rented an apartment at 1443 North Hayworth Avenue, while he leased a smaller one at 1403 North Laurel Avenue. Among his neighbors in the L-shaped complex were Lucille Ball, who was dating band leader Desi Arnaz, and Joyce Matthews, who would marry Milton Berle and then Billy Rose. Schwab's Pharmacy was two blocks east, where Scott would drink a chocolate malted, and Greenblatt's deli on the corner of Sunset and Hayward, where he and Sheilah ate blintzes.

Zelda wrote Scott weekly letters, but lacking his actual address sent them in care of his Hollywood agent, Phil Berg. She wanted a family reunion, and in spring of 1938, Scott organized one at Virginia Beach. It quickly unraveled after Zelda got into an argument with Scottie, and Scott headed for the bar. Afterward, during one of Scott's alcoholic tirades, Zelda wandered the corridors saying he was a dangerous lunatic in need of institutionalization. When doctors arrived to calm Scott down, it took him some time to convince them that she was the crazy one.

Another year would pass before they saw each other again, for the last time. After New Year's, Highland was organizing a trip to Cuba for a selected group of patients, but because Scott was late giving approval, Zelda remained behind. To make up for that, Scott planned a trip to Cuba in April after Paramount canceled *Air Raid*, the film on which he had been working. Today, a nonstop flight from Los Angeles to North Carolina might take six hours, but in 1939, it could take eighteen to twenty-one, with four stops en route. Scott drank during the entire trip, and by the time the Fitzgeralds reached Club Kawama in Varadero, Cuba, 140 kilometers east of Havana, he was incoherent. Once he and Zelda checked in, he took off alone and got into a brawl at a cockfight. Zelda managed to get them on a plane to New York, where Scott picked another fight with a cab driver, then collapsed at the Algonquin Hotel. After having him admitted to Doctors' Hospital, she boarded the train back to Asheville alone. Two weeks later, when Scott finally returned to Los Angeles, he was filled with remorse and wrote Scottie he was considering bringing Zelda to California for a visit. But after a week back at the studios, he realized how much his absence had set him back, and that his contract was in jeopardy. He wrote Zelda, "I don't know how this job is going; things depend on such hairlines here—one must not only do a thing well, but do it as a compromise, sometimes between utterly opposed ideas of two differing executives. The diplomatic part in business is my weak spot." As his six-month MGM contract end neared, with only one screen credit to his name, his agreement was not renewed. Scott's firing ultimately came down to money. That January, the studio was obligated to raise his weekly salary to $1,500 and felt he wasn't worth it. Though he had remained sober for long periods, when he did relapse and miss work, Hollywood labeled him an unreliable drunk.

Without his MGM salary it was impossible to meet even basic expenses, and he began drinking again. Empty liquor bottles filled the garbage bin, daily consumption starting with beer, up to six 6-packs a day, and ending with a quart of gin. There were no further studio assignments so he returned to writing *The Last Tycoon* about the men who controlled Hollywood's movie business and particularly Irving Thalberg, who two years earlier had died at thirty-seven. Its central female character, Kathleen, was based on Sheilah, and the narrator, Cecelia, who regards events from a distance of several years, modeled after Lois Moran. *Collier's* agreed to pay up to $30,000 after approving the first fifteen thousand words, but after completing the initial chapter, Scott only had six thousand and requested a decision on that. When editors were unwilling to commit, he struggled to complete the rest.

Kathleen, called Thalia in an early version, is portrayed as the archetypical outsider who belongs nowhere, not even in Hollywood, a sanctuary for outcasts. As might be expected, Scott drew on his relationship with Sheilah for narrative and dialogue. But she was less quotable than Zelda, as when she gushes that being with Stahr makes her feel fluttery, like on a day in London during a caterpillar plague, when a furry thing dropped in her mouth. Scott's notes for Kathleen's character imply his ambivalence about Sheilah: "Stahr cannot bring himself to marry Thalia, [Kathleen]. It simply doesn't seem part of his life. . . . Thalia is poor, unfortunate and tagged with a middle class exterior which doesn't fit in with the grandeur Stahr demands from life."

With no income, Scott fell behind in Highland's payments and wrote Dr. Carroll, "I hope you will find it possible to let things go as they are for another month, trusting me as you did before. It is simply impossible to pay anything even on installments, when one drives a mortgaged Ford, and tries to get over the habit of looking into a handkerchief for blood while talking to a producer. . . . I hope this does not mean Zelda will be deprived of ordinary necessities." Apparently it wasn't, for that November she and some other patients joined Dr. Carroll for a three-week visit to Sarasota, Florida, where Zelda took courses in drawing and clothes designing at the Ringling School of Art. "I'm tanning myself and happy in such a fine heaven," she wrote Scott. "In this part of Florida, life seems to have nothing further to worry about than to open its shutters to a bright and new bazaar or newly acquired aspiration." Still uncertain about Scott's home address, she sent the card to his Hollywood agent, but now wanted to know where he was living. "What is your actual address? S'pose I wanted to phone you—or do something unprecedented like that? . . . What would I do if I should have a bad dream, or an inspiration?" When he finally sent his apartment's address on North Laurel, he began receiving letters pleading for release. She had been at Highland almost four years and wanted to live in Montgomery with her mother. "Janno had indeed learned a lot of things about minding their [Highland's] rules by the time the apples blossomed," she wrote in *Caesar's Things*. "Now that she was able to cooperate in these very expensive obligations, what she wanted most on earth was to be free of them." She had long since given up making friends with fellow patients who somehow managed to get away, and her mental state had improved, so what was the point of staying there?

Nor could Scott afford to keep her at Highland. There were no future contracts or advances from Harold. Upset over the debt she was incurring, Zelda discussed the situation with her sister, Marjorie, who asked Scott why he remained insistent she remain. "If you can't pay her board, where is she to go? Or is Dr. Carroll to keep her free of charge? Zelda only wants to go home, because she also is worried about you, and thinks she could quit being such a financial drain on you." Scott discussed the possibility with Carroll, who rejected the idea and explained his reasoning: "The facts remain unchanged—that she has been mentally injured, that the central nervous system is peculiarly susceptible, and that she should be protected with the same intelligence that any family would expect to give a member who has suffered from a damaging tuberculosis. Our suggestions have been carefully thought out, and include her having short vacations of ten days to three weeks about once in two months during the year. She is not prepared to live comfortably with any of the members of her family." Although Zelda's sisters and mother continued requesting her release, Scott was uncertain if she could function outside the hospital and fearful of being held responsible should she bring harm to herself or others.

At this point, Zelda appears to have taken the situation into her own hands, for Dr. Carroll did an abrupt about-face. Why this occurred may be connected to a rape accusation from one of his patients. There is some suggestion that Carroll was intimate with several, and that Zelda was among this group. Dr. Irving Pine, another psychiatrist on Highland's staff, testified to that accusation, saying, "Dr. Carroll treated his women patients badly, including Zelda." Determined to use Carroll's legal difficulties as leverage for her release, Zelda wrote John Biggs, "The proprietor (Carroll) has been implicated in a rape case (which could no doubt be substantiated from legal records) and might be willing to compromise." In some fashion Zelda maneuvered the situation to secure her release and wrote the prerequisite farewell letter to Highland's staff: "That life should once again have become desirable is a matter of my deepest gratitude to Dr. Carroll. . . . For the gracious supervision and the careful guidance that I have received at Highland Hospital, I am once more, gratefully yours." Scott then wrote Zelda's mother. "This morning I have a letter from Dr. Carroll, in which he suggests for the first time, that Zelda try life in Montgomery. This is a complete about face for him, but I do not think his suggestion comes from any but the most sincere grounds."

Before approving her release, Scott insisted that Carroll provide him a formal letter absolving him of any responsibility in event of relapse and guaranteeing that Zelda could reenter Highland whenever necessary. It was an agreement he always wanted from Dr. Meyer but could never obtain. Now, everything hinged on that same issue. After much consideration, Carroll finally consented, and on April 15, 1940, Zelda boarded an early morning bus for Montgomery. In her purse was a letter from Scott, written with unfamiliar coolness: "I do hope this goes well. Wish you were going to brighter surroundings, but this is certainly not the time to come to me, and I can think of nowhere else for you to go in this dark and bloody world. I suppose a place is what you make it, but I have grown to hate California and would give my life for three years in France. So Bon Voyage and stay well."

• *11* •

A Mind Washed Clean

*N*ever having witnessed her daughter's illness firsthand, Minnie Sayre was shocked by its severity. Readjustment was difficult for Zelda, and on June 18 she wired Scott, "I won't be able to stick this out. Will you wire money immediately that I may return to Asheville." That same afternoon she wired again, "Disregard telegram. Am fine again." Scott wrote the Murphys about her return to Montgomery saying, "She has a poor, pitiful life, reading the Bible in the old-fashioned manner, walking tight-lipped and correct through a world she can no longer understand. . . . Part of her mind is washed clean+she is no one I ever knew." The transition was made harder by Montgomery residents who regularly invited her to parties. "I remember one she came to," recalled a friend. "Everyone was standing in the garden with drinks in their hands, and when Zelda saw them, she dropped to her knees in prayer. You can imagine how that ripped Montgomery." Although her sister Marjorie warned people not to offer her alcohol, they did anyway. "They know that she simply cannot drink, yet they insist on inviting her to parties where they know liquor will be served; 'Oh, a little sherry won't hurt you!' Then one thing leads to another, and it ends up that we get a phone call in the middle of the night, and find her in such a state, that we have to get a nurse and a hypodermic to calm her down!"

These initial months required all Zelda's resources, and she told Scott she wasn't writing or painting because her focus remained solely on staying out of the hospital. To pass time she read on the patio off the kitchen, tended her mother's flower garden, and played card games on the front porch with her mother and Marjorie, who lived next door. After a while, she set up her easel and completed a painting of Scott with a cat on his shoulder in varying hues of green, and a self-portrait in which her eyes dominated the composition. Both were exhibited at the Montgomery Museum of Art. As she adjusted to breathing freely, she resumed letter writing and in one to Ludlow Fowler offered a glimpse into her life. "Down here, the little garden blows remotely poetic under the volupes of late spring skies. I have a cage of doves who sing and woo the elements and die. This little house looks like something out of the three bears; it would be fun were life less tempestuous."

When her uncle died and willed her several hundred dollars, Zelda wanted to pay down the Highland bill, telling Scott that she disliked, as much as he, being in debt to people she considered scoundrels. He appreciated the gesture but suggested she buy something for herself. Although Scott's expenditures had lessened, meeting basic costs still was a concern, and that September he asked the Murphys for another loan, writing, "You saved me— Scottie and me. . . . I don't think I could have asked anyone else and kept what pride is necessary to keep." He carefully apportioned what they sent, sending some to Scottie and applying the remainder toward outstanding bills.

Although America had not yet entered World War II, it was escalating widely in Europe, and Scott kept track of its progress on a map above his desk. France was at the center of things and Edouard where history was being made, rescuing Allied troops from Belgian beaches. On the day Dunkirk was evacuated, Scott and Sheilah were taking the train to San Francisco, when they heard a radio broadcast about the rescue effort and joined other passengers cheering in the aisles. After fighting erupted in North Africa and Mussolini's troops invaded Egypt, French troops were dispatched to Tunisia, and Edouard was chosen to command a flotilla of fighter pilots at Bizerte, forty miles from Tunis and a strategic location on the Mediterranean.

Less than five months later, on November 28, Scott suffered his first cardiac spasm while buying cigarettes at Schwab's Pharmacy. Short of breath, he felt a crushing pressure in his chest and sharp pain in his shoulder. Then, doctors knew little about the physiology of heart attacks, and there were no thrombolytic drugs or bypass surgeries. They could not control or cure these conditions and patients did not expect they would. After giving Scott nitroglycerin under the tongue for pain, his physician took an X-ray and performed an EKG, testing electrical activity in the heart. He then ordered him to bed rest. With a clear understanding of his condition, Scott funneled the calamity into *The Last Tycoon*. "Dr. Baer was waiting in the inner office. . . . He was due to die very soon now. Within six months one could say definitely. What was the use of developing the cardiograms?"

Although the spasm had damaged a quarter of his heart, Scott continued working in bed, propped up against pillows. Not to worry Zelda, he minimized his condition, writing her on December 13, "No news except that the novel progresses and I am angry that this little illness has slowed me up. I've had trouble with my heart before, but never anything organic. This is not a major attack, but seems to have come on gradually, and luckily a cardiogram showed it up in time." Concerned, she replied, "Take care of yourself. Though you say the doctors say you're far better than they think, I know you're not given to very accurate estimates of your condition." Unaware of his living circumstances, she suggested he come east. "Maybe you would be better off in this climate where the mountains might help you find more resistance again. . . . Don't just stay there and drift away." He was more honest with Scottie, admitting that after seeing his cardiogram, the doctor had confined him to the house, and he couldn't go to the studios even if he wanted to. In what would be their last communication, he cautioned, "You have two beautiful bad examples for parents. Just do everything we didn't do and you will be perfectly safe."

Unable to manage the stairs to his third-floor apartment on North Laurel, Scott moved around the corner into Sheilah's ground-floor flat. Although not feeling up to it, he and Sheilah attended a dinner at the home of Nathanael and Eileen West on Friday, December 13. Dorothy Parker and Alan Campbell also were there, along with Nat's other literary friends, Elliot Paul, Frances Goodrich, and Hilaire Hiler. Scott didn't particularly like Nat, but had a good relationship with his brother-in-law, S. J. Perelman, and the evening ended happily with the guests singing "The Last Time I Saw Paris."

To bolster his deteriorating health, Scott stopped drinking and limited his smoking, but time had run out. On, December 20, after eating supper with Sheilah at Lyman's Deli and attending a performance of *This Thing Called Love* at the Pantages Theater, he lost his balance when leaving his seat and felt dizzy all night. Although the forecast called for clouds and rain, Saturday was a sunny day with an afternoon temperature of 78 degrees. Scott was in Sheilah's living room reading the *Princeton Alumni Weekly* and had just finished eating a chocolate bar, when he suffered a massive heart attack around 3 p.m. and died. The cause of death was occlusive coronary arteriosclerosis, a condition common in alcoholics, where the walls and linings of the heart gradually erode. It was the shortest day of the year, December 21, 1940, and Scott was forty-four.

To avoid any scandal that might damage her career, Sheilah quickly had Scott's body moved to Pierce Brothers Mortuary, where it was put on view in the William Wordsworth Room. Only a handful of people came to pay respects, Dorothy Parker and her husband among them. "It was terrible about Scott," she wrote. "If you'd seen him you'd have been sick. When he died no one went to the funeral, not a single soul came, or even sent a flower. I said, 'Poor son of a bitch,' a quote right out of *The Great Gatsby* and everyone thought it was another wisecrack. But it was said in dead seriousness."

Scottie learned of her father's death that evening at the Obers', where she was spending the holidays, and it was Harold who called Zelda. She was walking with Julia Garland and when she returned home, her mother broke the news. At first, she could not comprehend the information. It seemed impossible he was gone. Who would be there now to offer her hope? "She wasn't going to have him anymore . . . not to promise her things, not to comfort her, not to just be there as general compensation." After discussing burial arrangements with the Obers, Scottie telephoned Sheilah to learn the circumstances of her father's death and request she not attend the funeral. Sheilah did the next best thing. After learning that Scott's body was being shipped east aboard the *Santa Fe Super Chief* on December 26, she boarded that train and put an accidental spin on it for the press. "Just before New Year's Eve, I suddenly decided to go to New York. I learned on the train that Scott's body was also on it, being shipped to Baltimore where he would be buried, so in a way he was still with me. Sydney Perelman was also on the train, accompanying the bodies of Nathanael West and Nat's wife, Eileen, who had perished in a car crash several hours after Scott had died." Nat was an appallingly bad driver and the couple killed after he barreled through an intersection and smashed into an oncoming car.

The day before Scott's burial, Gerald Murphy wrote Alexander Woollcott that Scottie seemed bewildered and that he and Sara were flying to Maryland for the funeral. She had anticipated her father's death for years, but still was not ready for it. The memorial service was held at the Pumphrey Funeral Home in Bethesda, Maryland, with a eulogy offered by Episcopalian minister Reverend Raymond Black. This time the room overflowed with flowers. Zelda sent a basket of pink gladioli; the Princeton class of 1917, yellow roses; the Turnbulls, a wreath of white ones; John and Margaret Bishop, chrysanthemums; and Anna and John Biggs, lilies and snapdragons. Not well enough to attend, Zelda asked Newman Smith to oversee arrangements. Scott wanted to be buried with his Maryland ancestors at St. Mary's Catholic Cemetery in Rockville, but the bishop of Baltimore objected, because he was not a practicing Catholic and had not received last rites. Instead, the burial took place at the Episcopal Union Cemetery in Rockville. Twenty-five of Scott's friends and relatives stood in a cold rain that December afternoon as his coffin was lowered into the ground. Mourners commented about Zelda's absence and Scottie's stoicism, but she was skilled at hiding emotions. "Of course I was upset that my father was dead," she said, "but I don't believe in any public show of grief." Rosalind did not attend, but Richard Knight was there, perhaps at Zelda's request and later visited her in Montgomery; that year he also divorced his wife. John Biggs became executor of Scott's estate, but resented his continual linkage with the couple. A Delaware Supreme

Court judge who seldom was queried over his legal opinions, he endlessly got questioned over being Scott's Princeton roommate. After being appointed to the federal court by Franklin Roosevelt, he vented his frustration saying, "I'm a Federal Court judge. I know Presidents. But all people want to ask me is what my drunken roommate was like."

After Sheilah Graham returned to Hollywood, she went to Scott's apartment to gather her things, and while removing her photo from a frame, noticed he had written "Portrait of a Prostitute" on the picture's reverse. Probably inscribed after one of their arguments, it remained Scott's condemnation from the grave. Sheilah embraced that role by having numerous casual affairs and became pregnant from two of them, her daughter probably the offspring of British philosopher A. J. "Freddie" Ayer. Seven months after Scott's death, she convinced Trevor Westbrook, a British aeronautics engineer, that he was the unborn child's father, and they married, establishing her daughter's legitimacy and providing his essential name. Two years later she again gave birth, this time to a son named Robert, probably the child of Robert Taylor or Robert Benchley, who insisted on being the boy's godfather. When Westbrook began doubting whether son or daughter was his, he divorced Sheilah. She lived into her mid-eighties and wrote several books about her relationship with Scott, accurately predicting she would only be remembered, if at all, because of Scott. Their relationship became the highlight of her life, and credit due, she took care of him during difficult times.

Before his death, Scott had completed only seventy thousand words of *The Last Tycoon*, but he left copious notes about the story line, and Edmund Wilson edited the half-finished manuscript throughout 1941 so it could be published that November. After reading it, Zelda wrote Margaret Turnbull of how intensely she disliked the character of Katherine, whom she described as a woman who knows how to capitalize on the iceman's advances, and smells of the rubber shields in her dress. The cunning desire to achieve one's ends by any means was something she always loathed in women.

In Montgomery, Zelda continued working on *Caesar's Things*, telling Margaret Turnbull that she was trying to weave religious imagery into patterns of everyday life. Initially, she planned on writing about her incarceration in mental hospitals, combining her experience with that of Vaslav Nijinsky's, who also got branded as schizophrenic by Bleuler. The renowned dancer had suffered a psychotic break at about the same age as Zelda and was taken to see Bleuler in Zurich. Since the doctor did not speak Russian or Polish, and Nijinsky could not understand German, French, or English, their communication could only have been minimal. Yet, after a characteristically swift diagnosis, Bleuler told Nijinksy's wife that her husband was incurably insane, and he was taken to a Swiss sanitarium called Bellevue. There, his condition dramatically worsened, and like Zelda he was doomed to a lifetime of incarceration. Gradually, over several revisions, Nijinsky was dropped from the narrative, and her novel evolved into a complex layering of autobiography and religious allegory.

The first four chapters involve the heroine's upbringing in a Southern town and her older sisters' more glamorous lives, material Zelda previously had visited in *Save Me the Waltz*. Chapters 5 through 7 concern the heroine's marriage to a painter, their life in Manhattan and France, and her affair with a French pilot, mental breakdown, and rehabilitation through faith in God. The title alludes to two verses from the Bible: the Gospel of Matthew 22:21—"Pay back, therefore, Caesar's things to Caesar, but God's things to God"—suggesting that human laws not in conflict with God's dictates should be followed, and wise choices made between superficial things of this world, and more valuable elements of the spiritual realm, and Deuteronomy 30:28, in which the boundaries of what we know are examined; certain things are best left in God's hands, but to what is revealed, we must pay heed.

The final chapter occurs in France and contains a long section about the heroine's love for a French pilot and punishment for her betrayal. Although an important element of *Save Me the Waltz*, here the affair is paramount. In homage to Edouard, the main characters' names all begin with *J*: Zelda is Janno and Edouard is Jacques, the same name she gives her lover in *Save Me the Waltz*. Scott is Jacob, here portrayed as an artist rather than writer. Occupations aside, in both narratives, the heroine's feelings about her husband's work are identical: "Jacob went on doing whatever it was that Jacob did; he was always doing something with pencils or pieces of string or notebooks. . . . He was more important than Janno."

When the French aviator encounters Janno, he pursues her immediately. "One day she met Jacques . . . he told her to come to his apartment. Janno was vaguely baffled by the pleasurable expectancy she felt." Blinded by passion, she blames fate for her actions. Again, the image of honeysuckle is invoked: "There were lots of places to have champagne and hangovers around the garden. . . . The dust hung over the honeysuckle and night birds wept in the loneliness." Without Scott as censor, the physicality of the relationship is made evident. "She kissed Jacques on the neck. It didn't matter now. . . . The kiss lasted a long time and there were two of them. . . . She should never have kissed him. First, she should never have kissed Jacques, then she shouldn't have kissed her husband. Then, after the kissing, . . . there should not have been any more." But there *was*, and no way to go back.

Sometimes, one or two incidents make an indelible impact on our lives, and for the Fitzgeralds, the Jozan affair became that marker. Scott wrote about the betrayal until he died, and twenty-five years after its occurrence, Zelda still was agonizing over its ramifications. "It was a sad love affair holding no promise and too impassioned to be dignified," she writes in *Caesar's Things*. *"None* of them . . . remembered the fact that, what counts is not the kiss, but the loyalties which are broken, the threads of fidelity which are frayed."

As the war overseas expanded and America dispatched troops, Zelda assisted the military effort by folding bandages at the Red Cross, but there were no more suitors from local depots. She had promised Dr. Carroll to walk several miles each day and stuck to that regimen, but distance walking was uncommon then and townspeople considered it odd. Lawton Campbell recalled seeing her near his aunt's home, clutching a Bible and wearing old clothes.

> While I was conversing with them on topics of the day, I looked up Sayre Street and saw coming down the hill a forlorn figure. "There's something familiar about that woman coming down the street," I said. "Who is it?" My aunts turned to answer my question and said in unison, "That's Zelda." But it was a different, "That's Zelda" than they would have said in the old days. It had no overtone of shock or surprise. It had only the undertone of pity. As she moved down the street, I could get a good picture of her. She wore a crewman's cap, a dingy sweater, a nondescript skirt and tennis shoes. Her hair was straggly and had lost its burnished gold. I walked down the steps to meet her as she approached the house. She greeted me with kind recognition but no spark of even feigned excitement. It almost seemed as if I were talking to a lifeless, faded, wax image.

Some days were better than others, and Zelda remained alert to her fluctuating condition, sometimes excusing herself from situations by saying she was "feeling precarious." She continued posting evangelical texts to friends, sending several to Edmund Wilson and Carl Van Vechten, and warning John Biggs in another, that he would die within the year and should prepare accordingly. Although her proselytizing embarrassed some, faith instilled the comfort she had always sought in others, and she told Ann Ober, "I would not exchange my experiences for any other, because it has brought me the knowledge of God . . . to accept with grace the implacable exigencies of life." To Scottie, her mother's newfound religion seemed irrational, and she took to leaving her letters unopened on the entryway table. Although they corresponded, Scottie kept visits to a minimum, and when announcing her engagement to Samuel Lanahan, delayed inviting Zelda until it was impossible for her to attend. "I feel guilty about having left notifying my mother until it was too late," she admitted, "but she was not well enough at the time, and I feared, that if she was in one of her eccentric phases, it would cast a pall over the affair."

Son of a wealthy stockbroker, Samuel was a Princeton grad and the sort of which Scott would have approved as a husband for his daughter. The wedding took place on February 13, 1943, in Manhattan's Catholic Church of St. Ignatius Loyola. Ann Ober bought Scottie her dress and Harold gave her away. The newlyweds sent Zelda a piece of the wedding cake that she shared with John Dos Passos, who was in Montgomery visiting. Perhaps, with him she shared her true feelings; to the Obers, she simply sent apologies for not being of more assistance. "Giving Scottie away must have brought back the excitement of those days twenty-five years ago, when there was so much of everything adrift . . . so many aspirations afloat." In a gesture of reconciliation, that spring Scottie invited Zelda to New York and arranged her stay at the Obers' place. Andrew Turnbull took mother and daughter to a performance of *Oklahoma*, and John Biggs came up from Wilmington to escort Zelda to lunch. It was a tense visit in which the pattern was always repeated. "The first day she would seem so well," Scottie recalled, "you couldn't believe she was a mental patient. . . . Then, the second day, she would begin to be nervous and somewhat absent-minded, and by the third day you knew she was under strain. It was almost like watching a clock run down."

After returning to Montgomery, Zelda expressed appreciation and gave Scottie an update on her novel. "I wish that my realms of epic literature would spin themselves out to a felicitous end. I write and write and have, in fact, progressed. The book, *Caesar's Things* still makes little sense, but it makes it very beautifully and may find a reader or two eventually." She made a second visit north to see her new grandson, Tim, who was born in April 1946, but when it came time to leave, she did not feel up to taking the train back alone. So Ann Ober accompanied her, and they stopped overnight in Wilmington with John and Anna Biggs who recalled her odd farewell.

> John mentioned that it was time to catch the train back to Montgomery. Zelda didn't seem to pay any attention, and we stressed it a bit more obviously. It was late. Perhaps we'd better get into the car, and so forth. Zelda said we didn't need to worry; the train wouldn't be on time anyway. We laughed and said, perhaps, but it was a risk we didn't intend to take. "Oh no," she said, "it will be all right. Scott has told me. Can't you see him sitting here beside me?" When they got to the station, the train was running thirty minutes late.

In the 1940s, doctors were unaware that insulin shock therapy caused patients to have recurrent relapses. These rebound psychoses built gradually until anxiety, headaches, and insomnia became incapacitating and precipitated another breakdown. Insulin shock therapy was not the miracle intervention initially thought, and outcomes were sometimes worse than if patients had done nothing. Zelda returned to Highland three times during the eight years she lived in Montgomery: from August 1943 until February 1944, then for eight months beginning early in 1946 until late that summer, and from November 2, 1947, until March 10 of the following year. By fall of 1947, she was so emotionally fragile, even the smallest incidents brought her to tears. As the situation worsened, her mother encouraged her to take longer walks, and when all else failed, the two prayed by Zelda's bed, as they had when she was a child. But prayers brought little relief, and she wrote Rosalind, "I have tried so hard and prayed so earnestly and faithfully asking God to help me. I cannot understand why he leaves me in suffering." On November 2, 1947, she boarded a train and returned to Highland for the last time. Dr. Carroll had retired two years earlier and Dr. Basil Bennett was now director. To staff members who remembered Zelda from earlier stays, she seemed greatly changed, showed little interest in surroundings, and was given to long periods of solitude.

Two months after arriving she began a daily series of insulin shock treatments. The procedure followed a set pattern and was formulated to cause a specific response. After being injected in the buttocks, her breathing became short, her temperature rose, and she started sweating. The insulin injection reduced blood sugar levels and precipitated two shocks: a dry one ending in convulsion, and wet one resulting in anabolic coma. The amount of insulin was increased daily over a course of six injections with comas beginning after five days. By destroying nerve cells in the cerebral cortex, the goal was to produce a controlled brain lesion. Only, determining the correct dosage was complicated. The deeper the coma, the greater the destruction of diseased neurons, but doctors had to be careful, since keeping a patient in coma too long could result in unwarranted brain damage and sometimes death. This procedure was repeated up to twenty-five times with the intent of inducing fifty to a hundred comas over a three-month period. For heightened results, electric and Cardiazol shock sometimes were combined with insulin injections during the deep coma period. After the initial shock came a loss of consciousness accompanied by violent jerking, and following that, epileptic seizure. In contrast to his American colleagues, Manfred Sakel discouraged combining electroshock with insulin, believing the trauma and resulting brain damage was too severe. It produced changes similar to those incurred from traumatic head injuries, not only wiping out memories but entire periods of a person's life.

When the procedure did work, it brought immediate though temporary relief, and patients subjected themselves to the ordeal because there were few alternatives. Impatient with her slow pace of recovery, Zelda expressed frustration to her mother, who wrote Scottie, "I'm distressed Zelda does not improve. Her letters to me are cheerful and she seems interested in the activities of the hospital. She also gives directions about her garden as if she expected to return. She is now in the hands of professionals and I must not make suggestions. The electric treatment is now being used in all hospitals for mental trouble. It may do her good. At least we can hope so."

Aside from her slow improvement, Zelda was upset over her weight gain, as insulin lowered blood sugar, stimulated the endocrine system, and made people ravenously hungry. Invariably, patients emerged from treatments grossly obese, the average weight gain over six weeks being fifty pounds. Zelda told Scottie she had grown so heavy, she would need to borrow her maternity clothes. Scottie recently had given birth to a daughter, whom Zelda had yet to see, and as she waited to improve, she worked on a gift for her, as well as Bible illustrations for her grandson, Tim. With passing weeks, she began feeling better and on March 9, 1948, wrote Scottie, "Today there is promise of spring in the air and an aura of sunshine over the mountains. . . . I long to see the new baby." For her final series of treatments, she was moved to the fifth floor of Central Building, where patients carefully were monitored for delayed shocks. After four months she was finally seeing progress and had been given permission to leave, when she decided to remain an extra week, to make certain she was at her best. That was a fatal mistake.

On the evening of March 10 a fire began around midnight in the third-floor diet kitchen of Central Building and quickly spread up an elevator shaft to the fifth floor, spewing flames onto each landing. Mainly constructed from wood, the large frame structure, three stories in the front and five at the rear, became an instant inferno with flames roaring up the dumbwaiter shaft to the roof. Wooden fire escapes collapsed and the entire structure became a furnace. The building had no alarm system connected to a fire department, no warning bell or gong to rouse patients, and no fire extinguishers or sprinklers. All doors on the fifth floor were locked, and windows screened with mesh wire, steel sashes, and bars to prevent escape. As customary, between nine and eleven that evening, patients had been given sedatives, which made them less likely to respond to abnormal conditions. The alarm had not been turned in until thirty minutes after the fire began, and when firemen arrived, the building had been burning for forty-five minutes. They doused the flames with water but the heat was so intense, it had little effect. Along smoke-filled corridors and stairwells, firemen hacked their way through locked doors and carried some patients to safety, while attendants struggled to lead others through smoldering halls. Townspeople heard screams from those trapped inside and retrieved several women who had wandered into nearby woods, where remnants of a March snowfall still powdered the ground.

By four in the morning, floors and ceilings from the roofline to basement collapsed, outside walls toppled, and Central Building's structure was reduced to rubble. There were twenty-nine female patients in the building when the fire began and everyone on lower floors got out. Of the ten on the fifth floor, nine were consumed by fire; only one escaped.

Alison Carter jumped to safety but was badly injured. Permanently disabled, she sued Highland Hospital in Buncombe County Superior Court for $150,000. Two nurses—Willie Mae Hall and Doris Jane Anderson—were among the defendants. Alison's lawyers stipulated that Highland was unsuited as a hospital for mental patients. As their brief asserts, on the night of the fire, Willie Mae Hall was assigned as night supervisor in charge of all patients, and Doris Jane Anderson designated to oversee Central Building and its twenty-nine patients. As the only nurse on duty to attend their needs, Anderson could not possibly monitor all floors, and there was nobody else to unlock doors and assist patients in escaping. She had no training on what to do in case of emergency and had never performed duties of a night charge nurse until the evening of the fire; she had been at Highland only several days, for the sole purpose of undergoing training. According to Alison's attorneys, Doris Jane Anderson was inexperienced handling mental patients and incapable of performing assigned duties. Moreover, locked doors and barred windows were prohibited in all but Grade A hospitals, and Central Building was categorized as C. By restraining patients in rooms without means of escape and not having someone to assist them, Highland Hospital was deemed culpable.

Zelda and eight other women on her floor perished, Highland's only fatalities. The others were Miss Borochoff, Miss Defriece, Mrs. Engel, Mrs. James, Mrs. Womack, Mrs. Hipps, Mrs. Kennedy, and Mrs. Doering, identified only by her diamond ring and wedding band. Zelda's remains were determined by their location, dental records, and a single burned slipper wedged under her charred body. An inquest followed examining questions of the fire's cause. Chief J. C. Fitzgerald (no relation to Scott) testified that if the fire alarm been turned in thirty minutes earlier, it could have been contained with no loss of life. He also stated that it was the third fire at Highland in less than a year. Two others had broken out the previous April, one in a mattress and another mysteriously ignited in a pile of oil-soaked rags under a stairwell. Chief Fitzgerald initially had surmised the current blaze started with an electrical malfunction in the kitchen, but now suspected arson.

In a bizarre turn of events, two weeks after the fire, the night supervisor, Willie Mae Hall, walked into Asheville's police headquarters and asked to be jailed, saying she was afraid she would start more fires at Highland. When asked if she had ignited the March 10 blaze, she replied she wasn't sure.

A judge ordered a psychiatric evaluation, and when it became clear that she had some involvement, Helen Kuykendall, a nurse at Highland, accompanied Willie Mae Hall to Duke University for psychological examinations. Rumors circulated that Hall was pursuing some vendetta against the hospital, disliked certain patients on the fifth floor, and heard voices telling her to set a fire. Adele Nims Yelvington, herself a patient at Highland, revealed that Willie Mae Hall told her she had fallen asleep smoking on duty and started the fire accidentally. She also testified that Hall, raised as an orphan, previously had set fires at one of her orphanages. Not actually a nurse but an aide, Willie Mae Hall was one of the so-called interchangables at Highland. When Robert Carroll was director, he frequently hired former patients to become nursing aides, and it had become an accepted procedure. Such staff members often were women escaping unhappy marriages or romances, and a shortage of trained psychiatric nurses necessitated this practice. In 1949, the *Baltimore Sun* reported that in the entire Maryland mental health care system, there were only twelve registered nurses for over nine thousand patients, and the situation in North Carolina was worse.

At the time of the fire, Highland was attempting to remedy that shortage. Hildegard Peplau, a psychiatric nurse who had studied with Harry Stack Sullivan and Erich Fromm, was developing a postgraduate course in psychiatric training. Six students with degrees from hospital programs who wanted to specialize in this area had been accepted, and Doris Jane Anderson was among them. An interview Peplau gave to the *Journal of Psychosocial Nursing* brings us closest to the truth about the circumstances behind Zelda's death. She told Dr. Shirley Smoyak that prior to the fire, she had argued with the nursing director about students being used as fill-ins for regular staff. But, in her capacity as night supervisor, Willie Mae Hall objected to this decision and insisted on assigning the six new nursing students to night duty. When Hildegard Peplau objected, Hall wound up assigning only one student nurse, Doris Jane Anderson. On the morning before the fire, when Peplau saw Hall in a hallway, she appeared angry, and when Peplau heard alarms on the night of the fire, she feared Hall had caused some incident. Doris Jane Anderson told Peplau that instructions were above the phone about what to do in an emergency, but that Hall had told her to disregard them and call her first. In case of fire, she specifically instructed Anderson *not* to contact the fire department. When Anderson smelled smoke and tracked it to the elevator shaft, she followed instructions and called Willie Mae's number, but it rang busy, which is when she contacted the fire department. Their report confirms that Central Building had been burning between thirty and forty-five minutes before they were notified. Truth serum later was administered to Willie Mae Hall, who admitted involvement with the fire, as well as over-sedating patients on the fifth floor and locking them in their rooms. She was found guilty of arson and committed to another mental hospital. Each victim's family was awarded $3,000 in compensatory damages, which the Sayres declined to accept, and Highland's director, Dr. Basil Bennett, forced to resign. He was replaced by Dr. Carroll's adopted daughter, Charmian, a former nurse who had become a psychiatrist and served as director until 1963, when Highland was bequeathed to Duke University.

Meanwhile, Zelda disappeared into smoke. What were believed to be her ashes were sent to the Bethesda mortician who had supervised Scott's funeral, and the same Episcopalian minister was asked to officiate. Minnie Sayre agreed to have Zelda interred in Maryland rather than Montgomery, and on a sunny St. Patrick's Day, she was buried next to Scott in Rockville's Union Cemetery. Mrs. Sayre did not attend, but Zelda's sisters and Scottie were there, along with some of the Fitzgeralds' friends, including John Biggs, the Obers, Mrs. Turnbull, the Stanley Woodwards, and Peaches Finney. Afterward, Scottie wrote her grandmother, "I was so glad you decided she should stay with daddy, as seeing them buried there together gave the tragedy of their lives a sort of classic unity, and it was very touching and reassuring to think of their two high-flying and generous spirits being at peace together at last."

After the funeral, Marjorie Sayre, who also was a talented painter and draftswoman, cleaned out Zelda's studio and held a lawn sale. A Montgomery art dealer found a three-foot stack of Zelda's oils among the items, but Marjorie didn't want them to be seen or sold and instructed the yard man to burn them in the backyard. She thought they held bad memories, but Scottie suspected jealousy. Marjorie kept a few for herself including *Night Blooming Cereus*, which she bequeathed to her daughter, Noonie, who later sold it to John Haardt's daughter, Anton. Exotic plants like the cereus fascinated Zelda, and she appreciated their mysterious flowering. Its succulent vine spawns white blossoms with a lemony scent and blooms once a year in the hours before midnight, then dies the following morning and closes up for another twelve months. The Southern writer Eudora Welty founded the Night Blooming Cereus Club in her hometown of Jackson, Mississippi, its motto echoing Zelda's approach to life: "Don't take it cereus—life's too mysterious."

During her marriage with Samuel Lanahan, Scottie had two sons, Thomas (Tim) and Jack Jr. (Jacky), and two daughters, Eleanor and Cecilia, but never was close to any of them and repeated some of her parents' mistakes. "She couldn't seem to give anything except the things money will buy," said daughter Eleanor. "She sent us to camp, bought us nice clothes and gave us festive birthday parties, but in between, she wished we'd just be happy and leave her alone." At Scottie's birth, Zelda had made the strange observation,

"I hope she'll be a beautiful little fool," and Scottie's comment at the delivery of her son, Tim, was equally bizarre: "At last we have a baby to put down the incinerator." That became unnecessary since Tim would do that for himself. He always had psychological problems and as Scottie recalled, "a disorderly mind—so packed with irrelevant material that he was never able to cut a clear path through it."

Although she wrote for newspapers and magazines and was active in Democratic politics, like many children of famous parents, Scottie was disappointed with her own accomplishments and regretted spending so much time on her parents' legacy. Nevertheless, she acknowledged their celebrity had paid her way through life: "I have developed a rather thick layer of tough skin over the years, which enables me to hear about my drunken father and crazy mother with enough equanimity to collect the royalty checks and try to ignore it." In 1967 after a twenty-year marriage, she divorced Jack Lanahan and wed C. Grove Smith, only to have that relationship quickly sour. To distance herself from Smith and care for her aunt Rosalind, she moved to Montgomery in 1973, and became something of a celebrity in her mother's hometown. In November 1975, she finally was able to rebury her parents in the Fitzgerald family plot at St. Mary's Cemetery in Rockville, and have their caskets placed in a double vault. The headstone was inscribed with the last lines of *The Great Gatsby*: "So, we beat on, boats against the current, borne back ceaselessly into the past."

Years of heavy smoking and drinking took their toll, and Scottie was diagnosed with tongue cancer in 1976. Against the advice of doctors, she continued both habits acknowledging, "It was a very cruel joke God played when he put cigarettes and alcohol into the universe for us to hang ourselves with." By 1981, the cancer was back, this time in her breast, and for a second time, she underwent surgery and radiation. Three years later, as she was planning a move back to Washington, she was diagnosed with esophageal cancer and died on June 1, 1986. She was sixty-four and buried at the foot of her parents.

Many of the Fitzgeralds' friends also suffered calamity. Ernest Hemingway would divorce second wife, Pauline, in 1940 and marry twice more, asserting at the end of his life that Hadley was the only woman he truly loved. After receiving the Nobel Prize for literature in 1954, he struggled with bouts of depression and in 1961 underwent electroconvulsive shock therapy at the Mayo Clinic, interventions that severely compromised his memory. On July 2 of that year, he committed suicide by shooting himself in the mouth. While serving as a lieutenant colonel in World War II, Tommy Hitchcock Jr. was killed in a plane crash. Dr. Thomas Cummings Rennie died at fifty-two from a cerebral hemorrhage. Edmund Wilson suffered a nervous breakdown and was institutionalized in Clifton Springs, New York, where he almost became addicted to the sedative Paraldehyde. Alex McKaig died of late-stage parietal syphilis in his mid-forties at a mental hospital in Middletown, New York, and John Dos Passos lost an eye in an auto accident that decapitated his wife, Katy. Ring Lardner succumbed at forty-eight from tuberculosis aggravated by alcoholism, as did Lady Duff Twysden at forty-five. After the deaths of her son and husband, Lubov Egorova lost her finances through mismanagement and died in a home for the aged and indigent. Peyton Mathis and John Haardt both drank themselves to death. Robert Benchley succumbed to cirrhosis of the liver at fifty-six, and after being disbarred from practicing law, Richard Knight died from alcohol poisoning. Sara Haardt Mencken passed away at thirty-seven from tuberculosis, and Gerald and Sara Murphy lost both their sons as teenagers.

Sara Mayfield, who briefly married John Sellers in 1924, was incarcerated in a mental institution for seventeen years. Her unorthodox behavior and drug addiction got her diagnosed with the label of "moral insanity," frequently ascribed to women who disregarded prescribed roles. As the daughter of one Alabama State Supreme Court judge, and sister of another, she was considered an embarrassment to the family. As her cousin, Camilla Mayfield, explained, "It was never confirmed publicly within the family that Sara had lesbian relationships, though people had gotten a whiff of it from several places. . . . There are two things in the deep south which in that period would have been seen as deeply personal and shaming and would bring stigma on the family; one was anything sexual being homosexual or bi-sexual, and the other was anything that could be construed as psychotic behavior." Sara exhibited both. Compromised by her behavior and convinced of her instability, her brother committed his thirty-five-year-old sister to Sheppard Pratt, the same hospital in which Zelda was confined, later transferring her to Bryce Mental Hospital in Tuscaloosa, Alabama, at that time considered the worst asylum in America. She made the best of a horrific situation by using her journalism skills to establish a weekly newsletter called the *Bryce News* that reflected the concerns of patients and caregivers. After questions surfaced as to whether her seventeen-year commitment was justified, President John F. Kennedy intervened at the request of George Wallace and finally got her released.

Only Edouard seems to have survived intact. As intended, he immersed himself at the center of history, and when Zelda withdrew to Montgomery and Scott lived obscurely in Hollywood, he was commanding a French naval flotilla and rescuing troops from Belgium beaches. Two years later, he was fighting with the Free French Resistance against the Germans in the Pyrenees. Apprehended by the Gestapo near Luchon and imprisoned in Toulouse for five months, he was then transported to Eisenberg, a camp for political prisoners in southern Germany near the Czech border. He escaped from there, only to be recaptured and sent to Oranienburg-Sachenhausen, a training facility for SS soldiers and concentration camp for political prisoners. Fellow inmates included Stalin's oldest son, Yakov Dzhugashvili; the British Special Operations Executive agent Peter Churchill; and Paul Reynaud, France's last prime minister before its German defeat in 1942. For two and a half years Edouard was imprisoned there, a period in which fifty thousand inmates died from disease and malnutrition. He might also have perished but for food parcels from Queen Alexandrine of Denmark, a close friend of his mother-in-law. Family connections made a difference but could not save him from the Sachenhausen Death March in spring of 1945.

As the Red Army advanced during the war's final days, Hitler ordered the camp's evacuation, and early on the morning of April 21, 1945, thirty-three thousand prisoners started marching northeast in groups of four hundred toward Schwerin on the Baltic, where the SS planned to load them on ships to be sunk. In cold, wet weather, the columns trudged between twenty and forty kilometers a day, each man grappling with the overwhelming necessity to keep going, since anyone lagging behind was shot. Hungry and thirsty, weighed down by fatigue, Edouard and others trudged through windswept potato fields, up steep hills and forested valleys, until reaching Wittstock, where German guards deserted them on April 23 to flee American troops from the Seventh Tank Division. Only nine thousand men survived the ordeal, and Edouard was among them. With other French soldiers, he was taken to Paris, then Cannes, where he was reunited with his family.

When he returned to active duty later that year, his career gathered speed. After being assigned to Naval General Staff Headquarters, and then the cabinet of Edmond Michelet, minister for the armies, he was posted to Morocco and Tunisia as *préfet* of the marines and commander of the navy, then, as commandant of the Mediterranean Air and Marine Force, promoted to vice-admiral. At fifty-two, he attained the rank two years later than planned. In what would be the apex of his career, in 1954 he was assigned to Indochina as commander-in-chief of the French naval forces in the Far East.

With the end of World War II, France sought to reestablish their colonial presence in Indochina, establishing base operations at Dien Bien Phu near the Chinese and Laotian border. Military strategy was overseen by politicians in Paris who made two mistakes: entering Indochina without clear objectives and underestimating the Viet Minh's resolve to keep foreigners out. Their approval was required for larger military operations, and Edouard grew increasingly frustrated that progress was thwarted by incompetent bureaucrats. Unable to pacify the country or subdue the Viet Minh, when Dien Bien Phu fell, French involvement in Vietnam ended. The Geneva Accord divided Vietnam at the seventeenth parallel, with the north supported by Russia and China, and south backed by the Americans.

One final occurrence soured Edouard on the whole endeavor. In June 1955, Prime Minister Ngo Dinh Diem, having proclaimed himself president in a fraudulent referendum, announced that the South Vietnamese Navy would become independent from French authority. Edouard anticipated this, but not the appointment of Le Quang My as commander of naval forces. Because of Le Quang's corrupt reputation, Edouard blocked his appointment and threatened to withdraw personnel and logistical support if he assumed command, but it proved a hollow threat. Despite Edouard's opposition, Le Quang was appointed naval commander and immediately replaced all French personnel in supervisory assignments. Sidelined with only advisory functions, France pulled out the following year, leaving their former colony mired in conflict.

As American soldiers replaced French troops, Scottie's son Tim got assigned to South Vietnam as an enlisted man in the United States Army. Echoing Edouard's cynicism about the South Vietnamese military, Tim wrote his father, "I have fallen into the universal opinion of people here, that we ought to withdraw at once and leave the people to the Communists they are too cowardly to fight. If any South Vietnamese have died, it's while they were running away." Four years later, having transferred from the army to the navy, he shot himself through the heart in Diamond Head Park, Honolulu.

On his way back to France from Indochina, Edouard stopped in Hawaii as a guest of the United States Navy, attended a performance of *South Pacific*, and was given a ceremonial jar of macadamia nuts, the Island's signature export. From there, it was on to military ceremonies in Yorktown, Virginia, where La Fayette and French soldiers had fought alongside Americans in the last major land battle of the Revolutionary War. Unaware of Zelda's ties to the area, he would have been interested to know that her maternal grandfather, a prominent attorney and tobacco planter in Yorktown, had owned three thousand acres on the Cumberland River and represented Virginia in the Confederate Congress and United States Senate.

Edouard would return to America one final time as commander of the French Task Force, when ships under his command participated in an international naval review at Norfolk, Virginia. After a triumphant career, at the age of sixty, he retired as full admiral in 1959 and was appointed to the governing board of SNECMA, Societe Nationale d'Etude de Construction de Motors d'Aviation, the government-owned company that designed and manufactured airplane engines for the French military. He and Lucienne moved to Paris and purchased a country estate northeast of the city at Mezille, but it would prove a brief stay. After two years, he stepped back from active life and relocated to Cannes with his wife, who had inherited a magnificent apartment overlooking the Mediterranean.

Zelda and Edouard never spoke after their affair, but Lois Moran telephoned Scott on her wedding day, to announce her marriage to Clarence M. Young, then assistant secretary of commerce. Another pilot, he had flown bombers in World War I, then served as assistant secretary for aeronautics in Hoover's administration. After marrying, she briefly continued acting, but fame would come through her association with Scott, rather than a film career. She died in 1990 on July 13, the same day seven decades earlier on which Edouard had exited Zelda's life.

Although the Frenchman denied intimacy with Zelda and Lois disavowed any sexual relationship with Scott, both relentlessly were queried over that issue, and saw themselves repeatedly portrayed in Scott's fiction. Between 1926 and 1980, there were twelve French editions of *The Great Gatsby*, and Edouard may have recognized elements of himself in the protagonist, as well as being amused and annoyed by Scott's characterization of him as Tommy Barban in *Tender Is the Night*, which saw eight French editions between 1934 and 1980. His composure was tested in 1979, when a French television station interviewed him for a documentary on Scott and asked intrusive questions about Zelda. Not surprisingly, he stopped the filming and walked out.

His patience was further tested the following year when Tennessee Williams's play *Clothes for a Summer Hotel* opened on Broadway. Williams also was a Southerner and his sister, Rose, diagnosed as schizophrenic. Set at a North Carolina asylum where Zelda is being treated, the play takes place in one day. Edouard figures prominently as do Ernest and Hadley Hemingway, Gerald and Sara Murphy, and Zelda's ballet teacher, Lubov Egorova. In its opening scene, Scott mistakenly has been informed that Zelda is improved and flies east to see her. It is a chilly autumn day and he is wearing California clothes more suitable for a summer hotel. On seeing Zelda he recognizes nothing has changed. Conversant with Nancy Milford's biography and Sheilah Graham's memoir, in one scene Williams has Zelda pronounce, "I am not a salamander." And in another, Scott chides Edouard saying, "Let go of her hand, she isn't yours . . . remember you're just employed here. The name of this woman is still Mrs. F. Scott Fitzgerald." "As distinguished," interrupts Zelda, "from Lily Shiel?" When she cries out during lovemaking with the Frenchman, Edouard cautions her to be discreet, but she objects, accusing him of disregard: "You are reckless . . . *you* have a reckless nature." "No," he insists, "I know when to be careful, but do you? . . . This is not the way of the French; we know passion but we also know caution. With public caution, our passions can be indulged in private." Only Zelda won't be bettered and complains, "You know, I expected our affair to continue, no matter what the cost." She then asks what she always has wanted to know: "What *did* happen to you? After you left me that summer?" With wry humor he responds, "Well, gradually, as such things occur to most living creatures, Zelda, I—grew old."

When *Clothes for a Summer Hotel* debuted, Scott had been dead forty years and Zelda, thirty-two. Yet, the affair still was being discussed and Edouard's military career becoming eclipsed by Zelda's legendary status. Instead of being celebrated for his own impressive accomplishments, Edouard and his fame became linked to the Fitzgeralds in the literary cosmos. During Edouard's final years, along with Tennessee Williams's play, three additional Fitzgerald biographies were published, all of which speculated about the affair. While the public never ceased wondering, Edouard remained silent, having appreciated Zelda for whom she was, and walking away when it became necessary. During his fifty-year marriage to Marshall Gallieni's granddaughter, Lucienne, he fathered a daughter and four sons, one of whom attended his alma mater, Prytannee. He died in Cannes at age eighty-two on December 11, 1981, fifty-seven years after the affair.

Notes

PREFACE

1. **Of all the books I have read so far about the Fitzgerald saga:** Martine Jozan, letter to the author, January 23, 2003.
2. **I liked [Jozan] and was glad he was willing:** Sheilah Graham, *The Real F. Scott Fitzgerald*. New York: Grosset and Dunlap, 1976, pp. 61–62.
3. **I tried to explain to her that we couldn't do that:** *Trimalchio: An Early Version of "The Great Gatsby,"* ed. James L. W. West. Cambridge, England: Cambridge University Press, 2000, p. 89.
4. **They both had a need of drama:** Edouard Jozan, interview by Nancy Milford (January 11, 1967), *Zelda: A Biography*. New York: Harper and Row, 1970, p. 112.
5. **She had forgot all about that year:** Zelda Fitzgerald, *Caesar's Things*, Zelda Fitzgerald Papers, Col. 183, Box 2A, Folder 2, Princeton University Library (hereafter P.U.L.), cited by Sally Cline: *Zelda Fitzgerald: Her Voice in Paradise*. New York: Arcade Publishing, 2004, p. 40, also by Milford, *Zelda*, p. 360.
6. **When one really can't stand it anymore:** Zelda Fitzgerald, *Caesar's Things*, Zelda Fitzgerald Papers, Col. 183, Box 2A, Folder 2, P.U.L., also cited in Milford, *Zelda*, p. 367.
7. **All our lives, since the day of our engagement:** F. Scott Fitzgerald to Dr. A.C. Rennie, quoted in Milford, *Zelda*, p. 364.

CHAPTER 1: RECKLESSNESS IN THE MAKING

1. **The specialist to whom mama took her:** Rosalind Smith, unpublished documentation on Zelda, Sara Mayfield Collection, University of Alabama, Tuscaloosa.

2. **As long as I can remember and long before that:** C. Lawton Campbell, "The Fitzgeralds Were My Friends," unpublished essay, collection of the author, p. 11.

3. **A lemonade and a tomato sandwich:** F. Scott Fitzgerald, *The Beautiful and Damned*. New York: Charles Scribner's Sons, 1950, p. 161.

4. **Skated at breakneck speed down the Perry Street hill:** Sara Mayfield, *Exiles from Paradise: Zelda and Scott Fitzgerald*. New York: Dell Publishing Co., 1971, p. 13.

5. **She swam and dove as well as most of the boys and better than many:** Eleanor Addison, "Why Follow the Same Pattern," *Columbus Dispatch*. October 27, 1963, p. 4C.

6. **Zelda lived just around the corner from me on Pleasant Avenue:** Mrs. H. L. Weatherby, letter to the author, April 1963.

7. **Even in those days, both of them had dash:** Mayfield, *Exiles from Paradise*, p. 18.

8. **We played hooky almost every day:** Zelda Fitzgerald, interview by Sara Haardt at Ellerslie (1926), Wilmington, Delaware, now in the Enoch Pratt Library, Special Collections, Baltimore, Maryland.

9. **I am in the world to do something unusual:** Owen Johnson, *The Salamander*. Indianapolis, IN: Bobbs Merrill Company, 1914, p. 385.

10. **She comes from somewhere out of:** Johnson, *The Salamander*, p. 2.

11. **The man I marry has got to:** Johnson, *The Salamander*, p. 451.

12. **Each salamander of good standing counts from three to a dozen props:** Johnson, *The Salamander*, p. 15.

13. **Going to be outstanding:** F. Scott Fitzgerald, *The Beautiful and Damned*, p. 147.

14. **Alabama, you're positively indecent said the tall officer:** Zelda Fitzgerald, *Save Me the Waltz*, in *The Collected Writings of Zelda Fitzgerald*, ed. Matthew J. Bruccoli. New York: Charles Scribner's, 1991, p. 33.

15. **I saw her as she had looked at that last Christmas dance were together:** Sara Haardt, interview with Zelda Fitzgerald, p. 3.

16. **Already she is in the crowd at the Country Club:** Article in the *Montgomery Advertiser*, quoted in Nancy Milford, *Zelda: A Biography*. New York: Harper and Row, 1970, p. 15.

17. **She had superb courage, not so much defiance:** Sara Haardt, interview with Zelda Fitzgerald, pp. 1–2.

18. **Cannot be considered above reproach:** F. Scott Fitzgerald to Isabelle Amorous (February 26, 1920), in Matthew J. Bruccoli and Margaret M. Duggan, eds., *Correspondence of F. Scott Fitzgerald*. New York: Random House, 1980, p. 53.

19. **Built like an Olympic swimmer [with] large, appealing bright brown eyes:** John Peter Kohn Jr., *The Cradle: An Anatomy of a Town: Fact and Fiction*. New York: Vantage Press, 1969, p. 201. The title comes from Montgomery being called the Cradle of the Confederacy because it served as its first capital. A

Montgomery native, Kohn received his law degree from the University of Alabama in 1925, and after serving as county attorney, became a judge and then member of the Alabama Supreme Court. He was a year and a half younger than Zelda and in the same social circle as Peyton Mathis and John Sellers.

20. **One night, the police were questioning him about a naked woman:** Kohn, *The Cradle*, p. 202. Kohn married Margaret Patteson Thorington, who, like Zelda, was a famous belle of her time, the modern version of a trophy wife. Her relative, Chilton Thorington, was the Sayre family doctor who was treating Anthony Sayre Jr. at the time of his breakdown and suicide.

21. **They dared not take him to a doctor:** Mayfield, *Exiles from Paradise*, p. 177.

22. **In a hundred years I think:** Zelda Fitzgerald to F. Scott Fitzgerald (Spring 1919), in *The Collected Writings of Zelda Fitzgerald*, p. 446.

23. **She was so drunk:** Unsent letter from F. Scott Fitzgerald to Marjorie Brinson (December 1938), quoted in Scott Donaldson, *Fool for Love*. New York: Delta Press, 1983, p. 63.

24. **They went up to the haunted school-yard:** Zelda Fitzgerald, *Caesar's Things*, cited by Sally Cline, *Zelda Fitzgerald: Her Voice in Paradise*. New York: Arcade Publishing, 2000, p. 40; also by Milford, *Zelda*, p. 360. Original documentation in Zelda Fitzgerald Papers, Col. 183, Box 2A, Folder 2, P.U.L., pp. 40–41.

25. **There wasn't any more compensatory:** Zelda Fitzgerald, *Caesar's Things*. Summarized by Cline, *Zelda Fitzgerald*, p. 41.

26. **Always intensely skeptical about her sex:** F. Scott Fitzgerald, *The Beautiful and Damned*, pp. 234–35.

27. **Have a date with you on Saturday:** Note from Pete Bonner in Zelda Fitzgerald scrapbook, P.U.L.

28. **Frankly, it all seemed such a gamble to her:** C. Lawton Campbell, "The Fitzgeralds Were My Friends," pp. 12–13.

29. **I am very glad, personally, to be able to write to you that:** Maxwell Perkins to F. Scott Fitzgerald, quoted in Matthew J. Bruccoli, ed., *The Romantic Egoists: A Pictorial Autobiography from the Scrapbooks and Albums of F. Scott and Zelda Fitzgerald*. New York: Charles Scribner's Sons, 1974, p. 53.

30. **I am very proud of you:** Zelda Fitzgerald to F. Scott Fitzgerald, quoted in James R. Mellow, *Invented Lives: F. Scott and Zelda Fitzgerald*. New York: Houghton Mifflin Company, 1984, p. 79.

31. **I don't want to think about pots:** F. Scott Fitzgerald writing about Rosalind in *This Side of Paradise*, a character strongly reminiscent of Zelda. New York: Charles Scribner's Sons, 1931, p. 180.

32. **Darling—Mama knows we are going to be married someday:** Zelda Fitzgerald to F. Scott Fitzgerald (April 1920), Folder 12, Box 42, P.U.L., cited by Kendall Taylor, *Sometimes Madness Is Wisdom*. New York: Ballantine Books, 2001, p. 64.

33. **Mrs. M. W. Brinson, (Marjorie Sayre Brinson) accompanied by her sister Zelda Sayre:** News clipping in Zelda Fitzgerald scrapbook, P.U.L.

CHAPTER 2: SEEDS OF DISCONTENT

1. **Next time you're in New York I want you to meet Zelda:** F. Scott Fitzgerald to Ruth Sturtevant (March 26, 1920), quoted in *The Letters of F. Scott Fitzgerald*, ed. Andrew Turnbull. New York: Charles Scribner's Sons, 1963, pp. 458–59.

2. **There was no luncheon after the wedding:** Rosalind Smith, unpublished documentation on Zelda Fitzgerald, W. S. Hoole Special Collections Library, University of Alabama, Tuscaloosa, Alabama.

3. **Could play golf all day, dance all night:** Shelly Armitage, *John Held Jr.: Illustrator of the Jazz Age.* Syracuse, NY: Syracuse University Press, 1987, p. 72.

4. **I love Scott's books and heroines:** Zelda Fitzgerald, interview by *Louisville Courier Journal* (September 30, 1923), quoted in Matthew J. Bruccoli, ed., *The Romantic Egoists: A Pictorial Autobiography from the Scrapbooks and Albums of F. Scott and Zelda Fitzgerald.* New York: Charles Scribner's Sons, 1974, p. 112.

5. **He was tall, dark, and tweedy:** Jack Shuttleworth, "John Held, Jr., and His World," *American Heritage* 16, no. 5 (August 1965), p. 29.

6. **Loved each other, desperately:** Carl Van Vechten, *Parties.* New York: Avon Books, 1977, quoted in Kendall Taylor, *Sometimes Madness Is Wisdom.* New York: Ballantine Books, 2001 p. 89.

7. **His pockets often bulging with her clever observations:** An observation by Edmund Wilson, also noted by Lawton Campbell: "He, Scott, would hang on her words," quoted in Campbell, "The Fitzgeralds Were My Friends," unpublished essay, collection of the author, p. 20.

8. **He danced her around the gilded edges of many fashionable hours:** Zelda Fitzgerald, *Caesar's Things* ch. 7, Col. 183, Box 2A, Folder B, p. 235, P.U.L., cited by Sally Cline, *Zelda Fitzgerald: Her Voice in Paradise.* New York: Arcade Publishing, 2002, p. 108; also cited by Linda Wagner-Martin in *Zelda Sayre Fitzgerald: An American Woman's Life.* London: Palgrave MacMillan, 2004, p. 206.

9. **Standing regarding her, very quiet:** F. Scott Fitzgerald, *The Beautiful and Damned.* New York: Charles Scribner's Sons, 1950, p. 243.

10. **They interested me so greatly:** George Jean Nathan, quoted in Nancy Milford, *Zelda: A Biography.* New York: Harper and Row, 1970, p. 71.

11. **He said he had gained a lot of inspiration from them:** Milford, *Zelda*, p. 71.

12. **His business is the theater:** Ernest Boyd, *Portraits: Real and Imaginary.* New York: George H. Doran Company, 1924, pp. 199, 201.

13. **Most alluring to man is that woman:** George Jean Nathan, "On Women," in *The World of George Jean Nathan*, ed. Charles Angoff. New York: Alfred A. Knopf, 1952, p. 139.

14. **To a man, the least interesting of women is the successful woman:** Nathan, "On Women," p. 131.

15. **The calling of a husband's attention to a love letter addressed to his wife:** George Jean Nathan to Zelda Fitzgerald (September 12, 1920), quoted in Scott Donaldson, *Fool for Love: F. Scott Fitzgerald.* New York: Delta Press, 1989, p. 68.

16. **At present, I'm hardly able to sit down:** Zelda Fitzgerald to Ludlow Fowler (April 16,1920), F. Scott Fitzgerald Papers, Col. 183, Box 5, Folder 4, P.U.L. The cut on her tailbone caused by a broken bottle near George's bathtub required three stitches.

17. **In his biography on Fitzgerald:** George Jean Nathan, "Memories of Fitzgerald, Lewis and Dreiser," *Esquire*, October 1958, p. 148.

18. **He also made love to Zelda:** Arthur Mizener, handwritten note on Nathan's response to Mizener's letter of January 10, 1950, interview with Arthur Mizener by the author, Cornell University, Ithaca, New York.

19. **Sweet Souse: What happened to you:** George Jean Nathan to Zelda Fitzgerald (no date), Zelda Fitzgerald Papers, Col. 187, Box 5, File 18, P.U.L., quoted in Taylor, *Sometimes Madness Is Wisdom*, p. 78.

20. **The room was bedlam. Breakfast dishes were all about, the bed unmade:** Campbell, "The Fitzgeralds Were My Friends," p. 17.

21. **You just watch that elevator:** F. Scott Fitzgerald quoted in Milford, *Zelda*, pp. 73–74.

22. **He is afraid of what she might do in a moment of caprice:** Alexander McKaig diary (October 11, 1920), now in the possession of his nephew, attorney Robert Taft, Brighton, Fernald, Taft and Hampsey, Peterborough, New Hampshire, quoted in Taylor, *Sometimes Madness Is Wisdom*, p. 89. In one notebook entry, Fitzgerald writes, "She looked lovely, but he thought of a terrible thing she had said once when they were first married, that if he were away, she could sleep with another man and it wouldn't really affect her, or make her really unfaithful to him. This kept him awake for another hour, but he had a little fine deep restful sleep toward morning. In *The Notebooks of F. Scott Fitzgerald*, ed. Matthew J. Bruccoli, New York: Harcourt, Brace, Jovanovich, 1978, pp. 231–32.

23. **I like you better than anybody in the world:** Edmund Wilson, *The Twenties*, ed. Leon Edel. New York: Farrar, Strauss and Giroux, 1975, p. 55.

24. **Suddenly, this double apparition approached me:** Gilbert Seldes, quoted in Milford, *Zelda*, p. 97.

25. **If she's there, Fitzgerald can't work:** Alex McKaig diary (October 11, 1920), cited in Taylor, *Sometimes Madness Is Wisdom*, p. 100.

26. **In taxi Zelda asked me to kiss her:** Alex McKaig diary (April 17, 1921), cited in Taylor, *Sometimes Madness Is Wisdom*, p. 95.

27. **I suppose I ought to be furious because you've kissed so many men:** F. Scott Fitzgerald, *The Beautiful and Damned*, 181.

28. **Would have to make up her mind, whether she wanted to go into the movies:** Alex McKaig diary (October 11, 1920), quoted in Taylor, *Sometimes Madness is Wisdom*, p. 98.

29. **When I like men I want to be like them:** F. Scott Fitzgerald, *The Notebooks of F. Scott Fitzgerald*, p. 78, note 938, p. 146.

30. **Went up to Fitzgeralds to spend evening:** Alex McKaig diary (October 21, 1920), quoted in Taylor, *Sometimes Madness Is Wisdom*, p. 99.

31. **Seemed a little crestfallen:** Edmund Wilson to F. Scott Fitzgerald (June 22, 1921), in Edmund Wilson, *Letters on Literature and Politics 1912–1972*, ed. Elena Wilson. New York: Farrar, Strauss & Giroux, 1977, p. 63.

32. **I think it's a shame that England:** F. Scott Fitzgerald to Edmund Wilson, misdated by Andrew Turnbull as May 1921, quoted in *The Letters of F. Scott Fitzgerald*, ed. Andrew Turnbull. New York: Charles Scribner's Sons, 1963, p. 326.

33. **I'm glad it's a girl:** F. Scott Fitzgerald, *The Great Gatsby*. New York: Scribner's, 1925, p. 17.

34. **She *is* awfully cute, and I am very devoted to her:** Zelda Fitzgerald to Ludlow Fowler (December 22, 1921), quoted in Milford, *Zelda*, p. 114.

35. **The pictures prove to me that you are getting more beautiful every day:** George Jean Nathan to Zelda Fitzgerald (May 29, 1922), Zelda Fitzgerald Papers, P.U.L, quoted in James R. Mellow, *Invented Lives: F. Scott and Zelda Fitzgerald*. Boston: Houghton Mifflin Company, 1984, p. 151.

36. **I certainly miss you + Townsend + Alec:** Zelda Fitzgerald to Ludlow Fowler (November 1921), quoted in Milford, *Zelda*, p. 85.

37. **Zelda and her abortionist:** F. Scott Fitzgerald, Notebooks, no. 1564, F. Scott Fitzgerald Papers, P.U.L. Fitzgerald's notebooks were a workshop for his ideas. He organized them in 1932 while he was living at La Paix outside Baltimore. The originals are at Princeton in two spring binders with alphabetized index separators and typed on white paper. They are organized into seven categories: conversation and things overheard, feelings and emotions (without girls) descriptions of girls, ideas, moments, what people do, observations, scenes and ideas.

38. **Chill-mindedness of his wife:** F. Scott Fitzgerald, The Ledger of F. Scott Fitzgerald, P.U.L.

39. **It seems to me on one page, I recognized a portion of an old diary of mine:** Zelda Fitzgerald, "Mrs. F. Scott Fitzgerald Reviews *The Beautiful and Damned*, Friend Husband's Latest," *New York Herald Tribune*, April 2, 1922, reprinted in Matthew Bruccoli, *The Collected Works of F. Scott Fitzgerald*. London: Wordsworth Special Editions, 2011, p. 388.

40. **Withholding from her the first money she has ever earned:** F. Scott Fitzgerald to Burton Rascoe (April 1922), F. Scott Fitzgerald Papers, P.U.L., quoted in *Correspondence of F. Scott Fitzgerald*, ed. Matthew J. Bruccoli and Margaret M. Duggan. New York: Random House, 1980, p. 100.

41. **Are you going to act in *The Beautiful and Damned*:** H. L. Mencken to F. Scott Fitzgerald (May 18, no year), F. Scott Fitzgerald Papers, Col. 187, Box 51, Folder 9, P.U.L.

42. **Three or four years ago girls of her type were pioneers:** Zelda Fitzgerald, interview by *Louisville Courier Journal* (September 30, 1923), reprinted in Bruccoli, *The Romantic Egoists*, p. 112.

43. **I've studied ballet:** Zelda Fitzgerald, interview reprinted in Bruccoli, *The Romantic Egoists*, p. 113.

44. **He is a typical newspaperman:** Zelda Fitzgerald to Rosalind Smith, quoted in Lane Yorke, "Zelda: A Worksheet," *Paris Review.* Fall 1983, p. 219.

45. **Fascinated Scott in the Great Neck days:** Ring Lardner Jr., *The Lardners: My Family Remembered.* New York: Harper Colophon Books, 1976, p. 164.

46. **There was a porch on the side of our house:** Lardner, *The Lardners*, p. 163.

47. **Tilde and John did not forget Scott's rudeness:** Rosalind Smith, unpublished documentation on Zelda Fitzgerald, W. S. Hoole Special Collections Library, University of Alabama, Tuscaloosa, Alabama.

CHAPTER 3: THE FRENCH LIEUTENANT

1. **John is like a man lying in a warm bath:** Alan Tate, *Memoirs and Opinions, 1926–1974.* Chicago: Swallow Press, 1975, p. 72.

2. **Tanned and beautiful, often wearing:** Honoria Murphy Donnelly, *Sara and Gerald: Villa America and After.* New York: Times Books, 1982, p. 107.

3. **She was the only woman I've ever known:** Gerald Murphy, as quoted in Nancy Milford, *Zelda: A Biography.* New York, Harper and Row, 1970, p. 124.

4. **Violets and muguets (lily of the valley) and lilacs:** Zelda Fitzgerald, quoted in Sara Mayfield, *Exiles from Paradise: Zelda and Scott Fitzgerald.* New York: Harper and Row, 1971, p. 107.

5. **Here's a chance to become famous:** F. Scott Fitzgerald, *Trimalchio: An Early Version of "The Great Gatsby,"* ed. James L. W. West, Cambridge, England: Cambridge University Press, 2000, p. 85.

6. **She might dress like a flapper:** Gerald Murphy, quoted in Donnelly, *Sara and Gerald*, p. 151, and Kendall Taylor, *Sometimes Madness Is Wisdom.* New York: Ballantine Books, 2001, p. 137.

7. **It was all in her eyes:** Gerald Murphy, quoted in Donnelly, *Sara and Gerald*, p. 107.

8. **Scottie comes up to people when she meets them:** F. Scott Fitzgerald, *The Notebooks of F. Scott Fitzgerald*, ed. Matthew J. Bruccoli. New York: Random House, 1980, p. 80.

9. **I think St. Raphael (where we are):** F. Scott Fitzgerald to Tom Boyd, in *Correspondence of F. Scott Fitzgerald*, ed. Matthew J. Bruccoli and Margaret M. Duggan. New York: Random House, 1980, p. 138.

10. **Scott has started a new novel:** Zelda Fitzgerald to Xandra Kalman (June 21, 1923), quoted in Linda Wagner-Martin, *Zelda Sayre Fitzgerald: An American Woman's Life.* London: Palgrave MacMillan, 2004, p. 74.

11. **I have begun life anew:** Fitzgerald to Edmund Wilson (Summer 1924), in *F. Scott Fitzgerald: A Life in Letters*, ed. Matthew J. Bruccoli. New York: Simon and Schuster, 1994, p. 76.

12. **Alabama was much alone:** Zelda Fitzgerald, *Save Me the Waltz*, in *The Collected Writings of Zelda Fitzgerald*, ed. Matthew J. Bruccoli. New York: Charles Scribner's Sons, 1991, p. 79.

13. **All the young men fell a little in love with her:** Edouard Jozan, interview by Nancy Milford, *Zelda*, p. 108.

14. **She thinks I'm in love with every woman that I shake a cocktail for:** F. Scott Fitzgerald, quoted in Mayfield, *Exiles from Paradise*, p. 117.

15. **I don't think she liked many people:** Gerald Murphy, quoted in Donnelly, *Sara and Gerald*. p. 153.

16. **The flying officer who looked like a Greek God was aloof:** Zelda Fitzgerald, *Caesar's Things*, Zelda Fitzgerald Papers, Col. 183, Box 2A, Folder 2, P.U.L., p. 364, cited by Sally Cline, *Zelda Fitzgerald: Her Voice in Paradise*. New York: Arcade Publishing, 2004, p. 40, also by Milford, *Zelda*, p. 360.

17. **I don't somehow feel I ought:** Zelda Fitzgerald, *Caesar's Things*, ch. 4, Zelda Fitzgerald Papers, Col. 183, Box 2A, Folder 2, P.U.L., p. 2.

18. **My establishment would be honored:** Zelda Fitzgerald, *Save Me the Waltz*, p. 79.

19. **As her eyes met those of the officer:** Zelda Fitzgerald, *Save Me the Waltz*, p. 81.

20. **My work's getting stale:** Zelda Fitzgerald, *Save Me the Waltz*, p. 97.

21. **The French officer had quite a coterie of friends:** Zelda Fitzgerald, *Caesar's Things*, ch. 4, Zelda Fitzgerald Papers, Col. 183, Box 2A, Folder 2, P.U.L., pp. 7, 38.

22. **It is twilight as I write this:** F. Scott Fitzgerald, quoted in James R. Mellow, *Invented Lives: F. Scott and Zelda Fitzgerald*. Boston: Houghton Mifflin Company, 1984, pp. 209–10.

23. **Rene, who is twenty-three:** F. Scott Fitzgerald, quoted in Mellow, *Invented Lives*, p. 210.

24. **Rich and free, they brought into our little provincial circle:** Edouard Jozan, as quoted in Milford, *Zelda*, p. 108, also in Wagner-Martin, *Zelda Sayre Fitzgerald*, p. 83.

25. **A bit of an intellectual:** Edouard Jozan, interview by Nancy Milford (January 11, 1967), *Zelda*, p. 50.

26. **Really is criticizing Francis:** F. Scott Fitzgerald, notebook entry 1474, *Scenes and Situations in France*, "Where the French Outclass Us" (December 1926), reprinted in *Conversations with F. Scott Fitzgerald*, ed. Matthew J. Bruccoli and Judith Baughman. Jackson: University Press of Mississippi, 2004, p. 8. Edmund Wilson includes several of Fitzgerald's notebook entries in *The Crack-Up*, a collection of Fitzgerald's essays. New York: New Directions Press, 1945.

27. **What chance has a smart young Frenchman:** F. Scott Fitzgerald to Maxwell Perkins (October 10, 1924), in *Scott Fitzgerald*, ed. Andrew Turnbull. New York: Charles Scribner's Sons, 1963, p. 167, also quoted in *F. Scott Fitzgerald: A Life in Letters*, p. 82, and in *Dear Scott/Dear Max: The Fitzgerald-Perkins Correspondence*, ed. John Kuehl and Jackson R. Bryer. New York: Scribner's, 1991, as a postscript to Fitzgerald's letter about Ernest Hemingway.

28. **His English was more adequate about love:** Zelda Fitzgerald, *Save Me the Waltz*, in *The Collected Writings of Zelda Fitzgerald*, ed. Matthew J. Bruccoli. New York: Charles Scribner's Sons, 1991, p. 92.

29. **It didn't seem to make any difference about what she wanted to do:** Zelda Fitzgerald, *Caesar's Things*, cited by Milford, *Zelda*, p. 365.
30. **I am half feminine, that is, my mind is:** F. Scott Fitzgerald to Dr. Thomas A. C. Rennie, quoted in Thomas J. Stavola, *Scott Fitzgerald: Crisis in an American Identity*. New York: Barnes & Noble, 1981, p. 65, and in Milford, *Zelda*, p. 261.

CHAPTER 4: A MISTRESS NOT A WIFE

1. **Monday, 22 March 1915. One of us took out the candle and lit it:** Edouard Jozan, handwritten journal entry, collection of Martine Jozan Work.
2. **You'll realize that it's nothing serious:** Jozan, handwritten journal entry, collection of Martine Jozan Work.
3. **Weepy, watery flowers that might have grown from dead eyes:** Zelda Fitzgerald to F. Scott Fitzgerald, quoted in Nancy Milford, *Zelda: A Biography*. New York: Harper and Row, 1970, p. 45.
4. **I wouldn't go to war unless it was in Morocco the Khyber Pass:** F. Scott Fitzgerald, *The Notebooks of F. Scott Fitzgerald*, ed. Matthew J. Bruccoli. New York: Harcourt Brace Jovanovich, 1980, p. 312.
5. **Fall like flies:** Jean Hourcade to the author, November 16, 2005.
6. **What do you expect, we are so handsome:** Jean Hourcade to the author, December 11, 2005.
7. **He drew her body against him:** Zelda Fitzgerald, *Save Me the Waltz*, p. 86, quoted in Kendall Taylor, *Sometimes Madness Is Wisdom*. New York: Ballantine Books, 2001, p 139.
8. **It was an improbable affair full of passion:** Zelda Fitzgerald, *Caesar's Things*, Zelda Fitzgerald Papers, Col. 183, Box 2A, Folder 2, P.U.L., cited by Sally Cline, *Zelda Fitzgerald: Her Voice in Paradise*. New York: Arcade Publishing, 2004, p. 40, also by Milford, *Zelda*, p. 360.
9. **It was so low they could see the gold of Jacques' hair:** Zelda Fitzgerald, *Save Me the Waltz*, in *The Collected Writings of Zelda Fitzgerald*, ed. Matthew J. Bruccoli. New York: Charles Scribner's Sons, 1991, p. 84.
10. **Aren't you afraid when you do stunts:** Zelda Fitzgerald, *Save Me the Waltz*, in *The Collected Writings of Zelda Fitzgerald*, p. 88.
11. **The plane had come out of its dive:** F. Scott Fitzgerald, "Image on the Heart," *McCall's Magazine* 63, no. 7 (April 1936), p. 54.
12. **If things didn't work out, there would always be the memory:** Zelda Fitzgerald, *Caesar's Things*, cited by Milford, *Zelda*, p. 364.
13. **All our lives, since the days of our engagement:** F. Scott Fitzgerald to Dr. Thomas A. C. Rennie, as quoted by Milford, *Zelda*, p. 364.
14. **I believed I was a salamander:** Zelda Fitzgerald, quoted in Milford, *Zelda*, pp. 175–76.
15. **I haven't seen a paper lately, but I suppose there's a war:** F. Scott Fitzgerald, *Tender Is the Night*. New York: Charles Scribner's Sons, 1962, p. 39.

16. **You must believe what you do is worth your time and energy:** Edouard Jozan, as quoted by Martine Jozan in an interview with the author, March 22, 2003.

17. **Long roads wound implacably up and over into pine fragrant depths:** Zelda Fitzgerald, as quoted by Andrew Turnbull, *Scott Fitzgerald*. Grove Press, 2001, p. 136.

18. **A shining beauty, a creature who overflowed with activity:** Edouard Jozan, interview by Nancy Milford, *Zelda*, p. 108.

19. **There's a fruit store on our street:** Frank Silver and Irving Cohn, "Yes, We Have No Bananas," from the Broadway review, *Make It Snappy*, 1922. Sung by Eddie Cantor in the revue, it became a major hit in 1923.

20. **David walked to the beach to join Alabama for a quick plunge before lunch:** Zelda Fitzgerald, *Save Me the Waltz*, in *The Collected Writings of Zelda Fitzgerald*, p. 89.

21. **Alabama and David and Jacques drove in the copper dawn to Agay:** Zelda Fitzgerald, *Save Me the Waltz*, in *The Collected Writings of Zelda Fitzgerald*, p. 89.

22. **Jacques drove the Renault:** Zelda Fitzgerald, *Save Me the Waltz*, in *The Collected Writings of Zelda Fitzgerald*, p. 89.

23. **What will you say to your husband:** Zelda Fitzgerald, *Save Me the Waltz*, in *The Collected Writings of Zelda Fitzgerald*, p. 90.

24. **When we are married:** Zelda Fitzgerald, *Caesar's Things*, Zelda Fitzgerald Papers, Col. 183, Box 2A. P.U.L.

25. **I could have annihilated:** F. Scott Fitzgerald, speaking to Dr. Robert Carroll, quoted in Matthew J. Bruccoli, *Some Sort of Epic Grandeur*. New York: Harcourt Brace Jovanovich, 1981, p. 408; also cited in Taylor, *Sometimes Madness Is Wisdom*, p. 140.

26. **Jacques spoke steadily into Alabama's face:** Zelda Fitzgerald, *Save Me the Waltz*, in *The Collected Writings of Zelda Fitzgerald*, p. 91.

27. **It was inexpedient, unexpected and miserable that she should be in love:** Zelda Fitzgerald, *Caesar's Things*, quoted in Milford, *Zelda*, p. 365.

28. **How could she remain:** Zelda Fitzgerald, *Save Me the Waltz*, quoted in Milford, *Zelda*, p. 365.

29. **Feeling of proxy in passion:** F. Scott Fitzgerald notebooks, nos. 466 and 765, F. Scott Fitzgerald additional papers, Col. 188, P.U.L.

30. **Her affair with Eduard Josanne [*sic*] and mine with Lois Moran:** F. Scott Fitzgerald to Dr. Mildred Squires, cited in Milford, *Zelda*, p. 222.

31. **San Raphael was dead:** Zelda Fitzgerald, *Caesar's Things*, Zelda Fitzgerald Papers, Col. 183, Box 2 A, Folder B, P.U.L., p. 288.

32. **One day the Fitzgeralds left and their friends scattered:** Edouard Jozan, interview by Nancy Milford (January 11, 1967), cited in Milford, *Zelda*, p. 109.

33. **Alabama could not read the letter:** Zelda Fitzgerald, *Save Me the Waltz*, in *The Collected Writings of Zelda Fitzgerald*, p. 94.

34. **Why do you keep those letters:** Martine Jozan, interview by the author, July 7, 2006.

35. **She so hardly spoke the language:** Zelda Fitzgerald, *Caesar's Things*, ch. 4, Zelda Fitzgerald Papers, Col. 183, Box 2A, P.U.L., pp. 288, 294.
36. **He was not very interested in sex:** Oscar Kalman, quoted in Jeffrey Meyers, *Scott Fitzgerald*. New York: HarperCollins, 1994, pp. 151–52.
37. **Love is a funny thing:** Zelda Fitzgerald, *Caesar's Things*, ch. 7, Col. 183, Box 2A, folder 8, P.U.L., quoted in Cline, *Zelda Fitzgerald*, p. 426, note 69, also in Milford, *Zelda*, p. 367.
38. **This is to tell you about a young man named Ernest Hemingway:** F. Scott Fitzgerald to Maxwell Perkins (October 10, 1924), in *Dear Scott/Dear Max: The Fitzgerald-Perkins Correspondence*, ed. John Kuehl and Jackson R. Bryer, New York: Charles Scribner's Sons, 1971, p. 78.
39. **She had forgotten all about this year of her life:** Zelda Fitzgerald, *Caesar's Things*, quoted in Milford, *Zelda*, p. 360.
40. **I feel old too this summer:** F. Scott Fitzgerald to Ludlow Fowler, in *F. Scott Fitzgerald: A Life in Letters*, ed. Matthew J. Bruccoli. New York: Simon and Schuster, 1994, p. 78.
41. **Your wife doesn't love you. She's never loved you. She loves me:** F. Scott Fitzgerald, *The Great Gatsby*. New York: Scribner's, 1925, p. 131.
42. **Your wife does not love you. She loves me:** F. Scott Fitzgerald, *Tender Is the Night*. New York: Charles Scribner's Sons, 1962, p. 341.
43. **I'm very sad, old sport:** F. Scott Fitzgerald, *Trimalchio: An Early Version of "The Great Gatsby,"* ed., James L. W. West, Cambridge, England: Cambridge University Press, 2000, p. 89. This is an early and complete version of *The Great Gatsby*, the one Maxwell Perkins first saw and commented upon. Until its publication in 2000, it was virtually unknown. Besides Zelda, Scott, and Perkins, only a few members of Scribner's firm had seen it, along with some literary scholars. The first two chapters of the first and second version are almost identical, but chapters 6 and 7 are almost entirely different.
44. **Do you think I'm making a mistake:** F. Scott Fitzgerald, *Trimalchio*, p. 84.
45. **I would know Tom Buchanan if I met him on the street:** Maxwell Perkins to F. Scott Fitzgerald (November 20, 1924), quoted in *F. Scott Fitzgerald: A Life in Letters*, p. 86.
46. **Gatsby was never quite real to me:** F. Scott Fitzgerald to Maxwell Perkins, quoted in *Dear Scott/Dear Max*, p. 87.

CHAPTER 5: TRULY A SAD STORY

1. **I could sleep with Zelda any time I wanted:** Edmund Wilson, *The Twenties*, ed. Leon Edel. New York: Farrar, Strauss & Giroux, 1975, p. 297.
2. **Zelda was not so loose, nor Howard so dangerous:** Wilson, *The Twenties*, p. 298.
3. **We're moving to Capri:** F. Scott Fitzgerald to Maxwell Perkins (February 18, 1925), in *F. Scott Fitzgerald: A Life in Letters*, ed. Matthew J. Bruccoli. New York: Simon and Schuster, 1994, P. 96.

4. **A high white hotel scalloped around the base:** Zelda Fitzgerald, "Show Mr. and Mrs. Fitzgerald to ____," in *The Collected Writings of Zelda Fitzgerald*, ed. Matthew J. Bruccoli. New York: Charles Scribner's Sons, 1991, p. 422.

5. **We've had a hell of a time here:** Scott Fitzgerald to Harold Ober (March 1925), in *The Letters of F. Scott Fitzgerald*, ed. Andrew Turnbull. New York: Charles Scribner's Sons, 1963, p. 355.

6. **I feel this lack of complete realization:** John Peale Bishop to F. Scott Fitzgerald, in *Correspondence of F. Scott Fitzgerald*, ed. Matthew J. Bruccoli and Margaret M. Duggan. New York: Random House, 1980, pp. 167–70.

7. **You are right about Gatsby being blurred and patchy:** F. Scott Fitzgerald to John Peale Bishop (August 9, 1925), Matthew J. Bruccoli, ed., *F. Scott Fitzgerald's "The Great Gatsby": A Documentary Volume*. Vol. 219 of *Dictionary of Literary Biography*. Farmington Hills, MI: Gale Group, 2000, p. 183.

8. **Zelda has been too sick for a long overland trip to Paris in our French Ford:** F. Scott Fitzgerald to Roger Burlingame (April 19, 1925), in *Correspondence of F. Scott Fitzgerald*, pp. 159–60.

9. **The mouth worried you until you knew him, and then it worried you more:** Ernest Hemingway, "Scott Fitzgerald," in *A Movable Feast*. New York: Charles Scribner's Sons, 1964, p. 12.

10. **I did not like her, but that night I had an erotic dream:** Ernest Hemingway, quoted in James R. Mellow, *Ernest Hemingway: A Life without Consequences*. New York: Da Capo Press, 1993, p. 291.

11. **Of all the people, you need discipline in your work:** Ernest Hemingway to F. Scott Fitzgerald, cited in Mellow, *Ernest Hemingway*, p. 436.

12. **Nobody knew whose party it was:** Zelda Fitzgerald, *Save Me the Waltz*, in *The Collected Writings of Zelda Fitzgerald*, ed. Matthew J. Bruccoli. New York: Charles Scribner's Sons, 1991, p. 95.

13. **Damn good looking:** Ernest Hemingway, *The Sun Also Rises*. New York: Charles Scribner's Sons, 1966, pp. 29–30.

14. **It was a constant merry-go-round for them:** Scottie Fitzgerald Lanahan, as quoted by Eleanor Lanahan, *Scottie, the Daughter of . . . : The Life of Frances Scott Fitzgerald Lanahan Smith*. New York: HarperCollins, 1996, p. 39.

15. **They went to Bourget and hired an aeroplane:** Zelda Fitzgerald, *Save Me the Waltz*, in *The Collected Writings of Zelda Fitzgerald*, p. 96.

16. **Honoria's teacher is Madame Egorova:** Gerald Murphy to Zelda Fitzgerald (September 19, 1925), quoted in *Correspondence of F. Scott Fitzgerald*, p. 179.

17. **There are dozens of pictures of my mother and father and me:** Scottie Fitzgerald Lanahan, as quoted by Eleanor Lanahan in *Scottie, the Daughter of . . .*, p. 28.

18. **We have come to a little, lost village called Salies-de-Bearn:** F. Scott Fitzgerald to Harold Ober (February 4, 1926), as quoted in *F. Scott Fitzgerald: A Life in Letters*, p. 135.

19. **Whenever they fought, Zelda threatened to pack up and leave:** Sara Murphy as quoted in Nancy Milford, *Zelda: A Biography*. New York: Harper and Row, 1970, p. 123.

20. **We were swimming at the beach in front of the villa:** Archibald MacLeish, in conversation with the author, Conway, Massachusetts, August 14–15, 1963.

21. **Zelda was a finer wife to Scott than anyone else could have been:** Archibald MacLeish, in conversation with the author.

22. **One particular night we had driven over through the mountains:** Archibald MacLeish, in conversation with the author.

23. **At twenty-four in Europe, patient has a near peritonitis caused by an inflammation:** Dr. Gross and Dr. Martel, included in Dr. H. A. Trutman's medical report on Zelda Fitzgerald (June 1930), Zelda Fitzgerald Papers, Col. 187, Box 54, Folder 10A, P.U.L, quoted by Sally Cline in *Zelda Fitzgerald: Her Voice in Paradise*. New York: Arcade Publishing, 2002, pp. 260–61.

24. **Zelda was a very extraordinary woman:** Archibald MacLeish, in conversation with the author.

25. **There were notches cut in the rock:** Sara Murphy, as quoted in Milford, *Zelda*, p. 124.

26. **They collected people then as some collect pictures:** Ernest Hemingway expands further about Gerald and Sara Murphy in "The Pilot Fish and the Rich," in *A Moveable Feast*, New York: Charles Scribner's Sons, 1964, pp. 213–20.

27. **Our life has gone to hell:** Ernest Hemingway to F. Scott Fitzgerald (September 1926), quoted by Bernice Kert, *The Hemingway Women: Those Who Loved Him—the Wives and Others*. New York: W.W. Norton and Company, 1983, p. 179.

28. **Zelda said that the way I was built:** Ernest Hemingway, "A Matter of Measurements," in *A Moveable Feast*, p. 162.

29. **He told me . . . about their marriage:** Ernest Hemingway, "Scott Fitzgerald," in *A Moveable Feast* pp. 170–71.

CHAPTER 6: RETRIBUTION AND REMORSE

1. **This hotel is extraordinary. It is like living in London:** Carl Van Vechten to Fania Marinoff (January 19, 1927), in *Letters of Carl Van Vechten*. ed. Bruce Kellner. New Haven, CT: Yale University Press, 1987, p. 91.

2. **A breakfast food that:** Zelda Fitzgerald, quoted in Matthew J. Bruccoli, *Some Sort of Epic Grandeur: The Life of F. Scott Fitzgerald*. New York: Harcourt Brace Jovanovich, 1981, p. 258.

3. **I can't remember a thing he said:** Lois Moran to Arthur Mizener, quoted in Richard Buller, *A Beautiful Fairy Tale: The Life of Actress Lois Moran*. Pompton Plains, NJ: Limelight Editions, 2005, p. 112, also in the Arthur Mizener Papers, Cornell University, Ithaca, New York, letters from Lois Moran to Arthur Mizener, 1948–1951.

4. **My worship for him was based on admiration for his talent:** Lois Moran to Arthur Mizener, in Buller, *A Beautiful Fairy Tale*, p 106.

5. **The girls who mop the floors are beautiful:** F. Scott Fitzgerald to his cousin, Cecilia (Mrs. Richard Taylor), quoted in James R. Mellow, *Invented Lives: F. Scott and Zelda Fitzgerald.* Boston: Houghton Mifflin Company, 1984, p. 281.

6. **The weather here makes me think of Paris in the spring:** Zelda Fitzgerald to Scottie Fitzgerald, quoted in Nancy Milford, *Zelda: A Biography.* New York: Harper and Row, 1970, p. 128.

7. **Everybody here is very clever:** Zelda Fitzgerald to Scottie Fitzgerald, quoted in Mellow, *Invented Lives*, p. 285.

8. **In California, though, you would not allow me to go anywhere without you:** Zelda Fitzgerald, quoted in Eleanor Lanahan, *Scottie, the Daughter of . . . : The Life of Frances Scott Fitzgerald Lanahan Smith.* New York: Harper Collins, 1995, p. 43.

9. **Hollywood completely disrupted since you left:** telegram from Lois Moran to F. Scott Fitzgerald (March 14, 1927), F. Scott Fitzgerald Papers, Col., 187, Box 51, Folder 12, P.U.L., also cited in Kendall Taylor, *Sometimes Madness Is Wisdom.* New York: Ballantine Books, 2001, p. 190.

10. **Darling Scott, I miss you enormously:** Lois Moran to F. Scott Fitzgerald (March 1927), note written on eastbound train, cited in Buller, *A Beautiful Fairy Tale*, p. 139.

11. **When you asked mother about Fitzgerald:** Tim Young, Lois Moran's son, as cited in Buller, *A Beautiful Fairy Tale*, p. 132.

12. **Will you like me as a woman:** Lois Moran, journal entry (November 9, 1928), quoted in Buller, *A Beautiful Fairy Tale*, p. 141.

13. **My earliest formal education took place at Ellerslie:** Scottie Fitzgerald quoted in Lanahan, *Scottie, the Daughter of . . .*, p. 32.

14. **Thank God you escaped alive:** H. L. Mencken to F. Scott Fitzgerald (March 15, no year), F. Scott Fitzgerald Papers, Col 187, Box 51, Folder 9, P.U.L.

15. **We used to have riotous parties at Ellerslie:** John Biggs, quoted in Seymour Toll, *A Judge Uncommon: A Life of John Biggs, Jr.* Philadelphia: Legal Communications, 1993, pp. 98–99, originally quoted in Lee Reese, *The House on Rodney Square.* Wilmington, DE: *News Journal Company*, 1977, pp. 174–75.

16. **From the depths of my polluted soul:** Zelda Fitzgerald to Carl Van Vechten (May 27, 1927), quoted in Andrew Turnbull, *Scott Fitzgerald.* New York: Grove Press, 2001, p. 178.

17. **Those delirious parties of theirs:** John Dos Passos quoted in Thomas J. Stavola, *Scott Fitzgerald: Crisis in American Identity.* New York: Barnes & Noble, 1981, p. 59.

18. **His drinking and frustration while at Ellerslie worried me:** Rex Polier, "Fitzgerald in Wilmington: *The Great Gatsby* at Bay," *Philadelphia Sunday Bulletin*, January 6, 1974, Section 4.

19. **Spent one lost afternoon with him:** Zelda Fitzgerald quoted in Milford, *Zelda*, p. 249.

20. **Those little fish swimming about under a shark:** Zelda Fitzgerald to F. Scott Fitzgerald (early March 1932), *Dear Scott, Dearest Zelda: The Love Letters of*

F. Scott and Zelda Fitzgerald, ed. Jackson R. Bryer and Cathy W. Barks. New York: St. Martin's Press, 2002, p. 154.

21. **Zelda Fitzgerald is studying ballet dancing with an absorption and seriousness:** Zelda Fitzgerald, interview by Sara Haardt, unpublished article, Sara Haardt Collection, Enoch Pratt Library, Baltimore, Maryland, p. 1.

22. **I joined the Philadelphia Opera Ballet:** Zelda Fitzgerald to Carl Van Vechten (October 4, 1927), quoted in Turnbull, *Scott Fitzgerald*, p. 179.

23. **I really felt a little guilty dropping Zelda's name:** Harold Ober to F. Scott Fitzgerald, quoted in Bruccoli, *Some Sort of Epic Grandeur*, p. 273.

24. **One of the objects that caught her fancy:** Anna Biggs quoted in Toll, *A Judge Uncommon*, pp. 97–98, and Milford, *Zelda*, p. 136.

25. **Start at six or seven o'clock in the morning:** John Biggs as quoted in Toll, *A Judge Uncommon*, p. 98, and Reese, *The House on Rodney Square*, p. 174.

26. **I knew there was only one way for me to survive my parents' tragedy:** Scottie Fitzgerald Lanahan, quoted in Lanahan, *Scottie, the Daughter of . . .* New York: Harper Collins, 1995, p. 71.

27. **We want to go in May:** Zelda Fitzgerald to Carl Van Vechten, quoted in Turnbull, *Scott Fitzgerald*, p. 179.

28. **Scott and I had a row last week:** Zelda Fitzgerald, quoted in Sara Mayfield, *Exiles from Paradise: Zelda and Scott Fitzgerald*. New York: Dell Publishing Co., 1971, p. 131.

29. **First trip to jail, and dive in Lido:** Facsimile of F. Scott Fitzgerald ledger book, P.U.L., also cited in Taylor, *Sometimes Madness Is Wisdom*, p. 209.

30. **There's no use killing yourself:** Zelda Fitzgerald, *Save Me the Waltz*, in *The Collected Writings of Zelda Fitzgerald*, ed. Matthew J. Bruccoli. New York: Charles Scribner's, 1991, p. 138.

31. **I'm twenty-eight years old and I've already got sweetbreads:** Zelda Fitzgerald, quoted in Mayfield, *Exiles from Paradise*, p. 131.

32. **Two drinks puts him into a manic state:** Zelda Fitzgerald, quoted in Mayfield, *Exiles from Paradise*, p. 116.

33. **Am going on the water wagon:** F. Scott Fitzgerald to Maxwell Perkins, quoted in Ring Lardner Jr., *The Lardners: My Family Remembered*. New York: Harper Colophon Books, 1976, pp. 163–64.

34. **There was nothing in the commercial flat except the white spitz of his mistress:** Zelda Fitzgerald, quoted in Mellow, *Invented Lives*, p. 325, and in Milford, *Zelda*, p. 301.

35. **Are you jabbering about oil:** Ernest Hemingway, "Scott and His Parisian Chauffeur," in *A Moveable Feast*. New York: Scribner's Sons, 1964, p. 211.

36. **La vie de Naples n'est pas tres chere:** Julie Sedova to Zelda Fitzgerald (September 29, 1929), Zelda Fitzgerald Papers. A.M. 20502, P.U.L., also cited in Taylor, *Sometimes Madness Is Wisdom*, p. 214.

37. **Notre theatre est magnifique et il vous serrait tres utile:** Julie Sedova to Zelda Fitzgerald, cited in Taylor, *Sometimes Madness Is Wisdom*, p. 214.

38. **I have always felt that this frantic effort on Zelda's part:** Rosalind Smith, unpublished documentation on Zelda Fitzgerald, Mayfield Collection, University of Alabama, Tuscaloosa, Alabama.
39. **Diaghilev died; the stuff of the great movement of the Ballet Russe lay rotting:** Zelda Fitzgerald, *Save Me the Waltz*, quoted in Alice Hall Petry, "Women's Work: The Case of Zelda Fitzgerald," *Literature Interpretation Theory* 1, nos. 1–2 (December 1989): p. 82.
40. **We went (to) sophisticated places with charming people:** Zelda Fitzgerald, quoted in Milford, *Zelda*, p. 156.
41. **There were all sorts and varieties of strange fish swimming by the camera:** Gerald Murphy, quoted in Milford, *Zelda*, p. 155.
42. **I worked constantly and was terribly superstitious:** Zelda Fitzgerald, quoted in Milford, *Zelda*, p. 347.
43. **I found myself saying hateful things to her:** F. Scott Fitzgerald, quoted in Tony Buttita, *After the Good Gay Times—Asheville '35: A Season of F. Scott Fitzgerald*. New York: Viking Press, 1974, p. 170.
44. **We might all four take that Compagnie General trip to Tunisia:** Gerald Murphy to F. Scott Fitzgerald, F. Scott Fitzgerald Papers, Col. 187, Box 51, Folder 13, P.U.L., also cited in Taylor, *Sometimes Madness Is Wisdom*, p. 218.
45. **I would almost rather she die now:** Rosalind Smith to F. Scott Fitzgerald (July 1930), F. Scott Fitzgerald Papers, Box 54, Folder 11, P.U.L. also cited in Taylor, *Sometimes Madness Is Wisdom*, p. 230.

CHAPTER 7: LOCKED AWAY

1. **It is a question of *petite anxieuse*, worn out by her work:** clinical evaluation of Zelda Fitzgerald's condition, Craig House file, Zelda Fitzgerald Papers, Col. 745, P.U.L. Dr. Oscar Forel told Nancy Milford in 1966 that while schizophrenia had been his initial assessment of Zelda, his opinion gradually altered and she never manifested enough of the stereotypical schizophrenic symptoms to be diagnosed in that category. Sally Cline, *Zelda Fitzgerald: Her Voice in Paradise*. New York: Arcade Publishing, 2002, p. 445.
2. **I went of my own free will:** Zelda Fitzgerald to F. Scott Fitzgerald (May 1930), F. Scott Fitzgerald Papers, Col. 187, Box 42, Folder 57, P.U.L., also cited in Kendall Taylor, *Sometimes Madness Is Wisdom*. New York: Ballantine Books, 2001, p. 255, and in *Dear Scott, Dearest Zelda: The Love Letters of F. Scott and Zelda Fitzgerald*, ed. Jackson R. Bryer and Cathy W. Barks. New York: St. Martin's Press, 2002, p. 84.
3. **Two sisters have nervous breakdowns:** Malmaison Hospital and Valmont Clinic patient evaluations of Zelda Fitzgerald's condition, Craig House File, Zelda Fitzgerald Papers, Col. 745, P.U.L. Dr. H. A.Trutman, Valmont Hospital Report, also cited in Cline, *Zelda Fitzgerald*, pp. 260–61. Also in this file

is a résumé of the consultation between Dr. Oscar Forel and Professor Eugen Bleuler done on November 22, 1930. The Oscar Forel medical records at P.U.L., covering Zelda's hospitalization at Prangins from June 5, 1930, through September 15, 1931, were prepared and translated from French into English by Mme. Claude Amiel under Dr. Forel's supervision.

4. **You must try to understand how dreary and drastic is my present position:** Zelda Fitzgerald to F. Scott Fitzgerald, cited in Cline, *Zelda Fitzgerald*, p. 266.

5. **I am thoroughly humiliated and broken:** Zelda Fitzgerald to F. Scott Fitzgerald, cited in Cline, *Zelda Fitzgerald*, p. 263.

6. **For too long, your wife has taken advantage of our patience:** Dr. Oscar Forel to F. Scott Fitzgerald, cited in Nancy Milford, *Zelda: A Biography.* New York: Harper and Row, 1970, p. 179, and Cline, *Zelda Fitzgerald*, p. 286.

7. **I beg you to think twice, before you say anymore to them:** F. Scott Fitzgerald to Rosalind Smith (1930), F. Scott Fitzgerald Papers, AM 20502, Box 53, Folder 14A, P.U.L., also cited in Taylor, *Sometimes Madness Is Wisdom*, p. 232.

8. **You say you place the beginning of the change in her:** Rosalind Smith to F. Scott Fitzgerald (June 16, 1930), F. Scott Fitzgerald Papers, Box 53, Folder 14A, P.U.L.

9. **It was at this point that her smoldering quarrel with my father broke out:** Scottie Fitzgerald Lanahan, as quoted by Eleanor Lanahan, *Scottie, the Daughter of . . . : The Life of Frances Scott Fitzgerald Lanahan Smith.* New York: Harper Collins, 1996, p. 45.

10. **I know your ineradicable impression of the life Zelda and I have led together:** F. Scott Fitzgerald to Rosalind Smith (June 8, 1930), in *Correspondence of F. Scott Fitzgerald*, ed. Matthew J. Bruccoli and Margaret M. Duggan. New York: Random House, 1980, p. 236.

11. **Do me a single favor:** Draft of a letter from F. Scott Fitzgerald to Rosalind Smith, unsent, F. Scott Fitzgerald Papers, P.U.L., also cited in Taylor, *Sometimes Madness Is Wisdom*, p. 231.

12. **He would come back some day:** F. Scott Fitzgerald, *Babylon Revisited and Other Stories.* New York: Charles Scribner's Sons, 1971, p. 230.

13. **At one point, when things were not going well with my father:** Lanahan, *Scottie, the Daughter of . . .*, pp. 46, 301.

14. **She was concerned, quite simply:** Lanahan, *Scottie, the Daughter of . . .*, p. 45.

15. **Please don't write to me about blame:** Zelda Fitzgerald to F. Scott Fitzgerald (after June 30), *Correspondence of F. Scott Fitzgerald*, p. 238.

16. **I am a woman of thirty:** Zelda Fitzgerald to F. Scott Fitzgerald, in *Dear Scott, Dearest Zelda*, p. 97, and in Taylor, *Sometimes Madness Is Wisdom*, p. 241.

17. **I demand that I be allowed to go immediately:** Zelda Fitzgerald to F. Scott Fitzgerald, Zelda Fitzgerald Papers, AM 20502, Box 42, Folder 65, P.U.L., also cited in Taylor, *Sometimes Madness Is Wisdom*, p. 24.

18. **Shall I write to daddy that he should come over:** Zelda Fitzgerald to F. Scott Fitzgerald (Fall 1930), F. Scott Fitzgerald Papers, AM 20502, Box 42, Folder 63, P.U.L., also cited in Taylor, *Sometimes Madness Is Wisdom*, p. 241.

19. **If you think you are preparing me for a return to Alabama:** Zelda Fitzgerald to F. Scott Fitzgerald (Fall 1930), F. Scott Fitzgerald Papers, AM 20502, Box 42, Folder 64, P.U.L.

20. **He said it wasn't even a question:** F. Scott Fitzgerald to Judge Anthony Sayre and Minnie Sayre (December 1, 1930), in *F. Scott Fitzgerald: A Life in Letters*, ed. Matthew J. Bruccoli. New York: Simon and Schuster, 1994, pp. 202–4.

21. **My marriage, after which I was in another world:** Zelda Fitzgerald, summarizing the important emotional events of her life to Dr. Oscar Forel, psychiatric report (September 15, 1931), Zelda Fitzgerald Papers, Col. 745, Box 1, Folder 2, P.U.L., quoted in Milford, *Zelda*, pp. 174–76.

22. **Why do I have to go backward:** Zelda Fitzgerald to Dr. Oscar Forel (November 1930), Zelda Fitzgerald Papers, Box 5, File 3, P.U.L., also cited in Taylor, *Sometimes Madness Is Wisdom*, pp. 240–41.

23. **Panic seems to have settled:** Zelda Fitzgerald to F. Scott Fitzgerald (Fall 1930), F. Scott Fitzgerald Papers, AM 20502, Box 42, Folder 64, P.U.L., also cited in *Dear Scott, Dearest Zelda*, p. 91.

24. **I had a very nice time:** Zelda Fitzgerald to F. Scott Fitzgerald, F. Scott Fitzgerald Papers, AM 20502, Box 42, Folder 41, P.U.L., also cited in Taylor, *Sometimes Madness Is Wisdom*, p. 244.

25. **Here is where Scott and I lunched yesterday:** postcard from Zelda Fitzgerald to her mother, illustrated in Eleanor Lanahan, *Zelda: An Illustrated Life: The Private World of Zelda Fitzgerald*. New York: Harry N. Abrams, 1996, p. 27.

26. **We played tennis on the baked clay courts:** Zelda Fitzgerald, *Show Mr. and Mrs. F to Number—*, in *The Collected Writings of Zelda Fitzgerald*, ed. Matthew J. Bruccoli. New York: Charles Scribner's, 1991, p. 429.

27. **Was the Madeleine pink at five o'clock:** Zelda Fitzgerald to F. Scott Fitzgerald, quoted in *Correspondence of F. Scott Fitzgerald*, p. 238, also in Koula Svokos Harnett, *Zelda Fitzgerald and the Failure of the American Dream*. American University Studies, Washington: Peter Lang Publishing, A.C., 1991, p. 153.

CHAPTER 8: NO HOPE SALVAGED

1. **I had a violent quarrel with Amalia this morning:** Zelda Fitzgerald to F. Scott Fitzgerald, Zelda Fitzgerald Papers, Box 43, Folder 49, P.U.L., also cited in Kendall Taylor, *Sometimes Madness Is Wisdom*. New York: Ballantine Books, 2001, p. 250.

2. **I feel like a person lost in some Gregorian but feminine service here:** Zelda Fitzgerald to F. Scott Fitzgerald (December 1931), Zelda Fitzgerald Papers, Box 43, Folder 39, P.U.L., also quoted in *The Correspondence of F. Scott Fitzgerald*, ed. Matthew J. Bruccoli and Margaret M. Duggan. New York: Random House, 1980, p. 274.

3. **The . . . material which I will elect to write about:** Zelda Fitzgerald to F. Scott Fitzgerald (April 1932), quoted in *The Correspondence of F. Scott Fitzgerald*, p. 291.

4. **I do not seem to be strong enough to stand much strain at the present:** Zelda Fitzgerald to F. Scott Fitzgerald (Spring 1932), Zelda Fitzgerald Papers, Box 44, Folder 7, P.U.L., also cited in Taylor, *Sometimes Madness Is Wisdom*, p. 255.

5. **At no time have I been able to get any statement of the suspicious, paranoid ideas:** Dr. Mildred Squires to F. Scott Fitzgerald (February 17, 1932), Zelda Fitzgerald Papers, Col. 187, Box 51, Folder 50, P.U.L.

6. **Mrs. Fitzgerald does not accept any of the nurses' suggestions:** Dr. Mildred Squires to F. Scott Fitzgerald (February 17, 1932), Zelda Fitzgerald Papers, Col. 187, Box 51, Folder 5, P.U.L.

7. **Our sexual relations have been good:** F. Scott Fitzgerald to Dr. Mildred Squires, F. Scott Fitzgerald Papers, P.U.L., also cited in Taylor, *Sometimes Madness Is Wisdom*, p. 257.

8. **This card was designed and printed by Mrs. Fitzgerald:** Dr. Frederick Wertham, handwritten note on the back of Dr. Mildred Squires' Christmas card, made by Zelda Fitzgerald, Frederick Wertham Collection, Harvard University, cited in Taylor, *Sometimes Madness Is Wisdom*, p. 258.

9. **Please do not judge or if not already done even consider:** telegram from F. Scott Fitzgerald to Maxwell Perkins, quoted in Matthew J. Bruccoli, *Some Sort of Epic Grandeur: The Life of F. Scott Fitzgerald*. New York: Harcourt Brace Jovanovich, 1981, p. 32.

10. **It would be throwing her broken upon a world which she despises:** F. Scott Fitzgerald to Dr. Mildred Squires, quoted in Nancy Milford, *Zelda: A Biography*. New York: Harper and Row, 1970, p. 222.

11. **It's very expressive of myself:** Zelda Fitzgerald, *Save Me the Waltz*, in *The Collected Writings of Zelda Fitzgerald*, ed. Matthew J. Bruccoli. New York: Charles Scribner's Sons, 1991, p. 285.

12. ***Dans ces deux, il en fut ainsi:*** Marie de France, *Lais*, French Texts Service, new edition. London, England: Duckworth Publishers, 1966.

13. **It is a pity that the publisher could not have had a more accurate proofreading:** *New York Times*, October 16, 1932, news clipping in Zelda Fitzgerald's scrapbook, P.U.L.

14. **Mrs. Fitzgerald should have had whatever help she needed:** News clipping in Zelda Fitzgerald's scrapbook, P.U.L.

15. **We had a mad-man's ball today:** Zelda Fitzgerald to F. Scott Fitzgerald (Spring 1932), Zelda Fitzgerald Papers, Box 44, Folder 9, P.U.L., also cited in Taylor, *Sometimes Madness Is Wisdom*, p. 265.

16. **Scott likes it better than France:** Zelda Fitzgerald to John Peale Bishop, quoted in Milford, *Zelda*, p. 258.

17. **I had Scott and Zelda in my car:** John O'Hara, "In Memory of Scott Fitzgerald," *New Republic*. March 3, 1941.

18. **I wish I had a whole lot of money:** Zelda Fitzgerald quoted in transcript of Dr. A. C. Rennie, cited in Sally Cline, *Zelda Fitzgerald: Her Voice in Paradise*. New York: Arcade Publishing, 2002, pp. 324–34, and Taylor, *Sometimes Madness Is Wisdom*, p. 274.

19. **I am incapacitated for helping her:** Document from Zelda Fitzgerald addressed to Dr. A. C. Rennie, F. Scott Fitzgerald, Additional Papers, Col. 188, AM 10-10-32, Box 25, P.U.L., also cited in Taylor, *Sometimes Madness Is Wisdom*, p. 269.

20. **In her subconscious:** F. Scott Fitzgerald to Dr. A. C. Rennie, F. Scott Fitzgerald Papers, Col. 188, Box 25, File 1, P.U.L., also cited in Taylor, *Sometimes Madness Is Wisdom*, p. 269.

21. **She is working under a greenhouse:** F. Scott Fitzgerald to Dr. Adolf Meyer (April 10, 1933), F. Scott Fitzgerald Papers, Col. 187, Box 51, Folder 10A, P.U.L., also cited in Taylor, *Sometimes Madness Is Wisdom*, p. 272.

22. **Your complaint of futility of our conversation:** Dr. Adolf Meyer to F. Scott Fitzgerald (April 18, 1933), Craig House Files, Col. 745, P.U.L., also cited in Taylor, *Sometimes Madness Is Wisdom*, p. 273.

23. **It is the great humiliation of my life that I cannot support myself:** Zelda Fitzgerald, Rennie transcript, p. 104, also cited in Taylor, *Sometimes Madness Is Wisdom*, p. 275.

24. **The evenings are so terrible:** Taped conversation of the Fitzgeralds at La Paix, Sunday, May 28, 1933, 2:30 p.m., Rennie Transcript, F. Scott Fitzgerald Papers. p. 82, P.U.L., also cited in Taylor, *Sometimes Madness Is Wisdom*, p. 274.

25. **He made it impossible for me to communicate with my child:** Zelda Fitzgerald, cited in Milford, *Zelda*, p. 325, also in Cline, *Zelda Fitzgerald*, p. 328, in A. C. Rennie transcript, P.U.L., p. 11.

26. **Zelda—had almost a hundred doctors:** F. Scott Fitzgerald, Rennie transcript, P.U.L., pp. 11, 12, also cited in Cline, *Zelda Fitzgerald*, p. 328.

27. **I can think, of—well, say fifty:** F. Scott Fitzgerald, Rennie transcript, p. 12.

28. **As far as destroying you is concerned:** Zelda Fitzgerald, Rennie transcript, p. 6.

29. **Why do you think you met Leger:** F. Scott Fitzgerald, Rennie transcript, p. 27.

30. **If you write a play, it cannot be a play about psychiatry:** F. Scott Fitzgerald, Rennie transcript, p. 28.

31. **I am so God-damned sick of your abuse:** Zelda Fitzgerald, cited in Cline, *Zelda Fitzgerald*, p. 328.

32. **A woman's place is with the man who supports her:** F. Scott Fitzgerald, cited in Cline, *Zelda Fitzgerald*, p. 329.

33. **I don't want to live with you:** Zelda Fitzgerald, cited in Cline, *Zelda Fitzgerald*, p. 330.

34. **I am perfectly willing to put aside the novel:** Zelda Fitzgerald, Rennie transcript, cited in Taylor, *Sometimes Madness Is Wisdom*, p. 276.

35. **Attack on all grounds:** F. Scott Fitzgerald quoted in Scott Donaldson, *Fool for Love: F. Scott Fitzgerald*. New York: Delta Press, 1983, p. 86.

36. **I am going to be a writer, but I am not going to do it at Scott's expense:** Rennie transcript, p. 88, also quoted in Taylor, *Sometimes Madness Is Wisdom*, p. 276.

37. **They don't seem to think a lot about their children:** Scottie Fitzgerald Lanahan, "Daughter of Fitzgerald, Aged 12, Criticizes Heroines of *This Side of Paradise*, Holds Flappers Fail as Parents," *New York Times*, September 18, 1933, p. 17.

CHAPTER 9: AN AILMENT NO ONE COULD CURE

1. **Already with Thee:** Line from John Keats, *Ode to a Nightingale*, that continues, "But here there is no light, save what from heaven is, with the breezes blown through verdurous glooms and windy, mossy ways."
2. **Nicole did not want any vague spiritual romance:** F. Scott Fitzgerald, *Tender Is the Night*. New York: Charles Scribner's Sons, 1962, p. 323.
3. **Barban came over behind her:** F. Scott Fitzgerald, *Tender Is the Night*, p. 301.
4. **I *only* know what I see in the cinema:** F. Scott Fitzgerald, *Tender Is the Night*, p. 300.
5. **He was one of those men who had a charger:** F. Scott Fitzgerald, notebooks, note 982, P.U.L., also cited in *The Notebooks of F. Scott Fitzgerald*, ed. Matthew J. Bruccoli. New York: Harcourt Brace Jovanovich, 1978, p. 151. Stallions bred for battles, tournaments, and jousts, these Medieval war houses were highly prized and expensive to own.
6. **What made me so mad was that he made the girl so awful:** Zelda Fitzgerald to Dr. Thomas Rennie, quoted in James R. Mellow, *Invented Lives: F. Scott and Zelda Fitzgerald*. Boston: Houghton Mifflin Company, 1984, p. 425.
7. **Nicole is a portrait of Zelda:** F. Scott Fitzgerald, character notes for *Tender Is the Night*. Additional information on Virginia Foster Durr's accusation against Judge Sayre is found in Sally Cline, *Zelda Fitzgerald: Her Voice in Paradise*, fn 11, chapter 22. New York: Arcade Publishing, 2002; Jeffrey Meyers, *Scott Fitzgerald: A Biography*. New York: HarperCollins, 1994, pp. 44–45; and Virginia Foster Durr, *Outside the Magic Circle: The Autobiography of Virginia Foster Durr*, ed. Hollinger F. Barnard. Tuscaloosa: University of Alabama Press, 1990.
8. **An achievement which no student of psychobiological sources of human behavior:** Review of *Tender Is the Night* in *Journal of Nervous and Mental Diseases*, quoted in Matthew J. Bruccoli, *Some Sort of Epic Grandeur: The Life of F. Scott Fitzgerald*. New York: Harcourt Brace Jovanovich, 1981, p. 370.
9. **My reason for wanting to change:** Zelda Fitzgerald to Dr. Adolf Meyer, Zelda Fitzgerald Papers, Box 5, File 7, P.U.L., quoted in Kendall Taylor, *Sometimes Madness Is Wisdom*. New York: Ballantine Books, 2001, p. 285.
10. **It's so pretty here:** Zelda Fitzgerald to F. Scott Fitzgerald, Zelda Fitzgerald Papers, Box 44, Folder 30, P.U.L., quoted in Taylor, *Sometimes Madness Is Wisdom*, p. 286.
11. **She suffered from fatigue, was mildly confused, and mentally retarded:** Dr. Clarence J. Slocum to F. Scott Fitzgerald (April 11, 1934), Craig House Files, 0745, P.U.L., also cited in Taylor, *Sometimes Madness Is Wisdom*, p. 286.

12. **It has been our observation that she tires easily:** Dr. Clarence J. Slocum, letter to F. Scott Fitzgerald, Craig House Files, 0745, P.U.L.

13. **We try to have her rest as much as possible:** Dr. Clarence J. Slocum, letter to F. Scott Fitzgerald, Craig House Files, 0745, P.U.L.

14. **I would not like to make even a tentative diagnosis at this time:** Dr. Clarence Slocum to F. Scott Fitzgerald (April 11, 1934), Craig House Files, 0745, P.U.L., also cited in Taylor, *Sometimes Madness Is Wisdom*, p. 287.

15. **They are so lonely and magnificent and heartbreaking:** Zelda Fitzgerald to Dr. A. C. Rennie, Zelda Fitzgerald Papers, P.U.L., also cited in Taylor, *Sometimes Madness Is Wisdom*, p. 289.

16. **The exhibition, as she may have told you:** F. Scott Fitzgerald to Dr. Clarence J. Slocum (April 2, 1934), Craig House Files, 0745, P.U.L., also cited in Taylor, *Sometimes Madness Is Wisdom*, p. 291.

17. **I get a pretty highly developed delirium tremens at the professional reviewers:** F. Scott Fitzgerald to Mabel Dodge Luhan (May 10, 1934), in *F. Scott Fitzgerald: A Life in Letters*, ed. Matthew J. Bruccoli. New York: Simon and Schuster, 1994, p. 258.

18. **About my book, you and the doctors agreed that I might work on it:** Zelda Fitzgerald to F. Scott Fitzgerald, quoted in Eleanor Lanahan, *Zelda: An Illustrated Life: The Private World of Zelda Fitzgerald*. New York: Harry N. Abrams, 1996, p. 29.

19. **I cannot see why I should sit in luxury:** Zelda Fitzgerald to F. Scott Fitzgerald, Zelda Fitzgerald Papers, Box 44, Folder 4, P.U.L., also cited in Taylor, *Sometimes Madness Is Wisdom*, p. 293.

20. **You must realize that to one as ill as I am:** Zelda Fitzgerald to F. Scott Fitzgerald, Zelda Fitzgerald Papers, Box 44, Folder 46, P.U.L., also cited in Taylor, *Sometimes Madness Is Wisdom*, p. 293.

21. **I do not feel as you do:** Zelda Fitzgerald to F. Scott Fitzgerald, Craig House Files, 0745, Box 44, Folder 42, P.U.L., also cited in Taylor, *Sometimes Madness Is Wisdom*, p. 293.

22. **I hope Mrs. Fitzgerald reached Baltimore safely and comfortably:** Dr. Clarence Slocum to F. Scott Fitzgerald (May 19, 1934), Craig House Files, 0745, P.U.L., also cited in Taylor, *Sometimes Madness Is Wisdom*, p. 294.

23. **You have always told me, that I have no right to complain:** Zelda Fitzgerald to F. Scott Fitzgerald (June 1930), Zelda Fitzgerald Papers, P.U.L., also cited in *Dear Scott, Dearest Zelda: The Love Letters of F. Scott and Zelda Fitzgerald*, ed. Jackson R. Bryer and Cathy W. Barks. New York: St. Martin's Press, 2002, fn 322, p. 86, also Taylor, *Sometimes Madness Is Wisdom*, p. 298.

24. **Mrs. Fitzgerald has been moved to a closed ward:** Isabel Owens to F. Scott Fitzgerald, F. Scott Fitzgerald Papers. Col 187, Box 51, Folder 33, P.U.L., also cited in Taylor, *Sometimes Madness Is Wisdom*, p. 304.

25. **He gave back to me both times a woman:** F. Scott Fitzgerald to Dr. Harry Murdoch (August 28, 1934), F. Scott Fitzgerald Papers, Box 51, P.U.L., also cited in Taylor, *Sometimes Madness Is Wisdom*, p. 299.

26. **It is Dr. Meyer's feeling that this present condition:** Dr. A. C. Rennie to F. Scott Fitzgerald (May 27, 1935), F. Scott Fitzgerald Papers, Box 53, Folder 14A, P.U.L., also cited in Taylor, *Sometimes Madness Is Wisdom*, p. 303.
27. **My dear Scott, Poor Sara, I fear, is now gravely ill:** H. L. Mencken to F. Scott Fitzgerald (May 30, 1935), F. Scott Fitzgerald Papers, Box 53, Folder 14A, P.U.L.
28. **It occurs to me that you alone knew how we felt these days:** Gerald Murphy to F. Scott Fitzgerald (August 11, 1935), F. Scott Fitzgerald Papers, Col. 187, Box 51, Folder 13, P.U.L.
29. **You have been cheated (as we all have one way or the other):** Sara Murphy to F. Scott Fitzgerald, F. Scott Fitzgerald Papers, Col. 187, Box 51, Folder 15, P.U.L.
30. **She began to look different as most people with mental illness:** Eleanor Lanahan, *Scottie, The Daughter of . . . : The Life of Frances Scott Fitzgerald Lanahan Smith*. New York: HarperCollins, 1995, p. 39.
31. **Her present condition was a great shock to me:** Rosalind Smith to F. Scott Fitzgerald (June 4, 1935), F. Scott Fitzgerald Papers, Box 53, Folder 14A, P.U.L.
32. **One of the saddest memories I have:** Rosalind Smith, unpublished documentation on Zelda Fitzgerald, Sara Mayfield Collection, University of Alabama, Tuscaloosa, Alabama.

CHAPTER 10: ALL IN DISARRAY

1. **As one student nurse recalled:** More information about Dr. Carroll's personality can be found in Jeffrey Meyers, *Scott Fitzgerald: A Biography*. New York: HarperCollins, 1994, p. 267.
2. **She once became so possessive:** Landon Ray, interview by the author at Highland Hospital, June 21, 1963.
3. **An enthusiastic person with an active mind:** Graphological analysis of Zelda Fitzgerald's handwriting prepared by Dr. Robert Carroll for Mrs. Anthony Sayre, Zelda Fitzgerald Papers, P.U.L.
4. **An institution employing all rational methods:** Thirty-two-page prospectus for Highland Hospital, 1944, cover page, Duke University Medical Archives, Durham, North Carolina.
5. **Now, the head doctor had devoted considerable research:** Zelda Fitzgerald, *Caesar's Things*, cited in Sally Cline, *Zelda Fitzgerald: Her Voice in Paradise*. New York: Arcade Publishing, 2004, p. 310.
6. **Knowing this, patients (mostly) suppress themselves:** Zelda Fitzgerald to F. Scott Fitzgerald (Christmas, 1939), Zelda Fitzgerald Papers, Box 48, Folder 1, P.U.L., also cited in Kendall Taylor, *Sometimes Madness Is Wisdom*. New York: Ballantine Books, 2001, p. 316.

7. **The benefits of scientific treatment have been strikingly enlarged:** Dr. Robert Carroll, Highland Hospital Prospectus, p. 21.

8. **I realize that I am at the end of my resources:** F. Scott Fitzgerald to Harold Ober (May 1936), in *F. Scott Fitzgerald: A Life in Letters*, ed. Matthew J. Bruccoli. New York: Simon and Schuster, 1994, p. 330.

9. **At Asheville, where much of the institutional atmosphere was lost in pleasant lodgings:** Rosalind Smith, unpublished documentation on Zelda Fitzgerald, Sara Mayfield Papers, University of Alabama, Tuscaloosa, Alabama.

10. **I left the hotel for the hospital this morning:** F. Scott Fitzgerald to Zelda Fitzgerald (July 27, 1936), in *The Correspondence of F. Scott Fitzgerald*, ed. Matthew J. Bruccoli and Margaret M. Duggan. New York: Random House, 1980, p. 440.

11. **You don't believe me, do you? I'm Scott Fitzgerald:** Helen Northup, quoted in *F in Wolfe's Clothing*, note reprinted from the *University of Wisconsin Library News*, in the *Fitzgerald Newsletter*, Micro Card Editions, Washington, DC, no. 19 (Fall 1962), pp. 102–3.

12. **The choosing of what was then one of the five or six best-known rich girls' schools:** Scottie Fitzgerald quoted in Eleanor Lanahan, *Scottie, the Daughter of . . . : The Life of Frances Scott Fitzgerald Lanahan Smith* New York: HarperCollins, 1995, p. 76.

13. **What I need is a substantial sum:** F. Scott Fitzgerald to Harold Ober (May 13, 1937), in *F. Scott Fitzgerald: A Life in Letters*, p. 322.

14. **There are so many houses I'd like to live in with you:** Zelda Fitzgerald to F. Scott Fitzgerald, cited in Taylor, *Sometimes Madness Is Wisdom*, p. 316.

15. **There would be episodes of great gravity that seemed to have no build up:** F. Scott Fitzgerald to Dr. Robert Carroll, in *F. Scott Fitzgerald: A Life in Letters*, p. 354.

16. **He fell in love with her helplessness:** F. Scott Fitzgerald, "Image on the Heart," *McCall's Magazine* 63, no. 7 (April 1936), p. 8.

17. **Are you by any chance interested in this French boy:** F. Scott Fitzgerald, "Image on the Heart," p. 52.

18. **You didn't actually have to kiss him tonight:** F. Scott Fitzgerald, "Image on the Heart," p. 52.

19. **You were there, you saw:** F. Scott Fitzgerald, "Image on the Heart," p. 52.

20. **He had to decide now, not upon what was the truth:** F. Scott Fitzgerald, "Image on the Heart," p. 62.

21. **The telegram came today, and the whole afternoon was sad:** F. Scott Fitzgerald to Sara Murphy (January 1937), F. Scott Fitzgerald Papers, P.U.L., also cited in Taylor, *Sometimes Madness Is Wisdom*, p. 320.

22. **I was to have lunch with Edmond Wilson:** Carl Van Vechten, quoted in Andre Le Vot, *F. Scott Fitzgerald: A Biography*, trans. William Byron. Garden City, NY: Doubleday, 1983, p. 318.

23. **I must be very tactful, but keep my hand on the wheel from the start:** F. Scott Fitzgerald to Scottie Fitzgerald (July 1937), in Andrew Turnbull, *Letters to His Daughter*. New York: Charles Scribner's Sons, 1965, pp. 25–26.

24. **Don't you know that drinking is slow death:** F. Scott Fitzgerald, quoted in Billy Altman, *Laughter's Gentle Soul: The Life of Robert Benchley*. New York: W.W. Norton and Company, 1997, p. 343.

25. **So who's in a hurry:** Robert Benchley, quoted in Billy Altman, *Laughter's Gentle Soul*, p. 343.

26. **Let's get out of these wet clothes and into a dry martini:** Version of a comment made by Robert Benchley to Ginger Rogers in the 1942 movie *The Major and the Minor*.

27. **I like to drink a martini, but only two at the most, three I'm under the table, four I'm under my host:** Quatrain misattributed to Dorothy Parker, quoted in Bennett Cerf, *Try and Stop Me*. New York: Simon and Schuster, 1944.

28. **The skin with its peculiar radiance:** F. Scott Fitzgerald, *The Last Tycoon*. New York: Charles Scribner's Sons, 1995, published under Fitzgerald's original title, *The Love of the Lost Tycoon*, ed. Matthew J. Bruccoli, p. 73.

29. **Not in his league at all:** Robert Westbrook, *Intimate Lies: F. Scott Fitzgerald and Sheilah Graham: Her Son's Story*. New York: HarperCollins, 1995.

30. **Better take it now. It is your chance, Stahr:** F. Scott Fitzgerald, *The Last Tycoon: An Unfinished Novel*. New York: Charles Scribner's Sons, 1941, p. 136.

31. **The police have just called telling me they've recovered my car:** F. Scott Fitzgerald to Scottie Fitzgerald (June 20, 1940), in *Letters to His Daughter*, ed. Andrew Turnbull. New York: Charles Scribner's Sons, 1965, p. 132.

32. **I don't know how this job is going:** F. Scott Fitzgerald to Zelda Fitzgerald, quoted in *The Letters of F. Scott Fitzgerald*. ed. Andrew Turnbull, New York: Charles Scribner's Sons, 1963, p. 144.

33. **Stahr cannot bring himself to:** F. Scott Fitzgerald, in *Two Outlines*, letter written on September 29, 1939, explaining plans for the novel, included in notes, *The Last Tycoon: An Unfinished Novel*. New York: Charles Scribner's Sons, 1941, p. 164.

34. **I hope you will find it possible to let things go:** F. Scott Fitzgerald to Dr. R. H. Suitt (September 27, 1939), F. Scott Fitzgerald Papers, Box 53, Folder 14 A, P.U.L., also cited in Taylor, *Sometimes Madness Is Wisdom*, p. 335.

35. **I'm tanning myself and happy in such a fine heaven:** Zelda Fitzgerald to F. Scott Fitzgerald, Zelda Fitzgerald Papers, Box 47, Folder 7, P.U.L., also cited in Taylor, *Sometimes Madness Is Wisdom*, p. 330.

36. **What is your actual address:** Zelda Fitzgerald to F. Scott Fitzgerald (December 1938), Zelda Fitzgerald Papers, Box 46, Folder 51., P.U.L., also cited in Taylor, *Sometimes Madness Is Wisdom*, p. 331.

37. **Janno had indeed learned a lot of things about minding their rules:** Zelda Fitzgerald, *Caesar's Things*, Zelda Fitzgerald Papers, Col. 183, Box 2A, Folder B, P.U.L., p. 312.

38. **If you can't pay her board:** Marjorie Brinson to F. Scott Fitzgerald (October 20, 1939), F. Scott Fitzgerald Papers, Box 55, P.U.L.

39. **The facts remain unchanged—that she has been mentally injured:** F. Scott Fitzgerald to Mrs. Anthony Sayre (October 15, 1939), F. Scott Fitzgerald

Papers, AM 20502, Col. 183, Box 6, Folder 24, P.U.L., also cited in Taylor, *Sometimes Madness Is Wisdom*, p. 336.

40. **Dr. Carroll treated his women patients, badly including Zelda:** Dr. Irving Pine, interview by Sally Cline, as cited in Cline, *Zelda Fitzgerald*, note 26, ch. 14.

41. **The proprietor (Carroll) has been implicated in a rape case:** Zelda Fitzgerald to John Biggs Jr. (January, 1941), Col. 628, Box 2, Folder 11, P.U.L. Sally Cline elaborates on the issues of the case referencing several conversations with Dr. Irving Pine who told her that "Dr. Carroll treated his women patients badly and took advantage of them." In Sally Cline, *Zelda Fitzgerald: Her Voice in Paradise*, Arcade Publishing, New York, 2004, pp. 375, 376.

42. **That life should once again have become desirable:** Zelda Fitzgerald to the Highland Hospital staff, copy of letter in Zelda Fitzgerald Papers, Col. 187, box 48, folder 39, P.U.L.

43. **This morning I have a letter from Dr. Carroll:** F. Scott Fitzgerald to Mrs. Anthony Sayre, quoted in *The Correspondence of F. Scott Fitzgerald*, ed. Matthew J. Bruccoli and Margaret M. Duggan, New York: Random House, 1980, p. 587.

44. **I do hope this goes well:** F. Scott Fitzgerald to Zelda Fitzgerald (April 11, 1940), quoted in *F. Scott Fitzgerald: A Life in Letters*, p. 442.

CHAPTER 11: A MIND WASHED CLEAN

1. **I won't be able to stick this out:** Telegram from Zelda Fitzgerald to F. Scott Fitzgerald, F. Scott Fitzgerald Papers, P.U.L., also cited in Kendall Taylor, *Sometimes Madness Is Wisdom*. New York: Ballantine Books, 2001, p. 340.

2. **Disregard telegram:** Telegram from Zelda Fitzgerald to F. Scott Fitzgerald, F. Scott Fitzgerald papers, P.U.L.

3. **She has a poor, pitiful life:** F. Scott Fitzgerald to Gerald and Sara Murphy (Summer 1940), quoted in *F. Scott Fitzgerald: A Life in Letters*, ed. Matthew J. Bruccoli. New York: Simon and Schuster, 1994, p. 458.

4. **I remember one she came to:** Nancy Milford, "The Golden Dreams of Zelda Fitzgerald," *Harper's Magazine*, January 1969, p. 52.

5. **They know that she simply cannot drink:** Marjorie Brinson, quoted in Helen Blackshear, "Mama Sayre, Scott Fitzgerald's Mother-in-Law," *Georgia Review*, Winter 1965, p. 16.

6. **Down here, the little garden blows remotely poetic:** Zelda Fitzgerald to Ludlow Fowler (1946), Zelda Fitzgerald Papers, Box 5, File 4, P.U.L., also cited in Taylor, *Sometimes Madness Is Wisdom*, p. 34.

7. **You saved me—Scottie and me:** F. Scott Fitzgerald to Gerald and Sara Murphy, quoted in *The Correspondence of F. Scott Fitzgerald*, ed. Matthew J. Bruccoli and Margaret M. Duggan. New York: Random House, 1980, p. 554.

8. **Dr. Baer was waiting in the inner office:** F. Scott Fitzgerald, *The Last Tycoon: An Unfinished Novel*. New York: Charles Scribner's Sons, 1941, p. 127.

9. **No news except that the novel progresses:** F. Scott Fitzgerald to Zelda Fitzgerald (December 6, 1940), in *The Letters of F. Scott Fitzgerald*, ed. Andrew Turnbull. New York: Charles Scribner's Sons, 1963, p. 131.

10. **Take care of yourself:** Zelda Fitzgerald to F. Scott Fitzgerald (no date), Zelda Fitzgerald Papers, Box 42, Folder 38, P.U.L., also cited in Taylor, *Sometimes Madness Is Wisdom*, p. 342.

11. **Maybe you would be better off in this climate:** Zelda Fitzgerald to F. Scott Fitzgerald, Zelda Fitzgerald Papers, Box 47, P.U.L., also cited in Taylor, *Sometimes Madness Is Wisdom*, p. 342.

12. **You have two beautiful bad examples for parents:** F. Scott Fitzgerald to Scottie Fitzgerald, quoted in Eleanor Lanahan, *Scottie, the Daughter of . . . : The Life of Frances Scott Fitzgerald Lanahan Smith*. New York: HarperCollins, 1995, p. 130.

13. **It was terrible about Scott:** Marion Meade, *Dorothy Parker: What Fresh Hell Is This?* New York: Villard Books, 1988, p. 299.

14. **She wasn't going to have him anymore:** Zelda Fitzgerald, *Caesar's Things*, quoted by Nancy Milford, *Zelda: A Biography*. New York: Harper and Row, 1970, p. 367. Original documentation from *Caesar's Things*, "The Big Top," ch. 7, p. 14, Zelda Fitzgerald Papers, Col. 183, Box 2A, Folder 8, P.U.L. A partially typed manuscript of 135 pages divided into seven chapters, begun in 1942 and worked on until Zelda's death in 1948, it currently exists as a fragmentary manuscript in the Princeton University archives.

15. **Just before New Year's Eve, I suddenly decided to go to New York:** Sheilah Graham, *The Real F. Scott Fitzgerald: Thirty-Five Years Later*. New York: Grosset and Dunlap, 1976, p. 219.

16. **Of course I was upset that my father was dead:** Lanahan, *Scottie, the Daughter of . . .*, pp. 132–33.

17. **I'm a Federal Court judge:** Seymour I. Toll, *A Judge Uncommon: A Life of John Biggs Jr.* Philadelphia: Legal Communications, 1993, p. 23.

18. **Jacob went on doing whatever it was that Jacob did:** Zelda Fitzgerald, *Caesar's Things*, cited by Sally Cline, *Zelda Fitzgerald*, p. 142; Milford, *Zelda*, p. 361; and Linda Wagner-Martin, *Zelda Sayre Fitzgerald: An American Woman's Life*. London: Palgrave MacMillan, 2004, p. 206.

19. **One day she met Jacques:** Zelda Fitzgerald, *Caesar's Things*, cited by Milford, *Zelda*, p. 364. This material also appears in Zelda's last chapter of her unpublished novel, *Caesar's Things*, in which her affair with the French pilot is told in greater detail than it appears in *Save Me the Waltz*, Zelda Fitzgerald Papers, P.U.L.

20. **There were lots of places to have champagne and hangovers around the garden:** Zelda Fitzgerald, *Caesar's Things*, Zelda Fitzgerald Papers, Col. 183, P.U.L.

21. **She kissed Jacques on the neck:** Zelda Fitzgerald, *Caesar's Things*, cited in Cline, *Zelda Fitzgerald*, p. 150.

22. **None of them in their fervor and necessity:** Zelda Fitzgerald, *Caesar's Things*, cited by Milford, *Zelda*, p. 367.

23. **While I was conversing with them on topics of the day:** Lawton Campbell, "The Fitzgeralds Were My Friends," unpublished essay, collection of the author, p. 29.
24. **I would not exchange my experiences for any other:** Zelda Fitzgerald to Ann Ober, quoted in Milford, *Zelda*, p. 373.
25. **I feel guilty about having left notifying my mother until it was too late:** Lanahan, *Scottie, the Daughter of . . .*, p. 150.
26. **Giving Scottie away must have brought back memories:** Zelda Fitzgerald to Ann Ober, quoted in Cline, *Zelda Fitzgerald*, p. 396.
27. **The first day she would seem so well:** Lanahan, *Scottie, the Daughter of . . .*, p. 86.
28. **I wish that my realms of epic literature would spin themselves out to a felicitous end:** Zelda Fitzgerald to Scottie Fitzgerald, quoted in Lanahan, *Scottie, the Daughter of . . .*, p. 372.
29. **John mentioned that it was time to catch the train:** Anna Biggs quoted in Milford, *Zelda*, p. 375.
30. **I have tried so hard and prayed so earnestly:** Zelda Fitzgerald to Rosalind Smith, quoted in Jeffrey Meyers, *Scott Fitzgerald: A Biography*. New York: HarperCollins, 1994, p. 340.
31. **I'm distressed Zelda does not improve:** Mrs. Anthony Sayre to Scottie Fitzgerald (January 27, 1948), quoted in Lanahan, *Scottie, the Daughter of . . .*, pp. 179–80.
32. **Today there is promise of spring in the air:** Zelda Fitzgerald to Scottie Fitzgerald, quoted in Lanahan, *Scottie, The Daughter of . . .*, p. 181.
33. **I was so glad you decided she should stay with daddy:** Scottie Fitzgerald to Mrs. Anthony Sayre (March 19, 1948), F. Scott Fitzgerald Papers, Col. AM 20502, Box 25, P.U.L., also cited in Taylor, *Sometimes Madness Is Wisdom*, p. 359, and Lanahan, *Scottie, the Daughter of . . .*, p. 181.
34. **She couldn't seem to give anything:** Lanahan, *Scottie, the Daughter of . . .*, p. 253.
35. **At last we have a baby to put down the incinerator:** Lanahan, *Scottie, the Daughter of . . .*, p. 172.
36. **A disorderly mind so packed with information:** Lanahan, *Scottie, the Daughter of . . .*, p. 418.
37. **I have developed a rather tough layer of skin over the years:** Lanahan, *Scottie, the Daughter of . . .*, p. 337.
38. **So, we beat on, boats against the current:** F. Scott Fitzgerald, *The Great Gatsby*. New York: Charles Scribner's Sons, 1924, p. 182. What Fitzgerald thought they were "borne back to" were life's pivotal events that forever change us.
39. **It was a very cruel joke God played:** Lanahan, *Scottie, the Daughter of . . .*, p. 473.
40. **It was never confirmed publicly within the family that Sara had lesbian relationships:** Camilla Mayfield, interview by the author, and documented in the Mayfield Collection, W. S. Hoole Special Collections Library, University of Alabama, Tuscaloosa, Alabama.

41. **I have fallen into the universal opinion of people here:** Tim Lanahan, quoted in Lanahan, *Scottie, the Daughter of . . .*, p. 343.
42. **Let go of her hand, she isn't yours:** Tennessee Williams, *Clothes for a Summer Hotel: A Ghost Play*. New York: New Directions Publishing, 1983, p. 74.
43. **You are reckless. You have a reckless nature:** Williams, *Clothes for a Summer Hotel*, p. 37.
44. **I know when to be careful but do you:** Williams, *Clothes for a Summer Hotel*, p. 36.
45. **You know, I expected our affair to continue, no matter what the cost:** Williams, *Clothes for a Summer Hotel*, p. 44.
46. **What *did* happen to you? After you left that summer:** Williams, *Clothes for a Summer Hotel*, p. 47.
47. **Well, gradually, as such things occur to most living creatures, Zelda, I—grew old:** Williams, *Clothes for a Summer Hotel*, p. 47.

Bibliography

PUBLISHED BOOKS AND ARTICLES

Aaron, Daniel. "The Legend of the Golden Couple." *Virginia Quarterly Review* 48 (1972): 157–60.

Allen, Frederick Lewis. *Only Yesterday: An Informal History of the 1920s*. New York: Harper and Row, 1964.

Allen, Joan. *Candies and Carnival Lights: The Catholic Sensibility of F. Scott Fitzgerald*. New York: New York University Press, 1978.

Altman, Billy. *Laughter's Gentle Soul: The Life of Robert Benchley*. New York: W.W. Norton and Company, 1997.

Amory, Cleveland, and Frederick Bradley, eds. *Vanity Fair: A Cavalcade of the 1920s and 1930s*. New York: Viking Press, 1960.

Angoff, Charles. *H. L. Mencken: A Portrait from Memory*. New York: Yoseloff, 1956.

Appignanesi, Lisa. *Mad, Bad and Sad: Women and the Mind Doctors*. New York, London: W.W. Norton and Company, 2007/2008.

Arien, Michael J. *Exiles*. New York: Farrar, Straus & Giroux, 1970.

Arieti, Silvano. *Interpretation of Schizophrenia*. New York: Basic Books, 1955. Second edition, 1974.

Armitage, Shelley. *John Held Jr., Illustrator of the Jazz Age*. Syracuse, NY: Syracuse University Press, 1987.

Baker, Carlos. *Ernest Hemingway: A Life Story*. New York Charles Scribner's Sons, 1969.

Bankhead, Tallulah. *Tallulah: My Autobiography*. New York: Harper and Brothers, 1952.

Benstock, Shari. *Women of the Left Bank, Paris*. 1910–1940. Austin: University of Texas Press, 1986.

Berg, A. Scott. *Max Perkins: Editor of Genius*. New York: Pocket Books, 1979.

Blackshear, Helen F. "Mama Sayre, Scott Fitzgerald's Mother-in-Law." *Georgia Review*, Winter 1965, 445 ff.

Bode, Carl. *Mencken*. Carbondale and Edwardsville: Southern Illinois University Press, 1969.

Bowen, Catherine Drinker. *Biography: The Craft and the Calling*. Boston: Little, Brown, 1969.

Boyd, Ernest *Portraits: Real and Imaginary*. New York: George H. Doran, 1924.

Brown, Dorothy M. *American Women in the 1920s: Setting a Course*. Boston: Twayne Publishers, 1987.

Bruccoli, Matthew J., ed. *As Ever, Scott Fitz: The Letters between F. Scott Fitzgerald and His Literary Agent, Harold Ober*. Philadelphia: J.B. Lippincott and Co., 1972.

Bruccoli, Matthew J., ed. *F. Scott Fitzgerald and Ernest Hemingway in Paris*. Bloomfield Hills, MI, and Columbia, SC: Bruccoli-Clark, 1972.

Bruccoli, Matthew J., ed. *F. Scott Fitzgerald's "The Great Gatsby": A Documentary Volume*. Vol. 219 of *Dictionary of Literary Biography*. Farmington Hills, MI: Gale Group, 2000.

Bruccoli, Matthew J., ed. *The Romantic Egoists: A Pictorial Autobiography from the Scrapbooks and Albums of F. Scott and Zelda Fitzgerald*. New York: Charles Scribner's Sons, 1974.

Bruccoli, Matthew J. *Scott and Ernest: The Authority of Failure and the Authority of Success*. New York: Random House, 1978.

Bruccoli, Matthew J. *Some Sort of Epic Grandeur: The Life of F. Scott Fitzgerald*. New York: Harcourt Brace Jovanovich, 1981.

Bruccoli, Matthew J., and Judith Baughman, eds. *Before Gatsby: The First Twenty-Six Stories*. Columbia: University of South Carolina Press, 2001.

Bruccoli, Matthew J., and Jackson R. Bryer, eds. *F. Scott Fitzgerald in His Own Time*. New York: Popular Library, 1971.

Bruccoli, Matthew J., and C. F. Frazer Clark Jr., eds. *Fitzgerald/Hemingway Annual 1973*. Washington, DC: Microcard Editions Books, 1974.

Bruce, Brian. "Thomas Boyd and F. Scott Fitzgerald: A Brief Literary Friendship." *Scholarly Journal of the Ohio Historical Society*, Ohio History, 109 (Summer–Autumn, 2000): 125–43.

Brunton, Laurence L., Randa Hilal-Dandan, and Björn C. Knollman. *Goodman and Gilman's the Pharmacological Basis of Therapeutics*. New York: McGraw-Hill Publishing, 2001.

Bryer, Jackson R. and Stern Prigozy, eds. *F. Scott Fitzgerald in the Twenty-First Century*. Tuscaloosa: University of Alabama Press, 2003.

Buller, Richard. *A Beautiful Fairy Tale: The Life of Actress Lois Moran*. Pompton Plains, NJ: Limelight Editions, 2005.

Bullock, Alan, and R. B. Woodings. *20th Century Culture: A Biographical Companion*. New York: Harper and Row, 1983.

Burgess, Anthony. *Ernest Hemingway and His World*. New York: Charles Scribner's Sons, 1985.

Buttitta, Tony. *After the Good Gay Times—Asheville '35: A Season of F. Scott Fitzgerald*. New York: Viking Press, 1974.

Buttitta, Tony. *The Last Summer: A Personal Memoir of F. Scott Fitzgerald*. New York: St. Martin's Press, 1987.

Callaghan, Morley. *That Summer in Paris: Memories of Tangled Friendships with Hemingway, Fitzgerald, and Some Others.* New York: Coward-McCann, 1963.

Carey, Gary. *Anita Loos.* New York: Alfred A. Knopf, 1988.

Chesler, Phyllis. *Women and Madness.* New York: Doubleday and Company, 1972.

Clemens, Anne Valdene. "Zelda Fitzgerald: An Unromantic Vision." *Dalhousie Review* 62, no. 2 (Summer 1982): 196–211.

Cline, Sally. *Zelda Fitzgerald: Her Voice in Paradise.* New York: Arcade Publishing, 2004.

Cody, Morrill, with Hugh Ford. *The Woman of Montparnasse.* New York: Cornwall Books, 1984.

Conrad, Winston. *Hemingway's France: Images of the Lost Generation.* Emeryville, CA: Woodford Press, 2000.

Cooper, Douglas Marshall. "Form and Fiction: The Writing Style of Zelda Sayre Fitzgerald." Dissertation, University of Michigan, 1979.

Corrigan, Maureen. *So We Read On: How "The Great Gatsby" Came to Be and Why It Endures.* New York: Little Brown, 2014.

Courbin-Tavernier, Jacqueline. "Art as Women's Response and Search: Zelda Fitzgerald's Save Me the Waltz." *Southern Liberty Journal* 11, no. 2 (Spring 1979): 22–42.

Cowley, Malcolm. *After the Genteel Tradition.* New York: W.W. Norton and Co., 1973.

Cowley, Malcolm. *Exiles Return: A Literary Odyssey of the 1920s.* London: Bodley Head, 1951.

Cowley, Malcolm. *A Second Flowering: Works and Days of the Lost Generation.* New York: Viking Press, 1973.

Cowley, Malcolm, and Robert Cowley, eds. *Fitzgerald and the Jazz Age.* New York: Charles Scribner's Sons, 1966.

Dardis, Tom. *Some Time in the Sun.* New York: Charles Scribner's Sons, 1976.

Diehl, Gaston. *Pascin.* New York: Crown Publishers, 1984.

Diliberto, Gioia. *Hadley.* New York: Ticknor and Fields, 1992.

Donaldson, Scott. *Archibald MacLeish: An American Life*: Boston: Houghton Mifflin, 1992.

Donaldson, Scott. *Fitzgerald and Hemingway: Works and Days.* New York: Columbia University Press, 2009.

Donaldson, Scott. *Fool for Love: F. Scott Fitzgerald.* New York: Delta Press, 1983.

Donaldson, Scott. *The Impossible Craft: Literary Biography.* University Park: Pennsylvania University Press, 2014.

Donnelly, Honoria Murphy. *Sara and Gerald: Villa American and After.* New York: Times Books, 1982.

Dos Passos, John. *The Best Times: An Informal Memoir.* New York: New American Library, 1966.

Dos Passos, John. *The Fourteenth Chronicle: Letters and Diaries of John Dos Passos.* Edited by Townsend Ludington. Boston: Gambit, 1973.

Dupont. *Edgemoorings* (newsletter). July–August 1954.

Durr, Virginia Foster. *Outside the Magic Circle: The Autobiography of Virginia Foster Durr.* Edited by and Hollinger F. Barnard. Tuscaloosa: University of Alabama Press, 1990.

Eble, Kenneth. *F. Scott Fitzgerald.* New Haven, CT: Yale University Press, 1963.

Edel, Leon. *Writing Lives: Principia Biographica.* New York: W.W. Norton, 1984.

Eicher, Terry, and Jesse Geller. *Fathers and Daughters: Portraits in Fiction.* New York: Penguin Group, 1990.

Elder, Donald. *Ring Lardner.* Garden City: Doubleday, 1956.

Fairy, Wendy W. *One of the Family.* New York, London: W.W. Norton Company, 1992.

"The Far Side of Zelda Fitzgerald." *Esquire* 62, no. 6 (December 1964): 158–59.

Fass, Paula. *The Damned and the Beautiful: American Youth in the 1920s.* Oxford, England: Oxford University Press, 1977.

Faulkner, William. Interview by Jean Stein, *Paris Review,* no. 12 (Spring 1956): 1–4.

Fels, Florent. *Drawings by Pascin.* New York: Book Adventures, 1967.

Fenton, Charles A. *The Apprenticeship of Ernest Hemingway.* New York: Viking Press, 1954.

Fenton, Charles A. *The Apprenticeship of Ernest Hemingway.* New York: Viking Press, 1958.

Field, Andrew. *Djuna: The Formidable Miss Barnes.* Austin: University of Texas Press, 1985.

Fitzgerald, F. Scott. *Afternoon of an Author.* Edited by Arthur Mizener. New York: Charles Scribner's Sons, 1957.

Fitzgerald, F. Scott. *As Ever, Scott Fitz: Letters between F. Scott Fitzgerald and His Literary Agent, Harold Ober.* Edited by Matthew J. Bruccoli. Philadelphia and New York: J.B. Lippincott Company, 1972.

Fitzgerald, F. Scott. *Babylon Revisited and Other Stories.* New York: Charles Scribner's Sons, 1971.

Fitzgerald, F. Scott. *The Beautiful and Damned.* New York: Charles Scribner's Sons, 1950.

Fitzgerald, F. Scott. *Conversations with F. Scott Fitzgerald.* Edited by Matthew J. Bruccoli and Judith Baughman. Jackson: University Press of Mississippi, 2004.

Fitzgerald, F. Scott. *Correspondence of F. Scott Fitzgerald.* Edited by Matthew J. Bruccoli and Margaret M. Duggan. New York: Random House, 1980.

Fitzgerald F. Scott. *The Crack-Up.* Edited by Edmond Wilson. New York: New Directions, 1956.

Fitzgerald, F. Scott. *The Cruise of the Rolling Junk.* Bloomfield Hills, MI: Bruccoli, Clark, 1976.

Fitzgerald, F. Scott. *Dear Scott/Dear Max: The Fitzgerald-Perkins Correspondence.* Edited by John Kuehl and Jackson R. Bryer. New York: Charles Scribner's Sons, 1971.

Fitzgerald, F. Scott. *F. Scott Fitzgerald: A Life in Letters.* Edited by Matthew J. Bruccoli. New York: Simon and Schuster, 1994.

Fitzgerald, F. Scott. *F. Scott Fitzgerald's Ledger: A Facsimile.* Washington, DC: Microcard Editions, 1972.

Fitzgerald, F. Scott. *Flappers and Philosophers.* New York: Charles Scribner's Sons, 1959.

Fitzgerald, F. Scott. *The Great Gatsby.* New York: Charles Scribner's Sons, 1925.

Fitzgerald, F. Scott. *The Last Tycoon.* New York: Charles Scribner's Sons, 1941.

Fitzgerald, F. Scott. *The Letters of F. Scott Fitzgerald.* Edited by Andrew Turnbull. New York: Charles Scribner's Sons, 1963.

Fitzgerald, F. Scott. *Letters to His Daughter.* Edited by Andrew Turnbull. New York: Charles Scribner's Sons, 1965.

Fitzgerald, F. Scott. *The Notebooks of F. Scott Fitzgerald.* Edited by Matthew J. Bruccoli. New York: Harcourt Brace Jovanovich, 1978.

Fitzgerald, F. Scott. *The Stories of F. Scott Fitzgerald.* Selected and with an introduction by Malcolm Cowley. New York: Charles Scribner's Sons, 1953.

Fitzgerald, F. Scott. *Taps at Reveille.* New York: Charles Scribner's Sons, 1935.

Fitzgerald, F. Scott. *Tender Is the Night.* New York: Charles Scribner's Sons, 1962.

Fitzgerald, F. Scott. *This Side of Paradise.* New York: Charles Scribner's Sons, 1931.

Fitzgerald, F. Scott. *Thought Book of Francis Scott Key Fitzgerald.* Princeton: Princeton University Library, 1965.

Fitzgerald, F. Scott. *Trimalchio: An Early Version of "The Great Gatsby."* Edited by James L. W. West. Cambridge, England: Cambridge University Press, 2000.

Fitzgerald, F. Scott. *The Vegetable.* New York: Charles Scribner's Sons, 1976.

Fitzgerald, F. Scott, and Zelda Fitzgerald. *Bits of Paradise.* New York: Charles Scribner's Sons, 1973.

Fitzgerald, F. Scott, and Zelda Fitzgerald. *Dear Scott, Dearest Zelda: The Love Letters of F. Scott and Zelda Fitzgerald.* Edited by Jackson R. Bryer and Cathy W. Barks. New York: St. Martin's Press, 2002.

Fitzgerald, Zelda. *The Collected Writings of Zelda Fitzgerald.* Edited by Matthew J. Bruccoli. New York: Charles Scribner's Sons, 1991.

Fitzgerald, Zelda. *Save Me the Waltz.* Carbondale and Edwardsville: Southern Illinois University Press, 1967.

Fitzpatrick, Kevin C. *A Journey into Dorothy Parker's New York.* Berkeley, CA: Roaring Forties Press, 2005.

Flanner, Janet. *Paris Was Yesterday.* New York: Viking Press, 1972.

Ford, Hugh. *Publishing in Paris: A Literary Chronicle of Paris in the 1920s and 1930s.* New York: Collier Books, MacMillan Publishing Co., 1975.

France, Marie de. *Lais.* French Texts Service. New edition. London, England: Duckworth Publishers, 1966.

Francillon, Robert E. *Zelda's Fortune.* Boston: James R. Osgood and Company, 1874.

Fryer, Sarah Beebe. *Fitzgerald's New Women: Harbingers of Change.* Ann Arbor: University of Michigan Research Press, 1988.

Garafolo, Lynn. *Diagilev's Russes Ballets.* New York: Oxford University Press, 1989.

Gerald Murphy: Toward an Understanding of His Art and Inspiration. Washington, DC: Board of Governors of the Federal Reserve Board System, Program of art exhibit, (Sept 21-Dec 1, 1983.)

Gill, Brendon. *A New York Life: Of Friends and Others.* New York: Poseidon Press, 1990.

Gish, Lillian. *The Movies, Mr. Griffith, and Me.* Englewood Cliffs, NJ: Prentice Hall, 1969.

Going, William T. "Two Alabama Writers: Zelda Sayre Fitzgerald and Sara Haardt Mencken." *Alabama Review* 23 (January 1970): 3–29.

Goldhurst, William. *F. Scott Fitzgerald and His Contemporaries.* New York: World, 1963.

Graham, Sheilah. *Beloved Infidel.* New York: Grosset and Dunlap, 1976.

Graham, Sheilah. *College of One.* New York: Viking Press, 1967.

Graham, Sheilah. *The Garden of Allah.* New York: Crown Publishers, 1970.

Graham, Sheilah. *The Real F. Scott Fitzgerald: Thirty-Five Years Later.* New York: Grosset and Dunlap, 1976.

Graham, Sheilah. *A State of Heat.* New York: Grosset and Dunlap, 1972.

Grau, Reagan Jay. "Waging Brown Water Warfare: The Mobile Riverine Force in the Mekong Delta, 1966–69." MA Thesis, Texas Tech University, August 2006.

Griffin, Peter. *Less Than a Treason.* Oxford, England: Oxford University Press, 1990.

Haardt, Sara. *The Making of a Lady.* New York: Doubleday and Co., 1930.

Haney, Lynn. *Naked as the Feast: A Biography of Josephine Baker.* New York: Dodd, Mead and Company, 1981.

Hansen, Arlen J. *Expatriate Paris: A Cultural and Literary Guide to Paris of the 1920s.* New York: Arcade Publishing, Little-Brown, 1990.

Hardwick, Elizabeth. *Seduction and Betrayal: Women and Literature.* New York: Vintage Press, 1975.

Harnett, Koula Svokos. *Zelda Fitzgerald and the Failure of the American Dream.* New York: Peter Lang, 1991.

Harrison, Gilbert A. *The Enthusiast: A Life of Thornton Wilder.* New Haven, CT: Ticknor and Fields, 1983.

Hart, Livye Ridgeway. "A Profile of Zelda." Original manuscript. Sara Mayfield Collection, University of Alabama, Tuscaloosa, Alabama.

Hartnett, Koula Svokos. "Zelda Fitzgerald and the Failure of the American Dream." Paper presented at the annual meeting of the Southern Atlantic Modern Language Association, Louisville, Kentucky, November 1981.

Hayes, Helen, with Sanford Dody. *On Reflection: An Autobiography.* New York: M. Evans and Company, 1968.

Heilbrun, Carolyn G. "Discovering the Lost Lives of Woman." *New York Times,* Book Review, June 24, 1984, 1, 26, 27.

Heilbrun, Carolyn G. *Writing a Woman's Life.* New York: W. W. Norton and Company, 1988.

Heller, Adele, and Lois Rudnick. *1915: The Cultural Moment.* New Brunswick, NJ: Rutgers University Press, 1991.

Hellman, Lillian. *An Unfinished Woman.* New York: Bantam Books, 1980.

Hemingway, Ernest. *Ernest Hemingway: Selected Letters, 1917–1961.* Edited by Carlos Baker. New York: Charles Scribner's Sons, 1981.

Hemingway, Ernest. *A Farewell to Arms.* New York: Charles Scribner's Sons, 1929.

Hemingway, Ernest. *The Garden of Eden.* New York: Charles Scribner's Sons. 1986.

Hemingway, Ernest. *A Moveable Feast.* New York: Charles Scribner's Sons, 1964.

Hemingway, Ernest. *The Sun Also Rises.* New York: Charles Scribner's Sons, 1966.

Hemingway, Mary Welsh. *How It Was.* New York: Alfred A. Knopf, 1976.

Hendrickson, Paul. *Hemingway's Boat: Everything He Loved in Life, and Lost, 1934–1961*. New York: Alfred A. Knopf, 2011.

Hergesheimer, Joseph. *Cythrea*. New York: Alfred A. Knopf, 1922.

Honan, Paul. *Authors' Lives: On Literary Biography and the Arts of Language*. New York: St. Martin's, 1990.

Hook, Andrew. *F. Scott Fitzgerald: A Literary Life*. Basingstoke: Palgrave MacMillan, 2002.

Hooper, Edwin Bickford. *The United States Navy and the Vietnam Conflict: The Setting of the Stage to 1959*. Vol. 1. Washington, DC: Naval History Division, Department of the Navy, 1976.

Hotchner, A. E. *Papa Hemingway*. New York: Random House, 1966.

Hudgins, Andrew. "Zelda Sayre in Montgomery." *Southern Review* 20 (1984): 882–84.

Irwin, John T. *F. Scott Fitzgerald's Fiction: An Almost Theatrical Innocence*. Baltimore: Johns Hopkins Press, 2014.

Israel, Lee. *Miss Tallulah Bankhead*. New York: G. P. Putnam's Sons, 1972.

Jacobson E. "The Early History of Psychotherapeutic Drugs." *Psychopharmacology* 89 (1986): 138.

Johnson, Owen. *The Salamander*. New York: A. L. Burt, 1914.

Kazin, Alfred, ed. *F. Scott Fitzgerald: The Man and His Work*. New York: Collier Books, 1951.

Kellner, Bruce. *Carl Van Vechten and the Irreverent Decades*. Norman: University of Oklahoma Press, 1968.

Kelly, John. "Memories of Scott and Zelda." *Pittsburgh Press*, February 6, 1983, 16, 18.

Kennedy, J. Gerald. "Fitzgerald's Expatriate Years." In *Cambridge Companion to F. Scott Fitzgerald*, ed. Ruth Prigozy, 118–42. New York: Cambridge University Press, 2002.

Kert, Bernice. *The Hemingway Women: Those Who Loved Him—the Wives and Others*. New York: W. W. Norton and Company, 1983.

Kleinsinger, Fred. "Understanding Non-Compliant Behavior; Definitions and Causes." *Permanent Journal* 7, no. 4 (Fall 2003): 11–18.

Kluver, Billy, and Julie Martin. *Kiki's Paris: Artists and Lovers 1900–1930*. New York: Harry N. Abrams, 1989.

Kohn, John Peter, Jr. *The Cradle: An Anatomy of a Town*. New York: Vantage Press, 1969.

Kokotailo, Philip. *John Glassco's Richer World; Memoirs of Montparnasse*. Toronto: ECW Press, 1988.

Koplewicz, Harold S. *More Than Moody; Recognizing and Treating Adolescent Depression*. New York: G. P. Putnam's Sons, 2002.

Kramer, Peter D. "How Crazy Was Zelda?" *New York Times Sunday Magazine*, December 1, 1966, 106–9.

Lanahan, Eleanor. *Scottie, the Daughter of . . . : The Life of Frances Scott Fitzgerald Lanahan Smith*. New York. HarperCollins, 1996.

Lanahan, Eleanor. *Zelda: An Illustrated Life: The Private World of Zelda Fitzgerald*. New York: Harry N. Abrams, 1996.

Lanoux, Armand. *Paris in the Twenties*. Translated by E. S. Seldon. New York: Golden Griffin Books/Essential Encyclopedia Arts, 1960.

Lardner, Ring. *What of It?* New York: Charles Scribner's Sons, 1925.

Lardner, Ring, Jr. *The Lardners: My Family Remembered*. New York: Harper Colophon Books, 1976.

Latham, Aaron. *Crazy Sundays: F. Scott Fitzgerald in Hollywood*. New York: Viking Press, 1971.

Le Vot, Andre. *F. Scott Fitzgerald: A Biography*. Translated by William Byron. Garden City, New York: Doubleday and Company, 1983.

Lewis, Janet. "The Cruise of the Rolling Junk: The Fictionalized Joys of Motoring." *Fitzgerald/Hemingway Annual*, 1978, 69–81.

Lidz, Theodore. "Adolf Meyer and the Development of American Psychiatry." *American Journal of Psychiatry* 123, no. 3 (1966): 320–32.

Loos, Anita. *A Girl Like I*. New York: Viking Press, 1966.

Loos, Anita. *Kiss Hollywood Goodbye*. New York: Viking Press, 1974.

Loos, Anita. *The Talmadge Girls*. New York: Viking Press, 1978.

Luce, William. *Zelda*. Off-Broadway one-woman show. New York, November 1984.

Ludington, Townsend. *John Dos Passos: A Twentieth Century Odyssey*. New York: E. P. Dutton, 1980.

Mackenzie, Compton. *Extraordinary Women: Theme and Variations*. London: Martin Secker, 1928.

MacLeish, Archibald. *Archibald MacLeish: Reflections*. Edited by Bernard A. Drabeck and Helen E. Ellis. Amherst: University of Massachusetts Press, 1986.

MacLeish, Archibald. *Letters of Archibald MacLeish*. Edited by R. H. Winnick. Boston: Houghton Mifflin Company, 1983.

MacShane, Frank. *The Life of John O'Hara*. New York: E. P. Dutton, 1980.

Malcolm, Janet. *Psychoanalysis: The Impossible Profession*. New York: Knopf, 1981.

Martin, Diana. "The Rest Cure Revisited." *American Journal of Psychiatry*. 164 (2007): 737–38. doi: 10:1176

Mayfield, Sara. *The Constant Circle: H. L. Mencken and His Friends*. New York: Dell Publishing, 1968.

Mayfield, Sara. *Exiles from Paradise: Zelda and Scott Fitzgerald*. New York: Delacorte Press, 1971.

McLendon, Winzola. "Scott and Zelda." *Ladies Home Journal* 91 (November 1974): 58–171.

Meade, Marion. *Bobbed Hair and Bathtub Gin: Writers Running Wild in the Twenties*. New York: Harcourt, 2004.

Meade, Marion. *Dorothy Parker: What Fresh Hell Is This?* New York: Villard Books, 1988.

Meade, Marion. *The Screwball World of Nathanael West and Eileen McKenney*. Boston/New York: Houghton Mifflin Harcourt, 2010.

Mellow, James R. *Charmed Circle: Gertrude Stein and Company*. New York: Praeger Publishers, 1974.

Mellow, James R. *Hemingway: A Life without Consequences*. New York: Addison-Wesley Publishing Company,1992.

Mellow, James R. *Invented Lives: F. Scott and Zelda Fitzgerald.* New York: Houghton Mifflin Company, 1984.

Mencken, H. L. *In Defense of Women.* New York: Alfred A. Knopf, 1927.

Mencken, H. L. *The Vintage Mencken.* Gathered by Alistair Cooke. New York: Vintage Books, 1955.

Merkin, Richard. *The Jazz Age as Seen through the Eyes of Ralph Barton, Miguel Covarrubias, and John Held, Jr.* Providence, RI: Museum of Art, Rhode Island School of Design, September 25–November 10, 1968.

Meyers, Jeffrey, ed. *The Biographer's Art: New Essays.* New York: Amsterdam, 1989.

Meyers, Jeffrey. *Scott Fitzgerald: A Biography.* New York: HarperCollins, 1994.

Milford, Nancy. *Zelda: A Biography.* New York: Harper and Row, 1970.

Miller, Linda Patterson, ed. *Letters from the Lost Generation: Gerald and Sara Murphy and Friends.* New Brunswick and London: Rutgers University Press, 1991.

Mizener, Arthur, ed. *F. Scott Fitzgerald: A Collection of Critical Essays.* Englewood Cliffs, NJ: Prentice-Hall, 1963.

Mizener, Arthur. *The Far Side of Paradise.* New York: Houghton Mifflin Company, 1949.

Mizener, Arthur. *The Fitzgerald Reader.* New York: Charles Scribner's Sons, 1963.

Mizener, Arthur. *Scott Fitzgerald and His World.* New York: G. P. Putnam's Sons, 1972.

Moore, Lucy. *Anything Goes: A Biography of the Roaring Twenties.* London: Atlantic, 2008.

Moorehead, Caroline, ed. *Selected Letters of Martha Gellhorn.* New York: Henry Holt, 2006.

Nathan, George Jean. "Memories of Fitzgerald, Lewis and Dreiser." *Esquire*, October 1958, 148–49.

Nathan, George Jean. *The Theater, the Drama, the Girls.* New York: Alfred A. Knopf, 1921.

Nathan, George Jean. *The World of George Jean Nathan.* Edited by Charles Angoff. New York: Alfred A. Knopf, 1952.

Neret, Gilles. *The Arts of the Twenties.* New York: Rizzoli, 1986.

Nijinsky, Romola. *Nijinsky.* New York: Simon and Schuster, 1980.

O'Hara, John. *Selected Letters of John O'Hara.* Edited by Matthew J. Bruccoli. New York: Random House, 1978.

Pachter, Marc, ed. *Telling Lives: The Biographer's Art.* Washington, DC: New Republic Books, 1979.

Pattillo, Edward. *Zelda: Zelda Sayre Fitzgerald Retrospective.* Montgomery: Montgomery Museum of Fine Arts, 1974.

Pendleton, Thomas. *I'm Sorry about the Clock: Chronology, Composition and Narrative Technique in "The Great Gatsby."* Selinsgrove: Susquehanna University Press, Associated University Presses, 1993.

The Pensacola Journal, Pensacola, Florida (listed chronologically):

"French Plane Off On Flight to Pensacola," December 9, 1935.

"French Flying Boat at NATAL," December 20, 1935.

"Naval Officers, City Plan to Welcome French Plane," January 11, 1936.

"Giant French Aircraft to Arrive Today," January 14, 1936.

"Frenchmen to be Guests of Clubs Today," January 15, 1936.

"Derrick en Route to Port to Raise Capsized Plane," January 16, 1936.

"Derrick Coming to Raise Plane Lifted Engine," January 15, 1936.

"French Plane Brought to Surface, Overhaul to Begin Monday," January 18, 1936.

"Capsized French Plane Raised from Bay," January 19, 1936.

"Plane Righted, Put upon Truck at Navy Station," January 21, 1936.

"Damaged French Plane Will Be Sent to France on Ship Due Saturday," January 28, 1936.

"Tanker Leaves with Seaplane; Men Also Sail," January 29, 1936.

Perkins, Maxwell E. *Editor to Author: The Letters of Maxwell E. Perkins*. Edited by John Hall Wheelock. New York: Charles Scribner's Sons, 1979.

Petry, Alice Hall. "Women's Work: The Case of Zelda Fitzgerald." *Literature Interpretation Theory*, December 1989, 69–83.

Phillips, Gene D. *Fiction, Film and F. Scott Fitzgerald*. Chicago: Loyola University Press, 1986.

Piper, Henry Dan. *F. Scott Fitzgerald: A Critical Portrait*. New York: Carbondale: Southern Illinois Press, 1968.

Piper, Henry Dan, ed. *Fitzgerald's "The Great Gatsby": The Novel, the Critics, the Background*. New York: Charles Scribner's Sons, 1970.

Polier, Rex. "Fitzgerald in Wilmington: *The Great Gatsby* at Bay." *Philadelphia Sunday Bulletin*, January 6, 1974, section 4.

Pozharskaya, Militsa, and Tatiana Volodina. *The Art of the Ballet Russes: The Russian Seasons in Paris 1908–1929*. New York: Abbeville Press, 1988.

Ring, Frances Kroll. *Against the Current: As I Remember F. Scott Fitzgerald*. Berkeley, 1985.

Rogers, Marion Elizabeth, ed. *Mencken and Sara: A Life in Letters—the Private Correspondence of H. L. Mencken and Sara Haardt*. New York: McGraw-Hill Book Company, 1987.

Rothschild, Deborah. *Making It New; The Art and Style of Sara and Gerald Murphy*. Williamstown, MA: Williams College Museum of Art, 2007.

Runyon, Keith. "The Fitzgeralds of Montgomery, Alabama." *Courier-Journal and Times*, March 24, 1974, Today's Living Section, p. 14.

Salwak, Dale, ed. *The Literary Biography: Problems and Solutions*. Houndsmill, Basingstoke, Hampshire: MacMillan, 1966.

Schouvaloff, Alexandre. *Leon Bakst: The Theatre Art*. London: Sotheby's Publications, 1991.

Schulberg, Budd. *The Disenchanted*. New York: Random House, 1950.

Seymour-Jones, Carole. *Painted Shadow: The Life of Vivienne Eliot*. New York: Doubleday, 2002.

Shorter, Edward. *A History of Psychiatry: From the Era of the Asylum to the Age of Prozac*. New York: John Wiley, 1997.

Showalter, Elaine. *The Female Malady: Women, Madness and English Culture, 1830–1980*. New York: Pantheon Books, 1985.

Shuttleworth, Jack. "John Held, Jr., and His World." *American Heritage* 16, no. 5 (August 1965): 27–38.

Sklar, Robert. *F. Scott Fitzgerald: The Last Laocoon*. New York: Oxford University Press, 1967.

Smith, Frances Scottie Fitzgerald Lanahan. "My Father's Letters: Advice without Consent." *Esquire*, October 1965, 93–99.

Smith (Lanahan), Frances Fitzgerald. "Introduction." In F. Scott Fitzgerald, *Letters to His Daughter*. Edited by Andrew Turnbull, pp. ix–xvi. New York: Charles Scribner's Sons, 1965.

Smith, Scottie Fitzgerald. "Foreword." In *As Ever, Scott Fitz: Letters between F. Scott Fitzgerald and His Literary Agent, Harold Ober*, ed. Matthew J. Bruccoli, xi–xvi. Philadelphia and New York: J.B. Lippincott Company, 1972.

Smith, Scottie Fitzgerald. "Foreword." In *Bits of Paradise*, by F. Scott and Zelda Fitzgerald, xi–xvii. New York: Charles Scribner's Sons, 1976.

Smith, Scottie Fitzgerald. Foreword to *Zelda*, exhibition catalog. Montgomery: Museum of Fine Arts, 1974.

Spencer, Charles. *Leon Bakst*. New York: Rizzoli, 1973.

Spencer, Charles. *The World of Serge Diaghilev*. Chicago: Henry Regnery Co., 1974.

Spencer, Madera. "Museum Show to Feature Zelda Fitzgerald Art." *Montgomery Advertiser Journal*, September 29, 1974, section C.

Squires, Mildred, and Sidney Tillim. "A Clinical Evaluation of Hypoglycemic and Convulsive Therapy." *Psychiatric Quarterly* 16, no. 3 (July 1942): 469.

Squires, Mildred, and Sidney Tillim. "A Physiologic Concept of Hypoglycemia and Convulsive Therapy." *Psychiatric Quarterly* 18, no. 1 (1963): 92–104.

Statesville Record and Landmark. "Psychiatric Test for Nurse Called in Asheville Fire." April 14, 1948, 8.

Stavola, Thomas J. *Scott Fitzgerald: Crisis in an American Identity*. New York: Barnes & Noble, 1981.

Stein, Gertrude. *Selected Writings of Gertrude Stein*. Edited by Carl Van Vechten. New York: Random House, 1946.

Stewart, Amy. *The Drunken Botanist: The Plants That Create the World's Great Drinks*. Chapel Hill, NC: Algonquin Books of Chapel Hill, 2013.

Szasz, Thomas. *Schizophrenia: The Sacred Symbol of Psychiatry*. New York: Basic Books, 1976.

Tate, Allen. *Memoirs and Opinions, 1926–1974*. Chicago: Swallow Press, 1975.

Taylor, Frances Finne. (Kendall Taylor). "The Fitzgerald Myth: A Study of Zelda Sayre Fitzgerald." Master's Thesis. Vanderbilt University, 1964.

Taylor, Kendall. *Sometimes Madness Is Wisdom*. New York: Ballantine Books, 2001.

Thurber, James. *Credos and Curios*. New York: Harper and Row, 1962.

Tighe, Mary Ann. "Painting on the Other Side of Paradise." *House and Garden*, October 1983, 204.

Tillotson, Jerry, and Robbie Tillotson. "Zelda Fitzgerald Still Lives." *Feminist Art Journal* 4 (Spring 1975): 31–33.

Toklas, Alice B. *What Is Remembered*. New York: Holt, Rinehart, and Winston, 1963.

Toll, Seymour I. *A Judge Uncommon: A Life of John Biggs, Jr.* Philadelphia: Legal Communications, 1993.

Tomkins, Calvin. *Living Well Is the Best Revenge.* New York: E. P. Dutton, 1962.

Turnbull, Andrew. *Scott Fitzgerald.* New York: Grove Press, 2001.

Tytell, John. *Passionate Lives.* New York: Birch Lane Press Book, 1991.

Vaill, Amanda. *Everybody Was So Young.* New York: Houghton Mifflin Company, 1998.

Van Vechten, Carl. *Letters of Carl Van Vechten.* Edited by Bruce Kellner. New Haven, CT: Yale University Press, 1987.

Van Vechten, Carl. *Parties.* New York: Avon Books, 1977.

Van Vechten, Carl. *The Splendid Drunken Twenties: Selections from the Daybooks, 1922–1930.* Edited by Bruce Kellner. Urbana: University of Illinois Press, 2003.

Wagner-Martin, Linda. *Zelda Sayre Fitzgerald: An American Woman's Life.* New York: Palgrave MacMillan, 2004.

Warren, Carol A. B. *Madwives: Schizophrenic Women in the 1950s.* New Brunswick, NJ: Rutgers University Press, 1987.

Weissman, Myrna M., and Eugene S. Paykel. *The Depressed Woman: A Study of Social Relationships.* Chicago: University of Chicago Press, 1974.

West, James L. W. *The Perfect Hour: The Romance of F. Scott Fitzgerald and Ginevra King, His First Love.* New York: Random House, 2005.

Westbrook, Robert. *Intimate Lies: F. Scott Fitzgerald and Sheilah Graham: Her Son's Story.* New York: HarperCollins, 1995.

Whitaker, Robert. *Mad in America: Bad Science, Bad Medicine, and the Enduring* Mistreatment *of the Mentally Ill.* Cambridge, MA: Perseus Publishing, 2002.

Williams, Tennessee. *Clothes for a Summer Hotel: A Ghost Play.* New York: New Directions Publishing, 1983.

Wilson, Edmund. *Letters on Literature and Politics, 1912–1972.* Edited by Elena Wilson. New York: Farrar, Straus & Giroux, 1977.

Wilson, Edmund. *The Shores of Light.* New York: Farrar, Straus & Young, 1952.

Wilson, Edmund. *The Thirties.* Edited by Leon Edel. New York: Farrar, Straus, & Giroux, 1980.

Wilson, Edmund. *The Twenties.* Edited by Leon Edel. New York: Farrar, Straus & Giroux, 1975.

Wiser, William. *The Crazy Years: Paris in the Twenties.* New York: Atheneum, 1983.

Wiser, William. *The Great Good Place: American Expatriate Women in Paris.* New York: W. W. Norton and Company, 1991.

Wolfe, Travis. "Scott, Zelda: Fitzgerald Home in Montgomery is Now Museum." *Chattanooga Times,* June 9, 1989, section D.

Wolff, Geoffery. *Black Sun: The Brief Transit and Violent Eclipse of Harry Crosby.* New York: Random House, 1976.

Woolcott, Alexander. *The Letters of Alexander Woolcott.* Edited by Beatrice Kaufman. New York: Viking Press, 1944.

Yardley, Jonathan. *Ring: A Biography of Ring Lardner.* New York: Random House, 1977.

Yorke, Lane. "Zelda: A Worksheet." *Paris Review,* Fall 1983, 210–63.

Zeitz, Joshua. *Flapper: A Madcap Story of Sex, Style, Celebrity and the Women Who Made America Modern.* New York: Three Rivers Press, Crown Publishing, 2006.

"Zelda Fitzgerald Exhibits Dolls at Museum." *Montgomery Advertiser*, August 1941.
"Zelda Sayre Fitzgerald." *Montgomery Museum of Fine Arts Bulletin*, September 1989.
"Zelda Sayre Fitzgerald's Pictures on View at Museum." *Montgomery Advertiser*, May 10, 1942.
Zuckerman, George. *The Last Flapper*. Boston: Little, Brown and Co., 1969.

UNPUBLISHED MATERIALS

American Psychiatric Association Library, Archives on Schizophrenia, Washington, DC.
ARDHAN, Retired Pilots Association, Paris, France. Robert Feuilloy, secretary general. Materials on Edouard Jozan.
Campbell, Lawton. "The Fitzgeralds Were My Friends." C. Lawton Campbell papers, Princeton University Library, Department of Rare Books and Special Collections, Princeton, New Jersey.
Duke University Medical Archives. Materials on Highland Hospital, Asheville, North Carolina.
Fitzgerald, F. Scott, Papers. Special Collections Division, Manuscript Collections, Firestone Library, Princeton University, Princeton, New Jersey.
Fitzgerald, Zelda, Papers. #010116, Special Collections Division, Manuscript Collections, Firestone Library, Princeton University, Princeton, New Jersey.
Fitzgerald, Zelda. Collection of Zelda Fitzgerald artwork, Montgomery Museum of Fine Arts, Montgomery, Alabama.
George Jean Nathan Collection. Rare Book Department, Cornell University, Ithaca, New York.
Haardt, Sara. Unpublished interview of Zelda Fitzgerald for *Good Housekeeping*. Now in the Sara Haardt Collection, Goucher College, also in the H. L. Mencken Collection at Enoch Pratt Library, Baltimore, Maryland.
Hourcade, Louis. Correspondence regarding Edouard Jozan.
Lanahan, Scottie Fitzgerald. Letters to author.
Marine Nationale Service de la Marine. Vincennes, France. Materials on Edouard Jozan.
McKaig, Alexander. Naval logbook now in possession of his nephew, attorney Robert Taft, Brighton, Fernald, Taft and Hampsey, Peterborough, New Hampshire.
Pensacola Naval Archives. Pensacola, Florida. Materials on Edouard Jozan.
Rosalind Smith letters, Sara Mayfield Collection. Amelia Gayle Gorgas Library, University of Alabama, Tuscaloosa, Alabama.
Sara Mayfield Collection. Amelia Gayle Gorgas Library, University of Alabama, Tuscaloosa, Alabama.
Shafer, Carolyn. "To Spread a Human Aspiration: The Art of Zelda Fitzgerald." Submitted in partial fulfillment of the requirements for the degree of master of arts in the Department of Art, University of South Carolina, 1994.
Sheppard Pratt Hospital Archives, Baltimore, Maryland.

State of Alabama Department of Archives and History, Montgomery, Alabama. Materials on early residents.

Taylor, Frances Finne (Kendall Taylor). "The Fitzgerald Myth: A Study of Zelda Sayre Fitzgerald." Master's thesis submitted to the Faculty of the Graduate School, Vanderbilt University, Nashville, Tennessee, August 1964.

Weatherby, Mrs. H. L. Letters to author

Wertham, Dr. Frederic. Zelda Fitzgerald artwork, Wertham Collection, Fogg Art Museum, Harvard University, Boston, Massachusetts.

W. S. Hoole Special Collections Library, University of Alabama, Tuscaloosa. Materials regarding Zelda Fitzgerald, Sara Mayfield, John Sellers.

INTERVIEWS BY AUTHOR (IN PERSON, BY TELEPHONE, AND THROUGH ELECTRONIC COMMUNICATION)

Dr. Basil T. Bennett, former director, Highland Hospital, Nashville, Tennessee. August 22, 1963; February 11, March 3, 1964.

Dr. Otto Billig, Nashville, Tennessee, February 13, 1963.

Helen Blackshear, Montgomery, Alabama, December 14, 1994.

C. Lawton Campbell, Bronxville, New York, January 28–29, 1964.

William T. Carpenter, Dupont, Edgemoor, January 12, 2012.

Tom Daniels, March 17, 1994.

Robert Feuilloy, Paris, France, July 4–7, 2008; July 10–14, 2008.

Lillian Gish, San Francisco, California, February 12, 1966.

Anton Haardt, Montgomery, Alabama, January 22, 2008.

Mrs. George Hickson, employee, Highland Hospital, Asheville, North Carolina, June 21, 1963.

Helen Hopkins, nurse, Highland Hospital, Asheville, North Carolina, June 21, 1963.

Jean Hourcade, Paris France, December 2008.

Tom Johnson, West Point, New York, March 11, 1963.

Pierre Jozan, Lyon, France, September 11–12, 16–17, 2007.

Laura Kahler, Hagerstown, Maryland, August 12–13, 1994.

Norwood Kerr, Alabama State Archives, November 26, 2007.

Jessica Lacher-Feldman, curator, Rare Books, Special Collections, University of Alabama, March 11–12, 2007.

Scottie Fitzgerald Lanahan, Washington, DC, January 24–29, 1964.

Archibald MacLeish, Conway, Massachusetts, August 14–15, 1963.

Dorothea Malm, Westport Historic District Commission, Westport, Connecticut, April 11, 1995.

Peyton Mathis III, December 16–22, 2007; January 6–10, 2008; January 21, 2008.

Mary McCahon, Westport Historical Society, Westport, Connecticut, April 11, 1999.

James Mellow, April 23, 1995.

Arthur Mizener, Nashville, Tennessee, February 6, 1964; Ithaca, New York, January 23, 1966.

Mark Palmer, Montgomery, Alabama, February 7, 1995.

Ed Patillo, Montgomery Museum of Fine Art, Montgomery, Alabama, April 3, 1995.

Mary Porter, Asheville, North Carolina, June 21, 1963.

Landon Ray, employee, Highland Hospital, Asheville, North Carolina, June 21–22, 1963.

Carolyn Shafer, February 15, 1993; April 10, 1993.

Rosalind Smith, Montgomery, Alabama, July 12–14, 1963.

Wendy Smith, Dupont, Edgemoor, Delaware, January 23, 2012.

Lani Suchcicki, *Pensacola News Journal*, Pensacola, Florida, March 2013.

Robert Taft, Peterborough, New Hampshire, May 15–17, 1995.

Anne Tillinghast, Asheville, North Carolina, June 20–21, 1963.

Andrew Turnbull, Cambridge, Massachusetts, August 21–27, 1963.

Harold Weatherby, Nashville, Tennessee, March 21–24, 1964.

Martine Jozan Work, Malibu, California, 2003–2017.

Index

About the Author

Kendall Taylor, PhD, is a cultural historian who has taught at George Washington University, the American University, and State University of New York. She also served as head of the National Exhibitions Program at the Library of Congress, academic director of the American University's Washington Program in Art and Architecture, and vice president for Planning and Research at Friends World College in Huntington, Long Island. Widely published, her critically acclaimed biography about F. Scott and Zelda Fitzgerald, *Sometimes Madness Is Wisdom*, was nominated by Random House for a Pulitzer Prize and published in several languages. Recipient of numerous grants and awards, Dr. Taylor was also a Fulbright scholar and Smithsonian Doctoral Fellow. She lives in New York and Florida.